Sports Parenting

Revised Edition

Negotiating the Challenges of the Youth Sports Journey to Help Kids Thrive

Paul Gamble PhD

Sports Parenting (Revised Edition): Negotiating the Challenges of the Youth Sports Journey to Help Kids Thrive

Published by Informed in Sport Publishing, Penticton, Canada.

© 2026 Paul Gamble

Copyright held by the author. All rights reserved worldwide.

No part of this publication may be reproduced, stored in a retrieval system, or transmitted, in any form or by any means – electronic, mechanical, photocopying, recording or otherwise – without prior written consent.

ISBN (paperback):   978-1-7776086-5-1

Cover design by Paige Harwood.

Contents

Prologue 1

Mapping the Territory 1
    The Growing Needs of Kids 1
    Realising the Full Benefits of Youth Sports 12
    The Athletic Skills Gap in Youth Sports 24
    Over-Scheduled and Under-Trained 34
    Keeping Girls in the Game: The Necessity of Physical Preparation 43

Choosing the Best Path 52
    Go Quickly or Go Far? 52
    Guiding Participation: Sampling, Specialisation and Premature Professionalism ..64
    Using Biological Age and Stage to Inform Decisions 76
    What You See Is Not All There Is 85
    Free-Range Athletes 93

Finding the Right Environment 100
    Choosing the Right Programme 100
    Selecting the Support Team: Go Armed with the Right Questions 110
    Investing in the Right Tools 117
    Teach an Athlete to Fish 124

Creating the Conditions 131
    Parental Investment and Involvement in the Youth Sports Journey 131
    Instilling Belief and Helping Kids to Find Their Aim 145
    Keeping the Fire Burning 156
    Challenges and Opportunities of Adolescence 170
    Harnessing the Mind 185
    Considered Communication: Care, Caution and Candour 201

Equipping the Performer for the Journey 214
    Cultivating Courage, Grit and Resiliency in Young Performers 214
    Getting Things Wrong: Making New and Better Mistakes 225
    Strategies to Deal with Distraction 234

- Agency and Accountability 241
- Feeling Privileged and Practising Gratitude 249

Negotiating Obstacles Along the Way 256
- Navigating Talent ID and Selection in Youth Sports 256
- Separating the Circles 262
- Purpose and Meaning 268
- Adversity as Opportunity 273
- Finding a Way 281
- Concluding Comments 285

Appendix ....

Bibliography ....

Prologue

4am alarm calls. Freezing on the side-lines at an away fixture in winter. Organising the whole family's lives around the competition schedule. Behind every successful athlete is a dedicated sport parent. Parents are the ones who make it all possible.

So who is the *sport parent*? Parents naturally differ in what they are seeking from their child's involvement in sport. Some dream of sporting success at the elite and professional level. Certainly, there are a number who view high school sporting success as a potential route to college scholarships. Perhaps the majority place the greatest value on the life lessons and wider benefits for their child's future beyond sport.

Clearly the *sport parent* comes in a variety of guises. Parents' attitudes towards their child's participation are shaped by what aspects of engaging in youth sports they deem to be most important. The terms 'talent development' and 'youth development' are used to describe these different facets of youth sports participation. *Talent development* concerns realising athletic potential within the sporting domain specifically, whereas *youth development* captures the wider health, developmental, social and life skill aspects of participating in youth sports. Youth sports offer a rich environment for kids to develop skills, behaviours and habits that transcend the athletic realm. Some of the most meaningful experiences and lessons during the formative years will come from their participation in sport.

It is fair to say the life of a sport parent is far from glamorous. The reason that so many dedicate so much to support their kid's participation in youth sports is the hope that the experience delivers the many potential benefits.

THE PIVOTAL AND DEMANDING ROLE OF THE 'SPORT PARENT'

My experiences overseeing talent development pathways and operating in these environments within elite and professional sport and more recently in the private sector have taught me how vital it is to enlist parents as a partner in the process. To use business parlance, parents are certainly a key stakeholder, but they are also far more than that. Parents are quite literally the driver for their kid's participation in sport, providing both the opportunity and very often the transportation. Without the involvement and support of parents, the opportunities for kids to participate in youth sports are far more limited. In some cases, continuing in the sport is just not viable when parental support is not available or forthcoming.

Parenting a youth sports athlete is akin to a full-time job in itself, requiring no small sacrifice from the family and considerable investment of time, effort and money. Such a pivotal role naturally comes with a host of responsibilities. A parent may be expected to fulfil a variety of functions at different points. The sport parent effectively serves as an extension of the coaching staff, and during the course of the youth sports journey they may assume a number of different roles, including serving as trusted advisor and even the young athlete's agent.

Supporting a young performer is very much a collaborative effort – as the saying goes, it takes a village. Naturally, parents and coaches are key players, but the collective effort comprises a wider supporting cast, including peers, mentors and specialist support providers. The sport parent is the keystone of the supporting effort and often parents are forced to take the lead and assume responsibility for enlisting and coordinating the various support providers.

NAVIGATING THE YOUTH SPORTS INDUSTRY

Parents face mounting challenges in their quest to provide the best opportunities and ensure their kids experience all that youth sports have to offer. Youth sports are big business – it is estimated that the youth sports market is worth $15.3 billion in the United States alone. The 'youth sports industry' continues to see more and bigger commercial interests vying to exploit the desire of parents to support their kids' aspirations.

In these circumstances it becomes all the more important for parents to be discerning in their choices as a consumer. The quality of services rendered and the user experience vary widely, so parents must choose wisely. The search to find the right environment is fraught with challenges and parents must grapple with the uncertainty that comes with trying to navigate unfamiliar territory. Much the same applies when seeking out the best coaching and enlisting other support providers.

Giving the sport parent a fighting chance means arming them with the knowledge to avoid being manipulated by marketing. Peeling back the curtain and lending greater understanding is important to redress the imbalance.

KNOWLEDGE TO EXERCISE 'PARENT POWER'

Sport has the potential to provide myriad benefits, but we should acknowledge that the youth sport experience is not always universally positive. There are clear indications of where we are currently falling short – one incontrovertible sign is the precipitous drop in participation that we see across all youth sports once kids reach their early teenage years. Those who govern sport certainly have a responsibility to confront and remedy the situation, but it is parents and the young performers themselves who are faced with negotiating these problems and they cannot afford to wait for administrators to act. Any real change is likely to come down to individual efforts 'on the ground', hopefully assisted by forward-thinking coaches and practitioners (and frankly to date there is little evidence that sports organisations and administrators are in fact capable of resolving these issues).

It is parents who ultimately have the power to help create the conditions for their own child to experience all that youth sport has to offer. The more informed sport parents become, the better equipped they will be to use their influence. The immediate task of navigating a youth sports landscape that is fraught with challenges requires being clear in our aims and understanding what it is we are dealing with. At the very least we can help to avoid the common pitfalls and mitigate the factors that lead kids to disengage and drop out.

I strongly believe that the most potent way to drive change is to enable more savvy sport parents so that they can exercise their power as consumers. One of the most effective ways that parents can wield this power is by making wise choices in where they spend their money. With better understanding we can harness market forces in a way that acts in the young athlete's favour. Knowledge is power when it comes to applying the consumer pressure that will be necessary to drive change within the youth sports marketplace.

WALKING THE FINE LINE

Naturally, parents are invested in their child's youth sports participation. This investment often leads parents to become increasingly involved. There is however a sweet spot when it comes to parental involvement. On the one hand, parental support is crucial in affording the young athlete the opportunity to participate and pursue their goals in the sport. On the other, parental involvement can be a source of friction and may add to the pressure of competing, with potential adverse consequences for the young athlete's experience and their participation in the long run.

Not only is this a delicate balance but the fulcrum on the seesaw also shifts as we advance on the journey. The 'sweet spot' is a moving target and as kids mature this adds new layers of complexity. Wise parents know there comes a time to step back to permit the performer to assume more ownership and responsibility. If we are not careful, our involvement is something the young performer sees fit to rebel against, with the result that their participation in the sport suffers or is forfeited entirely.

SPORTS PARENTING FITNESS

Many coaches and parents alike will have witnessed the unfortunate instances when overexuberant parents overstep and misbehave! A friend who works in talent development and coaches youth (soccer) football in his spare time is fond of telling the story of how he keeps a stash of lollypops handy during matches. When parents on the sidelines start to get too worked up, he presents them with a lollypop. As the reader can perhaps imagine, being handed a lollypop sends a pretty clear signal that you are getting carried away! Ken reports that this tactic works a treat in prompting the offender to calm down and get themselves under control.

At the other extreme, more jaded coaches sometimes resort to excluding parents altogether or putting rules in place to keep them at arm's length. I have even heard reports of a youth soccer coach who instructed his players that they would be dropped to the bench if they spoke with their parents once they reported for duty with the team on match day. Clearly such extreme measures are as short-sighted as they are self-defeating. Nevertheless, what this does reveal is the tension that can arise between coach and parent.

Administrators and coaches alike acknowledge that a parent's actions are of great significance (for good or ill). A reflection of their profoundly influential role is that the 'fitness' of the sport parent may be a factor for selection. As talent identification processes become more evolved, teams and organisations are taking a more holistic approach to talent selection – a notable example is the consideration of *psychological talent predictors*. A natural extension of such an approach is to include evaluation of parental support and the health of the athlete-parent relationship in the criteria that sporting organisations employ for selection.

Having been part of these discussions I can attest that sport parenting fitness is something that is taken into consideration when selecting young athletes for talent development pathways. To share my own experience overseeing academy and youth programmes in professional sport and with national sporting organisations, we gave a great deal of attention to the parents as one of the critical success factors when assessing young athletes' long-term potential. Our evaluations in different cases ranged from potential liability to major prospective asset.

I can imagine many readers recoiling at horror at these revelations! Being a sport parent can oftentimes seem a hugely demanding and somewhat thankless task! Worst still, you now discover that you are being judged and this might affect your child's chances of selection! In my various roles it has long struck me that we should do more to assist and equip parents, as at times it appears we are setting parents up for failure. If administrators and coaches are going to ask and expect so much, we should at least give you a fighting chance!

BRINGING THE SPORT PARENT INTO THE FOLD

In view of the many and varied responsibilities that typically fall to them, it is unsurprising that many parents at times feel ill-equipped and unsure of how best to proceed. Part of the uncertainty stems from the difficulty in fully apprehending what the youth sport experience is like from the perspective of a talented young performer. Elements of the coaching process are also hard to fathom, especially as parents are often not briefed on the plan or given any explanation of the rationale behind what the coach is attempting to do.

Given the acknowledged importance of parents and the integral role they play in the talent development process, it is nonsensical that we do not routinely provide guidance and support for parents in the same way as we cater for coach education. More enlightened individuals and groups are now attempting to address this glaring omission, but this movement is still very much in its infancy.

To date these efforts have been hampered by the dogma that permeates much of the academic literature on the topic. A notable complaint is that there is a lack of nuance in what has been written on the topic. There is often a tendency to misrepresent parents' intentions and actions. More empathy is called for and fundamentally the sport parent deserves more respect.

FORGING AN ALLIANCE BETWEEN COACH AND PARENT

The overarching theme of this book is the all-important trinity of coach, parent and athlete. Successfully navigating the youth sports journey is a truly collaborative effort and this coach-parent-athlete axis needs to be functioning properly to keep things on track. Each must play their role and the role of each will evolve as we progress. As the grown-ups, not only must the coach and parent find ways to work together but we must also help the athlete to fulfil their own role, which is of course central.

Parents and coaches have much in common, not least the best interests of the young performer. The many parallels that exist between coaching and parenting is a theme we will return to many times in the chapters that follow. The fundamental task of coach and parent alike is to do all they can to ensure that the young person is able to fulfil their highest potential. The coach is primary concerned with fulfilling this role in the context of sport, whereas parents are generally more concerned with the game of life!

Coaches and parents alike must judge when to step back to allow the young performer to face challenges on their own and learn to become independent. The rather odd aspect of being either a coach or a parent is that the ultimate objective is to make yourself redundant! It follows that we should perhaps work together to figure out how best to achieve this paradoxical end.

Rather than excluding parents, more enlightened coaches recognise the value in enlisting the parent as a partner in the endeavour. Given their central importance and degree of influence, it is only logical that coaches should seek to engage parents in the process. In turn, coaches benefit from adopting a perspective that encompasses the wider interests of the athlete and making some attempt to deal with the whole human!

Coaches and parents have a duty to help each other in service of the collective effort to support the young athlete. At times as a coach I act in a quasi-parenting capacity, whereas an integral part of parenting is coaching the child! The paternal aspect of my role as a coach is something that I had long been conscious of to some degree, especially once I began to contemplate becoming a father.

I can cite innumerable instances where I have been able to support the parenting effort in my capacity as a coach. And as a coach I am always reliant on the parent to help support the mission during the majority of time that the young athlete spends away from the practice and competition environment.

SHARED CAUSES

Aside from the obvious overlap in remit and common interests, there are other facets of the life of a young performer where there is a clear need for coaches and parents to join forces. Having known the world before the advent of the internet and smartphones, we tend to be far more aware of the growing significance of youth sports as one of the last remaining bulwarks against the perils of the virtual world for young performers in the *i-generation*. Parents and coaches alike are grappling with how best to combat the pull of the smartphone and regulate social media use to mitigate its deleterious effects. This truly is a contest for hearts and minds – and it can often seem like we are fighting a losing battle! On this front in particular there is a need and opportunity for coaches and parents to unite our efforts.

There are those who claim e-sports offers an adequate replacement for engaging in sport *IRL* (yes – 'in real life' now has an acronym). I staunchly refute the validity of this claim (and for the record I strenuously oppose the push to include e-sports at pinnacle events such as the Olympic Games). Engaging with a screen is also inherently antisocial and whilst 'e-sports' might provide an escape, there is also a tendency to withdraw into the virtual world rather than confront the uncertainty and discomfiting prospect of engaging in real life. In stark contrast, there is a *prosocial* element to engaging in youth sports. The competitive and cooperative nature of sport allows kids to learn to regulate themselves and their interactions with others, such that participation develops psychosocial skills. What is increasingly vital is that organised youth sport also provides in-person interaction in a way that brings young performers into contact with other kids from different backgrounds, social standing and ethnicities, fostering interpersonal skills and even societal benefits.

Competitive sport in particular has its own unique value. Youth sport is one of the vanishing spaces where the young person is permitted to lose and win (under relatively low stakes). Entering the contest means acknowledging and accepting losing as a potential outcome. The fact that the young performer voluntarily agrees to these terms is significant in itself. The competitive realm affords the opportunity to test themselves, confront their own limitations and experience setbacks. The trials that young athletes face during practices and in the crucible of competition forge character. When handled in the right way these experiences make kids more resilient.

As many parents intuitively understand, the youth sports journey is rich with life lessons. The experience reveals that striving towards a future goal is inherently meaningful. Sport teaches the merits of persevering. Training and practice teach the value of investing effort and making sacrifices in the present in service of their future self. In this way, sport is an object lesson in delayed gratification. In an era where discipline and focus are becoming lost arts, participating in sport reveals the rewards of discipline and focused effort.

Parents and coaches share the role and responsibility of helping to elucidate these lessons. Together we can help more kids to realise the myriad benefits that the youth sports journey offers.

SIMILAR BUT DIFFERENT

Notwithstanding the notable similarities between parenting and coaching, it is important to recognise that they are not the same. I was most struck by this following the birth of my son! The total investment and all-encompassing commitment to the wellbeing of a child is a profound and necessary part of being a parent. A parent's love and engagement in the life of their child is unconditional.

When I relate this to my experiences of coaching and working with athletes, I think the most obvious difference is the luxury of being able to maintain some distance. As a coach I am certainly very much invested and committed to serving the best interests of the individual; however, it is necessarily conditional. Effectively I am serving the yet to be realised best future version of the individual and calling on the part of the athlete's self that would strive to realise the potential that I see in them. To that end, I can and will send an athlete out of a session on any given day if their behaviour is not up to standard. Ultimately, I reserve the right to walk away entirely if the athlete consistently fails to deliver on their part of the deal; indeed, the fact that both parties are aware that this eventuality is always on the table is one of the defining features of the coach-athlete relationship. Conversely, parents do not enjoy quite the same freedom: logistics make it difficult to banish a child on the days when they misbehave – after all, they live there! And walking away is of course not an option, no matter what happens.

Clearly there are important differences between the respective roles of coach and parent that need to be acknowledged and respected. Just as a well-functioning society relies on the separation between church and state, young performers must retain some separation between their involvement in sport and the rest of their life; this is never more evident than when it comes to their relationship with their parents. Whilst parents might play an integral role in the youth sports journey at various points, there must be a clear delineation to avoid parental involvement in one domain encroaching on the other. Simply put, it is crucial that the performer is clear at all times that their parent is first and foremost their parent, irrespective of whatever interactions take place in the context of their participation in sport.

One of the reasons why it is beneficial to delegate various duties to coaches and practitioners is to preserve the sanctity of the parent-child relationship. As we alluded to before, the sport parent can take advantage of the coaches and others who have the necessary separation to engage with the young performer in a more conditional manner.

UNIFYING THE EFFORT TO SUPPORT THE STUDENT-ATHLETE

Beyond chasing college scholarships, what is often overlooked is that engaging in sport can help kids to do well in school. There is often a perceived tension between sport participation and study commitments, such that the desire for scholastic success can lead parents to discourage and limit participation especially in high school. The message that is rarely heard is that youth sports have the potential to complement rather than conflict with the pursuit of scholastic achievement.

There are of course only so many hours in a day, so there is always a logistical challenge, especially as kids approach the business end of their time at school. Nevertheless, the benefits are such that it arguably becomes more important and worthwhile for young people to continue to regularly engage in sport to support their ability to study and learn, as well as improving their physical and mental wellbeing and helping to manage stress. Learning how to balance study and sport commitments is likewise an integral part of being a successful student-athlete – and certainly these time management skills will come to the fore as the young performer progresses in their journey through high school and potentially higher education.

Parents and coaches share a common goal in supporting the performer to learn how to manage their time successfully. More broadly we have a shared interest in the success and wellbeing of the young athlete, so it makes a lot of sense to align our efforts rather than inadvertently pulling in different directions!

ONTO THE BOOK...

The lack of concerted effort and dedicated resources for the parents who are so integral in supporting young performers has long baffled me. The motivation for writing this book was to fill this void in an effort to better support the underserved and somewhat underappreciated sport parent. My hope is that arming parents with a better understanding of how to navigate the challenges will ultimately enable more kids to experience the good parts of what youth sports can offer.

The functioning of the coach-parent-athlete axis is crucial to the success of the endeavour. This relies on all parties being informed such that they understand what their role is (and how it will evolve over time) and equipped to fulfil what is expected of them. Operating harmoniously further depends on each party being aware and having an appreciation of what the other parties are doing, not least so that they can do their part to support.

With this book I hope to contribute to the effort to bring coaches and parents together in service of the young performer. Even the most cynical coach cannot refute that the vast majority of parents have the best of intentions. If we want to better align our efforts then as coaches we must do our part to share the insights that will help parents to be better able to operate in this space. My experiences have taught me the merits of sharing with parents the perspectives of the coach and practitioner such that all parties are better able engage with each other. Once parents better understand what it is that coaches are trying to do, they are instantly better placed to contribute to the effort, so it is in the coach's interest to lend these insights. Whilst the primary audience for the book is sport parents, I hope that it also provides a resource for youth sports coaches and helps their efforts to engage and work collaboratively with parents.

To that end, the chapters that follow lend insight into the talent development process and shed some light on the parts that are more opaque. Certainly, there are aspects that seem counterintuitive at first glance, such that they need to be explained in a way that reveals the logic. By taking the time to explain we can bring some much-needed clarity and help parents understand how they can best serve the ultimate mission and the interests of the young performer's future self. Importantly the reader will also become better able to discern good coaching practice as a result.

The deeper intention behind this book is to help young athletes to flourish and realise their potential. To that end, a recurring theme is that it is the young performer themselves who is the agent in the arena and ultimately it their quest to pursue. As such, the most important role of both coach and sport parent is to help the young athlete to step into this central role and assume all the attendant responsibilities as they progress along their youth sports journey.

This book thus attempts to share insights and inside knowledge to equip the reader in a way that will help both parent and athlete to navigate the youth sports journey. Each section of the book aims to provide parents with an insider's perspective on coaching and athlete development so they can understand how best to support their child. Each chapter provides strategies and tips to help the reader to apply this knowledge in a practical context.

The book is divided into six parts, each of which focusses on a distinct theme. In the opening section we 'map the territory', with a broad overview of what needs we need to fulfil and the ways in which sport is so vital for helping kids to flourish. The second section seeks to elucidate what constitutes the best path for an aspiring young performer. We then move onto the question of what to look for when choosing the right environment for the young performer and how to make astute choices when selecting coaching and other specialist support. The fourth section goes to the heart of the matter of what we need to collectively put in place to create the conditions for young athletes to thrive. We then move onto the key tools that we need to help equip kids with as they progress through the youth sports journey. The final section explores the obstacles that young athletes will likely face along the way and how they might best tackle and overcome these challenges.

ABOUT THE NEW EDITION…

The original version of the book was released only a few months after I became a father. With the arrival of our son, the subject matter instantly took on much greater weight. I also now had a 360-degree perspective on the topics covered. I was never exactly detached, but as I start to contemplate our son embarking on his own youth sports journey it is certainly now much more personal.

One of the most interesting pieces of feedback on the original was that it was equally relevant to coaches and those who work in talent development. One host of a podcast even suggested that I change the title to make it more inclusive! In the years since the first book was published, I have continued to write for a mixed audience of parents, youth sports coaches, physical education teachers and those involved in talent development. The interactions with readers both online and in person has sharpened my understanding of the struggles that parents, youth sports coaches and young athletes themselves are facing.

These experiences have only strengthened my conviction that the book is important and necessary. Despite the books and resources that have been released since, I still feel that parents remain poorly served. While there have been genuine efforts to educate, sport parents have become recognised as a consumer and the information that is directed towards parents reflects this. At one extreme, the token parent education efforts offered by sports organisations tend to frame parents as the problem, whereas on the other we have various actors seeking to exploit parents' desire to help their kids with short cuts and advice on how to reach the pros.

Many are still searching for answers. The conversations I have had with parents and coaches indicate that the pain points are still the same. What is heartening is that there is an evident hunger for information from parents and youth sport coaches who are seeking to do the right thing. I have felt a growing sense of urgency to do more to reach the intended audience, which motivated me to revisit the book and update the content with a revised edition.

Soon after the release of the original it dawned on me that parents struggle to find time to read books! Reflecting this, the chapters are short bite-sized reads, allowing the reader to dip in and out of the book as time permits. So whilst the book is comprehensive, it is also easy to consume. The book is also designed to be a handbook, such that each chapter provides a standalone resource on the relevant topic that the reader can refer back to as they encounter different challenges.

The final piece of reader feedback was essentially a request to make it easier to quickly identify the guidance offered and make the content more actionable. To that end, the revised edition has new features to help the reader to identify the key recommendations, with more extensive summaries including practical tips on implementation and action items following each chapter.

This book is dedicated to two fathers and a son.

In cherished memory of my late father-in-law Tony: the epitome of a dedicated parent and supportive sport parent, who cultivated the extraordinary talents of my wife Sian, for which he was rewarded in life with the pristine relationship that the two of them enjoyed. You are fondly remembered and greatly missed.

In thanks to my dad, who similarly models all the best attributes that I describe in this book; having instilled in me a life-long passion for sport, my dad is also the person most responsible for encouraging and supporting my endeavours as a player and my subsequent career as a practitioner, coach and leader. I love you, Father.

Finally, this book is dedicated to my bright-eyed boy, Leo Gamble. Aside from giving me a crash course in parenting, your arrival and taking time out to take care of you has given me a new perspective on coaching and life in general. Mumma and Dada love you more than can be captured in words.

Mapping the Territory

The Growing Needs of Kids

The title has dual meaning: kids have needs that must be satisfied as they grow and mature to support their development; but there is a growing necessity to do more to ensure that these needs are being met. The trends in wider society are generally heading in the wrong direction from this perspective, placing a greater onus on parents to adopt countermeasures at a local level. Clearly this is important and advantageous from an athlete development perspective, but it applies more generally to our efforts to raise healthy, capable and social young people.

KIDS THESE DAYS…

The latest in a series of reports on the steeply declining levels of physical activity among children and adolescents was published in 2020. This most recent publication, commissioned by the World Health Organisation (WHO), reported on the present state of things on a global scale, based on nearly 300 surveys across 146 countries. The report also tracked trends over the past two decades, drawing comparisons to data collected in 2001. Based on data from 1.6 million kids aged 11-17 years, somewhere in the range of 76-80% of boys and 83-88% of girls reported insufficient levels of daily physical activity, based on WHO guidelines (60 minutes of moderate to vigorous activity daily) [1].

Against the backdrop of the general downward trend in regular physical activity among kids in general, there has also been a decline in active play (especially unsupervised active play) over recent years. Moreover, as kids progress through their school years they report a decline in daily moderate-vigorous activity and this is particularly evident among females [2]. 2017 was the first recorded year that the proportion of children aged 6-12 who reported participating in at least one sport for a minimum of one day in the past year started to decline. Across all sports there is a precipitous drop in participation once kids reach their early teens. Clearly this makes for grim reading for those involved in sport at all levels, but arguably the bigger issue for most parents is that each of these trends presents a problem for healthy development of body and mind.

From a personal perspective I have been a bit insulated from these trends. In my professional capacity I don't tend to come across many kids who are not physically active. Over the past decade I have also lived in parts of the world where kids (and adults) are generally more active. Nevertheless, there have been signs that things are not proceeding in the direction we would like. Notably, there have been consistent signals from athletic directors, coaches and physical education teachers at high school and junior level that the level of mastery of basic motor skills among young performers is in decline. The trends we observe coincide with wider societal factors, in particular the decline in free play and physical activity among children and adolescents, all of which has accelerated in the past decade since the advent of the smart phone.

BODY AND BRAIN DEVELOP IN TANDEM...

'By acting in the world children develop their cognition' [3]

We explore and move through the world with our body. We also interact with external objects and others using our body. Physical activity and exercise are accordingly associated with brain development and cognitive function in children. Just as we learn to move during the early years, we move to learn. This co-development of motor skills and cognitive skills is evident throughout childhood and adolescence [4]. We develop our brain through action: by engaging in play, exploring our surroundings and exercising our body.

Embodied cognition is a fancy term that describes how we perceive and understand the world in relation to our body and the possibilities for action. A primary motivation that drives how we perceive the world around us is to plot a path through it [5]. Similarly, we identify objects around us and perceive features of the environment in relation to our body and their potential utility – that is, what we can grasp, what we might climb on, a gap we might squeeze through, and so on.

What all this means is that the development of our brain and body are to some extent inseparable. A mind needs a body in order to function: how we think and what we perceive is inextricably linked to our body and its capabilities. We learn what our bodies can do by physically engaging with the world around us, which in turn changes our brain and alters our perception [3]. This is especially true during childhood and adolescence given that we are still growing and the dimensions and capabilities of our bodies are continually changing. As we grow and learn what our changing body can do, we continually update our embodied understanding of the world and the possibilities for acting in it [6].

NIMBLE BODIES, NIMBLE MINDS...

Something that is widely overlooked is that being physically active is not only good for developing motor skills; it also helps to develop cognitive abilities. For instance, children learn more by doing than simply watching [7]. Kids learn better when they are able to move their body and physically engage with the learning material [8].

Kids who are more active tend to learn better, in part due to the positive link between habitual physical activity and cognitive function [9]. A dose of physical exercise enhances brain function in ways that directly benefits learning and memory [10]. This has led to growing interest in the strategic use of physical exercise for the specific purpose of improving scholastic performance. Prospective studies have demonstrated that exercise interventions can improve academic outcomes (school examination scores) in children [11].

Regularly participating in strenuous play and vigorous physical exercise supports the ability to harness mental faculties, including attention and working memory. The link between physical fitness and academic performance in children is also present among teens [12], and the ongoing need for regular physical exercise to support academic performance during adolescence is especially pronounced in boys [13].

What is also noteworthy but perhaps less intuitive is that the degree of mastery of fundamental movement skill among kids is also positively related to their academic achievement. Better developed motor skills and higher fitness are each associated with scholastic abilities [14]. Engaging in quality physical education thus facilitates cognitive development and improves academic performance in children and adolescents [15].

In particular, proficiency in complex motor skills, such as those that feature in music and sport, is linked to the development of 'higher order' cognitive abilities [4]. Measures of intelligence (IQ) are similarly related to fine motor skills, which again affirms the relationship between cognitive and motor development. In a real sense, bodies with better coordination have more nimble minds [16].

These findings are especially pertinent to combating and managing attention deficit and hyperactivity disorder (ADHD). The link between motor skill development and cognitive development is particularly evident among kids diagnosed with ADHD [17]. Physical exercise is demonstrated to be highly efficacious in improving neurocognitive function in this population [18]. Providing strategically timed doses of moderate to vigorous physical exercise before and during the school day helps kids who exhibit ADHD-type behaviours to engage and focus in class [19].

Physical exercise has the greatest efficacy of all non-pharmacological treatment modalities for neurodevelopment disorders such as ADHD [20], providing short- and long-term positive effects that come without any negative side effects. Scheduling exercise breaks within the school day helps kids diagnosed with ADHD to behave in class, concentrate on what is being taught and study successfully [18]. Of all types of physical exercise, active play is especially beneficial in the management of ADHD in children and adolescents [21].

KIDS NEED TO PLAY...

Beyond the benefits of regular exercise, engaging in active play is necessary to support kids' development. Not only is engaging in play inherently pleasurable and rewarding but it also serves vital functions from a developmental perspective. Active play is a characteristic behaviour in youngsters, especially among mammals. The fact that this intrinsic drive to play exists across species speak to the importance of play in the developmental process and its role in learning to survive and thrive [22]. Humans have the longest period of infant dependency of all mammals, so it follows that play would have all the more prominent role during our extended childhood. In fact we have brain circuitry that is specifically devoted to play [23]!

Play is exploratory and inherently interactive. As they play, kids experiment with different ways of physically interacting with objects and their surroundings, discovering new possibilities and developing their capabilities as a result. Reflecting the range of functions it fulfils, there are different categories of play, such as locomotor play, object play and social play. In this way, play can take the form of physically interacting with their environment, external objects and other players.

Continuing the theme of brain and body developing in tandem, play not only develops motor control and coordination but it is also central to how the brain develops. For instance, play is specifically implicated in the maturation of frontal lobe brain structures and the prefrontal cortex in adolescents [24]. Hence play is integral to both motor and cognitive development for children and adolescents.

Satisfying the need to play is crucial if we want kids to develop properly. Studies from other mammals indicate that depriving juveniles of play hinders development in ways that negatively impacts cognitive, emotional and social functioning [23]. Play is imperative for young males especially [25]. Social play in particular is indispensable from a brain development perspective.

Sadly, opportunities to play and be active are increasingly restricted at school. Boys in particular often struggle when they are not able to satisfy their craving for regular physical exercise and active play, which increases the likelihood of behavioural issues. Coincidentally, boys are also twice as likely to be diagnosed with ADHD compared to girls [26]. Frighteningly, there is evidence to suggest that ADHD is presently over diagnosed in children and adolescents [27], implying that some proportion of these kids are simply manifesting a need to be active and play that is not being served.

It follows that providing opportunities to be physically active when not in class and outside school via extracurricular sport and unsupervised play has become all the more important. This is especially crucial given that the pharmacological solution that is increasingly favoured in different parts of the world (notably North America) acts in part by suppressing the brain circuitry involved with play [28]. We have no clear idea what effects this has from a developmental perspective, but I strongly suspect they are not positive. Conversely, as play is associated with the same areas of the brain that are implicated with ADHD, it follows that active play is especially effective as a therapeutic modality in this population [21] – plus there are no negative side effects!

As childhood progresses, play increases in complexity. Competitive sports are effectively just a more sophisticated and complex form of play. Whilst young children spontaneously engage in simple games and play activities with each other, over time youth sport increasingly fulfils the continuing need for play in older children and teens.

LEARNING TO NAVIGATE RISK…

Testing the limits of our capabilities and the boundaries of what is safe is another characteristic theme of play that is invaluable. Inevitably, as kids push into this frontier territory, they will encounter risks and some element of danger. In doing so they learn to recognise threats, assess risks and manage themselves accordingly. So-called 'risky play' serves a variety of functions, not least providing a means to confront fears and overcome anxiety.

Engaging in risky play is integral to how kids develop their ability to navigate risk, learning risk tolerance and honing their judgement. The developmental significance of risky play has been highlighted in mental health, emotion regulation and ability to handle social situations [29]. Unfortunately, over recent times well-meaning grown-ups have been increasingly getting in the way of this!

Paradoxically, there have been recent calls from public health researchers to restore opportunities for 'risky' outdoor play for children and youth. The move to promote risky play as a pillar of healthy development has become necessary to counter the growing prevalence of anxiety and risk aversion among young people, which has been the legacy of the *safetyism* that has taken hold in different parts of the world over recent times [30].

The desire to keep kids safe is eminently understandable, but when we deprive kids of the opportunity to learn how to navigate physical risks, we render them less capable of dealing with risk and more anxious as a result.

FIGURING OUT HOW TO PLAY NICELY WITH OTHERS…

Many of the developmental aspects described also help kids to negotiate other players. Whilst solo play allows kids to explore and experiment with different ways of interacting with the external world and objects, engaging in games that feature other players adds an extra dimension. It follows that play that involves others is especially crucial from a developmental perspective.

Social play develops the social brain. The socialising process is essentially learning how to play with others. Inviting others to play and asking to join in a game are how children form social bonds with other children and make friends. Social play teaches reciprocity – for instance, taking turns. Reciprocity is integral to all healthy and enduring relationships, so this is a key lesson!

Aside from the interpersonal aspects, play that involves others is linked to other facets of cognitive development that are concerned with self-regulation, decision-making, adaptability and creativity. Engaging in social play serves to foster kids' adaptability and permits them to acquire the coping skills to deal with ambiguity and handle challenges [22]. Playfulness is even shown to be important to forming short- and long-term relationships once children become adults [31].

Learning how to negotiate other players is an extension of figuring out how to operate within the rules of the game so that they are able to participate successfully. There is both a cooperative and a competitive element to play, just as there is in sport. We must learn to cooperate if we want to participate in a manner that ensures others want to play with us, starting with agreeing on a game that each party wants to play.

As we test out the limits of what our bodies can do, the games we play with others also serve to teach us where the boundaries are and how far we can push things with others. For instance, rough and tumble play teaches the line between 'playful' versus conduct that is deemed unacceptable. Engaging with different play partners (both boys and girls) also helps kids to learn to modulate their behaviour according to who they are playing with.

Playing with others provides the forum to experiment and develop a repertoire of behaviours and social skills. Play is typically not a one-off activity but rather something we engage in on a serial basis, such that the same participants are involved in successive games. We generally want others to agree to play with us again, so figuring how to conduct ourselves in ways that will be deemed acceptable by those we are playing with is highly valuable information.

LEARNING TO PLAY FAIR…

'The moral value of exercises and sports far outweigh the physical value.'

– Plato

Games typically involve rules, so participating in the game necessitates regulating impulses and modifying behaviour to operate within those constraints. Even if the rules are unspecified, as they participate in the game over and over again kids intuit what constitutes 'fair play'.

Without any intervention from the grown-ups, the young performer will be schooled by their peers on how to play in a manner that is permissible and conducive to their future participation. Moral and ethical behaviour thus tends to emerge spontaneously simply as a consequence of playing the game over and over again. Unsupervised play even helps to foster conflict resolution skills!

Competitive games (such as youth sports) serve other important functions. Through playing these games kids learn how to conduct themselves properly when they compete. Kids also learn how to respond appropriately and regulate their emotions when they win and lose. Kids are tacitly rewarded by their peers when they are magnanimous in victory and gracious in defeat. Sore losers and those who gloat when they win are far less well received.

Once again, arguably the biggest lesson that kids learn over time is reciprocity. In other words, they learn how to be a competitor who plays fair. Team games additionally teach us how to be a good team-mate as well as a fair opponent.

Naturally, all of this applies to kids' participation in youth sports. If navigated in the right way, youth sports have the potential to help foster moral and social beings. Youth sports are a vehicle to instil good values and foster empathy [32]. That said, the grown-ups have an important role in setting the right tone and modelling key tenets of fair play, not least in their treatment of competitors or the opposing team. Sadly, coaches and parents on the sidelines can equally have a negative influence on the attitudes and behaviours of young athletes [33]. The ethos within the organisation as it relates to sportsmanship and fair play should be important criteria when selecting a youth sports club.

BARRIERS TO ENTRY AND ENJOYMENT…

The more time kids spend engaged in outdoor active play, the more likely they are to be active throughout the day, such that they are less likely become sedentary [34]. If we want to encourage kids to adopt active and healthy lifestyles, then it is important that we acknowledge and address the barriers.

One of the major barriers is motor competence. The link between motor skill development in children and health behaviours during childhood and later life is well established. There is a direct connection between fundamental motor skill proficiency, habitual physical activity and physical fitness [35]. This relationship works both ways: less active kids have less well developed general motor skills; and kids with poor motor skills tend to be less active.

The increase in screen time even among young children means that kids are not only becoming less active but also demonstrating lower general motor skill development as a result. Over the past decade especially, digital technology and time spent engaging with a screen has also emerged as a major threat that is displacing active play. Perhaps the biggest consequence is that less kids possess the basic level of proficiency to enjoy engaging in sport, contributing to the decline in participation.

A certain level of motor competence naturally makes it easier to engage in active play – a well-coordinated kid can quickly pick up the rudiments of most games. Possessing a basic level of general motor skill proficiency greatly improves the experience and makes participating in activities inherently more enjoyable and less a cause for apprehension. Conversely, kids who perceive that their basic motor skills are not up to standard are understandably reticent to take part.

As well as being a barrier to entry, inadequate fundamental motor skill development is also a reason for kids dropping out of sport. Lack of competence (whether perceived or actual) makes it more likely that kids will withdraw and lapse into a sedentary lifestyle. This is especially the case as kids reach their teens and become more sensitive to social evaluation from their peers.

This is a classic example of a positive versus negative feedback loop. On the one hand, there is a virtuous cycle, whereby more proficient movers are more inclined to play and in turn likely to be more active overall, leading them to become more capable and ready to participate over time. On the other, kids who perceive themselves to be less proficient are less likely to participate, increasing the likelihood of being sedentary and causing them to fall further behind, such that they become even less inclined to participate as time goes on.

Most parents and coaches will attest to the fact that there is a steep drop off in participation numbers when kids reach their early teens in various sports. This is particularly the case for girls; many of whom cease to participate in sport entirely (and this mirrors the higher proportion of girls failing to meet daily physical activity levels compared to boys). There is an evident need to combat these troubling trends, as the consequences of the decline in participation over the adolescent years are bigger than we realise.

As an aside, perhaps this is part of what explains the rise of e-sports! A growing number of kids are more adept and certainly more comfortable manipulating an avatar on a screen with the aid of a handheld controller than moving their own body. For many this has become the easier and more compelling option than acting with their body and limbs to explore, play and compete in the real world. Sadly, such choices also rob kids of the most important benefits of active play, physical exercise and participation in sport.

To be clear, e-sports is a misnomer. I caused much consternation in my most recent role with a commercial sport and health organisation when they launched an e-sports venture and I refused to comply with an order to refer to e-sports players coming into the facility as 'athletes'. It may be that some athletes happen to participate in e-sports; however, playing e-sports does not make an athlete. The term 'athlete' should be reserved for and restricted to the physical realm. The fact this was a controversial viewpoint demonstrates how far from the path we have strayed...

WIDER IMPLICATIONS...

Satisfying kids' need to engage in physical exercise and play is not only important for their development during childhood and adolescence. Engagement in physical exercise, outdoor play and participating in sport (as opposed to e-sports gaming) throughout childhood and adolescence also influences lifestyle choices and habitual physical activity in adulthood. It is firmly established and widely recognised that childhood exercise is medicine (that is also free of the harmful side effects that come with pharmaceuticals). The benefits extend into adulthood and concern both body and mind. This does also mean that the consequences for failing to meet these needs are similarly extensive and lasting.

A prominent example is that the declining levels of physical activity among youth has coincided with greater mental health issues reported among children and adolescents particularly. There is much evidence to suggest that this is likely a causal relationship. Measures of physical fitness and mental health among children and adolescents are demonstrably related to each other [36]. Lower general motor skill competency is further linked to both reduced physical fitness and to worse mental health among adolescents [37].

The increasing hours that modern youth are spending on a screen correspond to less time spent engaging in physical activity such that it is linked to more sedentary behaviour. The rising use of digital technology since the advent of the smartphone has come at the cost of reduced social interaction with peers, which has led to a concomitant increase in reported loneliness among adolescents [38]. Worse still, screen time in general and the use of mobile digital technology in particular is a common cause of sleep disruption among children and adolescents [39]. The negative effects of screen time on psychological and emotional wellbeing are thus likely due in part to sleep disruption [40]. This is especially problematic for teens, in part because the adolescent brain is particularly sensitive to the negative effects of insufficient sleep [41].

Key Take-Home Messages

1. Body and brain develop together. Movement does not just develop motor skills but is also essential for cognitive function, learning and brain development.

2. Regular physical activity is vital for healthy development in children and the need for regular physical exercise and active play remains evident among teens [42].

3. Play is a fundamental need and essential for development. Play promotes motor skills, brain development, creativity, social competence, emotional resilience.

4. Physical activity supports academic performance and attention. Regular movement improves concentration, memory, problem-solving, and classroom engagement.

5. Risky play builds confidence and reduces anxiety. When children explore physical risk, they develop risk assessment, resilience, courage, and emotional regulation.

6. Social play shapes character, values and morals. By playing with others children learn fairness, cooperation, conflict resolution, emotional control and sportsmanship.

7. Fundamental motor skills are a gateway to participation. Competence in basic motor skills increases confidence and enjoyment.

8. Screen time is displacing active play and harming development. Excessive screen use reduces physical activity, sleep quality, mental health and social interaction.

9. Early activity habits influence lifestyle into adulthood. Lifelong physical and mental health are shaped by movement and play patterns established in childhood.

Practical Tips for Parents

✓ Aim for daily opportunities to be active and spend time outdoors (ideally in nature).

✓ Prioritize motor skill development: Use games, obstacle courses, outdoor play.

✓ Protect time for free and social play: Schedule playtime like any other priority. Encourage group games, backyard challenges, and outdoor exploration.

✓ Allow regulated risk-taking: Let kids climb, jump, explore, and test limits under supervision, without overprotectiveness. Help kids to manage risk rather than avoid it.

✓ Promote social interaction without screens: Encourage play with peers, team activities, and group problem-solving games. Limit isolation due to digital devices.

✓ Create a movement-friendly home environment: Provide simple equipment: balls, bikes, skipping ropes, bats, chalk, garden spaces.

✓ Choose active family activities (walks, hikes, bike rides, backyard games).

✓ Youth sports increasingly fulfil the need for play in older children and teens…
…however, youth sports do not have to be organised and supervised by grown-ups!

✓ Guide moral and social development through sports – parents and coaches shape values, so model the right behaviour and choose clubs based on ethos of fair play.

✓ Set the example by being active and engaged in the physical world and model responsible use of digital technology especially when kids are around.

✓ Regulate screen use at home. Set clear boundaries on digital technology. Limit screen time, keep devices out of bedrooms and protect pre-bedtime routine.

Action Items

» Build a daily movement habit as a family and strive to keep family life playful. Schedule unstructured play: reserve screen-free time and space for free play.

» Create opportunities for social play: Coordinate with other parents to provide options for drop-in free play and pick-up games for kids in your neighbourhood

» Explore setting up a chapter of the Let Grow project* to offer before and after school free play opportunities in partnership with your school and local community.

» Introduce managed risk: Allow climbing, exploring, jumping, rough-and-tumble play.

» Model fair play and sportsmanship in your sideline conduct and communication.

» Limit digital technology, especially during the early years. Maintain screen-free zones (bedroom, dining table) and limit screen use in the evenings, especially before bed.

* https://letgrow.org/

Realising the Full Benefits of Youth Sports

Parents intuitively understand that youth sport is worthwhile for the direct and indirect benefits it provides. On the other hand, signs of declining participation and the tendency for kids to opt out during the high school years indicate that parents and kids themselves might not fully appreciate how crucial sport can be to success in other realms and their wellbeing in general. It is a quirk of the human condition that we do not tend to appreciate what we have until it is taken away. In some ways it may have taken a global pandemic to highlight just what an important role sport plays in the lives of children and adolescents. The period of the pandemic revealed the full extent of what kids miss out on when deprived of these opportunities. Observing the host of ill effects that ensued ironically provided a vivid illustration of the myriad benefits that youth sport provides.

Organised sport (below the elite level) was a notable casualty of covid-19 and even once kids cautiously returned to school, youth sports and competitive school sport in particular remained off limits for many. Competitive seasons were suspended for an extended period. The disruption and uncertainty extended all the way up to college sports, which is the end-goal that many student-athletes aspire to. Against this backdrop, the numbers of kids attending practices (once they were able) declined dramatically. Whilst covid-19 might now be in the rearview mirror, participation in organised sports among younger children has failed to recover to pre-pandemic levels. We are contemplating a generation of high school kids who may be lost from participating in organised sport.

More generally, there has been a blinkered view of public safety that overlooks the wider impacts. The policy decisions, whilst understandable early in the pandemic, failed to weigh the costs of depriving kids of opportunities to participate in the name of safety. The detrimental second-order effects of these decisions and the associated harms soon became evident and are now impossible to ignore. Public health policy brought about an increase in sedentary behaviour among kids, with sport and physical activity being replaced with greater time spent engaged with screens, especially among adolescents [43]. Rates of childhood obesity have increased over the period [44] and these adverse changes in lifestyle and health-related behaviours have also been mirrored by a decline in wellbeing among children and adolescents [45].

Most of us are reluctant to look back on the period of the pandemic; however, beyond serving as a cautionary tale and it also offers a unique opportunity to reaffirm why and how participating in sport is more valuable than ever from a developmental perspective. Detailing the many ways that participating in sport can assist kids and adolescents in various aspects of their life will hopefully enable parents, coaches and performers to better appreciate all the potential good that sport can serve and prioritise accordingly. In this way the pandemic might yet prove to be the catalyst that reaffirms the role of sport in the lives of young people. We can hope that growing awareness might prompt more initiatives and greater collaboration from stakeholders to allow a greater number of kids to experience the benefits. For coaches and parents this will hopefully lead to more conscious efforts and greater cooperation to ensure that all the potential benefits are actually realised in practice.

SPORT CONNECTS PEOPLE…

With so much of a young person's life is being lived through their smartphones in the digital era, the propensity of sport to connect people has arguably never been more relevant or more necessary. Kids who have grown up in the smartphone era report less in-person social interaction with their peers compared to previous generations [38]. Kids who routinely exceed one hour of screen time each day are more likely to report worse psychological wellbeing and a host of related behavioural and social difficulties [46].

Organised youth sports serve as a forum for in-person interaction. Beyond that, engaging in sport also takes phones out of kids' hands. Anybody who has watched kids gathered together, but each glued to their screen understands this importance of this point. Sport represents one of the last bastions for young people to connect with each other and interact with people outside their usual social circle, without electronic devices getting in the way.

Sport is unique in its ability to bring together individuals from different social and ethnic groups. In this way, youth sports help benefit the local community and society in general. Participation in organised youth sports brings young people into contact with others from the local community and beyond – many of whom they might not otherwise interact with. On the field of play everybody is free to participate without favour. Sport is often the place where great friendships and lasting bonds are forged.

Whilst team sports are the obvious example of how sport teaches teamwork, all sports require kids to learn to engage cooperatively and competitively with others such that it is a vehicle for social and emotional learning. Participation in group-based sporting activities is especially beneficial for developing the self-regulation capabilities that help kids to manage themselves and regulate their interactions with others [47].

SPORT ENCOURAGES PROSOCIAL BEHAVIOUR…

Participation in sport positively impacts behaviour in children and youth. Youth sports foster *prosocial behaviour* (i.e. acting to help or benefit others of their own volition). Engaging in sport from an early age is beneficial for boys especially; those who regularly participate in sport and group play are less likely to develop behavioural problems later in childhood [48].

Those who participate in organised team sport in particular are less liable to lapse into antisocial and delinquent behaviours [49]. Among the benefits of outdoor sport participation within communities is a reduction in antisocial behaviour and even reduced involvement in criminal activity. High school students (of all ethnicities) who participate in sport report fewer disciplinary problems and are less likely to drop out from school [50].

SPORT HELPS KIDS TO PERFORM IN THE CLASSROOM...

The wider benefits of engaging in active play and participating in school sport and youth sport are similarly underappreciated from a learning perspective. There is an assumption among some parents that sport distracts from school. The data do not bear this out. Not only do large-scale studies fail to find any negative impact [51], participating in sport helps kids to pay attention in class. Consistent participation in extracurricular sport is associated with better classroom engagement in children aged 6-12 years and this is especially the case with boys [52].

When handled properly, participating in sport complements academic study in a way that has a net positive effect on grades. Far from being mutually exclusive, it is possible that investing time becoming better at sport can actually help kids to do better in school. Sporting participation in and out of school provides a structured environment that allows kids to channel their energy in a healthy and positive way, whilst simultaneously boosting brain function.

The type of moderate-to-vigorous physical exercise that features in sport confers particular benefits, in terms of neurocognitive performance and executive functions such as attention [53]. In addition to the transient enhancement of neurocognitive function following physical exercise, regular participation leads to beneficial and lasting changes over time in children and adolescents [54]. Each of these findings helps to explain how participation in sport benefits kids' academic performance on the whole.

Neuroplasticity describes how the brain changes its circuitry and makes new neuronal connections in response to the conditions experienced. Regularly engaging in sport and physical exercise supports and stimulates these processes that allow the brain to adapt its structure and function over time. Sporting activity that develops coordination and motor skills is therefore especially beneficial for neurocognitive development and the links between fundamental motor skill proficiency and academic achievement are particularly strong [55]. An illustration of how sport practice changes the brain is that the brains of elite athletes exhibit more grey matter, reflecting their repertoire of highly developed motor skills [56].

As many parents will attest to, boys have a particular need to run around and be active on a regular basis [57]. That said, it is equally important to promote opportunities and boost participation in sport among females given that overall girls tend to be less active and drop out from sport earlier.

It is evident that there is a specific need and a host of benefits that come from participating in sport for kids classified as *neurodivergent* [58]. Extracurricular sport is accordingly considered medicine for these kids. Participating in extracurricular sport during middle childhood is specifically advocated to ameliorate ADHD-type symptoms [59]. Once again, the pandemic highlighted that those most at need are also worst affected when deprived of these opportunities.

When opportunities to engage in physical exercise and organised youth sports become restricted this poses serious negative consequences that affect not just the fitness of young bodies but also young minds. Moreover, the loss or lack of these opportunities is not just a problem for children; the physical exercise and opportunities to develop motor skills provided by youth sports remain vital in adolescence. Participating in sport engages different facets of prefrontal cortex function, which is significant as this region of the brain is still in development in adolescents and is integrally involved in social and emotional intelligence as well as executive function [60].

SPORT SUPPORTS MENTAL HEALTH AND WELLBEING...

It is well established that physical activity and exercise enhance mood and wellbeing. Regularly engaging in physical exercise and sport are accordingly positively linked with mental health in children and adolescents [36]. Beyond these direct benefits of regular exercise, engaging in sport has ancillary benefits that further improve psychosocial wellbeing and *resilient coping* [61]. Regular physical exercise helps to manage and relieve life stress and youth sport provides a sanctuary from difficulties faced in other facets of life, providing periods of respite and serving as an outlet to blow off steam. Active play assists coping among children even in the most challenging times [22]. Adolescence is certainly a stressful and challenging period in the lives of many young people, especially in the present era, so the value of sport in supporting psychological and emotional health and wellbeing cannot be overstated.

As during the pandemic, the degree of the benefits of participation are most conspicuous when these opportunities are absent: the trajectory for health-related quality of life is objectively worse for kids who do not participate in organised sport [62]. Excessive time spent on screens was one of the biggest reasons for the decline in mental health during this period. Illustrating the psychosocial impact, kids in urban areas with low engagement in organised sports during the childhood years are twice as likely to become withdrawn and report depressive symptoms compared to those with high sports participation [63].

Data from Australia mirror these findings in adolescents: greater participation in team sports predicted lower incidence of depression and anxiety symptoms over time [64]. A large-scale study of high school students in Canada similarly reported that those who participated in varsity sport reported lower depression and anxiety symptoms [65]. These latter findings are highly pertinent given that adolescents represent an increasingly high-risk group from a mental health and psychosocial wellbeing viewpoint. Participation in organised sports during adolescence creates a virtuous cycle: engaging in sport fosters better mental health in teens; and better mental health in turn increases the probability that they will remain engaged in sport [66].

Adolescence represents a *neurobiological critical period* that is pivotal in shaping how the individual responds to stress. What conditions individuals are exposed to during the phase and what adaptation occurs in key structures of the brain as a result has a major bearing on their reactivity to stress during adulthood. The enduring benefits of regular exercise and participation in sport during this formative period serve a protective effect that make the individual more resilient to stress and less prone to neurological conditions in later life. An illustration of the prominent role of activity and its lasting effects is that level of physical activity during early adolescence is predictive of depressive symptoms reported three years later [67]. The reported effects were especially pronounced in boys: low physical activity predicted depressive symptoms, whereas high physical activity demonstrated a protective effect.

Regular physical exercise proved to be one of the few protective factors that mitigated the widespread negative impact on psychological wellbeing of the lockdowns and pandemic restrictions among children and adolescents. Young athletes are well placed to access these benefits and those who proved able to motivate themselves to engage in high-intensity training independently suffered less of a negative impact on their physical and mental health during the lockdown and ongoing restrictions [68].

Group-based activities and team sports are especially beneficial for psychosocial wellbeing, which makes it all the more unfortunate that these types of sporting activities were most restricted. Whilst authorities have been slow to acknowledge the public health time bomb created by policy decisions, public health experts have started to emphasise the need to provide opportunities and encourage kids to engage in sport and exercise as a countermeasure against the negative mental and physical health impacts of the pandemic [69].

That said, young athletes were not spared from the mental health impact. The suspension of organised sports had a marked negative effect on student athletes and naturally young performers who were approaching the culmination of their high school athletic career over this period were the hardest hit, not least due to the potential impact on their college prospects [45]. The prevalence of anxiety symptoms was higher among female student athletes compared to males [45]. Those who compete in team sport have been relatively more likely to report depressive symptoms, reflecting the prominent social element of team sports, which supports team sports athletes' wellbeing under normal circumstances. Ironically, the pandemic favoured athletes in individual sports from both these perspectives as they tend to be more accustomed to training solo and also less affected by the absence of social interaction.

SPORTS BUILDS CONFIDENCE AND BELONGING...

Sport fulfils a unique function for so many kids as the source of much needed opportunities to gain confidence and self-esteem. Sport can be a sanctuary where an otherwise shy and self-conscious young person is able to engage with others, express themselves and perhaps even excel. Regardless of social standing, if a kid can play their peers will welcome them.

Amidst the general flux and confusion of the teenage years, sport often provides something of a safe space where things remain predictable. The field of play is one of the few realms that remains constant. The terms of engagement are not opaque; everybody understands the rules of the game and generally operates in accordance with them. Much of the awkwardness that impedes interactions in other facets of life is thus avoided in the domain of sport.

Organised youth sports have become all the more crucial in combating the epidemic of loneliness among adolescents who spend less time socialising with each other in person than previous generations [38]. Sport creates enduring friendships and provides crucial social support that the young person is are able to lean on during challenging times. The friendships, banter and encouragement from peers are a big part of what makes the experience enjoyably and are frequently cited reasons why kids choose to participate and remain engaged in sport.

The social element of sport and exercise is particularly important for young females from the perspectives of motivating participation and deriving mental health benefits [67]. These interactions also provide a safety valve from the stresses encountered in the sport and beyond the sporting arena.

SPORT FOSTERS A HEALTHY LIFESTYLE...

Organised youth sports participation is associated with better health-related behaviours in children and adolescents. For instance, kids who play team sports are less likely to engage in smoking and drug use [49]. High school students who participate in organised youth sport are also less liable to engage in self-harm [70].

Engaging in organised sport during childhood and adolescence has lasting positive effects that carry over into the years that follow. For instance, a 12-year follow up study demonstrated that kids who participate in organised sport through middle school and high school retain the positive health habits such that they remain significantly healthier than their peers once they reach adulthood [71]. The tendency for youth sports participation to translate to higher physical activity and better physical fitness in early adulthood is especially evident among females [72].

Given the overwhelming benefits, it is helpful for us to be aware of the trends in youth sports participation and understand the points at which kids tend to drop out so that we can act to improve retention. A notable finding is that ages 6-9 years are crucial for getting girls involved in organised sport, as the trends suggest those who commence their participation in these years are most likely to remain involved in sport [73]. The data also indicate that if we miss that window, it is rare for girls to start participating in organised sport thereafter.

From a retention perspective, the 'tween years that bridge childhood and adolescence similarly appear pivotal in determining kids' participation in sports and general level of physical activity in the years that follow. It appears that kids break one of two ways at this point: some proportion remain physically active and choose to engage in a range of extracurricular activities; whereas the remainder lapse into more sedentary lifestyles, with increasing time spent engaged with screens (those two things being related) [74].

SPORT EQUIPS KIDS FOR THE GAME OF LIFE...

Something that parents prize is the potential for youth sports to teach life lessons and foster habits and behaviours that will help kids to be successful as adults [32]. It is notable that former competitive high school and collegiate athletes are well represented among leaders and high performers in different professions and fields such as business and commerce. Those who have engaged in competitive sport bring traits and capabilities that serve them well in the professional sphere. Former athletes characteristically possess skills that are highly prized by prospective employers. Many leaders in business and other domains share a history in college and high school sport, which naturally makes them quick to appreciate these qualities in their staff and in applicants when recruiting.

The experience of participating in organised youth sport has the propensity to develop productive behaviours and life skills. More specifically, competitive sport provides a forum to struggle, fail and overcome difficulties in a relatively low risk environment. Whilst their ego and body might take a few blows in the process, kids largely come through the experience of competing and testing themselves unscathed. Competitive sport also has the element of performing under pressure, which is a major asset in high stakes professional settings.

"You are not committed to something unless you are willing to sacrifice for it"

– Professor Jordan B. Peterson

Being successful in sport requires dedication. The process of training and practice teaches kids to apply themselves and exercise discipline. Young performers (hopefully) learn what it means to commit to a future goal and work diligently to attain it. In the process they come to understand the benefits that accrue from regular investment of effort over time and gain a genuine appreciation of the value of toil, tenacity and perseverance.

Key assets that young performers develop include the ability to *invest* themselves in working towards a long-term goal, *persist* in their quest and *resist* distractions along the way. It is worth highlighting that such qualities have become all the more important in the digital era and the benefits apply to achieving long-term goals in all competitive domains, not just sport. An illustrative example is the West Point military academy: neither physical fitness or academic grades predict success of new recruits entering the highly demanding selection process, but rather it is the attributes we have described, most notably measures of grit, that separates those who emerge successful [75].

Beyond developing key attributes, the process of purposefully preparing and practising and the experience of competition with all its attendant struggles, each serve to develop highly transferable skills that equip young people to strive and be successful in their professional and personal lives.

Regularly engaging in physical exercise in itself acts as a buffer that helps kids to regulate their own conduct and cope with challenge. The transient effects of exercise can help kids to navigate stressful situations and regulate the emotions they experience in response [76]. In addition to all the benefits that come from regular exposure to exercise, participation in youth sports confers other positive effects. Through sport kids learn self-regulation skills [77] that help them to adjust to school and other social contexts. Engaging in organised youth sports and other types of group-based activity during childhood is likewise associated with better emotional development [78].

Open skill sports (team sports, racquet sports) are particularly advantageous, as young performers are required to respond to constantly changing conditions, which in turn fosters cognitive flexibility and adaptability [79]. During practices and in the competitive arena kids become familiar with facing challenges, helping them to learn how to respond to setbacks in a positive and productive manner. The trials of competition likewise afford rich opportunities for young performers to develop resilience and the coping tools that are crucial for weathering life's storms.

REALISING THESE BENEFITS IN PRACTICE…

Whilst in theory each of the potential benefits we have described are available to all, we cannot assume that they are always realised in practice. Parents have a pivotal role here, not least when it comes to selecting the most conducive environment and a coaching set up that is capable of delivering these benefits, as we will explore in the next section. In turn, the coaches and practitioners involved share a responsibility to ensure that the environment, coaching input and support delivered provides full value. As noted in the previous chapter, part of this responsibility is making sure that kids are proficient and thus able to enjoy participating, as this will go a long way to ensuring that they remain active and retain the benefits of engaging in sport through the critical adolescent years.

Just as it is useful for parents and coaches to know the points when kids drop out, it is also helpful to be aware of the barriers to participation and understand how these change as kids progress through their journey. During the childhood years the challenges are mainly logistical – which reinforces why parents are so crucial in providing transport and the wherewithal for kids to attend. However, as we transition into the early adolescent years the reasons that kids drop out begin to change and it becomes more about what the experience provides (or not) [80]. The steep decline in participation in organised sport in the early teenage years, especially among females, suggests much work is to be done in this area. Beyond addressing logistical and financial barriers to participation and retention, we need to give more attention to ensuring that the experience is positive and meets the needs of young performers.

Practically, coaches, parents and the athletes themselves each have a role to remain mindful and do their part to ensure the youth sport experience delivers the good parts, whilst taking steps to avoid or otherwise mitigate the factors that can sour the experience. How young performers approach their participation is certainly part of the equation. What mindset they bring to the pursuit and how they appraise the ups and downs they encounter along the way will similarly have a decisive bearing on the experience and what benefits they derive.

As the grown-ups, we have a prominent role and share a responsibility to retain a healthy perspective and model the right behaviours. Whilst youth sport has the potential to be prosocial and foster good health behaviours, this does depend on the environment and the motivational climate surrounding the young athlete's participation. Excessive external pressure and a winning at all costs mentality can equally have a toxic influence and elicit negative behaviours [81]. How we conduct ourselves towards opposing teams and officials, how we react in different situations and how we respond when things go awry are all important from this perspective.

IN SUMMARY...

This chapter offers a reminder and perhaps a newfound appreciation of the wider value of youth sports. The benefits extend far beyond sport and the direct rewards of competition. Engaging in youth sports helps kids in multiple domains, from the classroom to their personal lives. The prospective advantages of participation include supporting academic achievement, developing life skills, providing social interaction, creating friendships and social support. The trials and experiences that youth sport provides are invaluable in fostering key skills and attributes that set kids up to be successful in life.

The dwindling opportunities for active play and decline in physical education, compounded by the catastrophic effects of the restrictions over the period of the pandemic represent a public health time bomb. Declining participation and the precipitous drop off in participation seen in many youth sports around early adolescence is likewise a problem that administrators, coaches and parents need to work together to solve. Restricting or discouraging youth sport participation risks taking away a key source of physical and mental health for children and teens. Should we fail to heed the warning and lessons provided by the pandemic, the harsh reality of the negative health consequences that are already starting to manifest themselves will soon become impossible to ignore.

Key Take-Home Messages

1. Youth sport delivers far-reaching benefits beyond physical fitness — including cognitive development, academic performance, emotional wellbeing, social skills, resilience, and lifelong health habits.

2. The full value of youth sport often goes unrealised unless it is intentionally supported by parents, coaches, and environments.

3. The pandemic exposed how crucial sport is for children's mental health, social connection, behaviour, and overall wellbeing.

4. Sport is a powerful platform for learning life skills such as perseverance, teamwork, discipline, coping with setbacks, and managing emotions.

5. Participation in sport protects against screen addiction, sedentary lifestyles, loneliness, anxiety, and depression.

6. The environment, mindset, and motivational climate matter — simply being involved in sport does not guarantee benefits.

7. Dropout from sport is highest in the early adolescent years, particularly among girls, and is influenced more by the quality of experience than by logistics.

8. Youth sport should be valued as a developmental pathway, not just as preparation for competition or performance.

Practical Tips

✓ Ages 6-9 = key window for commencing organised youth sports participation (especially for females) to improve the probability they will continue participating

✓ Emphasise the importance and wider benefits of youth sports to help kids recognise the value beyond sport

✓ Encourage exposure to competitive sport for the valuable lessons and experiences it offers

✓ Strive to model healthy attitudes and behaviours to create a positive motivational climate surrounding their participation

✓ Facilitate continued participation during the high school years for the developmental benefits it provides beyond sport

✓ Recognise and seek to overcome barriers. Watch for early signs of disengagement (loss of enjoyment, anxiety, reluctance.

✓ Resist external pressure or comparison with others. Focus on progress, development and personal goals.

✓ Encourage kids to reflect on what they are learning through sport — not just how they are performing.

✓ Emphasise the friendships, sense of belonging and emotional support that come from shared experiences in competitive sport.

✓ Recognise sport as a stress-relief outlet and a positive coping tool for children and teens that supports mental health and wellbeing.

✓ Help kids to understand how physical activity improves mood, focus, and resilience.

Action Items

» Actively promote sport as a key contributor to children's overall development, not just a leisure activity.

» Enrol kids in team sports for teamwork and cooperation

» Enrol kids in dynamic open skill sports for adaptability and cognitive flexibility!

» Foster life skills intentionally by highlighting how effort, discipline, resilience, teamwork, and problem-solving learned in sport apply to life, school, and work.

» Work collaboratively across parents, coaches, schools, and clubs to make sure kids experience the full benefits of participation.

» Monitor and protect mental health, especially during transition periods or after setbacks, injuries, or performance drops.

» Guard against excessive screen time and sedentary behaviour, using sport as a meaningful alternative for connection, activity, and wellbeing.

The Athletic Skills Gap in Youth Sports

Just as I was starting to write this book, I had a desultory conversation with an athletic director and one of the coaches at a local high school who were both bemoaning the lack of basic movement skills of the kids entering the school. The declining levels of fundamental movement skills among young performers is a common observation and a complaint that I have heard many times from coaches in various sports on my travels over recent years. However, what made the conversation a little troubling was the suggestion that by the time the kids reached high school there was little that could be done for them.

In previous generations kids acquired foundational motor skills (run, jump/land, throw/catch, etc.) through free play and exploration. In this way, kids expanded their movement skill repertoire by running around, climbing on things, jumping off them, etc. Over recent decades there has been a decline in unsupervised play, compounded by a trend towards 'safetyism' that has befallen playgrounds and other outdoor play spaces.

In part due to these trends, it is no longer safe to assume that kids have fully developed what coaches previously considered 'the basics'. The declining proficiency in fundamental movement skills among kids has a number of implications as we will explore, not least inhibiting performance and increasing the likelihood of injury for young athletes.

So, the aforementioned high school coach and athletic director were not wrong in their observations regarding the declining physical literacy of the student body. Where they were entirely wrong however is their suggestion that nothing could be done. Naturally, the earlier the coaching intervention to remedy the situation the better; however, there are no grounds to concede that we cannot salvage the situation. With the proper coaching, young performers can absolutely make meaningful improvements and become more athletic at any stage in their youth sports journey.

'NATURAL' ATHLETICISM IS NO LONGER A GIVEN...

Traditionally, practices and skill development in many youth sports have focussed almost exclusively on technical and tactical elements. For the most part, the need for dedicated development of athletic skills has been largely overlooked. In previous generations this was not a major issue as sports coaches were largely able to rely on the athleticism that young performers had developed on their own. Unfortunately, we are now forced to reckon with these omissions, as the level of 'natural' athleticism among young performers continues to decline at all levels and across sports. A question we need to contemplate is how we can help kids to acquire athletic movement skills and develop relevant capabilities?

Fundamental motor skills are universal (i.e. they are ubiquitous in all forms of human movement). Broadly these general motor skills can be stratified into locomotion skills (crawl, climb, run, jump), object control/manipulation skills (throw, catch) and stability skills (land, balance). These gross motor skills are both generic and generalisable, forming the building blocks for more complex motor skills. Examples of foundational movement skills that are easily recognisable include *run, jump, throw*. These component skills are often combined and sequenced in athletic movements and sport skill techniques (e.g. run up, plant foot, throw) [82].

The continuing decline in free play among children and adolescents that has been especially pronounced with the *i-generation* means that there is less and less opportunity for aspiring young athletes to acquire and hone these general motor skills organically. The downstream effects are increasingly evident and is something frequently commented on by colleagues who work in national sports organisations across multiple sports and in different parts of the world.

There is an ever-growing body of data from different parts of the world that support what coaches and practitioners have been saying [83]. Less than 20% of English schoolchildren aged 6-9 years met the standard for mastery in all four of the gross motor skills assessed [84]. A similar number (around 18%) failed to achieve the standard in any of the four. Girls generally fared worse than the boys – only 12% of the girls met the standard across all criteria.

This is far from an isolated finding. The trends in the data from children in the United States over recent decades paint a similar picture. Despite having been fairly stable over the preceding decades, there has been a consistent decline in general motor competence among children and youth since the year 2000 [85]. What is particularly worrying is that the deterioration has been most marked among 6–10-year-olds.

'It is alarming that adolescents aged between 12 and 13 years entering their first year of post-primary physical education do not display proficiency across nine basic movement patterns' [86]

Unsurprisingly, these concerning findings in primary school aged kids are reflected in the data from older kids and there is an indication that the situation worsens over time. One recent study of 12- and 13-year olds reported that only 1 in 10 demonstrated mastery of all nine fundamental movement skills assessed [86]. The evaluation of fundamental movement skills comprised tasks such as running, skipping, jumping, landing, throwing, catching, dribbling a ball (with the hands), and kicking a ball, which are very much representative of general athletic skills that are common across sports.

Once again, girls overall scored significantly worse than the boys in several of these skills, most notably running, kicking and throwing [86]. The deficits in certain locomotion skill elements and object control skills in general (striking, throwing, catching, bouncing) among school-aged females is a common finding [83]. This has major implications as lack of proficiency in these areas presents a barrier to participation in many sports. In particular, the lower performance on these measures contributes to the lower perceived competence and motivation to participate reported among girls relative to boys of the same age [87].

That said, whilst boys generally score higher on fundamental movement skills, they consistently score worse than girls on body control elements. Boys also tend to perform worse on certain locomotor skills such as skipping that involve different coordination patterns and elements of rhythm [83]. The evidence thus points to these being specific areas requiring remedial development for young males.

PHYSICAL EDUCATION...

Along with the decline in unsupervised active play, both the amount and quality of physical education provided in schools has also been in decline in many parts of the world over recent decades. Using the data from the United Kingdom as an example, the provision of physical education within state-funded secondary schools (ages 11-17) has decreased 16% over the recent period and scores on basic motor skills such as throwing and catching have declined in parallel [88].

Against this backdrop there has been a push to focus on *deliberate play* in early physical education. This policy rests on the assumption that engaging in play during physical education classes will be sufficient to spontaneously develop proficiency. Sadly, the hours spent on physical education within the school timetable has been steadily declining in many parts of the world. Certainly, results to date do not support that this offers an effective solution, at least in isolation.

The less ideological minority have called for dedicating time in physical education classes to develop proficiency in these fundamental movement skills, supported with appropriate instruction [89]. Happily, the deliberate preparation and the deliberate play approaches complement each other [90]. In other words, dedicated time spent developing athletic movement skills (with appropriate coaching input and feedback) in combination with unsupervised free play to put it into practice seems to offer the best way forward.

All the same, the trends in the data demonstrate that we cannot rely on what is delivered in physical education class at school, not least given the ground we need to make up. We should however adopt the *deliberate preparation* in youth sport practices, such that we can cater for athletic movement skill development, just as we do with other sport skills.

EVEN SPORTY KIDS REQUIRE REMEDIAL MOTOR SKILL DEVELOPMENT...

All kids have considerable scope to develop their general motor skills but the necessity for coaching intervention has been highlighted [35]. Reflecting anecdotal reports from my colleagues in different sports, even sporty kids increasingly require remedial development based on the substandard movement competency reported among many youth sports athletes in research investigations [91].

The advent of year-round competition in many youth sports, with a greater emphasis on supervised and coach-led practice from an early age, also increasingly deprives kids of opportunities to develop motor skills by engaging in other sports. Consequently, it is not uncommon to discover that a dedicated young ice hockey player may not be able to run, jump, or skip with any degree of proficiency. Neither can we necessarily expect that a high performing junior-level swimmer will demonstrate basic athletic movement competencies on land.

Participating in organised youth sports similarly does not guarantee 'natural' development of fundamental athletic skills to the same extent as the endless hours engaged in free play that used to be the norm (alongside organised sport). It is argued (and there is near consensus among academics on this point) that participating in a single sport from a young age further narrows the opportunity to develop the full range of athletic skills.

The data do support that children who engage in multiple sports exhibit higher levels of motor coordination compared to their peers who engage in a single sport, whether that sport is (soccer)football [92] or swimming [93]. That said, even athletes who participate in multiple sports may demonstrate shortcomings requiring remedial development. The selection of sports also matters given the array of different elements involved. The inclusion of certain sports such as gymnastics and track and field athletics proves particularly beneficial in this regard [94].

When we consider that specific instruction for athletic movement skills is not commonly included during regular sports practices, it is easy to see how 'natural athleticism' might be increasingly hard to come by without additional support. Extensive time spent in coach-led specialised sport practice is unlikely to confer comprehensive development of the respective motor skill elements.

As these general motor skills are the foundation of sports skills, kids' ability to pick up the rudimentary versions of the skills that feature in a given sport is heavily dependent upon their level of fundamental movement skill competency [95]. In other words, we can make a direct connection between foundational movement skills and sport skills: developing greater general motor skill proficiency makes it easier to acquire the skills and techniques that are specific to the sport. These athletic skills are also crucial to their ability to move effectively and efficiently on the court or field. If the young performer's general motor proficiency is not sufficiently well developed, they will inevitably struggle to cope with the demands of practices and competition especially as they progress on the youth sports journey [91].

The consequences for failing to provide opportunities to bring fundamental motor skills up to standard extend beyond impaired performance. Young performers who have deficiencies in one or more fundamental motor skills are also at heightened risk of various types of sports injury. In particular, the odds of non-contact injury and overuse injury are increased when young performers are lacking in stability and locomotor movement skill proficiency. This is especially evident with young female athletes as these issues become compounded once they hit puberty, as we will explore in the next chapter.

A NEGLECTED PIECE IN THE TALENT DEVELOPMENT JIGSAW...

Whilst long-term athlete development models and those engaged in talent development pathways might refer to fundamental skills and *physical literacy*, I would argue that they do not adequately make the case or indeed offer practical guidance on how coaches might deliver this type of instruction. It remains underappreciated by coaches, parents and the athletes themselves just how vital athletic skills are for aspiring high performers in youth sports.

The idea of *dexterity* is useful here. Let's use the analogy of playing a musical instrument. We would expect the manual dexterity of an aspiring young musician to be highly developed. Playing an instrument demands the ability to move the hands and manipulate the fingers with a high degree of precision, as well as exquisite timing and a well refined sense of rhythm. It is easy to recognise that this type of dexterity similarly applies to the fine motor skills that feature in the particular sport. *Object control* is a fundamental motor skill and one that is critical for sports that involve manipulating an external object or a ball (or both simultaneously such as controlling a ball or puck with a stick). We can equally apply the idea of dexterity to the athletic movement skills that permit the athlete to manipulate their own body, move around and intercept players and objects. There is much the same need for a high degree of control, coordination, precision, timing and rhythm.

Lower limb dexterity is linked to both performance and injury in athletes. Much like the example of dexterity being expressed in the controlling and manipulating an object, in this case the dexterity concerns the interaction between the supporting lower limb and the ground. Young team sports players who have better developed lower limb dexterity are more agile [96]. Conversely, lower proficiency on measures of lower limb dexterity is related to risk of non-contact injury. This makes some sense, as clumsy movers are more liable to fall over, have heavier sounding foot contacts and experience more jarring impacts when they land.

Adolescent female athletes often report lower scores on lower limb dexterity [97], which helps to explain the higher incidence of non-contact lower limb injuries in this population. Interestingly, such deficits in lower limb dexterity do not seem to be evident among elite-level female players, who exhibit similar proficiency to their male counterparts [98]. More highly developed lower limb dexterity differentiates the best performers in these sports, which again makes sense as better performers are recognisably quicker on their feet and more nimble in their movements.

We can apply dexterity to the whole body and all four limbs and call this *movement dexterity*. More dextrous movers are more capable at manipulating their body and manoeuvring themselves with a higher degree of precision, timing and smoothness, which is closer to what we might think of as *athleticism*.

From an athletic preparation standpoint, we need to ensure that young performers are capable of performing the full array of athletic movements that are demanded of them in the competition arena. The necessity of developing these capabilities also applies from a sports injury viewpoint, given that suboptimal movement mechanics are implicated in the non-contact overuse injuries that are common in youth sports. A greater level of athletic skill mastery not only reduces wear and tear but also allows performers to avoid high risk scenarios.

It has been clearly demonstrated that we can make a meaningful difference in improving movement competency and reducing injury risk. Such interventions are typically aimed at early physical education to take advantage of the fertile conditions of *central nervous system plasticity* in children of this age. It is similarly advocated that we commence movement skill training interventions early to inoculate young performers against future injury risk [99]. Logically it makes sense that the earlier we intervene the better; the best way to change the trajectory is to act before these deficits become too entrenched. Nevertheless, remedial movement skills training remains highly efficacious later on in the journey.

ATHLETIC SKILLS ARE SPORTS SKILLS...

Colleagues across sports and in different parts of the world readily attest that the fundamental athletic skills exhibited by athletes at high school and college-level are in decline. There is also general agreement that this trend become more pronounced over the past decade or so. What is striking is that technical sport skills (pitching, swinging, striking and ball skills) show no such decline: kids still exhibit good skills in the context of the sport and remain highly adept when it comes to technical elements. How can we explain this stark difference? It is actually quite simple: these are the elements that are coached and practised regularly, whereas athletic movement skills are typically overlooked.

There is a false separation between sports skills (fine motor skills relating to aspects of technique in the sport, such as swinging a bat or striking a ball) and athletic movement skills. General motor skills are the foundation of sport skills; hence they are referred to as foundational movement skills. These general motor skills serve as the building blocks for sport skills. Cultivating general motor skills also creates a virtuous cycle: the more capable a child becomes, the better able they are to enjoy participating, in turn increasing their desire to engage in sporting activity, which provides further opportunity to become proficient!

Something that reliably distinguishes the better performers in youth sport is a higher level of general motor skill proficiency. There are good reasons why assessments of athletic performance are employed for talent identification and selection. Superior scores on athletic performance assessments are among the few metrics that differentiates starters from non-starters at youth level [100]. If young performers want to stand out they should invest practice time honing these athletic skills. Dedicated athletic movement skill development confers a real performance advantage.

Logically it also makes sense that athletic movement skills merit the investment of time and effort given that for many sports the majority of playing time is spent engaging in these activities. Performers spend hours engaged in practice dedicated to sport skills, whereas the development of athletic skills is typically given only cursory attention or left to chance entirely. This seems all the more nonsensical when we examine the relative time spent engaged in respective activities on the court or on the field.

Let us take 'net' sports such as tennis or volleyball as an example. The relative time players spend interacting with the ball represents a small fraction of total playing time. The remainder of the time players are engaged in repositioning themselves as they react to where the opponent has struck the ball, covering the court to intercept the ball, getting into position to play the shot and then recovering to position themselves to receive the next shot in the rally. Each of these elements constitute athletic skills. If we apply the same analysis to team sports, the disparity between time spent in possession of the ball versus engaged in activity 'off the ball' is greater still.

A GAP IN THE SPORT COACHES' TOOLBOX...

Providing for this growing need and addressing these increasingly common shortcomings will require dedicating time and attention to developing the pillars of athleticism for children and youth, irrespective of the sport. In turn, this calls for coaching input and feedback to facilitate learning, placing the onus back on coaches to provide kids with the requisite athletic skills that they might have acquired naturally in previous generations.

Whether we are talking about conventional 'sport skills' or the generic athletic skills that players require in the sport, the concept of *deliberate practice* applies. The hallmarks of deliberate practice are that the performer engages in a directed manner and with a defined purpose (e.g. improving a specific element of the skill) [101]. As coaches we tend to assume too much when it comes to 'basic' athletic skills such as jumping and running. My experience is that performers frequently lack a clear understanding of what it is they are trying to do.

Whilst there might be some logistical challenges to catering to these generic athletic skills during sport practices, these are far from insurmountable. Arguably the bigger barrier is that sports coaches are not necessarily equipped to provide the requisite instruction and feedback.

IN SUMMARY...

In the absence of exposure to a variety of activities through active play and multi-sport engagement, young athletes are likely to have gaps in their general movement skill set. The athletic skills gap is not only evident in the declining fundamental motor skills of kids, but also in the deficits in physical education and coaching acumen in relation to athletic movement skill development. Sport coaches' natural tendency is to focus on technical skills and tactical aspects; moreover, many lack expertise when it comes to coaching 'generic' athletic skills. Whilst youth sports coaches with a physical education teaching background might be equipped to deliver generic movement skills instruction, for the most part coach education is generally unfit for this purpose, with little content dedicated to athletic skill development, particularly in team sports and racquet sports.

In view of these trends, we must make athletic skill development a priority for young performers. Whatever their main sport, it is crucial that young performers are afforded opportunities to develop their general motor skills and individual performers are well advised to devote practice time to this purpose. Athletic skills are sport skills, as well as being the building blocks of the technical skills in the particular sport. On that basis, the time invested will yield benefits from a sport skill development and performance standpoint, as well as inoculating against injury.

Kids can dramatically improve their general motor skills when given the opportunity and proper coaching input [102]. We know quality physical education helps develop motor competence in children. What is often overlooked is that adolescents likewise remain receptive and highly responsive to physical education. Whether delivered in class or as part of sports practices, dedicated movement skills training is highly efficacious with high school athletes [91], at least when delivered in-person [103].

All of this thoroughly debunks the notion that by the time young performers reach high school they are somehow a lost cause! Indeed even once performers reach the college level they remain able to improve their fundamental motor skills with appropriate coaching intervention and exposure to generic movement skill elements.

Beyond attending class, it is customary for conscientious students to invest time doing homework and in many instances enlist a tutor to engage in outside learning after the school day ends. It would make sense for aspiring young performers to adopt a similar attitude to their athletic development. In this case particularly there is a need to invest in dedicated practice and seek coaching input to fill in the gaps and develop the athletic skills that are most integral for their chosen sport.

Key Take-Home Messages

1. Fundamental movement skills (locomotor, stability, and object control) are declining due to reduced free play, increased screen time, limited physical education and early sport specialisation.

2. Many young athletes lack basic athletic move skill competencies (run, jump, land, throw, catch, balance), even if they are technically skilled in their sport.

3. Athletic movement skills are the foundation of sports skills — they are not separate from but rather integral to sport performance.

4. Deficits in foundational motor skills lead to poorer sport performance, lower confidence, reduced motivation and increased risk of injuries.

5. Girls tend to lag behind boys in object control and locomotor skills, while boys often lag in body control and balance skills.

6. It is never too late to develop athletic skills — significant improvements are possible at any stage, including during high school and college.

7. We assume kids acquire basic movement skills naturally — but becoming competent increasingly requires instruction, feedback and dedicated practice.

8. Simply participating in organised sport does not ensure comprehensive athletic skill development; movement skills demand specific attention.

9. Better movement dexterity (body control, timing, rhythm, coordination) facilitates better performance and reduced injury risk.

10. Physical literacy and athletic skills are a neglected but critical piece in talent development and long-term athlete development (LTAD).

Practical Tips for Parents

✓ Availability of quality physical education is an important criterion when selecting schools.

✓ Treat athletic skills (run, jump, land, change direction, catch, balance) as core skills — not extras.

✓ Identify gaps early — seek out relevant activities to fill the athletic toolbox.

✓ Seek out activities that develop body awareness and kinaesthetic (movement) awareness to help kids understand what good movement looks and feels like.

✓ Use games, challenges, obstacle courses, and circuits to build motor skills in fun, engaging ways.

✓ Aim for a mix of deliberate skill instruction and deliberate play — both are essential.

✓ Expose kids to a range of sports early on — especially those that develop control, coordination, rhythm, spatial awareness (e.g., gymnastics, track and field, martial arts).

✓ Parents can and should request that athletic skill development is catered for by the youth sports teams their child is enrolled in.

✓ Recognise how needs differ for girls vs boys — focus on locomotion and throwing skills for girls, and rhythm/body control for boys.

✓ Treat athletic movement skills as sport skills – strive for mastery and celebrate quality movement skill execution.

Action Items

» Facilitate active free play in a variety of environments.
» Seek out local clubs for track and field athletics (run, jump, throw), gymnastics and swimming during childhood to develop fundamental motor skill proficiency.
» Resist doing too much of one thing — variety develops the athletic toolbox.
» Lobby schools to improve the quality (not just quantity) of physical education, including recruiting specialist physical education teachers.
» Request that schools enlist high calibre coaches to deliver sessions and teacher training sessions to upskill the staff on foundational movement skills development.
» Ask sport coaches and academies to integrate athletic movement and gymnastic skill elements as part of regular practices and routine preparation.
» Seek out athlete development programs that focus on physical and athletic skills.

Over-Scheduled and Under-Trained

Each school year many kids face a schedule stacked with practices and competition, perhaps juggling multiple sports. As kids progress on their youth sports journey they face increasing pressure to invest more and more time (and money). Not only do the hours spent engaged in supervised practices tend to increase, they are also encouraged to attend camps and partake in extra coaching on top of the regular practice and competition schedule. Too often these added extras are pushed on parents and kids based upon the premise that they are necessary to get ahead or avoid falling behind their peers.

As commercialisation and premature professionalism continue to encroach youth sport, these pressures are arising earlier and earlier. During a recent conversation with a friend and colleague, he lamented that his kid's under-11 (soccer)football team were expected to attend four practices each week, in addition to playing games at weekends. Sadly, this is becoming increasingly common.

At the same time, it is advocated that kids should strive to participate in multiple sports. This is well-intentioned and sound in theory; however, the reality on the ground is rarely acknowledged and there is a lack of consideration of the opportunity costs. Whilst variety is beneficial, there are potential negative consequences if we do not first address the issue that the time commitment for any one sport is often excessive. When kids are attending multiple practices each week for one sport, adding more organised sport commitments leaves even less time to devote to general athletic development or physical preparation – or indeed playing with their friends without adults getting in the way.

MIND THE STRENGTH GAP...

An overlooked consequence of declining physical activity and outdoor play is that kids today are notably weaker than in previous generations. Physical performance measures requiring muscular strength have shown a steep downward trend over recent decades. Parents and kids often share the assumption that attending practice will provide the conditioning required to engage in youth sports, yet many young athletes are finding themselves ill-equipped for the physical rigours involved.

The ability to move effectively requires a threshold level of force-generating capacity at each link in the chain. These minimum requirements vary according to the athletic activity in question. More dynamic movements demand greater levels of strength and naturally the minimum requirements change with age, as limbs grow longer and young bodies become heavier.

A young person's experience of participating in youth sport will vary dramatically according to whether or not they possess adequate levels of strength for the demands involved. As long as they meet the threshold level of physical capacity they will be able to participate successfully. However, if they drop below that threshold they will find their ability to participate is compromised and they are liable to suffer more injuries.

Kids who lack strength are physically less robust, as muscular strength undergirds the body's resilience to the stresses and strains associated with sport. Strength deficits are thus implicated in the musculoskeletal injuries that are increasingly common in youth sports.

The reality is that young athletes increasingly need help to cope with the physical demands of youth sport. Dedicated dryland or off-field training becomes all the more necessary as practising and competing in the sport becomes more physically demanding. Sadly, this typically only becomes apparent once young performers start breaking down.

GROWING PAINS...

As we will discuss in the chapter that follows, puberty brings major challenges for young females. Without timely training intervention this sets off a cascade of secondary effects that hinder performance, contribute to girls dropping out of sport and render young female athletes increasingly prone to injury. We will unpack this all in the next chapter, but the implications are that girls should engage in regular dedicated physical preparation from around age 11 onwards to provide the boost they need to continue participating and avoid the negative downstream effects that otherwise occur.

Boys are generally more favoured by nature as puberty comes later and also brings free gains in lean mass, strength, power, speed and endurance (sadly girls are not so fortunate). All the same, pubertal males who participate in youth sports do face growing pains and heightened risk of overuse injuries as a consequence of the combined strains of rapid growth and stresses of practices and competition. Whilst adolescent boys do have the advantage of this 'neuromuscular spurt' to accompany the adolescent growth spurt, there is a lag before these natural gains in strength and function fully kick in. Naturally it also takes time to adapt to their changing bodies and recalibrate their motor control and coordination to adjust to their growing limbs and increasing mass.

Essentially, the danger zone for young male athletes coincides with the periods before, during and immediately following the adolescent growth spurt. It is during this period before they fully grow into their bodies that we see a higher prevalence of musculoskeletal pain and the precursors of common overuse injuries and developmental conditions affecting major joints.

TOO MUCH OF THE SAME, TOO SOON...

Excessive volumes of narrowly focussed sport practice on an immature skeleton can lead to growth-related injuries involving adverse changes to load-bearing bone and joint structures as a result of the repetitive stresses and strains involved. To give an example, cam deformity is a condition affecting the hip joints of young athletes that often leads to impingement, causing pain and altered function. Boys are most prone to suffering from this condition.

Regular sports participation between ages 10 and 14 is linked with this condition. Unsurprisingly it is most prevalent in sports that heavily involve the hip, such as ice hockey, basketball, soccer(football) and alpine skiing. Kids in these sports are 2-8 times more likely than their peers of the same age to develop cam morphology [104]. Lack of variety in sporting participation throughout the year (i.e. early sport specialisation) also makes it more likely that juniors will develop hip impingement due to load-related morphological changes [105].

Increasing the quantity of sporting activity raises the probability of developing these changes. Engaging in more practices per week and accumulating higher weekly volumes of training both increase the odds of suffering from growth-related injuries of this type [106]. Beyond the frequency and volume, the content of practices is also a factor. A narrow focus on specialised sports practice and sports-specific training contribute to the biomechanical overload that cause the maladaptation [107].

High performing juniors, i.e. the ones most likely to have a heavy burden of weekly practices and competitions, are most likely to be affected. Young athletes competing at national or international level are not only more likely to exhibit this condition, but the degree of morphological changes they display is also significantly greater compared to kids who compete at lower levels [108].

The sensitive period for developing growth-related injuries is during the phase of skeletal maturation prior to puberty, with the most pronounced adverse changes associated with cam deformity occurring between ages 11-12 years of age [109]. Once growth plates close no further changes are observed, so from around age 14 onwards the risk subsides for most young athletes, although late-maturing athletes remain at risk until they reach skeletal maturity.

Another factor that contributes to growth-related overuse injuries is that different tissues do not adapt to growing limbs in a uniform manner. Muscle is most responsive, whereas connective tissues tend to lag behind. To compound this, muscle responds to the moderate loading involved in sporting activity, whereas this may not be adequate elicit an adaptive response at the tendon [110]. The imbalance in development may be amplified by the effects of the hormones released during male puberty. All of this increases strain on tendon structures and increases the risk of tendon overuse injury. It is no coincidence that the attachment site between bone and tendon is a common site of the overuse injuries that pubertal male athletes are susceptible to.

The incidence of specific conditions depends on what sport(s) the young athlete participates in. Anterior knee pain (persistent soreness at the front of the knee, in plain language) is prevalent in court and field sports that involve frequent jumping, landing and running activity – hence it is often termed 'jumper's knee' or 'runner's knee'. Tendinopathy affecting the shoulder is common in throwing sports, whereas tendinopathy at the hip and lower leg is more often seen in artistic and skating sports.

As before, sport specialisation is associated with the incidence of overuse injury due to the high volumes of specialised sport practice with little variation in the weekly schedule and over the course of the year, resulting in repetitive stress and cumulative load that is concentrated on certain areas [111]. If left unchecked, such overuse conditions can develop into more severe overuse injuries involving microavulsion fractures at the region where tendon inserts onto the bone. These conditions are most prevalent among boys and include Sever's disease (affecting the heel where the achilles tendon attaches), Osgood-Schlatter's disease (knee) and 'Little League Elbow' [112].

The injury risk factors associated with these overuse conditions differ between boys and girls. Deficits in strength and consequent movement compensations primarily drive the increased risk in girls. Conversely, reduced flexibility is a major factor contributing to overuse injuries in boys, which is not typically the case with girls (if anything girls tend to suffer from too much flexibility rather than too little). For instance, restricted knee and hamstring range of motion is associated with anterior knee pain. Reduced quadriceps and upper calf flexibility coinciding with the adolescent growth spurt are likewise known risk factors for Osgood-Schlatter disease [113].

EASING THE STRAIN...

Care is required to help young athletes get through sensitive periods to development when there is known to be elevated risk. These sensitive periods encompass the phase of skeletal maturation prior to puberty (approximately ages 11-13 for boys), the period that coincides with peak height velocity (the phase of most rapid growth otherwise known as the adolescent growth spurt) and the 6-12 months that follow the adolescent growth spurt.

The overuse conditions associated with youth sports are due to biomechanical overload that overwhelms the body's natural adaptive response. It follows that modifying and managing loads is part of the solution to mitigate the risks. Being active daily is a good thing but moderation is key. Avoiding excessive volumes of repetitious activity means regulating the volumes of single sport practice. The best strategy to do this will differ according to the period in question. For instance, for age-groups up to under-12 for girls and under-14 for boys it seems prudent to put limits on weekly participation given the long-term risks associated with excessive loading prior to skeletal maturity.

Implementing load management measures to manage injury risk during later periods of rapid growth coinciding with puberty requires a more responsive and individualised approach. Two young male athletes on the same under-15 team can be as much as 3 years apart in biological age. Regular assessment of height (both standing and seated) and weight to track growth and maturation is the best way to identify periods of heightened risk for each individual. Having access to this information will help coaches to be alert to the situation so that they can adjust training and practice loads accordingly. The six months following the end of the adolescent growth spurt is another important time to monitor young athletes and modify loads to allow them to adjust and get through this period of heightened risk for traumatic injuries.

Sadly, this is far from standard practice, with some notable exceptions. Positive examples that might be used as a model include youth academies in professional (soccer) football that employ special measures in these age groups to better accommodate growth and maturation factors in an effort to reduce injuries. Outside of these more enlightened environments it will be up to parents to drive initiatives to implement a similar approach.

Variety in sports participation is also important to mitigate the risk of overuse injury in particular. Better distributing the stresses on the body throughout the week and through the year is a matter of scheduling and selection. An assortment of sports at different times of the year provides variety as well as permitting downtime. However, this requires parents to remain firm to ensure that sports remain seasonal rather than encroaching on the rest of the calendar.

Whilst it can be beneficial for kids to participate in multiple sports, this does create a coordination challenge for the respective sport coaches. The challenge of managing loads during key phases of development becomes impossible without knowing what else the young athlete is doing at other times in the week. Once again, this puts this onus back on the parent to be the point person who manages the overall schedule and communicates with each of the sports to regulate load on behalf of the young athlete.

Managing participation to ensure that the demands do not become excessive effectively requires parents and kids to more selective. If the weekly practice commitments for a given sport are too much then we should attempt to negotiate a different arrangement. For instance, if the under-11 team practices four times a week then it is reasonable to propose committing to consistently attending two of the four sessions. Such an agreement will allow the schedule to accommodate different activities throughout the week without stacking practices on top of each other.

Once symptoms start to occur early intervention offers the best outcome. Effective intervention involves modified activity rather than complete rest [114]. However, practically this does mean temporarily reducing participation in sports practices and reallocating some of this time to strength training and remedial exercise to resolve symptoms and restore function.

TAKING A MORE PROACTIVE APPROACH...

Whilst certain injuries and overuse conditions might be commonly associated with particular sports ('Little league elbow' being a striking example), the most important take-home message is that these injuries are preventable whatever sport(s) kids participate in. It is straightforward to identify the periods when young athletes are most vulnerable, we can anticipate the risks and we can take steps to mitigate them.

Beyond tracking growth and regulating practice volumes, steps can be taken to address specific needs and target vulnerabilities. Being proactive in addressing known risk factors is the best approach to guard against developing these conditions in the first instance. The preventive measures are quite similar to the countermeasures that we would apply for early intervention. Effective prevention includes dryland or off-field training to fortify the relevant tissues, create reserve capacity, increase tolerance to load and improve fatigue resistance.

The ideal situation is for coaches and parents to work together to be more economical with practices, so that we can use this time more wisely. This will make room to implement additional countermeasures to mitigate risks and address early warning signs. Importantly this will also allow us to dedicate time and resources towards kids' physical and athletic development especially as they approach key developmental windows.

The debate regarding the safety of youth resistance training is now effectively settled, thanks to the positive results of many years of research investigation. Based on this evidence the consensus among the relevant national and international bodies is that strength training under qualified supervision is safe, effective and highly beneficial for children and teens. Not only has the conversation moved on from debating the potential hazards of youth resistance training, what is even more notable is that the focus has now switched to the negative consequences if kids *do not* engage in strength training [115].

Physical preparation offers protection against growth-related conditions and overuse injuries. Training builds additional capacity to extend the failure limits of the tissues. Having reserve capacity provides a buffer during times of additional stress. Stronger muscles, bones and connective tissues are better able to tolerate load. Better conditioned athletes are also more resistant to fatigue. More holistic development of athletic capabilities can also serve to ameliorate and better distribute the stresses and strains on the body.

Strength training does not just build muscle but also stimulates bone growth and adaptation of connective tissues. Different modes of strength training moving through full range of motion under load including gymnastic exercises supporting weight in extended positions provide stimulus for tendons to adapt and will also support the effort to develop and maintain flexibility as kids grow. Increasing lean mass and strength likewise promotes bone development during growth and maturation.

Rapid growth reduces flexibility in boys especially. Easing the passive stress on the tissues during these periods means addressing soft tissue restriction with modalities to increase active and passive range of motion. Getting the regular dose required to achieve this means incorporating flexibility training (various forms of stretching) and mobility training (actively moving through full range of motion whilst supporting their weight) in the young athlete's daily routine. I have long been a proponent of a daily mobility regimen, especially with young developing athletes, and this should be first thing that a young athlete does when they arrive at practice.

CHALLENGES OF IMPLEMENTATION...

As it stands, too often it is only once recurring injuries have started to impede their ability to participate in sport that young athletes come to recognise the problem and become receptive to making changes to accommodate the necessary training interventions – by which point, there are additional complications to deal with. Clearly we should not wait to intervene until this realisation is forced upon them. The stakes are high, as experiencing their first significant injury is a common trigger causing young athletes to drop out from participating in sport entirely [116].

What is true is that left to their own devices, the majority of kids would opt to just play sport rather than seeking out opportunities to engage in off-field physical preparation and athletic development. Kids and parents often need to be helped to the realisation that they can either voluntarily invest time and resources in training, or else be forced to involuntarily take time out from sport due to injury and pay the costs in medical treatment. When viewed in this way, rather than fitting training in when they can find the time, the imperative becomes making the time to train on a regular basis so that they remain fit to participate without becoming injured.

Aside from finding the time, there are logistical challenges to putting this into practice. One such challenge is finding appropriate facilities that permit kids of this age to train and provide a conducive environment. The other major challenge is that when things get hectic with demands of sports and school, training tends to be the first thing that gets dropped. It is important to acknowledge these difficulties and recognise that hard choices need to be made. All the same, these are challenges that must be negotiated to serve the young athlete's best interests.

On the plus side, we are not talking about a huge amount of time. In the case of strength training, two sessions per week provides the necessary 'dose' for continued improvements (one session per week is adequate to maintain current levels). Each of these training sessions can be completed within an hour. On that basis, reclaiming two one-hour slots within the existing weekly schedule will go a long way towards achieving the desired outcome.

There are other complementary strategies that we can use to reclaim time within and around supervised practices, so that we can incorporate exercises to develop key capabilities. For instance, the warm-up offers a window of opportunity to provide a regular dose of 'neuromuscular training', encompassing mobility, body control, balance and coordination training. Similarly, a daily check-in and self-maintenance routine, comprising a series of mobility and balance exercises combined with the use of self-therapy tools as necessary, is a time-efficient and highly effective way to improve function over time as well as keeping on top of any musculoskeletal issues so that they don't develop into injuries. This requires minimal equipment and can be done either prior to practice or as a standalone session at home.

Key Take-Home Messages

1. Weekly practice loads, competitions, camps and added extras often exceed what growing bodies can tolerate.

2. Multi-sport participation is beneficial – but not when the time commitments in each sport are excessive. Accommodations must be made to make this work.

3. Sport practice does not ensure kids are fit and prepared to handle the physical demands.

4. Puberty introduces challenges and injury risks – the critical ages, risk profile and solutions differ for boys versus girls.

5. Overuse injuries in youth are largely preventable – the critical periods can be readily identified, the risks are easily anticipated and can be mitigated.

6. Certain developmental windows involve different risks: pre-pubertal phase of skeletal maturation, adolescent growth spurt and 6–12 months after the growth spurt.

7. Physical preparation is essential — not optional. Strength training, mobility work, and neuromuscular training build the resilience needed to tolerate sport load.

8. Parents must take an active role in coordinating schedules. Coaches rarely know the full picture; without parent oversight, total weekly load easily becomes excessive.

9. Early intervention prevents dropout. Waiting until injuries appear makes the problem harder to fix and many kids quit sport after their first major injury.

Practical Tips for Parents

✓ Monitor weekly workload across all sports. Count total hours of practices, games, travel, and conditioning across all sports.

✓ Protect free time, downtime and unstructured play. Kids need rest and recovery as much as they need daily activity.

✓ Track growth and maturation. Simple height/weight checks help identify when the child is entering a high-risk growth phase.

✓ Prioritise regular physical preparation. Two strength sessions per week is ideal; one session maintains progress.

✓ Include daily mobility and movement routines as part of warm up or as a standalone session on non-practice days.

✓ Choose sports that complement each other (e.g. summer and winter sport) and strive to limit overlap in competition calendars for respective sports.

✓ Negotiate with coaches when workloads are excessive. Examples: Attend 2 of 4 weekly practices, skip low-value or redundant sessions

✓ Watch for early signs of pain or overload — and act quickly. Modified activity + strength work is more effective than rest alone.

✓ Communicate with all coaches about total load. Parents must serve as the central coordinator.

Action Items

» Audit your child's weekly schedule. Avoid stacking multiple practices on same day.

» Reduce unnecessary commitments. Cut back on extra camps, clinics, and private coaching when the regular schedule is already heavy.

» Build two 1-hour strength sessions into the weekly routine. Treat them as essential appointments, not optional add-ons.

» Implement a daily mobility routine. Especially vital during rapid growth periods.

» Ensure one full rest day per week. No organised sport, no structured training.

» Track height monthly during puberty and alert coaches to growth spurts.

» Advocate for your child when needed. Regulate participation during high-load weeks and periods of rapid growth.

» Keep sports seasonal! Maintain seasonal boundaries and resist year-round participation.

» Seek help early if symptoms appear. Early intervention with strength + mobility + load modification can prevent long-term issues.

Keeping Girls in the Game: The Necessity of Physical Preparation

One day the grandfather of a young female athlete I was working with came along to the track and after the session asked me the question 'do girls run differently than boys?'. My answer was, 'yes – if we are not careful'. The unique circumstances faced by young female athletes are often overlooked from a physical development standpoint. Once girls hit puberty the challenges that emerge mean that dedicated physical development and athletic preparation essentially becomes a non-negotiable for female athletes. For some years I have been a crusade to make administrators and coaches aware that girls have unique needs and sports must do more to provide the support they need when they need it. Practically, parents are the key to making this happen. So here I will make the case that training is a necessity for girls if we want to avoid injury, prevent performance becoming hampered and keep young females in sport.

WHERE TRAJECTORIES DIVERGE…

Prior to puberty the trajectory of motor development for boys and girls is mainly determined by how active they are. In other words, boys and girls are similarly receptive so it is mainly a question of exposure and what opportunities they receive. That said, the tendency for boys to be more active can lead to differences motor coordination from around age 6 [117]. It is only once girls hit puberty that things start to diverge quite dramatically.

Boys are far more fortunate when it comes to the changes that accompany puberty (which also arrives a couple of years later than for girls). Male puberty is the source of a considerable portion of the athletic performance advantage that male athletes enjoy relative to females. Boys experience free gains in lean mass, strength, power and speed as they go through puberty [118]. On that basis, whilst training remains important, young male athletes enjoy performance benefits and get away with much more from a sports injury risk perspective simply due to the boost in various capacities and other advantages that nature bestows upon them.

Girls are not so fortunate: when young female athletes hit puberty they receive no such boost from nature. Worse still, in the absence of appropriate intervention, the changes that do occur mean that everything becomes harder as they enter their adolescent years. The trajectory for any performance measure you care to mention thus starts to diverge not long after girls hit puberty (circa age 12) and the gap widens significantly once boys reach puberty themselves (circa age 14) [119].

All in all, puberty sort of sucks if you're a girl. Whilst limbs become longer and hips become wider, most muscle groups do not spontaneously catch up, so young females can effectively become relatively weaker as the muscles are now at more of a mechanical disadvantage due to the longer levers they are operating with [120]. All of this makes it tougher to stabilise and young female athletes become less able to resist the internal and external forces they encounter during sport. The disparity in upper body strength between males and females also becomes much more pronounced with the onset of puberty [121].

Differences in motor patterns also start to emerge not long after girls go through puberty as they struggle to control longer limbs, a higher centre of mass and more mobile joints. Deficits in strength at key links in the chain (notably the hip) are the main driver for these changes.

COMPENSATE AND CARRY ON...

Naturally, girls make the best of things and come up with workaround strategies to overcome these challenges. One muscle group that does keep up with the changes that occur during puberty and becomes stronger are the knee extensors (i.e. quadriceps), reflecting their role as an *anti-gravity* muscle group (as girls become heavier the quadriceps in turn become stronger) [122]. Consequently, starting in early adolescence young female athletes tend to alter their movement strategy to favour the strongest link, opting to preferentially use their stronger quadriceps muscles when applying force to generate propulsion (when jumping, accelerating, changing direction). This is also reflected in the movement strategy employed to dampen forces, such that they preferentially use the knee joint to absorb energy when landing, decelerating, etc. [123]. Due to the strength deficits and accompanying compensatory strategies, spontaneous changes in movement mechanics become increasingly evident in female athletes as adolescence progresses and they gain mass [124].

Unfortunately, the compensatory changes and altered coordination patterns have a number of downsides. The quadriceps-reliant and knee-dominant movement strategy is not stellar from a performance viewpoint: jump height, jump distance, speed, and change of direction scores tend to plateau in adolescent female athletes during the years that follow puberty, in the absence of training intervention [119].

To add injury to insult, these characteristic changes in biomechanics during jumping, landing, running, and changing direction are implicated in the non-contact and overuse injuries that are prevalent among adolescent female athletes. Once they enter adolescence girls become more prone to injury, especially non-contact and overuse injuries involving the lower limb. The knee joint takes a lot of stress, so unsurprisingly female athletes become prone to knee injuries, but injuries to other joints, notably the ankle, also increase.

All of this means that female high school athletes not only suffer more injuries in general compared to male athletes in the same sports, but also have higher incidence of severe lower limb injuries that result in extended periods on the sidelines [125].

Adolescent female athletes also suffer more overuse injuries than their male peers in the same sports [126].

IMPLICATIONS FOR PARTICIPATION...

Oddly enough, the fact that things are becoming harder is not lost on young females. Unfortunately, these struggles come at a time in a young female's life when they are at their most self-conscious and hyper aware of social judgement. It is no coincidence that this phase of development brings a mass exodus of girls opting out of sport. A consistent finding is that girls disengage from participating in sport en masse as they reach their early teens (data in the UK indicate around 4 in 10 girls drop out around this time).

The explanation is that girls discover other interests, but another widely accepted claim is that many girls no longer wish to take part as a result of junior sport becoming increasingly competitive around this time. The common assumption that competitive sport is much less appealing for girls versus boys is seemingly based more on stereotypes than compelling evidence. The available data indicate that teenage girls' attitudes towards the competitive aspect of sport are not dramatically different to boys, especially among girls who consider themselves 'sporty' [127].

There is evidently more to the question of why sport becomes less rewarding once girls hit puberty. If we want to design and implement countermeasures that will have a meaningful effect, we must ensure we are in fact addressing the underlying causes. The lack of impact of initiatives to reduce dropout and improve retention suggest we are failing in this regard.

The best way to some shed light on what these factors might be is to go to the source and ask! A survey investigating teenage girls' attitudes towards sport in the United Kingdom are illuminating [127]. The steep drop off in participation among girls seems more driven by lack of confidence alongside feelings of insufficiency and the sense they are ill-equipped to compete.

The other major driving for girls dropping out of participating in sport is injury. Suffering their first significant injury is the most common reason cited by high-level young female athletes for ceasing to participate in sport [116]. In many cases this decision is forced upon them, as a considerable proportion find that they are unable to return to sport following the injury. To give an example, nearly half of adolescent female athletes who suffer ACL injuries fail to return to competitive sport [128].

TO THE RESCUE!

It does not have to be this way. we can do is tackle the reasons for girls dropping out of sport by taking steps to help girls feel more capable. The availability of quality coaching becomes all the more important to lend a sense of competence so that girls feel confident enough to continue. Having the support to improve and remain competitive will provide the assurance that girls require to remain involved in the sport.

Likewise female athletes who continue participating are also not doomed by fate to be prone to injury and having their performance flat-line once they reach adolescence. By taking appropriate countermeasures – specifically, physical and athletic preparation – we can mitigate and even eliminate these problems, permitting young female athletes to continue to improve their performance and avoid any increase in injury risk.

With timely and appropriate intervention, we can provide girls with a boost in various strength capacities and capabilities, essentially replicating what boys get for free. The deficits that drive the decline in function following puberty can be remedied with training. Lack of strength is the major predictor that explains the rise in traumatic knee injuries such as ACL injury among adolescent girls (which is not the case for boys) [129], so strength training intervention is essential. Training to provide the necessary boost in capacity also provides the foundation for coaching intervention to address the problematic movement mechanics and compensatory strategies that render adolescent females more prone to these injuries [130]. In fact, if female athletes commence training early enough, these movement compensations resolve spontaneously once we have provided the requisite boost in strength [131].

Sadly, early intervention remains the exception. Most often it is only once young female athletes start to experience issues that parents seek external help to salvage the situation. The athlete I described in the opening (a rockstar named Sophie) was one such case.

Sophie was (and remains) very active and participated in multiple sports but she had been plagued with recurrent injuries that were keeping her from doing what she loved. Sadly, this is a tale that will be familiar to many young female athletes and their parents, but fortuitously in Sophie's case the story had a happy ending. Serendipitously, a sports physician colleague of mine happened to be friends with Sophie's mother (they had daughters of the same age who also attended the same school) and so at Dr Forsyth's suggestion they sought out my help.

The remedy in these cases essentially involves a two-pronged strategy comprising both strength training and movement skills training. Both elements are required: it is not sufficient to just attempt to teach female adolescents how to move in a more optimal and less injurious manner. After all, they adopted the strategy they have for a reason (i.e., out of necessity) and so without strength training intervention to address the strength deficits that originally prompted the compensatory changes we cannot expect the new movement patterns to stick, especially under 'live' conditions.

In plain terms it is necessary to become stronger to be able to generate force to initiate movement and to resist the forces experienced when landing, decelerating, etc. More specifically, young females must possess the requisite strength to generate and dampen forces at each link in the chain; after all, they are only as strong as their weakest link. This means remedial strength training is an essential piece of the puzzle. Providing the requisite boost in capacity effectively provides the conditions to increase capability and permits us to work on movement skills. Directed strength training intervention serves as the gateway to enable the athlete to express the desired coordination patterns.

Sophie was a case study for this dual-pronged strategy. Sophie commenced strength training alongside regular sessions on track and turf that focussed on developing key capabilities as well as remodelling her athletic movement skills. As we developed Sophie's force-generating capacity at key links in the chain (hip, knee and ankle), we simultaneously worked on her capability to utilise this capacity to become more mechanically effective and efficient in her movement. Sophie's strength training progressed in parallel with her movement skill development, such that as she became stronger, we were able to progress to more challenging athletic movements involving higher force demands. Through her diligent efforts Sophie was soon able get back on the court, turf, pool, trails and snow. We continued to work together for some time and Sophie was able to resume her hectic sporting schedule without suffering any further injuries.

BUILDING STRUCTURAL INTEGRITY...

An important and under-recognised aspect of physical development for young athletes is developing their hardware for the rigours of sport and life after sport. An important objective of the physical development process for young athletes is ensuring that bones, joints and connective tissues grow and adapt in such a way that they are robust and resilient to the stresses and strains they will be exposed to when participating in sport. The *tempering* effects of different forms of physical training represent one of the most crucial aspects of physical development in serving to build resilience and bolstering the intrinsic strength properties of structures and tissues.

Clearly there is a genetic component in all this and it certainly helps to choose your parents well. All the same, *epigenetics* also makes a significant contribution. In plain language, what activities and conditions young bodies are exposed to during the developmental years has a profound bearing on the characteristics and qualities that are manifested. We can harness this positive interaction between training, growth and maturation processes to enable young athletes to express their genetic potential to the fullest extent.

Improving the structural integrity of bones, joints and connective tissues is important for young athletes in general but it is a priority for young female athletes. Given the high incidence of non-contact injuries and overuse injuries affecting joints and connective tissues (especially ligaments and tendons) among adolescent female athletes, a key pillar of the injury-proofing process is building structural integrity and increasing the failure limits of respective structures and tissues.

Timely training intervention during key developmental phases is especially potent as training adaptations are augmented by what is occurring naturally. In this way, training and the processes of growth and maturation combine to great effect to build stronger and more structurally sound bodies. Consistent application of a regular 'dose' of physical preparation has compounding effects that accrue over time. Once again for females the potential for training to bolster and fortify is all the more important given that they cannot rely on nature to give them a boost during puberty as boys can.

LIFE-LONG BONE HEALTH...

Beyond the more immediate concerns of performance and sports injury, there are longer term considerations that are typically overlooked with young female athletes. Females are more prone to bone health issues and conditions such as osteoporosis as they age. Female athletes in different sports are accordingly not only subject to bone stress injuries during their athletic career but may also be at heightened risk of degenerative conditions in later life. Promoting life-long bone health should be a priority in the physical development of young female athletes.

Being active during the formative years is one of the best ways that women can protect their future selves from these issues. Bone is *mechanoresponsive*, which simply means that it adapts its structure and fortifies itself in response to whatever loads and mechanically stresses it experiences. The young skeleton is at its most mechanosensitive due to the ongoing process of growth and maturation. In plain terms, growing bone is more responsive and shows more marked adaptation. Consequently, the developmental years when the young athlete is still growing represents a crucial window for laying down bone and building structural integrity of the developing skeleton.

Young female athletes in weight-bearing sports receive the benefit of regularly participating in the types of activities that prompt bones to adapt in a way that renders them more resilient over time [132]. Consequently, female athletes in high-intensity jumping and running sports report higher overall bone mass as well as greater bone mineral density in the bones and areas that experience the most load, as compared to their untrained and sedentary peers [133]. Training provides a supplemental and complementary stimulus that meets the threshold for promoting bone growth and adaptation. Activities and exercises that provide the mechanical stimulus to elicit bone growth are described as *osteogenic*. Notably this includes weight-bearing exercise on land with external loads, high muscle forces and/or higher impact. Strategic use of this type of training allows us to protect young female athletes from bone stress injuries and provides an important buffer against bone loss in later life, provided their energy intake and nutrition is sufficient.

'NEUROMUSCULAR TRAINING'...

A key part of the effective intervention and physical preparation for young females is described as 'neuromuscular training'. Essentially this comprises activities that promote body awareness, improve balance abilities, develop motor control and refine coordination patterns.

Strength training and neuromuscular training have a synergistic relationship, such that the best results are observed when they are employed in combination. As we described with Sophie, becoming stronger facilitates developing these capabilities. An integrated approach that combines neuromuscular training with strength training has proven efficacy in reducing injuries among young female athletes [134] and interventions of this type can also confer improvements in athletic performance [135].

Effective neuromuscular training regimens typically involve generic exercises that develop body control and the ability to balance and stabilise. Another feature is coordination exercise designed to develop *limb dexterity* and general *movement dexterity*, focussing on 'feel', precision, timing and rhythm. With a nod to the previous chapter, neuromuscular training includes dedicated generic athletic movement skills, notably jumping, landing, running and changing direction.

NECESSITY AND BENEFITS OF TIMELY INTERVENTION...

There are considerable benefits to starting early, such that the best approach is to commence strength training and structured athletic preparation prior to puberty. Not only are girls receptive to training at this time but this also catches them before things start to diverge. Commencing neuromuscular training before compensatory changes become evident is naturally a more straightforward proposition [134].

Time is also of the essence from the perspective of developing bone health. The developmental years when the young athlete is still growing represents a crucial window for laying down bone and building structural integrity of the developing skeleton. Performing osteogenic exercise and activity during the receptive periods of childhood and the transition to adolescence provides a way to strengthen bones and increase bone mass. The 'tween years' and early teens represent key windows of opportunity that young female athletes should be encouraged to take advantage of in service of their long-term performance health [136].

In an ideal world sports teams and organisations would be routinely following the advice that has existed for over a decade to implement *integrative training* (strength training and neuromuscular training in combination) with young female athletes, commencing prior to puberty [137]. Practically, this means beginning regular strength training from around age 11 for most girls, before the strength of various lower limb muscles start to plateau. Clearly we have some way to go, as this is far from common practice currently, despite the consensus in the sports science and medicine literature on the need, merits and demonstrated safety when undertaken with qualified supervision.

Nevertheless, we should not let the perfect be the enemy of the good. Even if we miss this window, the benefits are such that young female athletes should be encouraged to start strength training and seek out coaching input at any stage in the journey. All young female athletes stand to benefit from engaging in comprehensive physical and athletic preparation under supervision to realise the performance and injury protection benefits as well as laying the foundations for life-long bone health. I very much hope that parents reading this book will share this information and help spread the word to schools, sports clubs and other parents.

Key Take-Home Messages

1. Puberty presents unique challenges for girls, bringing physical changes (longer limbs, wider hips) without matching strength gains that make things more difficult.

2. Without intervention, girls become relatively weaker and adopt compensatory movement patterns, which limit performance potential and increase injury risk.

3. Lack of capability drives loss of confidence and dropout—not lack of interest. Many girls disengage from sport in early adolescence because they feel ill-equipped and believe they cannot compete—not because they dislike sport or competition.

4. Physical preparation is not optional but essential for girls. Strength training and neuromuscular training are necessary to build capacity, improve movement quality, protect against injury and enable female athletes to keep progressing.

5. Early intervention solves the problem at source. Commencing dedicated physical preparation prior to puberty (around age 10–11) prevents movement compensations as well as building resilience and structural integrity, including bone health.

6. Training replicates the neuromuscular spurt that boys get naturally. Through targeted training, girls can gain strength, power, movement control and resilience—essentially creating their own neuromuscular 'boost' that boys get for free.

7. Physical preparation builds the belief to continue. When girls feel capable, strong, and confident in their movement, they are more likely to remain involved in sport.

Practical Tips

✓ Seek qualified physical preparation coaches for your daughters. Prioritise strength and movement training from age 10–12. skill, balance, coordination).

✓ Keeping girls in sport requires a physical boost to ensure girls feel capable and confident to continue participating through the teenage years.

✓ Group-based physical and athletic preparation programmes are a good option as they provide the social aspect that young female athletes enjoy.

✓ Seek to ensure training provides strength and weight-bearing exercise (jumping, landing) to fortify bones, ligaments and tendons – the 'tween years and early teens are a key window for building strong bones.

✓ Supplemental osteogenic training is imperative for girls who participate in non-weight bearing sports such as swimming to promote life-long bone health.

✓ Strength training and movement skill coaching is beneficial at any stage.

✓ Dedicated training is all the more necessary if your daughter has had previous injuries to protect against future injury.

✓ Ensure injury management and rehabilitation includes training intervention to reduce the odds of reinjury when they return to sport

✓ Remedial strength and neuromuscular training (in combination) are essential with recurrent injuries to break the injury cycle .

Action Items

» Introduce dedicated physical preparation from around age 11 (or earlier) under qualified supervision.

» Seek out athletic development programmes that offer an integrative training approach that combines strength and neuromuscular training

» Lobby for the physical education at school to include specific provision to develop strength and fundamental movement skill training for the girls

» Request that coaches integrate physical preparation into weekly sessions, with a focus on building capacity, capability and movement skills

» Educate clubs and schools on why girls need training—not just sport practice.

» Spread the message with other parents. Work together to push for strength and neuromuscular training to be integrated into practices, such as during the warm-up

» Lobby sports organizations to provide training resources, female-friendly environments, and coach education on girls' developmental needs.

Choosing the Best Path

Go Quickly or Go Far?

When guiding aspiring young athletes we must carefully consider whether we are optimising for success in the short-term or the long-term. Put more simply, the question for a young performer is 'do you want to win now or win once you reach senior elite-level?'. At first glance it is not obvious that these two aims might be in conflict with each other. However, something that parents and young performers need to recognise is that chasing quick wins and prioritising early success may lead to decisions that prove detrimental to their chances of being successful over the long-term.

Given the growing external pressures it is no wonder that so many kids and parents are in such a hurry. It is also quite understandable that parents and young performers would direct their time and efforts towards being successful as a junior on the assumption that this will translate to long-term success. Indeed a big reason that kids and parents put so much weight on achieving success early on is that they take it as a sign that they are on the path towards success at senior level.

On the surface it seems reasonable to presume that the past or current performance of a junior athlete might indicate their future potential to perform at the senior level. However, the relationship between rankings in junior competition and competitive success at senior level is not as strong as we might think.

IS WINNING AS A JUNIOR CRUCIAL FOR LONG-TERM SUCCESS?

The importance of early success in junior competition is widely overstated. When we look at the data from different sports we typically discover it is only in the later age-groups that competitive results start to correlate with later success in senior competition to any meaningful extent [138, 139].

All in all, the conversion from top-performing junior to successful elite-level senior is actually surprisingly low. This begs the question, how much stock should we put in results from junior competition when evaluating the potential for future success at the senior level? To phrase this another way, to what extent does winning as a junior indicate that the young athlete is on track to reach the elite-level of senior competition?

A pivotal study that set out to address this question collated longitudinal data from athletes from different Olympics sports that included their results in junior competition as well as their later performances in the open-age category (i.e. senior-level competition) [140]. The analysis comprised data from over 13,000 athletes across an array of sports and included results and placings in national and international competition.

The major finding of the study was that the correlations between results in age-group junior competition and subsequent performance in the open-age category (i.e. senior level) were shockingly low. Moreover, the younger the age category, the less results in junior competition predicted later performance at the senior level. Based on their analysis the authors concluded that junior performance has little if any predictive value and explains very little of the variance in performance once athletes reach the senior level [140].

This is not an isolated finding. The same pattern is reported in studies of sports in which performance is measured in time and distance, such as track and field athletics. Only a small fraction of those who go on to be elite senior athletes (17-26% depending on the event) are rated as top junior performers between the ages of 14 and 17 [141]. Very similar findings are observed even in sports like swimming that are associated with early specialisation. It is only once swimmers in the sprint events reach their final year of junior competition (age 18 for boys, age 17 for girls) that their rankings start to reliably correlate to performance in senior level competition [139].

To explain these findings, we need to understand that age-grade competition favours kids who are relatively older in chronological or biological age. Being bigger and stronger naturally gives these kids a performance edge over their peers in the age group. Talent identification is notoriously unreliable at younger ages and naturally this is reflected in selection decisions. Selection for national age-grade representative squads and professional academies are biased towards those who are born in the first quarter of the eligibility period and early-maturing performers are likewise consistently over-represented in junior squads [142, 143]. All the same, this does not translate to success later on as growth curves converge and their physical advantages in relation to their peers are eliminated.

For an illustration of this we can look to elite level ice hockey. Data from Sweden show that early-maturing athletes enjoy early success at junior-level, as indicated by selection to age-grade national teams at the under 16 level [144]. However, these advantages diminish over time and the proportion of early maturing players is lowest in the age-group (under-20) prior to senior level. What is equally striking is that the group most disadvantaged at junior level – i.e. late-maturing athletes – prove more likely than early-maturing players to succeed in reaching the National Hockey League (NHL) [144].

The early advantages of relative age effects and being more advanced in biological age diminish over time and are not stable predictors of future success. Indeed, the top performers at junior level might be more advanced than their peers for a number of different reasons that are not necessarily reflective of their potential over the long term. For instance, early specialisation is another confounding factor. Kids who have spent more time practising the sport to the exclusion of others from a younger age may have a competitive edge in junior competition, yet this often comes at a cost to their later development in that it limits the scope for future improvements. Once again, junior performances in this case can give a false impression of their potential for future success.

In other words, it is unsafe to extrapolate from results in age-grade competition. Some proportion of the kids who dominate at the junior level are simply older or further along in their growth and maturation. Others have accelerated their development and maximised their performance, such that they tend to peak early. In either case, the subsequent performance trajectory does not follow the upward trend we might expect as these formerly successful juniors progress to the open-age category. Selection judgements made later in young athletes' development thus offer a more reliable indicator of an individual's potential to succeed in senior-level competition.

The data do not support the general presumption that success in junior competition is a prerequisite for success at the elite-level as a senior. Young athletes who aspire to reach the highest level do not necessarily need to be a top performer in age-grade competition, especially early on. Ironically, those who are overlooked due to relative age effects and biological maturation may prove most capable of succeeding at the senior level.

All the same, there is an understandable desire for success in junior competition to attract the attention of scouts and selectors (notwithstanding the fact that their judgements are also skewed by relative age effects and early maturation). Once again, something kids and those advising them should be aware of is that being identified as a talent early on is not necessarily advantageous to long-term success.

DOES EARLY SELECTION TO TALENT PATHWAYS CONFER AN ADVANTAGE..?

On the surface, earlier access to higher calibre coaching, training facilities and other forms of athlete support that come with being part of a talent development pathway should prove more beneficial in advancing young athletes' development over the long term. But in practice it is much less clear whether it is an advantage for young performers to be selected early for talent development pathways.

To answer this question, we can look to another research investigation that collated the findings from the available studies on the topic to assess whether being part of talent promotion programmes from a younger age was associated with higher levels of attainment in junior and senior competition, relative to their peers who were selected later [145]. The studies included in the analysis featured a range of sports, encompassing both individual and team sports. The 'talent promotion programmes' included national federation junior squads and regional youth academies. The measure of success was whether early age of selection showed a positive association with competitive performance at junior level and senior level, respectively.

Based on their analysis, the authors concluded that being selected to talent development programmes at an earlier age was associated with diverging outcomes in terms of subsequent performance in junior versus senior competition. Kids who entered talent promotion programmes at a younger age did appear to show accelerated development, based on their achievements in junior competition. However, this apparent advantage did not translate into competitive success at senior level. Conversely, young performers who were relatively older when they were selected may not have had the same level of success in junior competition but were ultimately more successful once they reached senior level.

We should note that these findings do not prove causation. It would follow that standout performers in age-grade junior competition would be more likely to be selected for talent squads and youth academies from an early age. It also follows that kids who do not have the same early success in junior competition would be selected later (assuming they were selected at all). What takes more explaining is why kids who were selected later should prove more to be more successful than their early-selected peers in senior-level competition.

Early selection to talent development pathways may also lead to paradoxical effects that can be detrimental to young athletes' development over the long term. Being marked out as talented confers status and this can influence the individual's attitudes towards their participation in sport in unhelpful ways. For instance, they might become more defensive in how they engage in practice, playing it safe and avoiding situations where they might fail, as they seek to preserve their status and protect their standing in the eyes of others. The treatment that precocious talents receive is also not necessarily conducive to developing the habits, attitudes and behaviours they need to continue to progress:

The impetus to select early is in part driven by the belief that earlier exposure to talent development pathways will provide advantages that can be expected to accrue over time. The fact that early selection was not associated with success at senior level challenges this assumption. Whilst selection offers opportunity, there are also costs. Being part of a talent pathway involves greater commitment from the young athlete, meaning more time spent engaging in the sport, probably for a greater proportion of the year and likely to the exclusion of others sports and activities. The earlier they take this step, the more they might miss out on. Clearly we need to account for these factors and acknowledge that there are potential downsides that need to be managed.

There is also the question of readiness. That is, are they ready and equipped to take advantage of the opportunity they are being presented with? This is an important consideration for those involved in talent development pathways, as it will have a direct bearing on whether the potential benefits are realised. It might be more prudent to adopt a 'wait and see' approach early on. Young performers who are selected later typically fare better, presumably because they are more mature and better prepared to take advantage of the opportunity.

In reality, the push to select early is also driven by competitive pressures and other interests. In team sports, youth academies attached to professional teams compete with each other to secure up-and-coming young talents. There is also competition between sports to try to ensure that promising young performers opt to pursue their particular sport rather than the alternatives. Commercial youth sports academies also exist (notably in North America) that are motivated more by financial interests than such niceties as what might be best for the young athletes' long-term development. These agendas and the incentives involved can act in direct opposition to adopting the long-term, 'slow and steady' approach that is seemingly more conducive to long-term success.

THE RECIPE FOR SUCCESS DIFFERS FOR JUNIOR VERSUS SENIOR LEVEL...

To elucidate the factors that contribute to success at junior versus senior-level competition and extensive investigation collated the data from a host of earlier studies, encompassing a sample of over 9000 athletes [146]. The analysis included key variables relating to their participation and practice during the junior years and examined the athletes' performance in junior- and senior-level competition to see how the success factors aligned and where they differed.

Based on this study, there are a few critical areas where the paths to success at junior- and senior-level seem to diverge. The standout performers in junior competition typically report beginning their participation in the sport at an earlier age, accumulate more time in the sport over their childhood and early teen years and attain performance milestones (e.g. first national team selection, first national championship) at earlier ages. In contrast, world-class performers at senior level are more likely to have commenced the sport when they were a little older, spent less time in the sport in their early junior years (and more time engaged in other sports) and typically attain key performance milestones relatively later.

Those who go on to enjoy success at senior level tend to emerge as top performers relatively later in their junior career. Conversely, those who achieve breakthrough success early on most often find that this is the pinnacle of their achievements and they are not able to replicate this success once they make the transition to the senior ranks. This indicates that early success in junior competition may come at a cost.

What brings early success in junior competition seems to be distinctly different to what ultimately leads to success at senior level. Starting early and engaging in more coach-led practice in a single sport provides the conditions for rapid progression and success in junior competition. Conversely, more varied participation and more moderate volumes of coach-led practice result in less rapid but more consistent progress throughout the developmental years, which is seemingly more conducive to long-term success at the elite level. In other words, the factors associated with success at junior versus senior level appear to be at odds with each other.

The recipe for success in junior competition is not necessarily conducive to attaining long-term success. What confers an advantage at junior level may not be consistent with what it takes to succeed once athletes reach the senior ranks.

All things considered, it is better to fly under the radar and break through later in the youth sports journey. Parents need to be a steadying influence. Young performers who have early success are likely to be bombarded with invitations and it pays to be selective and consider the costs that accompany the prospective opportunities.

We should note that the athletes who do go on to reach the highest level are nonetheless above average at the junior level. An important difference is that the successful individuals tend to have a reservoir of yet to be realised potential that they can draw upon. This is part of what allows them to emerge as high performers later in their development and ultimately prevail at the elite level - assuming they are given the opportunity.

WIN NOW OR WIN LATER WHEN IT REALLY MATTERS?

In view of these discrepancies it seems we must decide: is the objective to be a top-performing junior or is the aim to reach the highest level of senior competition? It is important that we are clear on the ultimate aim, as this will determine what approach we take. If we are primarily concerned with success as a junior then there is a case for going all in and amassing a lot of practice in the chosen sport. However, if the young performer has aspirations of reaching the highest level as a senior then we must take a different route.

Whilst there will be some trade-offs, in reality the slow and steady approach that allows for more variety in participation and practice during the junior years will bring athletic benefits that will become more evident as young performers mature. As such, these young athletes will become increasingly competitive as they progress through age-grade competition, whereas their previously more successful peers may start to falter.

Importantly, these findings should provide some assurance for parents of young performers. Many parents are anxious to avoid their kids falling behind and this can be exploited, especially in North America where youth sports has become a multi-billion dollar industry. Understanding that moderation offers the best route over the long-term will help to ease this anxiety and permit parents to resist the continual pressure to sign their kids up for more camps, extra coaching, travel teams and year-round competition.

The metrics we use to gauge success matter in this regard, as they will influence our approach and our decision-making. If junior rankings and performances in age-grade championships are key performance indicators then this will inevitably lead coaches to optimise for short-term success. In contrast, if we judge the success of a talent development pathway on how many athletes make a successful transition to the senior ranks then we will be more inclined to prioritise long-term success.

In my capacity overseeing support for athletes in the talent development pathway for Scottish Squash, we emphasised to the young athletes that whilst it was nice when they had success in junior competition, what we really cared about was them winning once they reached senior level. Likewise, we had a great deal of humility about our ability to predict what a young player might be capable of achieving, so we tried to ensure that a door remained open to them.

WHAT IS THE BEST ROUTE TO LONG-TERM SUCCESS..?

Raw physical attributes and performance in junior competition are not good predictors of future success, at least until late adolescence once growth curves even out. Technical skills, tactical awareness and character traits are generally more reflective of future potential in young performers [147].

Time spent engaged practising and playing the primary sport during the childhood years yields benefits from the perspective of developing technical skills and tactical awareness or 'game sense'. Using the example of (soccer) football, hours engaged in supervised practices and informal play between the ages of 6 and 12 years reportedly differentiate those players who go on to secure senior professional contracts in the sport [148].

There is likely a sweet spot for the amount of time spent engaged in the relevant sport during the junior years that is adequate to elicit continued improvements but not excessive to the extent that it comes at a cost of compromising the young athlete's long-term athletic development and their future prospects at the senior level. Youth sports coaches should strive to be more economical with practices, not least as this will help with retention and avoid burnout. The young athletes can help themselves in this regard by being mindful and attentive to ensure that they get the most out of the practice time available (more on that in a later chapter entitled Harnessing the Mind).

A far more reliable indication of a young athlete's long-term potential is their year-to-year performance progression throughout the junior years. It follows that this is what we should be aiming for, rather than chasing quick wins. A study titled 'what makes a champion' examined data from those who go on to become world class in senior-level competition and found that these individuals typically progressed less quickly than their counterparts as juniors [149]. The most important factor that differentiates those who emerge and have success once they reach senior level is sustained progression throughout the junior years. In other words, the rate of improvement matters less than avoiding a plateau in their performance and stalled development.

Based on data on the transition from junior to senior competition in track and field athletics it has similarly been argued that annual improvement in performance through each year of junior competition from ages 13-18 is the best predictor making a successful transition to elite level as a senior [150]. Likewise, the progress that occurs after athletes make the transition to senior-level is another aspect that differentiates those who are ultimately successful at the elite level [141].

Beyond the specialist skills of the sport, more evolved talent ID and development systems are also starting to recognise the value of general movement proficiency or *athleticism*. As with skills and character, these qualities are less biased by the transient influence of growth and maturation, making them much more reliable indicators of future potential (as well as crucial assets) regardless of the sport [151]. From the aspiring performer's perspective, developing the foundations of athleticism represents a very good investment in the future.

Success in junior competition is fine as long as it can be sustained. All the same, it remains crucial that this is not to the detriment of developing the capacities, capabilities and skills that will be required to be successful once they reach senior level. To that end, we should urge moderation, emphasise quality rather than quantity and seek to develop their range of skills and abilities rather than opting for narrowly focussed practice and intensive preparation.

MORE ≠ BETTER AND THE PERILS OF PREMATURE PROFESSIONALISM...

What brings rapid progress as a junior can prove detrimental over the long-term. Early on, improvements can be achieved simply by doing more of the same. However, the effectiveness of this brute force 'more is better' approach inevitably diminishes over time as the easy wins and low-hanging fruit become exhausted. Aside from diminishing returns, there is also risk. Months and years of high volumes of the same activity without much variety or variation is a recipe for overuse injury.

Prominent voices have sounded the alarm on the 'premature professionalism' that is encroaching into talent development pathways and even school sports. Academies attached to professional clubs and affiliated commercial organisations are scouting kids from earlier and earlier ages. In many cases, the coaches attached to these programmes are retired professional players. This is also creeping into the independent school sports sector, where it is becoming increasingly common to hire former professional players for coaching positions in the belief that their profile and prestige will help recruitment. Formal education in the coaching sciences is not generally a prerequisite, so it is unsurprising that recently retired athletes would tend to recreate what they were exposed to in their professional career. When the content and delivery of practices and off-field training seeks to replicate what the professionals are doing, by definition it is no longer age- and stage-appropriate. Not only is this not optimal but may be detrimental for young athletes who are still growing and learning the sport.

Whilst doing more of the same does allow kids to progress more rapidly, which makes them more competitive as a junior, there are costs to this approach that are only revealed later. Consequently, chasing short-term success in junior competition can hinder the young performer's long-term prospects. As parents and coaches clearly we need to overcome these misapprehensions so that we can guide aspiring young performers to invest their time and efforts more wisely.

On that basis, rather than chasing rapid development, we should be striving for steady but consistent progress that is sustained through the developmental years. As coaches and parents, it is important that we take the long view so that we are not in too much of a hurry. The defining characteristic of development coaching is that it emphasises building the foundations for medium- and long-term success over quick wins and short-term performance outcomes.

THINKING LONG-TERM...

With aspiring young performers we should be thinking long-term. The long-term perspective also applies to the manner in which practices and training is delivered. Whilst there is need for the grown-ups to be somewhat directive when kids are still learning and developing, it is also important that we afford ample opportunities to play, explore and discover the possibilities. The over-riding objectives are learning and lasting improvements.

'to improve athletes' long-term senior performance, youth training strategies should primarily focus on the expansion of youth athletes' potential for future long-term performance improvement through adulthood, rather than primarily seeking to accelerate their short-term junior performance.'

Ultimately, we want to elevate and expand a young athlete's long-term potential, rather than merely exploiting their existing strengths. Rather than accelerating their development so that they reach their ceiling earlier, we should be striving to push the ceiling ever higher!

Fundamentally, it is our duty to build young athletes to last. If you want to build a cathedral you spend the first number of years laying the foundations rather than concerning yourself with the decorative details that will adorn the exterior. Much the same applies to the developmental process for an aspiring young performer. Building excellent foundations should be the priority for the major part of the youth sports journey, especially during the early and middle stages when the athlete is still growing and developing physically.

Practically, this means investing the majority of time and attention to the fundamentals. Something that differentiates those who are successful at senior level is that they spent a relatively longer time engaged in the fundamentals stage during their developmental years in the sport compared to their competitors. The importance of building a sound foundation equally applies to athletic skills, as we noted in an earlier chapter.

To bring this together, the youth sports journey calls for a blend of variety and consistency. On one hand, building solid foundations and mastering the fundamentals requires consistency - in other words, ultimate success is built by doing the right things in the right way over a sustained period of time (measured in years not months). On the other hand, it is important that there is variety. That said, it is equally important that there is coherence, especially in relation to physical and athletic development. In these areas in particular what we are looking for is variation on consistent themes.

Finally, compounding is another principle that investing and training have in common. The fruits of our daily efforts are not immediately apparent but as long as we stick with it these incremental gains accrue and their effects compound over time in a way that yields big gains and dramatic improvements over the medium- and long-term. Staying on the right track demands patience and keeping faith in the process. Performers may not register the gains and improvements they have made in real-time, so periodic assessment is helpful to provide a tangible sense of progress and offer some assurance that their efforts are being rewarded and the training is bringing the desired improvements.

Whilst this might sound straightforward, there are some challenges to implementation. In the competitive world of youth sports, kids and parents are often in a rush to get an edge and wiser heads must prevail. It seems inevitable that these pressures will only grow as youth sports become ever more commercialised. Social media is awash with gurus parading flashy-looking 'advanced' exercises and hacks to get rapid results, so it is vital that parents and the young performers themselves have the knowledge and perspective to resist the allure.

To end on a positive note, one of the gifts that sport provides is helping kids to learn that working hard on a consistent basis will bring all kinds of benefits over time. The physical nature of the work and effort involved makes this so much more tangible. The idea that their future self will reap the rewards of the efforts they diligently invest today nonetheless applies to all aspects of their life, not least when it comes to schoolwork!

Key Take-Home Messages

1. • Early junior success is not a reliable indicator of future elite performance.

2. Relative age, early maturation and early specialisation can create short-term advantages, but these rarely translate to senior-level success.

3. Late developers and late-selected athletes often outperform early stars at senior level due to greater long-term growth potential.

4. The recipe for junior success differs from senior success — early specialization and intensive training may help win now, but broad development and moderation help win later.

5. Steady, sustained year-to-year progression is a better predictor of future potential than early age-group performance or rapid improvement.

6. More does not equal better — high volume, year-round, repetitive training increases burnout, injury risk, and limits long-term potential.

7. Focus should be on building strong foundations — technical, tactical, athletic, cognitive, and character skills.

8. Long-term development requires variety, moderation, patience, and consistency, not short-term pressure or acceleration.

9. Youth sport should be about raising the ceiling of long-term potential, not exploiting current abilities.

10. Patience, quality practice, and compound gains over time are the keys to sustained development.

Practical Tips

✓ Prioritise long-term growth over short-term wins.

✓ Avoid pushing early specialization — encourage multiple sports and variety during practice and training.

✓ Be cautious of early selection, talent labels, and premature high-performance environments.

✓ Promote quality of practice over quantity — mindful, purposeful, engaging sessions.

✓ Provide emotional support to reduce anxiety about "falling behind".

✓ Resist commercial pressures, year-round travel teams, and excessive competition schedules.

✓ Recognize that late bloomers often have the greatest long-term potential.

✓ Focus on improving consistently year after year rather than achieving instant results.

✓ Work on fundamentals, movement skills, decision-making, and game sense.

✓ Embrace challenges, new sports, and varied training — these build adaptability and resilience.

✓ Stay patient — progress is not linear, and late development is normal.

✓ Track progress through skills, learning, and habits — not just wins.

Action Items

» Shift the Goal Move from "Winning now" to "Developing to win when it matters".

» Track key development indicators: Year-to-year improvement, technical skills, tactical awareness, athleticism, movement quality, Learning attitude, habits, resilience

» Integrate multiple sports, unstructured play and skill-based training — especially ages 6–14.

» Practice moderation to support learning, enjoyment, and retention.

» Instil and reinforce a long-term view – keep the focus on development and progress

Guiding Participation: Sampling, Specialisation and Premature Professionalism

The most fraught questions for a sport parent concern the choice of what sports to participate in and what other activities they should be directing young performers to engage in. Survey data indicate that many parents believe that their child's chances of reaching the highest level will be improved by focussing their time and efforts on a particular sport from an early age [152]. The available data indicate that kids come to share this view, perhaps even more strongly than their parents [153]. In contrast, most authorities advocate against *early specialisation* (participating in one sport to the exclusion of others) in youth sports on the grounds it may impair their long-term development and increase injury risk.

So who is right? As in most things, it depends – and the truth lies somewhere in the middle.

DIFFERENTIATING EARLY ENGAGEMENT FROM EARLY SPECIALISATION ...

The intuition that getting started early will improve a kid's chances of success in a given sport is not entirely false. There is clear evidence that exposure at an early age is a factor for long-term success in certain sports and we should not pretend otherwise. This is especially the case in sports that involve unconventional environments, such as aquatic sports and snow sports. For instance, early entry age is one factor that predicts competitive success of junior swimmers once they enter senior-level competition (age 18) [154].

But early exposure is one thing – early specialisation is something else entirely and premature professionalism is a step beyond even that. The key distinction is that *early engagement* simply means being exposed to a given sport early on. In contrast, what constitutes *early specialisation* is that extensive time is spent in one sport to the exclusion of other sports.

Taking a step back, the early specialisation path looks like a minefield. First of all, how do you decide? Is it appropriate to take this step before the young athlete is in a position to make an informed decision? Are kids even equipped to make the decision to commit to one sport at such an early stage? Can they really anticipate the interests of their future selves, especially when they have not yet had adequate opportunity to explore and assess the available options? If it is the grown-ups who are effectively making the decision on the behalf of the young athlete then this is even more problematic.

In addition to the dangers of early specialisation from an injury standpoint, there are also considerable opportunity costs. In many cases kids are pushed into this decision before they have had the chance to try out other sports that they might conceivably have greater affinity for. One reason that kids (and parents) are pushed into this is the fear that they might be left behind by their peers who have jumped early and committed to that particular sport. In other words, rather than making the decision out of a firm preference, many make the decision reluctantly but feeling that they must.

Whilst early exposure is important for long-term success in certain sports, patience is a virtue when it comes to settling on the ultimate destination for the sporting journey. In other words, kids should not be in too much of a hurry to put all their eggs in one basket. It makes a great deal of sense to defer the decision to commit to any one sport to the exclusion of others.

Aside from exploring the options, sampling multiple sports has its own merits, not least in helping to develop more capable athletes. Yet it has been reported with some consternation that despite the consensus among the experts, parents and young performers themselves still believe that specialising will help their long-term prospects in the sport. Rather than blaming parents, this should prompt some introspection given the evident failure to communicate the message effectively. What we have clearly failed to do is make a compelling argument to provide parents with the justification and assurance to take a different route. On a more practical level, those parents who are sold on the merits of sampling have not been provided with clear guidance on how to make this work.

If we want to offer better guidance, then one thing we need to clarify is how long should we seek to defer the decision. When presented with the evidence, most parents can accept that early specialisation is best avoided given the downsides and potential hazards, but surely this does not mean we should delay specialisation indefinitely? What is an appropriate age to commit to one sport? Does this depend on the sport in question?

WHAT AGE DO ELITE ATHLETES START AND SPECIALISE..?

One way to assess the practical significance of starting versus specialisation age as developmental factors is by looking at what age successful senior athletes commence their participation and what age they opt to focus their efforts on their primary sport. Fortuitously, one study did just this and also examined how the characteristic patterns of participation (i.e. starting age and specialisation age) vary with different sports. The authors surveyed nearly three thousand Olympians representing a diverse array of sports from a host of countries across the world [155]. By virtue of the methodology this study captured only data from athletes who had succeeded in reaching the pinnacle of senior level competition. On that basis, we might tentatively conclude that the route that these athletes took facilitated or at least did not impede their ascent and successful transition from junior to elite senior level.

The average starting age reported by this sample of elite Olympic athletes was 10.6 years, albeit there was considerable variation between sports. Likewise, the average age at which these elite senior performers chose to specialise was 15.6 years – but again, this differed markedly according to the sport. On average, these athletes typically practiced other sports alongside their eventual chosen sport for around 5 years before they made the decision to specialise. This multi-sport sampling period prior to specialisation ranged between 2-8 years depending on the sport; however, it is worth noting that some of the lower values were actually reported for the late specialisation talent transfer sports, such as bobsled and triathlon. In other words, these athletes had already participated in multiple sports prior to commencing in their eventual chosen sport.

Interestingly, almost none of the sports would be considered 'early starting' according to the criteria offered by prominent talent development models, as the typical starting age for these elite senior athletes was over six years of age. This underscores that, irrespective of the sport, parents do not need to be in too much of a hurry to enlist their young children into formal practices if they have aspirations of their offspring becoming future Olympians!

Early specialisation according to the strict definition (before 12 years of age) was also rare among these world class senior athletes. Early specialisation was only seen in a select few sports, namely artistic gymnastics, rhythmic gymnastics and synchronised swimming. Once again, this is a hugely consequential finding that should strengthen the resolve of parents and those advising young performers to resist the pressures to commit to year-round participation in only one sport prematurely.

For a number of sports, the reported specialisation age was earlier among the female athletes. This makes some sense, as girls reach puberty around two years earlier than boys, meaning that adolescent females are effectively two years further along in their development from a growth and maturation perspective. It follows that we should take into account the differing growth and development curves of females versus males when thinking about what age it might be appropriate to specialise in a given sport. That said, the specialisation ages among elite senior female athletes was still typically above 12 years of age, even in sports such as tennis and swimming that we tend to think of as early specialisation sports for female athletes especially. Most commonly the specialisation ages reported by elite females in different sports was in the range of 14-17 years of age.

To date, authorities have largely advocated against early specialisation rather than making the positive case for the advantages of delaying specialisation. Aside from the scolding tone, the positions adopted have been theoretical and even ideological, rather than offering practical evidence for the superiority of diversified sports participation based on what works in practice. Understandably these arguments have rung hollow as they failed to satisfy the genuine concerns of parents who just wish to give their kids the best chance to succeed.

The findings of this study make a far more compelling case for why they should wait and continue participating in more than sport across the year. We now have an empirical basis to advocate delaying the decision to go all in on participating in one sport year-round. There are credible data suggesting this may offer the best path for those seeking to reach the pinnacle of senior level competition.

THE CASE FOR SAMPLING...

The arguments in favour of sampling as an alternative to early specialisation are essentially that this approach will render the performer more adaptable, more resilient to injury and in the long run allows them to perform better in their chosen sport.

The rationale for sampling from a talent development perspective is twofold. The first part is straightforward: an extended period to explore and sample an array of sports will afford greater opportunity to assess and ultimately decide what sport is for them. The second reason is that this diversified participation will also better equip them to excel in whatever sport they ultimately choose. It is this part that needs a fuller explanation.

One of the central benefits ascribed to *sampling* is that exposure to a variety of sports is likely to make more proficient sportspeople by developing relevant abilities and transferable skills. To some degree motor skills and tactical elements are generalisable and somewhat applicable to other sports. Naturally, this works best for sports that are somewhat similar – for instance, different invasion sports – and sport skills that are related (e.g. overhead striking in tennis and volleyball) [156]. In this way, a diverse sport background can conceivably help kids to readily pick up other sport skills and equip them to perform well in other sports. There is some empirical support for this – based on coach assessments athletes who spent more time engaged in other sports during childhood were rated as more capable at learning new skills [157]. The capabilities young athletes acquire through their experiences in various sports thus prove to be an asset in whatever sport(s) they eventually settle on.

The other major argument regarding the merits of sampling is that engaging in a range of activities and sports develops a more complete repertoire of athletic skills. In other words, sampling a variety of sports and activities during the developmental years makes for more capable athletes. What constitutes the best combination of sports for the sampling years is a question that is worth unpacking. The ideal selection of sports would encompass the full assortment of foundational motor skills.

When explained properly this all makes sense to most parents and young performers. However, whilst this all sounds good in theory, putting it into practice is not a straightforward proposition. There are logistical challenges that must be solved. Successfully deferring the decision to invest all their time and efforts in one sport prematurely effectively means opting out as necessary. Kids who enjoy early success and become marked out as talented are especially likely to find themselves pushed or pulled into ever-growing practice and competition commitments, often involving greater travel.

We also need to confront reality and concede that there are also opportunity costs with the sampling approach. Participating in multiple sports means a busy schedule and less free time. This is true for everybody involved (notably parents), such that family life often ends up revolving around sporting commitments. Sacrifices will need to be made, as this will inevitably restrict travel and leave less time for non-sport related social activity.

We must also acknowledge that there are trade-offs that must be grappled with. Whilst it is likely to better serve them in the long run, both kids and parents need to understand that dividing their time between different sports throughout the year may mean they do not progress as fast as those kids who invest all their time and efforts in one particular sport. We should be up front about this to manage expectations. Prioritising steady but consistent progress over early competitive success does require parents and the young performers themselves to adopt a longer-term perspective. Kids are more likely to remain patient if they have faith that it will pay off in the long run.

The experts emphasise the developmental benefits of sampling an array of sports to justify their assertion that kids should participate in multiple sports for as long as possible. Rather than taking the maximalist position, what we are rather arguing against is going all-in on a particular sport while the aspiring young athlete is still a child. As we discovered in an earlier, there are also very practical reasons to delay specialisation until kids reach skeletal maturity so that they are no longer prone to maturation-related overuse conditions.

The data in favour of delaying specialisation to participate in multiple sports for longer come from studies comparing elite senior athletes to their non-elite peers. It is however worth noting the respective ages of the groups. For instance, a study of athletes in Olympic sports reported that the elites committed to their chosen sport around age 14, compared to 12 years of age for the early specialisation group [158]. Similar, in another study the elite group who enjoyed long-term success specialised in their sport at age 15 versus 13 years of age for the sub-elite group [159]. This offers a more realistic picture for sport parents, rather than the notion that kids should strive to keep participating in multiple sports indefinitely.

A rigid insistence on sampling in the form of multi-sports participation has its own drawbacks. there are likely to be trade-offs that are not conducive from a talent development perspective. Unless accommodations are made then attending practices in multiple sports means a stacked schedule that does not allow any time to engage in unsupervised play and independent practice (or indeed have a social life), which is not favourable to developing talent and risks burnout in other ways. Attempting to juggle multiple sports often does not leave any time to devote to their physical development. This is especially problematic for young females given the necessity of physical and athletic preparation in this population. Too much time spent competing and attending practices for the respective sports and too little time training itself poses risk for injury.

There are some practical considerations that govern how long it is possible to participate in two or more sports. For instance, it is a far more viable proposition to pursue two main sports if the respective competition seasons do not overlap - for example, a summer sport and a winter sport.

Nevertheless, participating in multiple sports is only sustainable for so long. The constraints of time and resources (not least financial) mean that some choices will have to be made with respect to which sports to continue with. The pressures of competing priorities (not least schoolwork) become more prominent as kids get older. As young performers reach adolescence there is also a growing imperative to make room for physical preparation in the weekly schedule (this should be viewed as a non-negotiable for girls especially).

Inevitably, young athletes will reach a point where balancing sport with other commitments (notably school) means that decisions must be made. The crunch point will come when it is no longer practicable to maintain participation in multiple sports given the competing demands on their time. What point in the youth sports journey this comes somewhat depends upon the sport(s) in question. Sports such as swimming and gymnastics are notoriously 'early specialisation' sports, in part due to the very high time demands involved.

Other complications include the growing commercialisation of youth sport and the encroachment of 'premature professionalisation' into talent development pathways.

PERILS OF PREMATURE PROFESSIONALISM...

Aside from what sports kids participate in, the type of activity that they engage in during practices for the sport also matters. One of the reasons that early specialisation may prove detrimental to the quest in the long run is the tendency for preparation and practice to become too narrowly focussed and specific to that single sport. A related phenomenon involves young performers engaging in highly structured formal practices from an early stage – which has been described as *premature professionalism*.

Premature professionalism encompasses the trend for academies in professional sport and commercial youth sports organisations to commence intensified and highly specialised practice at younger ages [160]. In an earlier chapter we described this problem as too much of the same too soon. Here we have two separate but related problems –a lack of variety, plus excessive practice demands.

Getting too specific or specialised too early is akin to building a castle on sand. Coaches, parents and the athletes themselves need to play the long game and commit to investing the time and effort to build solid foundations for later success. Whilst these kids might experience a rapid ascent in the short-term, the limited range in what they're exposed to leads to gaps in their toolkit which often curtails their improvement over the longer-term.

When practice demands become excessive this also proves harmful for younger athletes especially. Famously, it has been reported that when the number of hours of weekly organised sports participation exceed the young athlete's age in years, the odds of injury increase [161]. Likewise, when the ratio of organised youth sports participation to free play exceeds 2:1, there is a marked increase in injuries [162].

Commencing intensified practice prematurely is also not advantageous for long-term development. Juniors who peak early amass practice hours through intensified training from a relatively early stage. Those who reach the top accumulate practice hours more gradually through their developmental years and then catch up later on, such that this tends to equal out by the time they reach the latest age-group prior to the transition to senior level [163].

ADVANTAGES OF ATHLETICISM...

To my knowledge, there is not a sport for which better developed athleticism is not an asset. Logically this might have some bearing on the selection of sports that we encourage young performers to participate in early in their development. For instance, there is a strong case to be made for encouraging all performers to participate in both gymnastics and track and field athletics early on. We might even take this a step further and adopt a checklist approach to guide our initial selection to tick off the various categories of fundamental motor skills and cognitive/perceptual elements. For instance, I might seek to include a racquet/bat/stick sport (object interaction), a team sport (object control, reactive open skills, multi-player environment), gymnastics/dance/wrestling/climbing (body control, whole-body dexterity, equilibrium), a locomotion sport, such as athletics, snow/ice sports (locomotion skills) and an aquatic sport, such as swimming (aquatic motor skills).

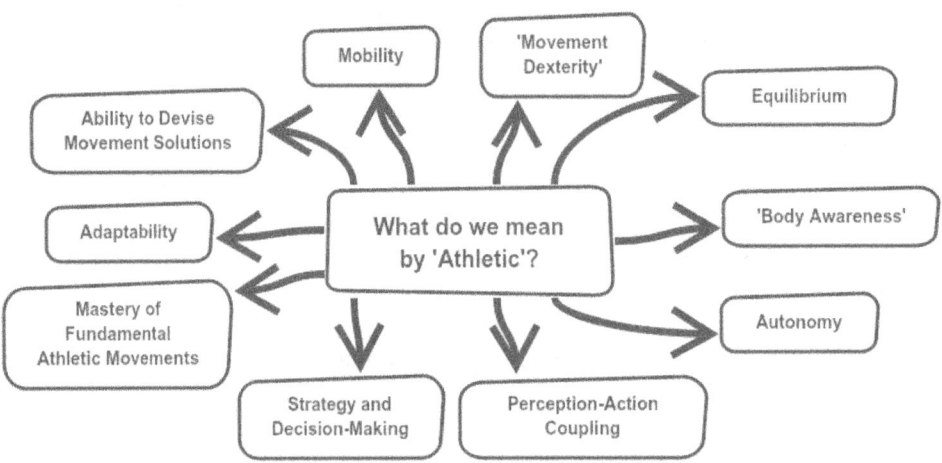

Reprinted with permission from *Informed: The Art of the Science of Preparing Athletes* [164], published in 2018 by Informed in Sport publishing

The merits of becoming an athlete first before engaging in highly specialised preparation for a specific sport are illustrated by the host of prominent examples of top performers who achieve extraordinary success and become stars despite being latecomers to their eventual chosen sport. What helps to account for their meteoric rise after making the switch is that these individuals possessed a high degree of athleticism and other generic and transferable skills that prove to be major assets in the newly chosen sport. The medal successes that have come from talent transfer programmes are another example of this phenomenon.

When we reach the point in the youth sports journey when it is no longer feasible to participate in a variety of sports our focus should switch to ensuring that all the necessary elements are accounted for. If these aspects are not provided for in the sport practices (as is often the case) a sport parent is well advised to seek out a programme that specifically caters for physical and athletic development. Similarly, in addition to diligently attending practice, young performers should be encouraged to devote time to developing their athleticism outside of sport practices, just as they do with their sport skills. Moreover, these athletic capabilities are increasingly part of what coaches are looking for when it comes to talent identification and selection.

There are also generic aspects of athletic preparation that merit inclusion irrespective of the sport. Developing general motor proficiency and other pillars of athleticism confers a competitive advantage in the short- and long-term. There is good evidence that *neuromuscular training* comprising various forms of balance training and movement skills development is effective in improving global motor proficiency in young performers. The focus for these studies is generally safeguarding against injury but there are also demonstrable performance benefits. Generic athletic skill such as jumping, skipping, landing, dynamic balance/stabilisation, and locomotion movements in all planes and axes should be a regular feature of young athletes' practice sessions, whether we are on the track, on turf, or on the court.

Whilst there is merit to being a specialist when it comes to the skills of the sport, performers benefit from being a generalist when it comes to movement skills. Performers and those who support them should recognise the value in seeking to become an athletic virtuoso in the context of their chosen sport (whatever that proves to be). Beyond regularly engaging in activities that develop relevant qualities on a regular basis, parents and performers might consider enlisting coaching support to develop athletic skills. For the most part, this expertise is uncommon even among sports coaches, so parents and young performers must choose well (I would recommend not simply settling for a personal trainer but rather seeking out somebody with the requisite skills – a background in track and field or gymnastics is a good start!).

As we introduced in an earlier chapter, more athletic kids will have an advantage when it comes to picking up new sport skills. Athletic kids generally find they can *play*, whatever sport they are thrown into. Performers who possess superior athleticism are also better able to express their technical and tactical skills during game scenarios. To use the example of racquet sports, the player who is able to move to the ball quicker, get into a better position to play the shot and retain their balance not only has a greater array of options but also a better chance of executing the shot successfully.

DIVERSIFIED PRACTICE AND PREPARATION...

Rather than continuing to contest the specialisation versus sampling argument, the better question is how do we ensure that young performers have the necessary variety to develop athleticism and other transferable skills irrespective of what choices they make regarding their sporting participation?

Whatever age a young athlete chooses to specialise, we should strive to ensure that they are able to access the benefits associated with sampling and diversified participation. Practices and training sessions should seek to incorporate the variety of activities that is necessary to develop the full repertoire of fundamental motor skills, rather than a narrow focus on sport-specific training. Young performers should similarly be encouraged to explore every opportunity to sample within their chosen sport, such as trying out different events, playing a range of positions, etc.

Sampling and variety *within* the sport also proves to be beneficial for long-term success. Whilst swimming exemplifies the importance of early engagement, swimmers benefit from competing in different events encompassing multiple swim strokes during the junior years [154]. Track and field athletics offers another example of the benefits of sampling multiple events within the sport. For instance, in the Netherlands young athlete are encouraged to practice and compete in multiple disciplines throughout the junior years and many of their top performers have competed in multi-events up to senior level before switching their focus to a single event.

Irrespective of the sport, young performers benefit from a balanced and varied practice menu. It is entirely possible to provide the necessary diversity of practice activities and preparation within a single sport. In fact, this may develop better performers in that sport in the long run. For instance, sport coaches might employ complementary 'donor' sports during practices to help with skill development whilst providing variety.

A diverse mix of activities encompassing different challenges makes performers more adaptable and ultimately improves their level of game sense and tactical problem-solving. This should be part of the criteria when selecting the coaching environment.

We have already described the benefits of *within sport sampling* in the early specialisation sport of swimming (the take-home message being we should encourage young swimmers to compete in different swim strokes throughout the junior ranks), so let us consider another example from football (soccer for those in North America). Ajax Amsterdam is arguably the most famous football academy is professional football. As has become customary in professional football, Ajax recruits players from an early age. What separates Ajax is their innovative and pioneering approach. One such innovation was to routinely rotate academy players to play different positions on the field and to continue to do so right up until players reach senior level. For many years the Ajax academy produced more senior professional players than any other academy in professional football, with graduates going on to play for the Ajax club and other top professional teams as well as the Dutch national team.

IN CLOSING...

We cannot know which sport a young performer will eventually choose if given the opportunity, so it pays to keep our options open. Young performers should be encouraged to try out other sports during their childhood years to see what captures their imagination and provides the best fit. Whilst early exposure is beneficial, a sampling approach and a diversified portfolio makes most sense during the early years.

A good adage for sports participation during the childhood years is *buffet not binge*. Extending the food metaphor, forward thinking sport parents should aim for a varied and balanced diet of sports and activities to cover all the relevant bases from a motor skills development standpoint. Over the youth sports journey we should aim to equip young performers with an extensive toolkit and transferable skills that they can bring to bear to whichever sport they ultimately opt to pursue.

There are considerable long-term rewards for young performers who have the foresight to invest time and effort in developing the foundations for later success, including universal assets such as general motor skills and athleticism that are applicable to all sports. As with investing, the best strategy is to have a diversified portfolio. For approximately the first two thirds of their youth sports journey, we should be aiming to expose kids to a diverse array of sports and a variety of activities, as this will best develop the various facets of athleticism. Every aspiring young performer stands to benefit from being exposed to track and field athletics (run, jump, throw) and gymnastics to build the foundations of athleticism for whatever their eventual chosen sport might be.

These findings underscore the importance of remaining patient and not chasing short-term success during the early junior years. Whilst engaging in more practice in the main sport to the exclusion of other sports from an earlier stage might allow more rapid improvement as a junior, delaying intensified practice until later is more conducive to success at senior level [149]. Those who go on to be elite continually improve through their junior years and reach their peak performance at an older age, so this is what we should be aiming for.

We should certainly encourage kids to participate in multiple sports for as long as it is feasible. However, we should be pragmatic rather than dogmatic on this point! The logistics of balancing sport and school whilst also leaving room for regular physical and athletic preparation mean that they will need to commit to their chosen sport at some stage. Thereafter we should strive for diversified practice and sampling within the sport, in service of continuing to develop motor skills and abilities. 'Diversified training' throughout the developmental years pays dividends in terms of later performance.

Key Take-Home Messages

1. Early exposure (engagement) to sport can be beneficial, but early specialisation (one sport to the exclusion of others) is rarely necessary and often harmful.

2. Adopt a "buffet, not binge" approach to participation throughout childhood — maintain moderation and variety, sampling the available options.

3. An extended sampling period in multiple sports before specialising is typical among elite athletes.

4. Athletes who go on to reach elite level typically specialise later (age 14-15).

5. Early specialisation before age 12 is rare among elite athletes, with very few exceptions (e.g., artistic/rhythmic gymnastics, synchronized swimming).

6. A multi-sport background during childhood develops important assets that give young athletes an advantage in whatever sport they ultimately choose.

7. Premature professionalism (overly structured, intensive, sport-specific training too soon) can lead to burnout, injury and limits skill development.

8. Becoming an athlete first — building broad movement skills — is an advantage in acquiring sports skills and specialising in the sport later on.

9. Seek variety within the sport (different positions, events, strokes, disciplines).

10. Diversified training, athletic development and motor skills are beneficial in every sport, especially after specialising.

Practical Tips

✓ Encourage participation in multiple sports through childhood, especially before adolescence.

✓ Build broad motor skill foundations to develop better athleticism, adaptability, injury resilience and long-term performance potential.

✓ Look for youth sports programmes that include athletic development, movement skills, balance, coordination and strength — not just sport-specific drills.

✓ Aim for a diversified portfolio — seek range (different sports) and variation (varied activities within sports).

✓ Avoid year-round single sport participation before adolescence.

✓ Use complementary or "donor" sports to support learning (e.g. gymnastics for soccer, tennis for cricket, athletics for most sports).

✓ Seek moderation and variety in sports participation and content of sport practices.

✓ Protect time in the schedule for physical preparation (non-negotiable for young females especially).

✓ Late(r) specialisation in many sports realistically means deferring the decision on which sport to commit to until after age 14, rather than age 12 or before

✓ Once it becomes necessary to commit to one sport, maintain variety through within-sport sampling and diverse practice activities.

✓ Be a generalist when it comes to athletic skills.

Action Items

» Design a sampling menu to explore options and see what they have affinity for.

» Make a simple map or checklist of sports and recreational activities that cover:

Locomotion (run, jump, cycle, swim, climb)

Body control (gymnastics, climbing, dance, swimming)

Object interaction (racquet/bat/ball/stick sports)

Cognitive/perceptual skills (team sports, racquet sports, martial arts)

» Delay Specialisation. Avoid specialising before age 12. For most sports, aim for specialisation after age 14.

» Audit the number of hours and content of weekly sports practices – number of hours per week engaged in organised sport should not exceed athlete's age in years.

» Promote "Athlete First" Mindset. Make athletic development a priority throughout.

» Consider seeking qualified support for athletic skill development — look to coaches with a gymnastics or track and field athletics background.

Using Biological Age and Stage to Inform Decisions

Fundamentally, our approach to physical and athletic development with young performers needs to be age-appropriate. We cannot simply copy what elite athletes at senior level are doing, but rather take our lead from what they were doing at the corresponding stage in their development. Beyond recognising that we must build the foundations and emphasise the fundamentals, we also need to meet the young athlete where they are and tailor our approach accordingly. In order to do so, we must first get a handle on the young performer's present status from a developmental perspective. What constitutes 'age-appropriate' comes down to *biological age* and what stage they are at on their individual growth curve – we cannot simply rely on chronological age. All of which means we need a reliable indication of where they are in terms of their relative stage of maturation to give us the proper frame of reference for determining what approach is most appropriate and offers the best way forward.

For coaches and to some extent parents this information is also vital to calibrate our judgements regarding a young athlete's current performance and future potential. The kid who is big for his age might dominate early on but may not necessarily be a top performer once his peers catch up and he can no longer rely on his superior physicality. The reality is that young performers competing at age-grade level are far from a homogenous group and kids competing in the same age group can be at very different points in their trajectory. This is manifested both physically and in the performance capabilities that they exhibit. A big reason why talent identification and selection goes awry in practice is due to a failure to account for these differences and the effects they have on performance at a given point in time.

Whilst individual growth curves eventually converge, during their formative teenage years young performers can differ dramatically in how they present and what they are capable of tolerating. Effectively this precludes a blanket approach when programming physical development and from a talent development perspective. To navigate these differences it is vital to have a sense of where each individual is so that we can determine how best to proceed and what to prioritise.

ESTABLISHING BIOLOGICAL AGE AND STAGE...

Clearly, it is important that we are able to determine where a young performer is on their individual growth trajectory. Aside from helping to parse genuine differences in ability versus maturation effects, on an individual level this information is necessary to guide decisions on how to best support the young performer. In this chapter we present a tool to estimate biological age and relative stage of maturation and describe how to use this information to inform the priority areas for development and guide training for the young performer.

One of the practical challenges for evaluating biological age and stage of maturation for young performers in the field is that the methods of direct assessment involve the use of medical scans to assess skeletal age or invasive quasi medical examination (known as Tanner staging) that is based on visual assessment of secondary sex characteristics. Each of these approaches has logistical and ethical issues that make them unfit for purpose in a field setting.

The alternative presented here simply involves measuring the young performer's height, both standing and seated, along with their body mass. Aside from these quick and simple measurements, the only other information required is the young athlete's date of birth. As such, it is far more practical as it requires minimal equipment and takes very little time, which also makes it far more feasible to undertake repeated measurement at regular intervals to refine our estimate.

BROAD BRUSH STROKES...

Before we present the tool, one important caveat is that this is a field assessment which provides an estimation. In other words it should be used as a general guide rather than a precision instrument, but the information does provide a broad 'ballpark' indication to guide decisions and inform training priorities.

In addition, we should acknowledge the limits of confidence in the estimate, particularly as it relates to different populations. The regression equations that the tool employs were originally derived from a sample population with a particular set of demographics. As such, whilst it has been validated with other populations it naturally fares best with individuals who share similar demographics to the original group. Consequently, there is a need to exercise caution and perhaps add an asterix when applying this tool with kids of different ethnicity to the predominantly white European kids who featured in the original sample.

The precision of this estimate can also vary according to the age of the young performer and how far away they are from their adolescent growth spurt (termed 'age at Peak Height Velocity' as it refers to the steepest part of their growth curve). This can however be mitigated by repeating the assessment at regular intervals, so that we are not relying on a single snapshot. A related approach is to cross reference the estimate provided by the maturation assessment against another method. A straightforward method of comparison that does not require any additional measurement simply involves expressing the performer's measured standing height as a percentage of their predicted adult height based on 'mid parent height' (the average of biological mother and father's height) [165].

HOW TO USE THE TOOL...

The reader can find the online assessment tool here:

https://drsianallen.shinyapps.io/AthleteMaturationCalculator/

The assessment takes very little time. The young performer's *chronological age* is calculated automatically from their date of birth and the date of the assessment. The only other data we need to input is the athlete's body mass (weight in kilograms) and height measurements (in centimetres) both standing and seated. If using a stadiometer, the seated measurement is taken with the athlete sitting up tall on top of a box with their back against a wall and the height of the box is then deducted (i.e. seated height measured from the floor minus the height of the box they are sitting on). If using a tape measure, the set-up is the same (sitting tall with back against a wall) and the distance from the top of the box to top of the athlete's head is measured.

The first step is to enter the relevant dates and athlete's details (including whether they are male or female), then input the relevant body mass and the two height measurements and the results will be displayed automatically.

APPLYING THIS INFORMATION TO GUARD AGAINST INURY...

One the most important applications of the individual maturation assessment is identifying periods of risk for growth-related injuries to regulate participation in organised sports and manage workloads. Certain stages of maturation relative to the adolescent growth spurt are associated with risk for specific growth-related injuries [166]. As we discovered in an earlier chapter, during the phase of skeletal maturation prior to the onset of the adolescent growth spurt young athletes are prone to overuse stress conditions involving the primary growth plate that can lead to adverse and permanent changes. In turn, the period coinciding with peak height velocity (the main adolescent growth spurt) is associated with various growth-related overuse injuries at the site where tendon inserts onto bone.

In this regard it is very helpful to have an individualised maturation assessment, as this will allow us to more precisely determine the period of heightened risk for the individual. To give an example, the approximate age range corresponding to the sensitive period for adverse morphological changes that are precursors of hip impingement are 9-11 in girls and 12-14 in boys [167]. However, this sensitive period will arrive earlier for early maturing athletes, whereas late maturing athletes will still be at risk beyond the age when their peers have attained a stage of skeletal maturity where they are protected.

Having an estimate of the approximate age at which the young athlete is likely to hit their adolescent growth spurt helps us to identify the period during which we will need to more closely monitor them. As this period approaches, parents should measure standing height and seated height on a more regular basis. Both the timing of growth spurts and rate of growth are relevant from an injury risk perspective [168].

Serial measurements allow us to more precisely capture these periods of rapid growth. Changes in leg length in particular (easily calculated from standing height minus seated height) and height are associated with overall injury incidence and specific growth-related overuse injuries [169]. For the most part, it will be up to parents to share this information with coaches, so that they can make the necessary modifications. During these times it is important to prioritise physical preparation (especially daily mobility exercises for boys) and be economical with practices, eliminating anything that is not essential.

Pre PHV >0.5 years prior to estimated age @ PHV
- Primary growth plate injuries (e.g. hip morphology, shoulder)
- Growth related injuries to foot/ankle (e.g. Sever's disease)

Mid PHV <0.5 yrs pre to 1.5/2yrs post estimated age @ PHV
- Growth-related injuries to knee (e.g. Osgood-Schlatter's)
- Biomechanical overload conditions (e.g. knee pain, tendinopathy)

Post PHV >1.5/2 years post estimated age @ PHV
- Acute muscle strains
- Ligament injuries

Finally, the individual assessment will help us to individualise the guidelines regarding weekly practice volumes. The general rule of thumb is that weekly hours of organised youth sports participation should not exceed the athlete's age in years. However, what is most relevant is biological age rather than chronological age. Two athletes in the same under-15 squad might be 3 years apart in biological age. What each of these athletes is able to tolerate is likely to be markedly different. This has major implications for late-maturing athletes especially. Not only do they remain prone to growth-related injury and overuse injury, but they are also less ready for the intensified training that comes as they advance through age-grade competition.

In view of these factors, it is perhaps unsurprising that late-maturing athletes tend to report higher incidence of injury [170]. Parents of late-maturing athletes thus have a particularly vital role to play in providing guidance and support to manage and mitigate these risks. The maturation assessment is an important tool to make parents aware of the situation in advance. Having this information and the growth tracking data to share with coaches will likewise be helpful when advocating on their behalf. Practically, parents will also need to take the lead in regulating participation and ensuring weekly commitments do not become excessive. Investing in physical preparation is also an important means to confer protection and build resilience for these young athletes especially.

GUIDING TRAINING PRESCIPTION...

Bio-banding is a practice that is growing in popularity as an alternative way to organise competition at youth level. Assigning kids to competition grades by biological age is becoming more common, notably in junior (soccer) football leagues in Europe. Rather than using chronological age-grades, bio-banding classifies and groups players based on relative stage of maturation. Age at peak height velocity (PHV), i.e. the age at which the individual hits their adolescent growth spurt, is the reference that is used to group kids and categorise the tiers of junior competition in a way that corrects for individual growth curves. So instead of under-13, under-14, etc., the biological age grades or bio-bands are expressed as PHV minus 2 years, PHV minus 1 year, and so on.

Pre PHV — **>0.5 years prior** to estimated age @ PHV
- Discovery, Exploration, Interaction
- Learning, Acquiring Capability

Mid PHV — **<0.5 yrs pre to 1.5/2yrs post** estimated age @ PHV
- Relearning, Recalibrating, Refining
- Developing Capability

Post PHV — **>1.5/2 yrs post** estimated age @ PHV
- Challenging Capability
- Developing Capacity

Originally published in *Informed: The Art of the Science of Preparing Athletes* [164]. Reprinted with permission.

We can implement this general approach to how we deliver physical and athletic preparation. Practically, the best way I have to found to do this is to stratify young performers into three broad bands that align with the major phases of development. This approach has been field tested in the wild – for instance, I adopted this structure with a commercial athletic development academy in my role as coaching director during my time in New Zealand. We sorted the kids who were enrolled into three groups using the assessment described and then tailored our approach and programming for each group accordingly. The groups aligned to the three major stages: pre-adolescence (Pre PHV), the interval following onset of puberty (Mid PHV) and the later phase that follows the adolescent growth spurt, termed post peak height velocity or post PHV. The priorities for physical and athletic development differ according to each stage, as depicted below. The manner in which this support is delivered also changes as young performers progress through each tier.

The approach described also works on an individual basis. Parents and coaches supporting a young performer can use the same tools and framework to guide training objectives and programming for their physical and athletic development.

UNPACKING THE PRIORITIES WITHIN EACH PHASE…

During the earliest pre-adolescent or *Pre-PHV* phase that precedes the onset of puberty young performers are most receptive to motor learning. During this phase kids can certainly gain strength but mainly this is through becoming better able to harness what they have; until puberty hits we will not see marked gains in muscle mass.

To explain the top line in the figure, the onus at this stage is discovering and developing movement capabilities and motor skills in service of acquiring fundamental movement skills and general athleticism. In general, this calls for a less structured approach and kids at this stage in their development tend to be more receptive when given some freedom to explore rather than more formal training. To that end, athletic and physical development will feature activities that challenge them to figure things out, such as negotiating obstacles and playing games for learning as well as conditioning. That said, there will likely be a subgroup that is willing and ready for more formal instruction on strength training techniques and fundamentals of sprint mechanics, jump technique, and the like. Girls especially can derive huge benefit from getting a head start on strength training in particular.

Following the onset of puberty we do start to see more marked changes, with spells of rapid growth especially for boys. As well as growing in stature, boys further benefit from free gains in strength, lean mass and speed. That said, this is a pretty volatile time – and during the multiple spells of rapid growth the respective structures of the growing limbs are under additional strain. Rapid growth also poses an ongoing coordination challenge, as the young performer must continually adjust and recalibrate to accommodate the changing dimensions of their body and limbs. All of which means that whilst we can and should introduce more formal strength training and athletic preparation during this phase we need to keep things relatively consistent and the focus should remain on maximising the quality of every repetition rather than pushing to increase load and maximise strength gains. There is a continued emphasis on general motor skills, which affords the young athlete the opportunity to continually refine and recalibrate coordination and body awareness as they adjust to their changing body and learn to harness the horsepower they are acquiring in the process.

As we discovered earlier in the book, for girls the picture is somewhat different, so a different approach is called for. Not only does puberty occur much earlier (on average commencing around age 12 but there is individual variation), the changes that occur during this phase are a lot different. Girls certainly grow in stature, gain mass and limbs become longer, but these changes are not accompanied by the free gains in strength and other capacities that boys enjoy. Consequently, this is a key window for strength training intervention to provide the necessary boost, as we explored in an earlier chapter. At the very least strength at respective links in the chain must be able to match the extra length and inertia of the limbs and body segments. Without this strength development female performers are compelled to adopt compensatory movement strategies, which is not optimal for performance and also predisposes to injury as we highlighted previously. On that basis, as well as helping young female athletes to surf the puberty wave and managing the attendant stresses and strains, we must seek to develop strength throughout this period, with a focus on bolstering the weaker links (notably hips and hamstrings). In addition to strength training, the other priority is developing relevant capabilities to accommodate changes in mass and limb length as well as refining movement skills.

The *post-PHV* phase commences when the period of rapid growth ends and things become relatively less volatile. For girls, this is typically around a year and a half following the main adolescent growth spurt (on average this equates to roughly 14 years of age but this will vary according to the individual). For boys, we typically need to wait a little longer (2+ years post PHV on the individual growth curve), so it is more a case of monitoring seated and standing heights and exercising professional judgement in deciding how long to delay until things stabilise. Once they hit this phase, we can start to double down on strength training and other aspects of physical preparation with a view to making gains in strength, speed and fitness in pursuit of whatever performance goals are identified by the performer.

Adolescence is a pivotal and formative phase for young people, so we should expect that they will assume a more prominent role and greater responsibility over this period. Hence by the time they reach this stage in their journey there will accordingly be an expectation that they are steering their own ship and that they are prepared to invest the necessary time and effort to pursue the goals they have identified. In the later teenage years young performers will typically nominate their chosen sport and define their long-term aspirations in sport. Now that we are dealing with young adults, the training process thus starts to more closely resemble the physical and athletic preparation of senior athletes, albeit with appropriate accommodations for the fact that they are still developing.

Key Take-Home Messages

1. Training and development for young performers should be based on biological age and maturation stage, not just chronological age. Kids of the same age can be at very different stages of development, physically and in their performance capabilities.

2. Understanding where an athlete is on their individual growth curve provides a better reference for guiding programming and development.

3. Field-based assessment using height (standing and seated), body mass, and date of birth offers a practical, non-invasive way to estimate maturation and guide decisions.

4. The assessment is an estimate and accuracy varies by demographics and proximity to peak height velocity (PHV), so measures should be repeated over time.

5. Individually predicted age at peak height velocity helps to identify the phase when we will need to monitor growth to more precisely capture periods of rapid growth and adopt countermeasures.

6. Biological age is more relevant than chronological age for regulating training load and participation in organised sport.

7. Three broad stages (Pre-PHV, Mid-PHV, Post-PHV) have distinct training priorities:

- Pre-PHV: Motor learning, movement exploration and coordination skills.
- Mid-PHV: Manage growth-related volatility, focus on mobility, movement quality, body control and coordination.
- Post-PHV: Seek gains in strength, speed and fitness with more intensive training.

Practical Tips

✓ Avoid rigid chronological age-based programming— use individual maturation assessment to determine participation and training priorities.

✓ Use simple field measurements (standing height, seated height, body mass, date of birth) to estimate individual biological age and track stage of maturation.

✓ Repeat assessments periodically to refine estimate.

✓ When predicted age at PHV is approaching, start to regularly monitor seated and standing height to more precisely track growth.

✓ Watch for signs of rapid height or leg-length change and share information with coaches to make necessary adjustments.

✓ Prioritise general motor skill development throughout early and mid PHV stages.

✓ Prioritise mobility and load management during mid PHV phase, especially for boys.

✓ For girls commence strength training ideally prior to PHV and continue to prioritise thereafter

✓ Use maturation assessment and growth tracking to engage athletes in conversations about their own development journey.

Action Items

» Use the online assessment tool to estimate and monitor biological age and stage of maturation*.

» Identify whether your child falls into Pre-PHV, Mid-PHV, or Post-PHV band.

» Use the framework to determine priorities and adapt training accordingly.

» Use the information to monitor injury risk and manage training loads.

» Use biological age assessment to regulate weekly practice loads (hours of organised sport per week should not exceed their biological age in years).

» Track growth and leg length changes using standing and seated height, especially in the period approaching and during PHV (adolescent growth spurt).

» Protect athletes during periods of rapid growth: Limit weekly practice loads, eliminate non-essential training, prioritise recovery, mobility and movement quality.

» Explore whether bio-banded competition is available for your child's sport.

» Seek coaches and training environments that tailor their approach to biological age and stage of maturation of the young performers within the group

» If they are not already using some type of maturation assessment encourage them to implement the tool provided in this chapter

* https://drsianallen.shinyapps.io/AthleteMaturationCalculator/

What You See Is Not All There Is

> "The fight is won or lost far away from witnesses — behind the lines, in the gym, and out there on the road, long before I dance under those lights."
>
> — Muhammad Ali

Most kids have a false impression of what life is like for the high performers they see on the television screen or social media. By extension many young performers have a wildly distorted notion of the work that went into the ascent and what they need to do to emulate the success of their sporting idols. The common cognitive bias encapsulated as 'what you see is all there is' describes the tendency to take what we see at face value and trust that it constitutes everything we need to know. Whilst this spares us a great deal of cognitive work it also leads us to overlook what is not visible or readily apparent. Unless prompted to do so, we do not tend to question our assumptions or consider the possibility that there could be additional unseen factors at work which might provide an alternative explanation for what we are seeing. The uninitiated are especially prone to this – after all they do not have any concept of all that goes on behind the scenes. This phenomenon certainly applies to sport. Aside from the need to address the distorted perceptions of would-be athletes, the unseen parts also have implications for coaching and parenting.

LOOKING BEYOND THE HYPE…

When we watch top performers competing on the screen most of us do not fully consider what goes on behind the scenes. In reality, the moments that athletes spend competing under the lights are a tiny fraction of the thousands of hours they invest in the endeavour. This realisation is crucial for young aspiring athletes. The analogy of an iceberg is often used to illustrate the unseen aspects of athlete life when the cameras are off. Beneath the surface the vast majority of the time is spent practising, preparing and recovering in between the glimpses we see in the competition arena.

If a young athlete wishes to pursue the path to elite level, they must understand the reality beyond the bright lights. In contrast to the glamorous depiction in the media, for the most part the life of an elite performer is rather more mundane.

In the digital era the social media accounts of elite (and not so elite) performers arguably provide a glimpse of sorts into this life. Yet one of the ironies of the social media age is that whilst top performers and those who work with them are sharing more 'behind the scenes' than ever, the public perception of what goes into preparing and performing has perhaps never been more distorted.

It is important to recognise that what practitioners and performers choose to post on these platforms is carefully curated – for the most part it is staged and only the stuff that looks cool or glamorous tends to get shared. Rarely does this provide an accurate representation and at times it is a total misrepresentation. The social media version is very far from the reality! Unless the person watching happens to be familiar with the reality on the ground it is very easy to get a skewed or even entirely inaccurate impression.

THE LESS GLAMOROUS REALITY BEHIND THE SCENES AND WHAT COMES AFTER…

Most parents who are eager for their kid to become a professional athlete would be well served by having a glimpse behind the scenes. If they had the opportunity to observe first-hand what an athletic career looks like, I suspect they might be less enthusiastic about the prospect and certainly more concerned with preparing the young athlete for their second career after sport.

What is not apparent from the outside is how precarious life is for a professional athlete. Whilst the stars in certain professional sports might be highly paid, this is not the case for everybody. In the Olympic sports especially, the financial rewards are considerably less. Funding is not particularly generous and not very secure, so athletes must seek sponsorships and endorsement to supplement their income. Whatever their earning potential in the sport, the window for accumulating wealth during their athletic career is short and uncertain.

What we certainly do not see is the reality that athletes face once their professional career is over. Athletic careers are short, so the years after sport represent a far greater proportion of their life. Whilst a successful career in sport opens doors and confers skills and attributes that are an asset in professional life, the career options available once the athlete retires from sport are nevertheless determined by the academic studies and vocational training they have undertaken earlier.

There is a growing onus on dual career development in the talent development literature, recognising that the support for promising youth athletes should also cater to their career prospects alongside and after sport. More forward-thinking talent development environments emphasise holistic development, with accommodations and support to help them undertake their studies alongside training and competing.

All the same, the degree to which young student-athletes are successful in balancing sport and school commitments comes down to their priorities and how they allocate their time and efforts. Most aspiring young athletes have their sights firmly fixed on their imagined future at the pinnacle of the sport and their thinking rarely extends beyond that. As the grown-ups, coaches and parents have a crucial role to play in helping them to contemplate what comes after. Shining a torch on the realities that professional athletes face once their athletic career comes to an end is crucial in helping them to the realisation that they must invest time and make preparations in the here and now for life after sport.

#THEGRIND

Just as the content of what is shared on social media is often misleading, so too is the subtext. The reason I object so much to the trend among athletes to refer to training as #thegrind is that this reduces training and practice to mere drudgery and just something to get through. This entirely misses the mark: the pursuit itself not only has value but is also a source of purpose. Athletes who fail to find meaning in the process will struggle to have enduring success. It is revealing that athletes who have long and successful careers frequently comment that they enjoyed being in the training environment and found the process of preparing and honing their craft rewarding in itself.

'Elite performance is achieved by doing the right things in the correct way over a consistent period'

– Andreas Behm, track and field coach to Olympic athletes (including Olympic gold medallist and world record holder in the 110m hurdles Aries Merritt)

It is true that the process of practising and preparing is by its nature somewhat repetitious. That said, it is far from mindless. Indeed the more engaged the athlete is during practice and training, the better and more lasting the fruits of their labours tend to be. Whilst there are those who live to compete, something that many athletes who enjoy long and successful careers at senior level have in common is that they genuinely enjoy the parts in between and remain captivated by the process of striving to get better. Aspiring high performers would do well to heed their example and learn to embrace and enjoy the process, not least as the lion's share of their time will be spent engaged in preparation.

Older athletes can be an invaluable resource in providing a more honest account for impressionable young performers. Naturally it pays to choose your role models wisely – ideally those who model the approach and attitude that it takes to be successful. In some instances these athletes can also share hard-won wisdom that we can all learn from. An example that comes to mind is an athlete I worked with during the first decade of my career, who was actually the reason I took up coaching track and field athletics. Mhairi had perhaps the best attitude to training of any athlete I have encountered. She was a young mother and this gave special meaning to our sessions on the track and in the gym; they were precious to her, on the basis that these were essentially the only times in the week that were dedicated exclusively to herself. What made this all the more striking is that Mhairi was a 400m runner and so most of our track workouts were pretty unpleasant and not what most would consider relaxing 'me time'. Mhairi brought a smile and a fabulous attitude to every session, despite the inclement weather that Scotland is notorious for, and it remains one of my most cherished coaching experiences.

AGE-APPROPRIATE AND FIT FOR PURPOSE...

A common complaint among colleagues in the field is that young performers (and even parents) frequently come into the weights room asking about an exercise they saw on Instagram. Performers (and parents) falling for the nonsense shared by 'virtual experts' and influencers on Youtube is becoming the bane of many coaches and practitioners' lives in the digital era.

Returning to the iceberg analogy again, the flashy and eye-catching glimpses shared on social media do not provide an accurate representation of the training and practice habits of a senior athlete. However, even if an aspiring young performer were to get an unedited behind the scenes view of the training performed by elite athletes, the reality is that it would not be applicable to their own training.

"The man at the top of the mountain did not fall there"

– Vince Lombardi

Everything we see from athletes operating at the senior-level is built upon a foundation of thousands of hours of practice. Their physical and athletic prowess is the accumulation of countless repetitions and the compounding effects of years of training. The awe-inspiring displays of skill and athleticism are the culmination of a great deal of time spent becoming proficient in the fundamentals.

By definition, the foundations of physical and athletic development and the pillars of sport practice comprise pretty basic exercises. Attaining proficiency in what coaches term *the fundamentals* means extensive time and effort spent diligently repeating variations of these basic exercises and core skills. It might not be glamorous or fancy, but this is where aspiring young performers should be investing the bulk of their time, rather than trying to emulate what they see on Instagram or Youtube.

As it happens, even experienced senior athletes at the elite level continue to drill the fundamentals and do not stray too far from the basics in their physical preparation. Ironically the practice and preparation that actually makes the difference is generally not what is shared in the media or on social media – after all, it is not eye-catching and makes for pretty dull viewing.

FACTORING IN THE UNKNOWN AND UNSEEN PARTS ...

Returning to our original theme, an extension of the 'what you see is all there is' fallacy is that the more visible or easily quantifiable tends to be given most credence. Just because something is not readily observable or widely shared does not mean it is of lesser importance. Ironically, it is these less tangible aspects that are often what make the difference for performers.

Considering the parts that we do not see is crucial from a talent development perspective. It is important to acknowledge that much of what an athlete's day to day activities happens beyond the watchful gaze of the coaching staff. Even during the times when I was working full-time with a team or with an individual athlete, the extensive time the athletes spent in my company still only represented a fraction of their day. This includes practice, training and self-management – some proportion of which is often undertaken in the athlete's own time.

It is important that young performers realise the significance of the solo and unsupervised practice undertaken by high performing athletes as these are elements that have an important bearing on success. In many ways the ultimate test of the individual performer's commitment is how they behave when the coach is not there. A related element that differentiates higher performers is what they choose to practise of their own accord: better athletes voluntarily work on their areas of weakness, whereas lesser performers tend to opt to practise the skills that are relatively strong [171].

There is also much that is beyond the purview of coaches, practitioners and indeed parents. The day-to-day choices that an individual makes and how they conduct themselves beyond the training facility can make a dramatic difference to the outcome. Sleep and nutrition are two variables that profoundly affect how performers respond to training, their ability to recover between sessions and their capacity to perform on any given day. Clearly meal times and sleep mostly occurs on the athlete's own time and away from the gaze of the coaches. Whilst parents can exert some influence in this regard, it is ultimately up to the young performer particularly as they get older. And this is as it should be; after all, this is their show.

NAVIGATING WHAT WE CANNOT SEE WITH YOUNG PERFORMERS...

As coaches of humans (inclusive of parents, teachers and others) we are always working with incomplete information. Inevitably there are unknown or unseen factors in play at any given time with any given individual. The intricacies of a young athlete's life beyond the practice or competition environment will never be fully knowable for a coach. To some extent this is also true for parents, especially as kids reach their teens and start making more frequent forays out into the world on their own. Parents and coaches alike ultimately have to exercise judgement and trust their intuition to fill in the blanks.

All the unknowns and the miscellaneous elements that are beyond our control naturally pose challenges for planning and programming. The inherent uncertainty means that there needs to be some readiness to adapt the plan as the situation evolves and the picture emerges. The willingness of the coach to make such accommodations and the flexibility of the programme are accordingly important considerations when deciding on the best environment for a young performer.

By extension we need to be responsive to the athlete's state on any given day. As a wise friend and fellow coach shared, the best monitoring system is a coach who pays attention. It is here that the human element of coaching comes to the fore. Being attentive and attuned to verbal and nonverbal cues similarly provides a good early warning system during instances when external events or non-training stressors are taking a toll on a performer. Parents are well placed to detect when something is amiss, albeit kids can be fiendishly good at hiding things from their parents if they are motivated to do so. Nonetheless, if the coach and parent are both keeping an eye on things and sharing intelligence it makes it less likely that something important will be missed.

Enlisting the athlete as an integral part of our information-gathering is likewise crucial. By definition, they are the richest source of information. Clearly the only person in a position to register how their body is feeling is the performer themselves – after all, only they have access to what is going on in their own mind! Sharing this information does however require a level of trust that must be developed over time and ultimately the choice of what and how much to share remains with the individual. In some instances the young athlete might be reticent to divulge certain information to a parent, whereas they are willing to confide in a coach, teacher or another member of the support team with whom they have good rapport. The converse is also true – for instance a young athlete might be unwilling to admit something to a coach that might affect their selection.

It is also an ongoing process to help the athlete to become more attuned to their own body (what practitioners term 'body awareness') so that they are better able to discern and report back on how things are feeling with a greater degree of specificity. Naturally the more *body aware* the performer becomes and the better they understand their own body and how it responds, the better able they will be to regulate themselves.

Key Take-Home Messages

1. What we see of elite athletes (on screen or social media) is only a glimpse — most of the crucial work happens behind the scenes.

2. Social media provides a curated, often misleading impression of training and athletic life; young athletes must learn to distinguish image from reality.

3. Elite performance is grounded in mastery of fundamentals, accumulated over years of consistent and purposeful practice.

True performance is built on thousands of hours of repetition, fundamentals, recovery, lifestyle discipline, and self-directed practice.

4. Appreciating and enjoying the process — training, preparation and growth — is crucial for sustaining long-term success.

5. The unseen elements (sleep, nutrition, mental preparation, attitude, self-discipline, solo practice) often make the biggest difference over time.

6. Athletes who are body aware and able to self-regulate and communicate honestly are better equipped to sustain their development and improve their performance.

7. Coaches and parents never have the full picture, so we must be attentive and observant to remain attuned to what's going on and responsive to changing circumstances.

8. Trust and body awareness must be developed over time so athletes can accurately communicate how they feel and what they need.

Practical Tips

✓ Help young athletes understand that success at the elite level is built upon diligence, consistency, excellent fundamentals and taking care of their body.

✓ Use trusted role models (ideally older athletes with maturity and wisdom) to share insights that reflect the reality of what the journey looks like behind the scenes.

✓ Encourage athletes to find meaning and satisfaction in daily training — not just in winning or public recognition.

✓ Shine a torch on what life looks like for a professional athlete to highlight why they need to invest in academic studies and make preparations for their career after sport.

✓ Promote athlete life skills and healthy off-field habits — sleep routines, nutrition, hydration and self-care — as part of everyday process, not just optional extras.

✓ Encourage athletes to take ownership — especially when the coach is not there — by practising weaknesses, not just strengths.

✓ The best athlete monitoring tools are conversation and observation, paying attention to verbal and nonverbal signs.

Action Items

» Use the iceberg analogy to have conversations with young athletes about what is not seen on social media and what real training looks like.

» Find ways to show your kids the reality behind the screen, such as enlisting older athletes to share their insights and first-hand experiences.

» Help kids to appreciate the wider aspects of athlete life beyond the training and practice environment, notably sleep and nutrition

» With the help of the coach, make sure your child is able to appreciate the importance of the fundamentals to better understand the purpose of practice

» Reinforce the importance of consistency and compounding — explain why and how they are the key ingredients for progress over time.

» Seek out talent development environments that promote a dual career focus and coaches who recognise the importance of school for life after sport.

» Prompt kids to reflect on how they practice — ask them whether they are as diligent when no one is watching and what they choose to practise.

» Help young athletes to implement a daily self-check protocol to cultivate body awareness, prompt them to listen to their body and take action to remedy minor complaints and soreness.

» Plan regular check ins with the coach and keep communication channels open to share timely updates and relevant information (sleep, stress, social pressures).

Free-Range Athletes

> "I trained 3-4 hours a week at Ajax (Ajax Amsterdam Football Club) when I was little but I played 3-4 hours a day on the street. So where do you think I learnt to play football?"
>
> — Johan Cruyff

The concept of *free-range kids* popularised by author (and parent) Lenore Skenazy [172] is highly pertinent to youth sports parenting and also readily applicable to how we coach young athletes. In each case, participating in free play and other activities without adult supervision are essential parts of how children and young athletes develop. Given the myriad benefits and essential role in developing adept athletes and capable humans, it seems baffling that we have systematically eliminated opportunities for kids to freely engage in activity without grown-ups being present. So here we will make the case for applying the free-range perspective to youth sports participation and talent development to help young athletes to be more engaged and better able to operate autonomously.

WHEN THE GROWN-UPS STEP AWAY...

When compared to previous generations, today's youth are sadly less accustomed to engaging in free play and unsupervised 'pick-up' games with others in their neighbourhood and with their peers at school. Nevertheless, the urge to play with others comes quite naturally, so we can expect that they will soon figure it out once provided the opportunity. The onus is on us as coaches and parents to collectively permit young athletes the space and time to roam, explore and interact without intervention from the grown-ups.

As we noted in an earlier chapter, freely engaging in play is central to how we explore and learn to navigate the world. More particularly, voluntarily participating in games with others (without intervention from the grown-ups) is how kids learn to engage with others, conduct themselves in a social context and interact with peers in a competitive and cooperative manner. A less structured environment where the kids themselves decide the playing area and the rules of the game affords the opportunity to apply what they have learned, explore different tactics and engage in trial and error. As such, free play and unsupervised games are particularly rich in opportunities to acquire and adapt sport skills and develop game sense.

A case study involving youth (soccer) football in North America illustrates kids' appetite for free play and the benefit of permitting them the space and opportunity to organise themselves. A group of coaches instituted a pilot whereby the first 10-15 minutes of practice was devoted to free play, rather than the standard coach-led drills, so that the opening part of the session was entirely led, managed and refereed by the kids themselves. This is akin to what is described in the physical education literature as *deliberate play*. The pilot intervention (or rather suspension of intervention) proved wildly successful and popular, so much so that other kids started to flock to the club. Not only was there greater enjoyment and engagement, but the coaches also observed the young players becoming more creative. The kids also became more adept at working autonomously rather than constantly looking to the grown-ups for direction or intervention. The resounding success and boost in player enrolment following the pilot has since led other youth sports (baseball and softball) at the same facility to adopt this policy.

A CASE STUDY OF HOW NOT TO DO IT: YOUTH SOCCER IN CANADA…

Firstly, this is necessarily a generalisation, but what I have observed since arriving into Canada with youth soccer and the numerous commercial academies has made for grim viewing. Being from the UK, I grew up playing and watching football (fun fact: my dad signed with a club in the top tier of English professional football back in the day), so it is a sport I am very familiar with. The reason that football is the world's game is that you only require a ball and a patch of ground to play. On that basis, what I have found so striking is how rarely I see kids kicking a ball around on their own. On the contrary, what I do see almost exclusively is even the youngest kids being over-coached in rigidly structured supervised practices that largely comprise scripted drills.

One sight that still haunts me is watching a professional coach (in the sense he was being paid) instructing 6- or 7-year-old kids to dribble up to a static dummy – PICK UP THE BALL WITH THEIR HANDS – throw the ball over said dummy, then run around to shoot into an empty net. I should note that the first kid to attempt the drill declined to pick up and throw the ball – rightly so, given that is against the rules in the sport – and was promptly castigated for failing to do so. All the more upsetting is that these poor kids' parents were paying significant sums of money for the privilege of subjecting their kids to these crimes against football. In itself this is baffling for a sport does not have any significant barrier to entry in most other parts of the world.

To be clear, there is absolutely a role for instruction and (competent) coaching to help kids learn the technical skills and acquire the necessary tactical understanding. The more proficient a kid becomes at executing the basic skills and the better they understand the game, the more they are able to enjoy playing it. Where we run into a problem is when closed skill drills and overcoaching restricts opportunities to play during practices. Likewise, whereas formal practices in the past might have constituted a fraction of the total time spent (I refer the reader to the Johan Cruyff quote we opened with), supervised practices under the command and control of the coach are almost exclusively what kids in Canada seem to be engaging in.

With the burgeoning youth sports industry, notably in North America, financial incentives are certainly part of what drives the trend for excessive time spent attending supervised practices. The other reasons why participation in formal practices is seemingly to the exclusion of playing the sport unsupervised are open to debate. Perhaps what kids experience makes them less inclined to engage in the sport of their own accord outside of supervised practice and competitions. It is also true that young student athletes' engagement in extracurricular activity is increasingly heavily scheduled, meaning that they have less free time to engage in sport for fun or otherwise.

PRACTICE THAT INHIBITS THE ABILITY TO *PLAY*...

Whatever the reasons, operating almost exclusively under external constraints and constant supervision is not conducive to developing the ability to play the game under live conditions. Clearly this is a major omission – after all, once the player takes the field it is up to them. Whatever instructions or game plan are provided beforehand, as soon as the game kicks off they must read and continuously respond to what is unfolding in front of them. Developing the expertise to make decisions, improvise solutions and respond spontaneously to what team-mates and opponents are doing in real-time is essential.

For kids to develop *game sense* they must acquire the necessary tactical understanding and an ability to read the game. Honing the specific cognitive and perceptual capabilities that underpin these aspects requires hours upon hours of engaging in the sport under dynamic and unpredictable conditions akin to what they will encounter in a match [173]. In other words, if we want to develop kids who can *play* we must provide ample opportunities for them to practice and compete under live conditions without getting in the way.

At the macro level, how we design and conduct practice at different stages in development matters. This assumes greater importance as opportunities to engage in free play and unsupervised practice become more restricted. Much the same applies with the game plan and instruction when kids compete – the coach must strike a balance between providing enough structure and organisation, whilst also affording the necessary freedom to be creative and respond to what is happening in front of them. At the micro-level, how the coach runs practice sessions clearly also matters. Intervention needs to be regulated, not least the volume and frequency of instruction and feedback that is provided.

The downstream effects of failing to account for these aspects of practice design are becoming noticed at the elite level. One of the top coaches in professional football in England recently commented on a growing trend he has observed whereby players continually look to the sidelines for guidance. He specifically traced this back to practices employed in the professional academy pipeline that lead players to become reliant on constant direction from coaches.

DELIBERATE PRACTICE, DELIBERATE PREPARATION AND SELF-DIRECTED LEARNING...

Simply attending supervised practice and being exposed to drills under the direction of a coach does not necessarily mean that any learning is taking place. Mindlessly following commands and performing prescribed drills does little to develop adaptive skills or may not transfer to the ability to execute in a competition environment.

Deliberate practice is the term used to differentiate the type of highly purposeful practice where the performer themselves has a central and active role rather than simply being a passive recipient of instruction from the coach. Deliberate preparation extends this concept to all facets of youth athlete development to provide a similarly deliberate and intentional approach to developing proficiency in global athletic skills in much the same way as sport skills.

A common assumption with deliberate practice and deliberate preparation is that this requires the constant presence and involvement of a coach. It is true that there needs to be adequate provision of external feedback and coaching input to guide learning; however, this can be provided periodically and in a variety of ways, including video feedback and input from peers. There is no necessity for the coach to exclusively lead proceedings or even be in attendance at all times.

In fact, from a talent development perspective it is important that as the young athlete advances on their journey they are afforded greater opportunity for *self-directed learning* [174]. In other words, the young athlete should be expected and encouraged to take more ownership and assume more responsibility to do the work of their accord and in their own time without relying on the coach to be there.

"Everything I know about football I learned on the street. My friends and I were always trying to think up a new feint. If anyone invented something new, they had to show it to the others. That is what street football is all about."

— Zinedine Zidane

It was more usual in previous generations for young athletes to spend hours practising alone or with friends (without any adults being present to supervise or direct proceedings). One of the paradoxical effects of having sports participation supervised and directed by a coach is that kids defer responsibility to the grown-ups.

Interestingly, young (soccer)football players at grassroots level in less wealthy nations engage in more solo practice [175], suggesting that this a first world problem and seems especially prevalent in North America. Moreover, it is the higher weekly hours of solo practice during childhood and early adolescence that differentiates the more skilled young players from less skilled players – both groups otherwise engage in comparable amounts of coach-led practice, peer-led play and organised matches.

Other studies investigating the developmental activities in team sports including football and hockey report that it is the 'enthusiasts' who voluntarily engage in considerably higher volumes of peer-led free play during childhood that ultimately prove most successful in reaching the highest level [176, 177].

Free-range athletes are more likely to retain the intrinsic motivation to engage in this type of solo and unscheduled practice [178]. When the grown-ups are out of the picture young performers are also more inclined to step up to coach and help each other, which benefits learning for all parties.

WIDER IMPORTANCE FOR THE JOURNEY IN SPORT AND BEYOND...

The benefits of taking more of a free-range approach extend beyond sport. As in a parenting context, affording performers the opportunity to operate independently develops *self-efficacy* – that is, a sense of capability and confidence in their ability to cope within a given context. Returning to the positive example of the soccer academy, it is a show of confidence when the coaches opt to turn over control to the young athletes and give them responsibility for coming up with the rules and collectively resolving contested calls without a referee. Moreover, young performers respond to challenge and find it motivating to have the onus placed back upon them (after all this is meant to be their show). Over time this approach helps to develop self-reliant athletes and capable individuals.

When provided with the equipment, rudimentary skills and a place to play the kids will likely figure out the rest for themselves. There is certainly value in helping them to become proficient in the basic skills but beyond that often the best thing we can do is stand aside and let them play with and against other kids. Cooperation and competition are integral features of sport and vital to what makes it engaging. The competitive element must be preserved, regardless of fashionable but misguided ideas of fairness held by well-meaning teachers and parents. This is another reason that the grown-ups should get out of the way at regular intervals – when left to their own devices, kids will opt to compete with each other.

Greater recognition of the role of free participation in talent development among youth sports coaches and sport parents will hopefully lead to more initiatives incorporating a free-range approach and ongoing efforts to enlist young performers in the process. This is likely to go some way to reigniting young performers' desire to engage in the sport spontaneously for the simple joy of doing so. In turn, unsupervised pick-up games with their friends may yet see a resurgence. From this perspective, adopting more of a free-range approach to coaching youth and sport parenting is likely part of the solution to address the growing drop-out rates we see across youth sports in the early- and mid-teenage years.

Key Take-Home Messages

1. Free play and unsupervised activity are essential for developing adaptable, creative, and confident young athletes.

2. Modern youth sport environments tend to over-emphasise structured, coach-led sessions at the expense of meaningful free play.

3. Playing under live, unpredictable conditions develops game sense, decision-making and problem-solving far more effectively than scripted drills.

4. Excessive supervision can undermine athlete autonomy, ownership and intrinsic motivation.

5. Self-directed learning and solo practice meaningfully differentiate higher-performing youth athletes from their peers.

6. Granting kids ownership to set rules, run the games and resolve disputes themselves builds self-efficacy and interpersonal skills.

7. A free-range approach supports lifelong engagement in sport and may help reduce dropout during adolescence.

Practical Tips

✓ Use questioning rather than constant direction to stimulate thought process and guide decision making rather than being too directive.

✓ Encourage athletes to take ownership of their development beyond organized sessions.

✓ Facilitate free play with peers, providing time, space and simple equipment.

✓ Resist the urge to organise every activity.

✓ Avoid overscheduling — keep space for individual practice and peer-led play.

✓ Support spontaneous sport participation (e.g., kicking a ball in the yard or park).

✓ Value fun, autonomy and problem-solving over competitive outcomes.

✓ Encourage kids to practice and explore skills independently.

Action Items

» Emphasise to kids that they do not need to attend a supervised practice or organised competition to engage in sport.

Find ways to incorporate deliberate play in the schedule.

Facilitate the conditions to spontaneously engage in independent practice and play.

» Praise kids when they engage in practice of their own accord

Encourage kids to take the initiative to organise opportunities to play sport with their friends rather than always making arrangements on their behalf

Coordinate with other parents to create options for drop-in free play and pick-up games in your neighbourhood

Request that coaches involve the athletes during practices, such as athlete-led warm-ups.

» Evaluate programs to ensure athletes have adequate exposure to performing under dynamic and 'live' conditions to foster game sense.

» Challenge kids to take more of a lead in directing their own practice.

» Celebrate showing initiative and coming up with ideas.

Finding the Right Environment
Choosing the Right Programme

Environment is all important for developing talents and young people. Parents are naturally highly motivated to find the programme that provides most optimal conditions to allow their child's talents to flourish. Looking past the sales pitch and making the right choice is however not a straightforward proposition. Being successful on this endeavour begins with understanding the key features that make for the most conducive setting to enable young performers to realise their athletic potential. In this chapter we aim to provide parents with some criteria to guide the search.

CONSUMER CHOICES AND MARKET FORCES...

Depending on the sport and what part of the world you happen to be in, the talent development environment might include community sports clubs, commercial academies, national development programmes or academy systems linked to professional sports teams. Schools are another crucial environment for inspiring and nurturing sporting talent, not least as they are often the setting where kids are first exposed to the sports that they subsequently choose to pursue. In turn, certain schools prize their reputation for excellence in particular sports such that they invest in facilities, coaching and support staff – and some even go as far as recruiting kids who excel in a targeted sport.

It pays to be a discerning consumer when it comes to choosing the training environment, given what rests on the decision. The 'user pays' model is prominent in North America and the 'youth sports economy' is estimated to be worth over $15 billion in the United States alone. This introduces market forces, for good or ill, which makes it all the more important that sport parents are well informed in their consumer choices. Giving the customer what they want can easily be hijacked by aggressive and misleading marketing that seeks to tell the customer what they should want. As a jaded youth soccer coach recently told me, young athletes are a renewable revenue source – each year, there is another cohort of unsuspecting kids (and parents) to exploit.

A more optimistic view is that by providing sport parents with the knowledge to make wiser consumer choices we can make the market forces work in the favour of young athletes, rewarding more reputable organisations in their recruitment and retention of kids, such that they outcompete the less scrupulous opposition. Certainly kids are already voting with their feet, based on the rates of drop out in participation. In particular, the steep decline once kids reach their teenage years indicates that there is a glaring gap in the market for those with the foresight to provide an alternative that better meets the needs of young performers.

RECOGNISING THE GOOD, THE BAD AND THE UGLY...

A characteristic feature of a functional talent development environment is that there is a dual focus on personal development and athletic development. This is expressed in a commitment to developing the personal qualities and attributes that will enable kids to flourish in addition to athletic capabilities and sport skills. Another good indication is their readiness to support the young student-athletes to be successful in their studies as well as their sporting endeavours.

Two essential elements of a conducive long-term athlete development programme are that the emphasis is *long-term* and the approach is geared towards *development*! The final part is that both the content and how it is delivered are geared to the age and stage of the young *athlete*! What constitutes 'age-appropriate' depends on the maturity of the individual from both a biological and emotional perspective. There should be some effort to assess each of these and meet the young athlete where they are.

What constitutes 'optimal' with respect to training content likewise depends on our timeline. The question then becomes what training will yield best results next month or next year (or the years after that)? In the case of youth sports, clearly we should be thinking on a longer timeline.

It takes foresight to recognise that highly specialised types of training which appear to transfer most readily to performing the sport are generally not what will develop the foundations to enable superior performance in the medium- and long-term. Parents should beware programmes that promise rapid results. Equally, parents need to be patient and adopt an appropriately long-term view to avoid adding to the demand for short-term results and quick wins.

Without doubt the most common mistake with youth sports athletes is getting too specialised too soon. When parents and kids (even some coaches) hear the term *sport-specific* many naturally assume it means that every exercise employed in training should simulate or mimic the sport. This is arguably the biggest misconception that parents need to guard against when assessing potential options. Unethical commercial programmes and opportunistic coaches and trainers are all too ready to take advantage of this misapprehension.

```
        Sport-specific
         'transfer
         training'

       Athletic Capability

      Foundational Capacities
```

'All functionality is context-dependent... one has to examine every exercise in terms of the neuromuscular and metabolic functions that it is intended to improve'

– Mel Siff

As described in the quote above, an exercise does not necessarily have to resemble the sport skill to be applicable. Many exercises that do not appear sport-specific at first glance are nevertheless highly effective in developing capacities and capabilities that are directly relevant to the sport. A good example is the practice of engaging in 'donor sports' and related training activities, such as gymnastics, to develop relevant capabilities. Clearly, we need to take a wider view of specificity, especially with youth sports.

There are universal capacities and capabilities that are foundational and thus necessary for any sport. Developing fundamental motor skills and the pillars of global athleticism are essential for young athletes regardless of their chosen sport. It follows that these should be the mainstay even of programmes that are designed for a specific sport.

"Don't rob Peter to pay Paul."

– variously attributed

Parents should be very wary of facilities and programmes using marketing slogans such as 'train like the pros!'. The trend for prominent private schools with a reputation for sport to hire high profile ex-players to coach their school teams is an example of a similar scenario creeping into school sports. At present it is beguilingly easy to succumb to what has been described as *early professionalism* [160]. Aside from being the opposite of age-appropriate, this is ultimately futile if it is at the cost of sacrificing enjoyment and harming their long-term prospects.

Parents and young athletes alike need to keep the notion of not robbing Peter to pay Paul very much at the forefront to avoid being drawn in by marketing. The youth sports industry, for that is what it is, is fraught with these issues. Parents must resist the allure of premature professionalism and seek out programmes that focus on establishing the bedrock capacities and developing the scaffolding of capability to support the young athlete's ability to perform at a higher level in the future. In the long run this will yield a far better outcome.

The final threat we need to guard against can be encapsulated as 'too much too soon'. What is highly revealing is that young athletes who are selected to talent squads at an early stage in their development also tend to exit the pathway earlier [158]. We might expect that kids who receive dedicated support and intensified training earlier on would progress quicker than their non-selected peers, whereas the objective data indicate that this is not necessarily the case. The evidence suggests that talent promotion programmes only become a conducive environment for developing talent once young athletes have attained a certain level of maturity.

Given the apparent trade-offs, there is a need for careful consideration we should not be in too much of a hurry. In general, parents would be well advised to wait until they are sure the young athlete is ready and equipped to cope with everything that comes with being part of a formalised talent development pathway.

FACILITIES VERSUS ENVIRONMENT...

My travels around the world have taught me that beyond meeting certain minimum requirements to run a viable programme, impressive facilities and state of the art equipment does not confer 'high performance' status. In fact, something that many talent hotbeds in different sports have in common is that they are often rather spartan and well worn.

Certain nations consistently succeed on a world stage in spite of a lack of facilities and resources. One example is Kenya who are a longstanding powerhouse nation in distance running. Another is the Pacific Island nation Fiji in rugby union – at the time of writing, the Fijian men's team are reigning Olympic Sevens rugby gold medallists (the women's team won bronze). Kenya and Fiji not only remain competitive but consistently achieve extraordinary success without the modern facilities, high-tech equipment and sports science support enjoyed by other leading nations.

Clearly, we do need to parse the effects of genetics and other aspects of environment, such as climate and altitude. We should also acknowledge that what constitutes minimum requirements from a facilities and equipment point of view varies a great deal depending on the sport. Unlike distance running and rugby, there are certainly sports where access to facilities and availability of specialised equipment can be a decisive factor.

Growing up I vividly recall watching on with envy at the acres of sports fields, courts, athletics track, swimming pool and world class training facilities boasted by the private schools in the town in England where I attended school (the state school I attended had neither the means nor the will to compete on this front). On the surface such advantages seem to be borne out by the data indicating that a disproportionate number of athletes who compete for Team GB at world and Olympic level are products of the independent (fee-paying) private school system in the United Kingdom. However, if we delve deeper the apparent differences in outcomes we see in the UK example are not simply attributable to facilities. Another crucial point of difference with these independent schools is that they affirm their commitment to sport by investing in quality coaching [179]. Sport and physical education are also prioritised in the school timetable, which contrasts sharply with state schools that continually cut back on the time allocated to physical education. We should also note that the same data from the UK reveal that there are other sports such as (soccer) football and rugby league that demonstrate no such over-representation of independent school educated athletes.

Facilities alone do not necessarily confer competitive advantage and certainly do not guarantee success. An illustration is that the elite sport schools in central European countries have failed to yield the expected returns in terms of national team representation and success at senior level. The empirical data fail to support that attending the German elite sport schools increases the likelihood of success at senior level [180]. A large survey of elite athletes in Belgium similarly reported that whilst they rated the facilities at the elite sport schools as superior, what was delivered and the outcomes for graduating student-athletes were not rated as meaningfully different to attending a mainstream school [181]. Finally, a retrospective analysis indicated that attending the 'top talent schools' in Holland made no difference to young performers' level of performance or highest level attained in junior or senior competition [182]. Aside from the lack of apparent benefit, another worrisome finding was that those who attended these elite sport schools also performed worse academically.

Clearly facilities alone are not a reliable guide, so a sport parent seeking to identify the best programme for a young performer needs to look beyond the amenities that they see on a tour. Creating an environment that reliably cultivates talent is not straightforward. As the sport school example illustrates, investing in facilities and attempting to bring the highest performing kids of their age together does not necessarily confer success! I have observed first-hand that what actually makes the difference are the less tangible aspects of the environment, which are predominantly created by the coaching staff along with the athletes themselves.

INCUBATOR, CLASSROOM AND CRUCIBLE...

The talent development environment must fulfil a variety of functions at different times. Each of the following elements will feature, albeit the blend and the relative emphasis shifts over the course of the journey.

An **incubator** to inspire and nurture talent. Performers should be encouraged to aspire and strive towards the highest goal they can envisage. The role of the individual in the process is paramount, so those involved need to ensure young performers retain a sense of agency. They should be reminded often that it is their choice to be there and it should remain clear that what they invest each day is ultimately up to them.

A **classroom** to instruct and inform. The programme must satisfy certain key objectives with clear outcomes that can be assessed. The time spent in the practice environment should develop the young person's *sporting IQ* – depending on the sport this might include game sense and decision-making faculties. Likewise, the staff in the training environment should help teach the performers how to look after themselves. For instance, there should be some effort to educate the performers on relevant aspects of *athlete life* and *performance health*, much of which concerns the choices they make beyond the environment, including nutrition and sleep habits.

A **crucible** to forge young performers and test their mettle. An important function of a talent development environment is to equip kids to cope with the challenges they will face. Part of the function of training and practice is to bring out their innate strength and render them more resilient both in body and mind. Youth athletes should be encouraged and afforded ample opportunity to voluntarily challenge themselves to perform under pressure under relatively low stakes so that they are prepared to do so when it matters in competition. Aside from preparing the performer to execute under competitive conditions, they should be provided guidance and support to develop coping strategies.

NECESSARY INGREDIENTS...

The coaches and staff naturally play a big role in shaping the training and practice environment. Those leading the programme naturally set the tone, but everybody involved contributes to the environment that is created. The staff share the responsibility for setting the standard both in what they ask of the performers and what conduct they accept. What is expected from all parties should be made clear and explicit. From day one there should be clear terms of reference and mutually agreed terms of engagement.

Both the content and manner of delivery matter from this perspective. When evaluating a prospective programme parents should take note of what is communicated and how instruction, input and feedback is delivered. Beyond what is said, equally important is what behaviours are modelled and tacitly reinforced, so it also worth noting how the coaches and staff conduct themselves. How they engage with the athletes is of course crucial; the interactions with the athletes and between the staff send clear and powerful signals, for good or ill. In addition to routine day-to-day interactions, it is also illuminating to observe how staff act in decisive moments. A notable example is how coaches conduct themselves on the side-lines and how they engage with athletes in the heat of battle.

Exceptional coaches are a rare breed and throughout my journey I have gone out of my way to seek out and spend time with these individuals. To give an example, since arriving in Canada I have connected with the head coach for the Tennis Canada hub for the province of British Columbia, the exceptional Oded Jacob. Following an engaging conversation over coffee, a former colleague and I were invited to come along and check out a training session at the regional centre.

On the surface the facilities are no more or less what you would expect to see at any indoor tennis centre and certainly no different to plenty of other facilities both public and private in the city, especially in the more affluent areas. That said, one court at the Vancouver centre does boast the innovative and very impressive *SmartCourt* technology, which automatically captures and catalogues players' movements and shots in each rally, via multiple cameras mounted around the court, supported with 'smart' machine learning algorithms.

Gadgets aside and returning to the important stuff, I was most impressed to see how the young players were practising: it was all purposeful and intelligent, rather than mindless drills. Watching Oded interact with the athletes collectively and individually similarly reinforced my initial impression that he is a coach of the highest pedigree. Whilst there was an assistant coach and a trainer present, it was clear who was running the show; however, it was a quiet authority that Oded exercised with a light touch. The fact that he had an audience that afternoon made no apparent difference – there was no bravado and the lack of ego on display was utterly refreshing. I was also impressed when he intervened (with the minimum of fuss) with a brief but very clear signal to the trainer (a stand in who was covering for their usual trainer on the day) who seemed to like the sound of his own voice a little too much.

The other major 'tell' was how the players conducted themselves. We were greeted with a smile and a 'good afternoon' by one of the young players as we arrived who enquired if he could help direct us. Without exception the players practising that afternoon were highly engaged and laser focused while on court and unfailingly polite and respectful during the breaks in between.

STEEL SHARPENS STEEL...

Aside from the grown-ups, the peer group around the young athlete are often instrumental in creating the conditions to bring out their best. Motivated kids will push each other, as well as lending encouragement and providing social support. In other words, those who the young performer practises with and competes against play as big a role as any in helping them to harness their latent potential.

The peer group in this sense includes team-mates and members of the training group as well as competitors. With individual sports these may be one and the same. For instance, during my tenure with the Scottish Squash programme those training at the national centre would practise together year-round, compete against each other at the national championships and those selected would be team-mates at the European and World team championships.

Those with older siblings in the sport benefit in a host of different ways. An older sibling can variously serve as a role model, an arch rival and wise counsel sharing the benefit of their knowledge and experience. An illustration of the advantages this brings is that having an older sibling in the sport makes it more likely that a young athlete will reach elite level [183]! Other competitors in the sport who are a year or two older can fulfil a very similar role (minus certain aspects of sibling rivalry!).

How kids conduct themselves and interact with each other naturally makes a big difference to the experience. What we are aiming for is an environment where the young performers challenge and support each other. To that end, the grown-ups in charge play an important role in their stewardship over the environment. How the coaching staff regulate conduct and respond to misbehaviour is important. A code of conduct goes a long way, with clear standards and explicit expectations that are signed up to by the parents and the performers themselves. Equally these standards much be enforced. A discerning eye is needed to differentiate between good-natured banter and conduct that crosses a line.

TRAINING ENVIRONMENT AS SANCTUARY...

During difficult times the training environment provides an important sanctuary for athletes. For instance, when an athlete is going through a slump in performance the training facility is where they go to regroup and channel their energies in positive way. In much the same way during periods out of action due to injury the training environment is the lab where athletes go to rebuild and direct their efforts towards coming back stronger. In both instances, the training environment takes on added significance as the place where the athlete can continue to feel productive and experience a tangible sense of progress. At such times practitioners and training partners alike play an important role in providing light relief and social support.

To give an example, a couple of years ago a former student-athlete (a talented rugby union player) who I worked with some years ago reached out to me. Seumas wanted to thank me and express his gratitude for helping him through challenging times during an extended injury lay off. He went on to say that the help and guidance over that difficult period had strengthened him mentally, such that our time together had an enduring benefit on his life since then.

The ankle injury Seumas suffered initially seemed innocuous (he lost his footing on a damp pitch), but as time went on the pain did not resolve. For almost a year, despite quality medical care, physiotherapy and extensive imaging, we did not have a definitive diagnosis. Exploratory surgery eventually revealed not one but two underlying issues, but in the meantime Seumas was unable to tolerate any running activity and this was essentially the situation for over two years.

During this extended period of frustrations and pain, our training sessions in the weight room provided a rare outlet where Seumas could invest his energies in a positive way. For those two years the weight room essentially became his sanctuary and our sessions together assumed additional significance.

Key Take-Home Messages

1. Ethos and approach are all important – seek programmes that prioritise long-term athlete development over short-term wins.

2. Flashy facilities do not guarantee quality; as long as the facility meets minimum standards, the calibre of coaching, culture of learning, attitudes of coaches and conduct of peer group are far more crucial.

3. Coaches' behaviours, values and communication set the tone — observe what they model, not just what they say.

4. The best environments inspire and encourage (incubator), teach essential knowledge (classroom), and challenge kids to become better (crucible).

5. The best environments strike the right balance between challenge and support.

6. A competitive and cooperative peer group is integral to creating conditions that promote striving, such that they push each other and pull each other up.

7. The training environment should double up as a sanctuary — a place where young people can feel productive, supported and secure, especially during setbacks or injury.

Action Plan

Priority	What to Do	What to Look For
Check their online profile	Scrutinise marketing material and social media	Check that marketing and social media posts are free of obvious red flags
Do a site visit	Evaluate facilities	Check facilities are adequate, necessary equipment is available and everything is well maintained
Observe coaching	Attend a session	Effective communication, quiet authority, teaching moments, role-modelling of standards
Evaluate training content	Check training is age- and stage-appropriate	Prioritises foundational motor skills, equipment is scaled to fit, programming accommodates individual differences
Assess the culture	Talk to existing parents/athletes	Motivation, respect, focus, enjoyment, work ethic
Check workload & philosophy	Discuss monitoring, accommodations for injuries and school/sport demands	Appropriate progression, attentive to daily state, plan B workouts and modifications, self management
Review attitude to challenge	Ask how athletes are encouraged to test themselves	Opportunities to struggle and overcome, build resilience and learn coping strategies
Evaluate the peer group	Observe interactions and peer group influence	Athletes push each other but also support each other
Confirm support in tough times	Ask about injury protocols and transitions	Training environment doubles as sanctuary for rebuilding confidence and ability

Selecting the Support Team: Go Armed with the Right Questions

Among the most consequential decisions for the sport parent is choosing the right people to coach their child and assist them along the way. Given what is at stake it is important to be as rigorous and discerning as possible when selecting professionals to support the mission. Especially if a young performer has high aspirations then naturally we will want to assemble the best team available to give them the best chance of succeeding. Over the course of the journey this might include a network of specialists to provide guidance and additional support as needed.

As with facilities, when embarking on the search it is helpful to be clear on the criteria. The calibre of the coach is naturally a good criterion to start with; however, this may take some work to establish. For instance, beyond credentials and their coaching resume, it is equally important that we consider what type of climate the coach creates for aspiring young performers under their care. Given all we need to consider it follows that parents need to do their due diligence prior to making the selection. To that end, there are a host of pertinent questions that must be asked and answered in order to make the best choice. In this chapter we attempt to walk through the steps that will improve the odds of finding the right fit to meet the needs of the young performer.

NARROWING THE SEARCH...

It can be a daunting task to trawl through the dizzying array of coaches, providers, gurus and therapists across different disciplines that you are likely to be faced with when beginning the search with a casual google enquiry, or surf on social media. Depending on the discipline, the professional body or certifying organisation is often a good place to commence the search for qualified providers in your region. From there, a good strategy is to seek out recommendations in order to draw up a long list of local options.

Making discerning consumer choices requires some ability to make an informed judgement on professional competency. When we come across a great coach or practitioner the difference is striking and immediately evident. However, unless you have been fortunate to come across one of the good ones and seen first-hand how they operate, it is difficult to form a reliable impression of what 'great' or even 'good' looks like. So whilst the opinions of other parents is helpful up to a point, without the necessary frame of reference it is difficult to sort the wheat from the chaff.

What sport parents greatly benefit from is a discerning eye to filter the options and narrow the search. Naturally somebody with specific expertise in the area is best placed to provide this assistance, so it serves to ask around other professionals.

REAL-LIFE REPUTATION BEATS SOCIAL MEDIA PROFILE...

In the social media era, commercially savvy coaches, practitioners and therapists increasingly maintain a strong social media presence. Given this is essentially now the norm, the fact that a practitioner might be active on social media is not necessarily a bad thing. Equally, the nature and tone of what they share on these channels can provide some indication of how they operate, so it is worth casting a critical eye on what content they post.

To give an example, providing content in the spirit of educating the viewer is broadly a good sign. It is also worth paying attention to how they refer to current and previous athletes. Celebrating their successes is one thing; however, if they are constantly and shamelessly claiming credit for their achievements then this is a red flag.

Certainly, in isolation social media profile is not a great measure of credentials or real-life credibility. Word of mouth recommendations from those with first-hand knowledge or personal experience are generally a much better indicator, especially when it comes from a fellow professional. The community of coaches and therapy providers working in sport is typically small and interconnected. Even if two coaches or practitioners have yet to cross paths directly, in general there are at most only a couple of degrees of separation connecting them.

On that basis, a good strategy to establish whether somebody is credible and well regarded among their peers is to ask around the local network. If a selection of people you ask have never heard of the coach or therapist you have found on google or social media, this doesn't necessarily mean they are not credible, but it should give you pause. Conversely, the endorsement of a respected fellow professional should carry some weight.

Beyond their reputation as a professional, another important criterion is whether the coach or practitioner in question is a good human. Once again, personal recommendations from former athletes can provide insight into an individual's ethics and professional manner. To that end, it is worth seeking out former clients who might be willing to speak about their experience. One critical question to ask is whether they felt the practitioner concerned was truly invested in helping them, independent of any payment received. Another thing to query is the extent to which they demonstrated that they genuinely cared about the person they were coaching or treating.

Naturally this approach does rely on the person in question being forthcoming. When it is a fellow professional a sense of duty can sometimes limit the degree to which they are comfortable being candid. To overcome this understandable reticence, one test that a fellow coach uses when deciding whether to pass on a recommendation for another coach is 'would I want this person to coach my child?'. Not only is this question directly applicable here, but it is also a good way to establish what the person really thinks about the professional expertise and personal qualities of the provider you are enquiring after.

GRACE UNDER QUESTIONING...

Once we have concluded our search and undertaken some due diligence, ultimately the only way to establish whether the particular coach or provider is a good fit is to try them out. Equally, there are critical questions to ask during this trial phase to provide further illumination. Aside from what answers they give, how the practitioner reacts to being questioned is highly instructive.

Good coaches and practitioners are essentially teachers. As such, the good ones are characteristically open to question and keen to share their coaching philosophy. You should be able to ask them about their approach. They should be open to sharing their position on hot button topics such as early specialisation. They should be willing to get into specifics and ready to explain the reasoning behind a particular drills or workout. In general, they will welcome the opportunity to educate and engage the athlete and their parent on their process.

In contrast, if the practitioner bristles at being questioned as if they perceive this as a challenge to their authority, this should be viewed as a red flag. Clearly there is a time and place and naturally questions should be asked in a respectful way. Assuming those conditions are met, if the coach or practitioner does not respond favourably to questioning then I would suggest exploring other candidates.

ARE THEY READY FOR A FOLLOW UP QUESTION...?

Beyond being open to being questioned, the provider should also be willing to engage beyond their initial answer, not least so you can verify what you have understood from what they have told you. You are entitled to expect the provider to have a clear and well thought out rationale for what they are doing. Part of the due diligence is establishing the soundness of their approach.

The most critical and revealing questions relate to the 'why'. Peeling back the layers, they should be able to explain what purpose the particular intervention is serving. More specifically, they should be able to tell you how it relates to the identified objectives and specific needs of the human in front of them.

Clearly, we also want to establish the depth of their knowledge. To that end, whatever the initial response, you should feel free to interrogate their reasoning beyond superficial answers. If they are able to give a cogent response as you ask follow up questions to go a couple of layers deeper, they are probably a keeper. If not, it might be time to carry on the search.

WHAT IS THE PLAN..?

When enlisting the help of a specialist provider typically there is a shelf life to their involvement. Their assessment and initial recommendations should be sufficient for them to demonstrate what value they can provide in the short term to address immediate needs and resolve any current issues. Beyond that, the question then becomes whether to continue working with them once the immediate needs have been met or the specific issue has been resolved.

When it comes to considering ongoing specialist support it becomes necessary to establish whether the provider has a plan beyond their initial intervention. To that end, parents should seek to establish what the next steps might be and whether they have a longer-term vision on how to help the performer to progress towards their ultimate objective.

Whatever the case, it is important that all parties are clear on what their remit is and what designated purpose they will serve on the journey ahead. To be clear, if the provider does not have a long-term plan or vision this is not a failing; it just means that they are more of a resource to be called on as and when the need calls for it.

WHAT IS THE TRANSITION PLAN (OR IS THERE ONE)..?

As with a specialist support provider, the involvement of any coach or practitioner will necessarily come to an end at some point. It is critical to establish from the outset that the provider or coach does in fact have this mindset, rather than seeking repeat business or reflected glory.

A good illustration of this is sports injuries. Returning from injury can be a daunting prospect and therapy providers play a crucial role in the initial stages particularly in managing the athlete's care and putting them back together. The practitioner should operate with the stated aim of moving the athlete onto the next stage in their journey, at which time their involvement will become reduced or cease entirely. As the rehabilitation process progresses there should be a readiness to pass over the reins to other providers. This becomes especially crucial during the latter stages to guard against developing a sense of dependency and to improve the chances of making a successful return. It is therefore critical that questions are asked on when and how this transition will take place.

These principles equally apply with coaching, particularly at the development level. Development coaches must have the mindset of doing everything they can to assist the young performer on the present stage of their journey and prepare them for whatever comes next. Sadly, there is a need to guard against the tendency for some coaches to cling to successful young athletes. The expectation should be that they step away when the time comes and pass the baton to whomever is best able to serve them on the next stage in their journey.

'A big factor into why I am throwing today is because of my original coach, Ian Baird, who gave me a lot of energy and motivation... It was Ian who passed on my passion for throwing'

– Tom Walsh, Oceania record holder, 2017 world champion and Olympic medallist in the shot put

Of the coaches I have come across on my travels, perhaps the person who best embodies these virtues is somebody that very few people will have heard of. Ian Baird is a track and field coach from Australia who lives and coaches in a small town in New Zealand. Without doubt Ian has the knowledge and expertise to coach senior athletes at the highest level but his passion lies is developing young athletes. Once his part is done, Ian actively seeks to move the athlete onto another coach to take the next step into the senior ranks. What is remarkable about Ian is that he does not feel any need to remain involved; he shows no desire to partake in the reflected glory when the athletes he has coached go on to achieve great things at senior level. This is best exemplified by Ian's relationship with multiple world and Olympic medallist Tom Walsh. Tom and his coach decided to honour Ian's contribution by awarding him the coach's medal when Tom won the world championships in 2017.

Once again, for parents and athletes at youth level it is critical to have these conversations to verify that the coach is doing it for the right reasons and motivated to act in the best long-term interests of the athlete. To that end, the coach should affirm their readiness to make the right decisions with respect to their own involvement. These negotiations should establish terms of engagement, specifying the conditions for their involvement with a clear commitment from each party (coach, parent, athlete). Make sure that the coach has a transition plan and is willing to assume the duty of facilitating the handover when the time comes.

Action Plan

» Draw up a shortlist of potential coaches using trusted networks and professional accreditation sources.

Narrowing the search:

- Word of mouth recommendations from other parents – competence, character, care
- Seek opinions from fellow professionals in the local network (would they be happy for this person to coach their kid?)
- Scrutinise the content on their social media
- Interview in person using a structured question checklist*.
- Give them a trial run

The test:

- How do they respond to questioning?
- Are they ready for a follow-up question?
- What is their plan? Do they have a clear rationale for their approach?
- Are they motivated by reflected glory or genuinely doing what is in the long-term best interests of the young athlete?
- Do they have a transition plan and a commitment to hand-over when the time comes?

*Questions to Ask a Prospective Coach or Specialist

1. Coaching Philosophy & Environment

What is your coaching philosophy when working with young athletes?

What is your position on early specialisation?

2. Individualisation & Relevance

How will you assess my child's needs?

What is the plan?

How does this support their specific goals?

What outcomes should we expect — and in what timeframe?

How will you measure and communicate progress?

3. Reasoning & Expertise

Can you explain the reasoning behind your approach in a couple of layers of detail?

How do you stay updated with coaching best practice?

4. Openness & Collaboration

How will we communicate — and how often?

How do you involve athletes and parents in decision-making?

5. Professional Standards & Ethics

Can you put us in touch with former athletes/clients who might be willing to share their experience?

What steps do you take to ensure a secure and supportive environment?

6. Roles, Remit & Long-Term Planning

How will your role evolve over time?

What is the plan beyond the initial phase of involvement?

7. Transition & Athlete-First Mindset

What happens when it is time for a new coach or provider to take over?

How do you ensure a smooth handover, so the athlete keeps progressing?

Investing in the Right Tools

One important question faced by aspiring athletes and the parents who support them is how to make best use of finite financial resources in the quest to improve performance and avoid injury. Deciding which tools merit the investment is not altogether straightforward. It is easy to be swayed by marketing, especially when stars in the sport are paid to endorse certain products in mainstream and social media. Even if they are not taken in by the hype directly, young performers may feel undue pressure to match their peers and keep up with competitors. Parents are motivated to help their child to succeed, so it can easily turn into a costly arms race in the attempt to get the best kit and provide a competitive edge.

EQUIPMENT SELECTIONS AND SPORTS INJURY…

Part of the rationale for investing in quality gear is that cheap equipment might be faulty and more likely to malfunction, which has the potential to cause injury. Certainly, build quality and structural integrity are key criteria when purchasing equipment (including shoes). By extension, from both injury and performance viewpoints it is important to take appropriate care and attention to make sure that equipment is maintained properly to avoid malfunction and ensure it remains in good working order.

That said, spending a lot of money to buy the latest name brand equipment is not in itself a guarantee of quality. A recent example that drew a lot of media attention was the very high-profile injury knee sustained by number one NBA draft prospect Zion Williamson when his Nike shoes split apart as he pivoted on the court during a televised college game. These shoes were certainly not cheap (and they had the player's name on the side), so what this does illustrate is the need to look beyond the manufacturer's logo and the price tag.

Build quality aside, there are some notable instances (many involve footwear) whereby advances in design features that were intended to improve performance have actually caused more injuries. In one such case, sports shoes that were designed to improve traction on turf proved so effective that they directly contributed to ankle and knee injuries, as players who wore these cleats often found their foot became 'stuck' on the turf.

Protective equipment is an obvious example of the use of equipment to safeguard against injury. The highly positive trends associated with the growing use of helmets among recreational skiers and snowboarders in reducing not just head injuries but other injuries exemplify the overall positive effects [184]. That said, whilst helmets and other gear certainly provide some protection and tend to reduce the severity of many injuries, the outcome is not always universally positive. Wearing padding and other protective equipment in contact sports can in some instances encourage reckless and dangerous play. A related phenomenon is the paradoxical tendency for the heightened sense of protection when wearing safety equipment to lead to more risk-tasking behaviours in outdoor sports. Clearly, equipment alone is not the whole answer when it comes to safety.

MANUFACTURERS' CLAIMS...

Running shoes and other athletic footwear can be one of the biggest expenses for parents and performers. Perhaps the biggest cautionary tale regarding manufacturers' claims about sporting equipment preventing injury concerns running shoe technology and design features. The very high rates of running injuries among recreational runners especially came to light some decades ago and has fuelled the arms race for running shoe manufacturers to devise technologies and engineering solutions to solve the problem. The running shoe industry has grown to monstrous proportions during the period since (athletic shoe sales represent a $20 billion industry in the US alone) and the quest to reduce running injuries also supports a mini-industry of stores and experts to prescribe the right running shoe for the individual.

Sadly, despite the hype, none of this has had any meaningful impact on reducing rates of running injury over the past few decades. Paradoxically the extra cushioning provided by expensive running shoes makes it more comfortable to run in a way that is mechanically unsound [185], whereas when we run barefoot we very quickly adapt our gait mechanics to attenuate impact forces – and we spontaneously do this because it is painful to do otherwise. Thus it appears the increased comfort provided by running shoes can actually facilitate the poor mechanics that cause injury.

There are similarly indications that other engineered design features not only do not necessarily solve the identified problem but may prove injurious. A related inconvenient finding is that some runners report more pain when they run in the type of running shoe prescribed for their needs (such as 'support' or 'pronation control'), compared to running in a randomly assigned or neutral shoe without specialised engineering features [186]. All of this somewhat undermines manufacturers' claims regarding the design features of their shoes and also raises questions about the practice of in-house experts prescribing a particular type of running shoe [187].

Ironically, rather than feeling compelled to buy expensive sports shoes, there is good evidence that parents might be better advised to have their kids go barefoot as much as possible. When I moved to New Zealand I was intrigued to discover that this was part of kiwi culture, even in the most affluent Auckland suburbs. Schoolchildren especially habitually run around barefoot, including when playing sports. There is some indication that this practice benefits fundamental motor skill development, as children who spend a lot of time barefoot when growing up report superior jumping performance and balance skills compared to those who wear shoes [188]. Perhaps unsurprisingly, regularly going barefoot is also advantageous for developing the structure and function of the foot in children and adolescents, whereas constantly wearing shoes seems to lead to flatter foot arches [189]. Another indication of the benefits for developing motor skills is that regularly performing barefoot running and sprinting training also appears to help children to learn sound running technique [190].

CHOOSING KIT TO FIT...

One aspect of equipment selection that does matter with young performers is making sure it is sized properly. Naturally we want apparel and footwear to fit. On that note, after 30 years of research study the best practical guidelines regarding running shoe selection is to choose a neutral running shoe that fits your foot and otherwise base the selection on weight (lighter is better) and comfort [191].

The need to select kit to fit the young athlete also applies to sporting equipment. The importance of scaling the dimensions of the playing area and equipment to young performers as they grow is emphasised in the skill acquisition literature [192], not least as this helps the young performer to enjoy all the sport has to offer. This seems quite a fundamental point and yet it is often overlooked. Most of us can readily call to mind the comical sight of a child grappling with an adult sized racquet or bat that seems almost as big as they are, or striving gamely to shoot a full-sized basketball into a hoop set to adult height.

Scaling the set up and ensuring equipment is sized to fit the young performer also makes a considerable difference from the perspective of acquiring skills. Using oversized equipment requires kids to adopt different techniques to cope, whereas adult-sized pitches and goals similarly affect how they play the game. By making the necessary modifications so that everything is scaled to the performer we help kids learn how to perform the skills of the sport in a way that will transfer and translate to the adult game as they grow. In addition to technical skills, this will benefit tactical development and game sense. Simply put, kids will learn to play in a way that will still work when they become older.

The most important consideration is that equipment is fit for purpose. For sports that involve extensive equipment, it makes more sense to invest in used equipment that fits rather than buying expensive equipment that the young athlete will soon grow out of. It might not look as flashy, but equipment does not need to be box fresh, as long as it has been well maintained and is still in good condition. This approach is certainly far more sustainable and relieves some of the financial stress when the time comes to purchase the next size up.

When making our selection we also need to be clear on what purpose we are seeking to fulfil – that is, we need to decide if our objective is short term advantage or long-term benefit.

MARGINAL GAINS...

Given the less than stellar record of the running shoe industry, one of the most striking things about the recent advent of miracle running shoes is that they have actually proven to be effective in producing a measurable benefit in performance (seemingly worth around 4 minutes over marathon distance if you're Eliud Kipchoge). The impact on the sport of distance running and track athletics of this revolutionary running shoe technology has been dramatic, akin to the swim suit technology that led to hundreds of records being broken in the pool. Like the swim suits, the appropriate response when equipment has this degree of impact is to ban it.

That said, below the elite level we should realise that the margins are far greater and so even if the equipment does yield a performance advantage it is far less of difference maker. Most readers will have observed the 'all the gear and no idea' syndrome in different sports, which is arguably the best illustration that purchasing the best equipment does not make you a good athlete or proficient at the sport. Aspiring young athletes should not feel any need to rely on such technological assistance. There is a strong case to be made that we should encourage developmental athletes to train and compete with standard equipment and the most basic gear. This approach will allow young performers to focus on developing their sports skills, athletic skills and physical qualities without any external aids.

RETURN ON INVESTMENT...

Part of the reason for the furore over the Nike running shoes is that the manufacturer guidelines state they are good for about 300km for the average runner. To put this into context, serious distance runners might log in excess of 100km in a week, so given that these shoes retail at over $300, the cost per kilometre is fairly exorbitant. All in all, a pretty extravagant purchase for three weeks' use! Those who opt to reserve the miracle shoes just for racing will equally have to contend with having to rapidly adjust to the shoes – and they are very different (a bit like having a small canoe on your feet), which will likely negate much of the potential benefit.

What people choose to spend their money on is also illuminating. I am always struck by the sight of recreational cyclists (generally middle-aged men) who have invested thousands of dollars on a carbon fibre bike because it is a few hundred grams lighter, yet it is apparent that they are themselves carrying kilograms of excess body weight.

REDIRECTING RESOURCES TO THE REAL DIFFERENCE-MAKER...

Our own body is the ultimate athletic tool we possess – it is an unmatched triumph of engineering. Whilst the dimensions and potential upper limits are somewhat dependent on choosing our parents well, what is unique about the body that further separates it from conventional equipment is that we can modify it to suit our purposes. We can also improve its load tolerance, capacities and capabilities – there is no tool on the market that can match its adaptability. Even with the advances in technology, no equipment compares to the human body from an engineering standpoint.

Whilst the human body is an extraordinary tool, we need to keep in mind that unlike other equipment we cannot simply replace it if it breaks or wears out (we only get one). Happily, whilst we cannot replace our hardware, it is highly adaptable and we can upgrade it with the right kind of training. We can also update and upgrade the software on an ongoing basis – and this is a far swifter and more straightforward proposition.

With athletes I use the analogy of the body as a race car. Physical preparation offers the means to boost horsepower and fuel economy, regular maintenance keeps everything in good working order and with the aid of coaching intervention we can improve its manoeuvrability, handling, and performance!

When faced with the choice of where to invest precious time and resources, the young performer's own body is the logical option. Regardless of what other equipment we might buy, investing in improving the capacities and capabilities of the body has far greater potential to positively impact performance. Beyond protective equipment, we can also fortify the body from the inside out, such that with the right coaching and preparation we can make the young performer more durable and resilient to injury.

Key Take-Home Messages

1. Money spent on sports gear does not always translate into better performance or reduced injury risk. Marketing can be persuasive, but it doesn't guarantee meaningful benefit.

2. Build quality and proper maintenance matter more than brand names or price tags when it comes to safety.

3. Equipment innovations designed to improve performance can sometimes increase injury risk or encourage reckless behaviour.

4. Footwear choices are often over-emphasised. Evidence shows expensive "engineered" running shoes haven't reduced injury rates. Comfort, fit, and technique matter most.

5. Properly sized and scaled equipment enables skill development, better game sense, and enjoyment—especially for growing athletes.

6. Performance-enhancing gear yields only marginal gains and often distracts from real development priorities.

7. The most valuable investment is in the young athlete's body—their strength, movement skills, and resilience.

Practical Tips

✓ Be sceptical of manufacturer's claims – ask coaches, practitioners, older athletes to share their insider knowledge and discern what is worth paying attention to

✓ Prioritise fit, function and build quality over labels.

✓ Choose neutral footwear that feels comfortable and allows natural movement

✓ Maintain all equipment carefully—functioning gear is safer than high-end kit that's poorly looked after.

✓ Scale equipment and playing environments to the child's size and stage of development.

✓ Seek out used equipment for fast-growing kids to make it more viable and cost-effective to move to the next size up.

✓ Encourage kids to practice with standard equipment to build skill and physical competence rather than relying on technological assistance.

✓ Upgrading, maintaining and future-proofing the young athlete's own body is generally the best long-term investment of all!

Action Items

» Audit current equipment: Check fit, condition and whether items are still appropriate for the child's size and skill level.

» Set a clear strategy and allocate resources to items that will deliver the greatest long-term development benefits.

» Redirect spending towards coaching, training and physical development instead of chasing incremental equipment upgrades.

» Encourage kids to lose the shoes and go barefoot on a regular basis to build strong and healthy feet and support fundamental motor skill development.

» Encourage kids to invest time and attention in their own body, including care and regular maintenance.

» Educate young athletes to help them understand that no piece of equipment substitutes for skill, effort, and preparation.

» Regularly reassess needs and review equipment inventory as the athlete grows and progresses.

Teach an Athlete to Fish…

"Give a man a fish, you feed him for a day. Teach him how to fish and he will feed himself the rest of his life"

— Proverb (variously attributed)

When we do something for a performer that they could do for themselves we deprive them of an opportunity. In some small way what we are effectively doing is impeding their progress towards becoming self-sufficient. Whilst this might seem insignificant at the time, if we extrapolate this out, consistently doing this small thing over time compounds into a major issue. Sadly this may only become apparent once the performer finds themselves alone and confronted with a situation that requires them to act independently, only to realise that they are entirely unprepared to do so.

A recent and particularly vivid example of this was the covid-19 lockdown. Suddenly performers found themselves without access to the facilities, direction, supervision and support they were accustomed to – they were on their own. It was notable that some performers coped admirably and even thrived when they found themselves with greater autonomy. Clearly this was great credit to the individuals concerned and reflects very well on their intrinsic motivation and resourcefulness, but it was also testament to the coaching environment they had been exposed to beforehand. However, what was perhaps more revealing is how so many others proved incapable of organising themselves during their time away and in turn faced a very steep path when organised practices and competitions resumed. This was evident even at professional and elite level. Many clearly struggled upon their return and there was a massive injury spike in many professional leagues following the enforced break, reflecting what a shock to the system it was for those who had failed to maintain some semblance of their normal routine. The disruption was of course far more lasting below the elite level and these performers also lack the same access to support, so they faced a much tougher struggle, with many falling by the wayside.

Clearly the pandemic was an unprecedented event but nevertheless this should serve as something of a wake-up call. In the starkest terms, what was exposed is how ill-prepared many performers (including professional athletes) proved to be when events required them to take care of themselves.

A less extreme and more common scenario is for kids to take a backseat and allow parents or perhaps the coach to direct operations on their behalf for longer than is appropriate. For a time this can seem like a pretty good arrangement, so long as they do their part by dutifully following commands and applying themselves as directed. However, by abdicating responsibility or simply being accustomed to having others steer the ship for them, they find themselves completely unmoored when confronted with a situation where it is up to them. For instance, these are the young performers who struggle the most with the transition from high school sport to competing at collegiate or university level.

COACHING AND PARENTING...

As a coach or a practitioner, the most revealing test of the job we have done is what happens when we are not there. One of the striking parallels between coaching and parenting is that the long-term objective is that we make ourselves redundant. As a coach if an athlete in my care is unable to cope and is incapable of performing when I am not there, then ultimately this constitutes a failure on my part. The job of a parent is similarly to equip their offspring to operate independently and ensure that they are self-reliant by the time they venture out on their own.

Whether in the role of the coach or as a parent, we need to be mindful of the ultimate mission. Looking ahead to when they go out into the world or step into the arena, our focus should be ensuring that the performer has the tools and capabilities to cope with whatever challenges they might face. Such considerations should shape how we interact with performers, including how much we intervene.

From this perspective, 'over-coaching' ultimately does more harm than good, as it renders the performer less capable and in turn more vulnerable when they step into the arena. In much the same way, well-intentioned 'over-parenting' has the potential to cause unintended second-order effects that are contrary to the desired outcome – that is, raising an independent, self-reliant and self-sufficient grown-up.

"Spoon-feeding teaches nothing but the shape of the spoon"

— E.M. Forster

When we do something for a young athlete that they could do for themselves we deny them the opportunity to exercise their agency. More importantly, we deprive them of the chance to become competent in taking care of themselves. The risk is that in doing so, we simply set them up for failure when the time comes that they must fend for themselves.

When it is framed in this way, what appears at first glance to be kindness can start to seem more like negligence. Most often this is a situation we stumble into inadvertently and with the best of intentions. Rather than any lack of care, in most instances it is motivated by a desire to help and results from our somewhat overzealous efforts to do so.

WHO'S SHOW IS IT ANYWAY?

Parents are instrumental in providing the means to participate and providing direction early on in the youth sports journey. Children's interests can be capricious, so part of the negotiation during the childhood years is making sure they follow through on commitments and attend practices for an agreed upon length of time before they are allowed to give up. Likewise, a recalcitrant young performer might need some encouragement to attend practice or stay on task during training from time to time. All the same, whether operating in the capacity of a coach or as a sport parent, we must recognise that this is not our show but theirs. By extension, there needs to be a shared realisation that it is their journey and it is up to them. The young athlete must be permitted define their own quest. Over time they should then be allowed to assume greater ownership of the pursuit.

'If it is to be, it is up to me'

William H. Johnsen

We must acknowledge that once the performer enters the arena and steps up to perform they are on their own – and this is as it should be. As parents and coaches we need to agree to these conditions. This means accepting that they might fall short on occasion. When things go awry, it is equally crucial that we realise it is not in their long-term best interests to intervene and try to fix things for them. Just as we need to afford performers the opportunity to figure things out in the competition arena, by extension we need to create an environment and provide ample opportunity to acquire the necessary skills and tools to problem-solve during practices, training sessions and in the times in between.

"The best teachers are those who show you where to look but don't tell you what to see."

– Alexandra K. Trenfor

A big part of coaching (and parenting) is teaching. Rather than simply telling what to do it is important that the coach explains the rationale behind each element in the training programme or practice session. To support the learning process, we should do our best to ensure the young athlete understands the reasoning process behind everything. On a more practical level, we cannot expect a young athlete to diligently practice something if they have no idea why it is important and how it will help them.

Likewise, rather than doing the cognitive work for them and telling them the answer, it is far better to act as their guide as they work through the problem and arrive at the solution through their own efforts. That way, we can be sure that they have actually learned something and it is far more likely that they will retain this newfound knowledge.

Whilst we do need to do our part to let them know why and how it is important, we should realise that it is always a choice. Supervision is certainly helpful, but we can only add value up to a certain point and we cannot do it for them. When we stand over a performer to make sure that they do something, we fail to consider that there is much that is beyond our ability to control or enforce, such as what attention and other mental resources they invest. Such a domineering approach also fails to guarantee that the performer will bother to train and practise when we are not around.

One of the biggest conundrums when raising kids in general and operating in the role of sport parent in particular is deciding when to step in versus when it is best to let them get on with it (and deal with the consequences).

HANDS-OFF VERSUS HANDS-ON...

Part of the strategy for preparing young players that is employed by a friend who heads up the Tennis Canada regional high performance squad here in British Columbia is to periodically send the kids away for spells training and competing in Europe. During their stay the young players are exposed to a higher standard of tournament play and the fiercely contested competition environment that is found in Europe. Beyond that, these trips serve a larger purpose from a talent development perspective: to some degree they constitute a rite of passage, or at least a dummy run to prepare the young performers for the trials that await them. Leaving the comforts of home and the extensive support that they are accustomed to is an essential part of these formative experiences. Whilst there are responsible grown-ups on hand, each player is expected to take care of themselves and do their part to handle the travel and logistics that are usually taken care of by parents and coaches on their behalf.

That said, the solution is not to just leave them to it. Returning to the proverb, the onus is on teaching the performer to fish, rather than simply handing them a rod and sending them on their way. We must help performers learn to fend for themselves. This is all the more crucial for those young performers who have aspirations of competing at the elite level, where it is survival of the fittest.

From the outset this involves instructing the performer on the fundamentals and making sure they understand the key tenets. Over time our job is to enable them to attain a greater level of mastery and provide a deeper understanding with further input and feedback under supervision. Imparting knowledge and lending the performer the benefit of our experience and expertise is an integral part of the process throughout the journey.

To be successful the performer will require a variety of skills and knowledge across multiple domains, not least *athlete life skills* so that they can organise themselves and manage other commitments. As described with the junior tennis players, developing all the necessary capabilities to operate independently will involve periodically immersing the performer in environments that bring their coping skills to the fore as well as strategic exposure to challenges and situations that place the onus on them.

CAPABILITY AND PROGRESS BUILD CONFIDENCE...

Part of coaching young athletes for competitive sport is preparing them to perform under competition conditions. Learning to perform under pressure and developing the capability and composure to execute when it matters should be viewed as integral elements of the process. It is vital that these aspects are catered for. Much of the anxiety experienced by performers stems from a sense of being unprepared and ill-equipped.

Whilst we might encourage them, the competition element of youth sports is something that kids must freely choose to take part in. It is helpful to periodically remind the performer that this is an arrangement that they enter into knowingly and of their own volition.

Attempting to artificially engineer conditions to protect the performer from the stress of competing is not only futile and ultimately doomed to fail but is also contrary to the spirit of the endeavour. We can however make it a less daunting prospect by working to ensure that the young performer feels prepared and gains a sense of *self-efficacy*. What we are striving for is a feeling of mastery, confidence and the sense that they are able to cope with challenge within that specific domain.

Put simply, the best way to safeguard the performer is to instil the belief that they possess the necessary tools and capabilities to cope with the trials that are a feature and an integral part of competitive sport. Equally it is important to establish a genuine basis for this belief! Developing a feeling of preparedness includes providing opportunities for the performer to test themselves in practice and competition environments that are more forgiving to allow them to rehearse and refine strategies and tactics.

IN CLOSING...

If we want to produce intrinsically motivated, capable and confident young performers then as coaches and parents we must permit them the necessary space to grow. Performers must be afforded the freedom and opportunity to try things, such that they can test out different strategies and solutions. They must also be given licence to make mistakes and even allowed to fail.

There is also merit to strategically and systematically exposing young performers to situations that require them to deploy their problem-solving and coping skills. There is however still room for us to add value and the advice of the grown-ups remains important so that we can help performers make best use of these experiences. Regrouping in between and engaging in *after action reviews* with trusted people in their circle is similarly important to help the performer to make sense of things and elucidate the lessons that they can take moving forwards.

As the performer progresses on their journey, the trials they encounter and the problems to be solved tend to increase in complexity. This places a growing onus on their ability to deal with ambiguity and face the unknown. Whilst these are trials that the young performer must increasingly face alone, we nevertheless remain on standby to provide counsel as required.

Key Take-Home Messages

1. Long-term success in sport depends on the performer's ability to operate independently — not under constant direction from adults.

2. When coaches or parents routinely do things a young performer could do for themselves, they unintentionally hinder development of self-reliance and capability.

3. Over-coaching and over-parenting create dependency and leave performers vulnerable when they enter the arena on their own.

4. The youth-sport journey must belong to the young athlete — it is their quest, their effort, and ultimately their responsibility.

5. Challenge, struggle, and occasional failure are essential experiences to build competence, confidence, and composure under pressure.

6. Our role evolves from directing and instructing to guiding, questioning, and preparing athletes to think and act independently.

Practical Tips

✓ Provide regular opportunities to allow kids to become more self-sufficient

✓ Find coaches who are willing and able to explain the purpose behind what they are doing, so the young performer is able to learn and understand why it matters.

✓ Guide problem-solving instead of giving them the answer — support the thinking process rather than replacing it.

✓ Step back deliberately — allow athletes to organise themselves and make decisions within safe boundaries.

✓ Resist the urge to continually bail out your kid by coming to their rescue when they forget kit – weigh up the cost versus benefit – there is merit to letting them learn the lesson and experience the consequences under relatively low stakes.

✓ Create autonomy-supportive environments — give choices, encourage responsibility, and invite athlete voice.

✓ Mirror the demands of competition in practices so athletes rehearse independence in progressively challenging situations.

Action Items

» Before stepping in, ask — Can they do this themselves? If 'yes', step back. If unsure, give them a chance to try.

» Reallocate responsibilities over time: transition these duties to the athlete in a phased manner, such as packing equipment, communication, planning and logistics.

» Use purposeful exposure to independence – engineer opportunities to travel and compete without direct parental support to practise self-management.

» Conduct regular after-action reviews: Help the performer reflect — What went well? What will you try next time?

» Use language that prompts the young athlete to come up with solutions "What do you think is the best approach?" before offering suggestions or issuing instructions.

» Educate kids on contingency planning! Walk them through scenarios (what could go wrong?) and prompt them to come up with a plan B for certain eventualities.

» Keep the end goal in sight: Aim to make yourself gradually less needed as the athlete matures.

Creating the Conditions

Parental Investment and Involvement in the Youth Sports Journey

We want the best for our kids. As parents we are naturally inclined to dedicate resources and make sacrifices to give our offspring the best chance to survive and ultimately thrive. One notable area where parents strive to give their kids the best opportunity is youth sports. Whatever benefit we are seeking for our kids through sport, we clearly need to make sure that they are on board! We also need to choose wisely in where, when and how we invest our energies and resources in the pursuit. Much like with coaching, we must also exercise judgement when it comes to the extent and nature of our involvement. This includes deciding what input to provide, how much assistance to offer and when to intervene.

Parents put time and resources into supporting their child's youth sports journey in the hope that it will all pay off sometime in the future. The hoped for return on investment might be direct in the form of future success in sport, such as a professional contract. Alternatively, parents might view youth sport as a route to other opportunities, such as a good education through a sports scholarship and a means to open doors that will improve their future career prospects. For many parents, the main driver is the ancillary benefits of sport in supporting healthy physical, cognitive and social-emotional development, in the hope that the experience will help their kids to thrive in all aspects of their life.

INVESTING WISELY...

The willingness of parents to invest in their kids' success is the source of enormous commercial opportunity. Youth sports has become an industry, especially in North America. In the United States alone, the youth sports market is estimated to be worth between 19 and 30 billion dollars annually and it continues to expand year-on-year. Pay-to-play travel leagues, youth sports academies, camps and miscellaneous services are marketed to parents as offering a way to give their child a head start or a competitive edge on their peers. Those offering these services frequently play on parents' anxiety that their kids will fall behind it they do not participate.

Given the clear profit motive, it is imperative that parents are discerning in their consumer choices. Choosing wisely in where and how we spend our money can help drive market forces in a way that incentivises providers to serve young athletes' best interests rather than exploiting kids and ripping off parents.

Ultimately the best guide is whether or not the investment will help kids to realise their potential in the long run. In accordance with this, it is important that we are using the appropriate timeframe when assessing the prospective return on investment. By definition, when we are dealing with kids we should be investing for the long-term. Chasing short-term results or quick wins is often to the detriment of a young athlete's long-term development.

It is important that both parents and young performers understand the principle of compounding, as the immediate return on effort invested may be hard to discern. Small incremental gains yield large and very significant returns over the long-term. This applies especially to physical preparation. To experience the real benefits and reap the rewards it is necessary to commit to the process long enough to accrue these gains, which become quite substantial over time. Consistently doing the right things in the right way over a sustained period of time is the best recipe for long-term success.

Another principle from investing that is highly salient to parental support during the youth sports journey is the law of diminishing returns. Once we go beyond a certain level each additional unit of input yields less and less, such that the extra time and effort we put in brings lower and lower returns. If we push past that we can even get into the realm of negative returns, whereby our contribution becomes counterproductive and produces negative effects.

The principle of diminishing (and negative) returns helps to illustrate how parental involvement and investment can have detrimental effects if it becomes excessive. For instance, if we are too involved this can discourage kids from assuming their proper role and associated responsibilities. Once again, we need to be mindful in where, when and how we invest our time.

RESOURCE ALLOCATION...

The level of direct parental involvement that is appropriate shifts as kids progress in their youth sports journey. Early on it is necessary and appropriate that we have a prominent role. However, once kids reach their teens it becomes more important that they assume greater responsibility and adopt a more active role in making decisions and steering their own course. At this stage it is generally wise to step back and consider delegating our advisor duties to other trusted figures who they look up to. In doing so, we avoid the worst case scenario, whereby our being too invested and too involved becomes the reason that kids disengage or act out in ways that sabotage their own success just to assert some independence.

Finally, when we think of investing resources our minds typically go to money or time; however, our attention is the most highly valued currency. From the recent experience of taking an impromptu sabbatical to look after our son full-time for the past couple of years (he recently started preschool), I can attest that what he craves more than anything is his parent's attention. With all the distractions in the digital age, this most valued resource is increasingly at a premium and it is beguilingly easy to fritter it away on devices and digital junk food that are custom-designed to hijack our attention. Moreover, the context matters. If kids start to perceive that youth sports is the best or only route to getting our undivided attention then this can put too much weight on the whole endeavour. It is important that we devote just as much of our attention to them at home as in the sporting arena and express that we are equally invested in their schoolwork and supporting them in pursuing their other interests beyond sport.

THE EVOLVING ROLE OF THE PARENT...

Parents are obliged to assume a number of roles and responsibilities over the course of the youth sports journey. Especially early on, parents must take the lead in providing the opportunity to participate in extracurricular sports and as such they have a hand in deciding which activities their kids try out. Thereafter, parents often remain integrally involved in their child's participation in youth sports in various capacities. As we described in the previous section, it typically falls to the parent to direct various aspects of the young performer's participation in organised youth sports, including critical decisions regarding the right programme and coaching set up to provide the most conducive environment and best opportunities for the young performer. Naturally younger performers will tend to defer to their parents on matters of importance and on a practical level they remain reliant on their parents for logistical matters such as transport and finance even as they enter their teens.

How much of a role parents should play is not a straightforward question. What constitutes an appropriate level of parental involvement is therefore a moving target. During the early years, parents naturally take the lead and we make most of the key decisions when it comes to participation. At this stage there is merit in coaches and parents being more directive. Children's interests are notoriously capricious and on occasion parents will need to cajole the young performer to stick with whatever sport they are involved with rather than simply following their whims and giving up prematurely.

"We forced him to swim and we have a strong belief that all children should swim because it's a life-saving skill."

– Caroline Peaty (mother of Adam Peaty)

One of the most famous examples concerns the parents of Adam Peaty who had to force him to get into the pool every time he went for swimming lessons as a child – young Adam was terrified of water (he even hated having a bath). For those unfamiliar with the name, Adam Peaty is multiple Olympic, world and European champion and current world record holder in the 50m and 100m breaststroke. That said, we should also note that Adam's parents' actions were primarily motivated by water safety, rather than a desire for sporting success.

In any case, there are instances where parents should encourage and even insist that kids follow through for a reasonable period (perhaps a season). The negotiation might involve switching to a new coach or team to account for the possibility that the environment is the issue rather than the sport itself.

All the same, the respective roles of sport parent, coach and the young performer themselves should evolve as we advance along the youth sports journey. It follows that the extent and nature of parental involvement and intervention must also change over time to reflect this evolution.

THE PARENTAL URGE TO PROTECT...

For a parent to seek to keep their child out of harm's way is entirely natural. What is less intuitive is that there are paradoxical adverse effects when we protect or intervene too much. Any short-term benefit of lending support must be weighed against the potential risk of impeding learning or enabling behaviours that are ultimately not in the performer's best interest.

It is important to recognise that kids learn from direct experience, particularly during the childhood years, as executive function and reasoning abilities are not fully developed until later in adolescence. What this means is that indirect learning experiences, such as warnings about potential dangers or observing the travails of others, sadly may not suffice – some things must be learned first-hand. It is often only after the child burns their hand on a hot stove that they fully assimilate the lesson.

Often the most important learning experiences are negative or unpleasant ones, so the desire to protect kids from them is eminently understandable. Nevertheless, these are important lessons that must be learned. Shielding kids from confronting situations only defers it for a later date. In general, it is best to learn crucial lessons in a timely fashion before the stakes become too high.

Likewise, it is only natural that we are inclined to take our child's side in any dispute. Equally, stepping in or standing up for them can mean that they do not face any reckoning for their own role such that they fail to take responsibility for their actions.

HELICOPTERS AND LAWNMOWERS...

At times parents will inevitably feel a natural urge to intervene, particularly when it appears that the child is not receiving fair treatment. Youth sport coaches all have stories of being harangued by parents advocating on behalf of their child. Most of us will also have witnessed parents remonstrating with officials during competitions.

It is very hard to stand aside when we can see that a young performer is struggling. Just as coaches should beware solving the puzzle for the athlete, parents must temper their urge to step in, not least as there are real consequences when do so too readily. The reader will be familiar with the cliché of 'helicopter parents', hovering close by, ready to come to their child's aid at a moment's notice. Well intentioned as it may be, this denies kids the opportunity to figure out how to solve problems on their own and handle conflict.

Encountering obstacles, experiencing difficulties are integral to how we learn important lessons and fortify ourselves to withstand future hardships. As we will discuss at length in a later chapter, the bumps in the road serve a vital role in the young athlete's journey to elite level and prove invaluable from a talent development perspective. This has important implications for the well-meaning actions of what have been dubbed 'lawnmower parents' who seek to smooth the path for their child. We should help kids to take full advantage of the opportunity presented by these trials rather than trying to avoid or minimise them. By seeking to spare kids from upset we inadvertently deprive them of the experiences they need to build confidence in their ability to cope with adversity.

Ironically, insulating kids from these trials ultimately serves to make them more anxious and less adept at detecting and responding to potential threat [193]. The paradoxical effects of over-protection renders kids less able to cope, so that with time they become more fragile and less resilient. At a deep unconscious level, kids understand this; and it becomes a growing source of disquiet as they anticipate future challenges without the requisite tools in their armoury.

REGULATING INVOLVEMENT AND INTERVENTION...

As parents often assume a great deal of the organisation and administrative duties it is beguilingly easy to get into the habit of making decisions and acting on the young performer's behalf. Over time we run the risk that the young performer grows accustomed to delegating responsibility rather than taking an active role.

If the role of the coach or parent is too dominant then this becomes an impediment to the young athlete taking ownership of all that their continuing participation requires. As with over protecting, excessive intervention can constrain development and render the individual less capable when they ultimately come to face these challenges alone. Parental involvement and intervention can similarly inhibit self-expression, particularly as young athletes mature.

Whilst the appropriate level of input will depend on the stage in the journey as well as other factors, there are some indications where the sweet spot might be when it comes to parental involvement. For instance, a study in high-level volleyball highlighted that parenting style and involvement were factors that separated the performers who were more successful [194]. A common finding among those who were successful was that they described *moderate* parental involvement, which they characterised as supporting their autonomy. Conversely, those who were less successful described their parents' involvement as excessive.

What is certainly true is that excessive command and control on the part of the coach or parent is not conducive to the athlete having any sense of agency with regards to their participation. Over time the young athlete's sense of control and perceived ownership over their own sporting journey can become eroded, harming their engagement and investment in the process. Ultimately when everything seems to be dictated by others this can lead to a feeling of detachment or even alienation.

WHEN THE YOUTH SPORT EXPERIENCE SOURS...

There is a pronounced shift in the nature of the young athlete's engagement in sport as we advance along the youth sports journey. What motivates participation and the behavioural responses that are manifested vary with age and stage of development, such that what the young athlete regards as being 'rewarding' (or threatening) changes as they mature.

These trends are broadly reflected in how kids respond to parental involvement. Whereas having a parent present is a source of reassurance during childhood, this is increasingly no longer the case once the young athlete enters adolescence. Indeed the presence or involvement of a parent may start to induce additional stress from the young athlete's perspective. It is not uncommon for parents to be a perceived source of pressure and expectation. For instance, heightened awareness of the financial investment that parents have made in supporting their participation in the sport can weigh on the young athlete, adding to the sense of obligation and parental pressure in a way that makes the experience less enjoyable [195]. Parents must be vigilant that interactions with their child do not revolve around youth sport activities to the extent that the relationship becomes too entwined with their involvement in sport.

The most vivid example I can recall features a brother and sister I will call Johnny and Amy who I came across during my tenure as coaching director for a commercial athlete development academy. Both Johnny and Amy performed in the sport of BMX (Amy also played soccer) and their parents were highly involved – their dad to the extent that he had started competing in BMX at master's level. They were both in their mid-teens when I met them. Johnny was the older sibling and he was particularly shy and withdrawn. Yet Johnny was a very gifted athlete – he would occasionally forget himself and give glimpses of what he was capable of (I remember one day we tested the group and he blew everybody away on the sprint test), but on the whole he preferred to stay under the radar. Johnny preferred to train alongside his sister and resisted my attempts to pair him up with another one of the older boys as a training partner. This was all very strange and when I spoke to Johnny's coach he was similarly perplexed and lamented Johnny's reticence to compete at the higher level that he was capable of.

When I eventually met their parents I finally got a sense of what might be behind it all – both mum and dad were insistent that I should be hard on Johnny and Amy during sessions and not give them an inch, especially Johnny as he was 'lazy'. In the end I came to the conclusion that Johnny had made a rational calculation – it was an unfavourable situation and the stakes were such that his solution was to quietly disengage rather than risk trying, judging that it was ultimately not worth it. The story does not have a happy ending. Johnny dropped out of school early to start an apprenticeship and gave up riding at the same time. Amy was a year or two younger, so she remained involved with the academy for a little longer, but in due course she also gave up both BMX and soccer. When I last spoke to Amy at her final session she told me she had plans to travel overseas (a move she freely admitted was at least in part motivated by a desire to escape her parents).

As the young athlete progresses on their youth sports journey, the associated challenges and obstacles to continuing participation also start to change. Notably, external factors can start to encroach. High school is a notoriously difficult time as teenagers seek to establish their identity and strive to navigate a complex and unforgiving social environment. All the external baggage, social pressures and expectations add to the stress and anxiety of competing, such that it colours their attitude towards participating in sport.

BEING CLEAR ON WHO AND WHAT WE ARE DOING THIS FOR...

Recognising that our role in relation to the young performer's participation in sport will necessarily shift over time, we need to be careful that we do not become the primary driver for the young performer's participation in sport. The road is long, so nourishing the intrinsic motivation to participate of their own accord is perhaps the most important contribution that parents can make towards the long-term success of the young athlete.

Mitigating outside influence to minimise interference becomes crucial from the perspective of preserving the premise that young athlete is doing it by their own choice and under their own volition. The endeavour needs to be separated as far possible from external obligations and expectations. Parents have a huge role in this, as one of the most likely sources of these perceived obligations and expectations from the athlete's perspective.

Parents can help by maintaining a degree of equanimity and consistency in their behaviour, to reinforce that affection, praise, and the parent-child relationship itself are not contingent upon the outcome or success achieved in the sport.

THE SPORT PARENT SELF-AUDIT...

Parents gravitate towards youth sports as a healthy and productive outlet for kids to invest their time and energy. For their part, what motivates some parents to become actively involved in organised youth sport is the opportunity to spend time and bond with their kids [196].

For the most part, parents and parent-coaches start out with the best of intentions but somewhere along the way things can go awry. It is easy to get carried away in the moment. Once we have tasted success we can get caught up in the excitement and lose sight of who and what we are doing it all for.

Part of our duty of care as sport parents is to periodically examine the motivation behind our own engagement and why we are invested in our child's participation in youth sports. Whatever our reasons for being involved, the grown-ups share a responsibility to keep the needs and interests of the young athlete at the forefront. Returning to the cautionary tale of Amy and Johnny, we must remain attentive to our own behaviours that might prove to be demotivating.

MINDFUL CONDUCT…

For coaches and parents alike it is important that we are aware that the tone of our interactions with the athlete can have a profound impact on their psychological and emotional state. In either case, how we conduct ourselves in the context of the sport has a profound effect on the young performer. Parents' conduct on the sidelines naturally receives a lot of attention as this is where the worst misbehaviour usually occurs!

A particularly revealing finding is intentions are not necessarily matched by actions. In the heat of the moment parents can find themselves engaging in behaviours that are not conducive or aligned with their stated goals for their child's participation in sport (e.g. enjoyment, learning) [197]. This is something we need to be cognisant of, not least given that we might not be fully conscious of these lapses or aware of their effects. Allowing for the possibility that there might be a discrepancy between how we recall our own behaviour versus what others observe, there is merit in periodically engaging in some self-reflection and eliciting candid feedback – not least from the young performer themselves!

Becoming more conscious of our actions is a necessary first step to practising better self-control. The coaching staff and sports parents who attend competitions (and practices) each have responsibilities as role models for young performers. Modelling better side-line behaviours has wider benefits and parents have been specifically identified as a key part of initiatives to improve young athletes' conduct towards both team-mates and opponents [198]. Understanding that emotions will get the better of us sometimes it also pays to have an agreement with other parents to help us keep ourselves in check and let us know when we are in danger of transgressing.

THE PARENT-COACH RELATIONSHIP…

The link in the coach-athlete-parent triad that too often gets overlooked is the relationship between sport parent and coach. As with any relationship that gets neglected, there is often misunderstanding and we can easily find ourselves in a situation where both parties feel disgruntled and dissatisfied.

In general, parents get a rough deal - they are often overlooked and in many cases intentionally side-lined. Parents are an easy scapegoat and a popular punchbag for administrators and commentators alike, who are quick to point to instances of parents misbehaving. Sadly, too many coaches fall prey to this lazy thinking and use it as a convenient excuse for not engaging. For their part, parents cite coaches as the biggest source of stress in relation to their child's participation in organised sport.

The parent-coach relationship is hugely influential in shaping not only the course of the youth sports journey but also the young athlete's experience along the way. Fostering a collaborative and respectful relationship between parents and coaches is vital in supporting the development of young athletes. When parents and coaches are able to work together this provides a supportive environment and creates the conditions to allow the young athlete to thrive.

In order to make this a reality, we must proactively address the common areas of dispute and sources of friction between coach and parent. Much of the cause of disputes and conflict comes down to misaligned expectations. To shed some light on the reasons for this, it is worth delving into the nature of the relationship. With the increasingly commercialised nature of youth sport, notably in North America, the relationship between parent and coach can become more akin to consumer and service provider. Naturally this affects expectations and the dynamics of the relationship, not least in terms of the stresses placed on it.

Whilst academies exist in professional sport, notably (soccer)football), for the most part, coaching at the youth level is professional only in the sense that parents are paying for these services. At the community level most coaches are paid very little if at all (and are often parents themselves), but the fact that parents are paying for the privilege nonetheless leads to certain expectations.

In sports where private coaching is more common, it is easy for the parent-coach relationship to be transactional. It can also create a set of incentives that prioritise short-term results to help secure repeat business, rather than doing what is in the young athlete's long-term best interests. Conversely, in the case of academies in professional sports and to some extent national development squads in Olympic sports, the power resides with the coaches and selectors, and as a result parents are often kept on the outside.

Whilst the nature and power dynamics of the relationship may differ, the solution in each case is for both parties to rise above the default situation and build trust to create a genuine partnership. A healthy and enduring relationship relies on mutual respect. Each party needs to acknowledge that the role of the other party is vital and recognise the value of their contribution.

JOINT COMMITMENT...

The coach-parent axis is crucial – and each party needs the other. Acknowledging this and the many goals we have in common, we have a strong basis for dialogue and a more collaborative approach. When things are working well, parents act as a de facto extension of the coaching team and a trusted coach serves as an extension of the parenting effort.

To secure the joint commitment to building the relationship, both parent and coach must acknowledge that they share a responsibility to the young athlete. Each has a prominent role to play in developing the young person and supporting them through the journey. Rather than vying for dominance, both parties must commit to cooperating in this shared mission and putting the athlete's needs first.

To that end, the parent and coach should seek to find areas that they can agree upon. Hopefully, both parties can agree that they are each committed to serving the young athlete's best interests. Establishing common goals is another important step to establishing a working relationship. Once we are aligned on the aims we can agree on the priorities. If both coach and parent are operating on the same horizon then we can prioritise long-term development and strive for consistent progress over the junior years, which is the best route to long-term success.

It is also helpful to highlight areas of shared responsibility. For instance, both coach and parent must recognise they each have responsibilities as a role model for the young person. How we conduct ourselves, notably during emotionally charged moments surrounding competitions, sends powerful signals to the athlete about how to handle challenges, interact with others and approach the sport. We have a duty to model the values and behaviours we wish to see the young athlete adopt. It is vital that coaches and parents are aligned on these values and agree on the behaviours that we are seeking to encourage!

As such, each of us has a duty to avoid pulling the athlete in different directions. It is healthy to have disagreement and it is important that each side feels secure enough to voice their concerns. There is a time and place for questioning. That said, it should be done in a respectful way and in the proper forum. Disputes should not be aired in public, but rather in private without bringing the athlete into it. As far as possible, both parties should avoid contradicting each other in front of the athlete. We should seek to minimise conflict and resolve disagreements in an amicable and civil way. We each have a duty to act like grown ups and avoid speaking negatively about the other party when they are not present.

The parent and coach must also share the common aim of developing a capable young person who can advocate for themselves, operate independently and deal with whatever circumstance they might face. It follow that there needs to be a shared commitment to fostering autonomy. Both parties have a responsibility to facilitate the athlete stepping into their rightful role in the process. Each has a duty to ensure that the athlete assumes greater ownership and responsibility over time. Practically what this comes down to is not doing for an athlete what they are capable of doing themselves. At each stage in the journey we must give the young athlete every opportunity to become more independent.

COLLABORATION IS CRUCIAL...

The roles of parent and coach are complementary, with each having duties in different domains. Both coach and parent can team up to monitor and reinforce key behaviours and uphold standards both within the sporting arena and beyond. To facilitate collaboration, it is helpful for parents to gain an understanding the coaching process. Conversely, coaches benefit from having an appreciation of parenting duties. Once the parent understands what the coach is trying to do, they can do their best to support it - and vice versa.

Role clarity is a precondition for minimising the potential areas of conflict. Clear boundaries and defined roles are crucial to avoid confusion and minimise friction. We must first define what the boundaries are if we are to ensure that both parties respect them. The coach and parent should take the time to specify and agree on their respective roles and responsibilities.

As with any relationship, communication is vital. Parents should feel comfortable asking questions. For their part, coaches should be receptive to being questioned - and in fact welcome the opportunity to explain the why behind what they are doing and educate the parent. Effective communication is key to maintaining and deepening the relationship. Both parties must work to ensure there are regular opportunities to have these exchanges. We can avoid unnecessary friction with explicit agreements on key matters such as channels for communication and protocols for the practice and competition environment.

Within a given context it should be mutually agreed and understood that there can be only one voice – and all parties should be clear on who that person is. In the competition and practice environment the designated person is the coach or practitioner leading the session. It is important that this is understood and respected, not least to avoid confusing or conflicting messaging. I can recall one instance where a parent came into the weights room as the session was coming to an end and proceeded to instruct his daughter on her squat technique (he only did it once).

Parents are the lead person for essentially everything beyond the practice and competition environment. Notably, coaches rely heavily on parents to take the lead on matters of critical importance such as nutrition and sleep, which have an outsized influence on how performers' respond and recover between workouts and their readiness to train. Coaches and practitioners likewise rely on parents to reinforce messages and encourage behaviours that support the mission when at home.

BRINGING IT ALL TOGETHER...

Clearly it is crucial to meet the young performer where they are when it comes to the nature and tone of our involvement. What young performers need from their parents and coaches naturally evolves as they progress on the youth sports journey. There are many good reasons for encouraging young people to be involved in youth sport but despite our best intentions there are adverse consequences when our involvement or intervention becomes over-bearing.

Just as over-coaching proves to be unhelpful for young performers, there are negative consequences to over-parenting. Nobody is more invested in the success and happiness of the young athlete than their parents. Enthusiastic and supportive parents are a huge asset; however, as the young performer progresses on their journey there is a growing need to support their autonomy and ownership. We need to understand the unintended second order effects of our intervention. When parents become too involved this can present other problems, especially as young performers enter adolescence and start to find their way in the world. In some ways it is better to err on the side of doing too little than too much!

Arguably all intervention, be it from coaches, practitioners or parents must be calibrated and carefully regulated. Too much support can create dependency, too much direction can be disempowering, too much input can constrain exploration and excessive instruction can inhibit learning.

The parent-coach relationship has a major influence on the young athlete's experience. It follows that in the young performer's best interest we share a responsibility to foster and maintain good relations. The parent-coach partnership is also a reciprocal relationship: the coach can be a key ally for the parent; and vice versa. All parties should have a clear set of ground rules and establish their expectations going in so that we can cooperate and collaborate effectively. By working together we can harness and direct the young performer's energies to favourably impact their trajectory and allow them to enjoy the significant ancillary benefits of participating in youth sport.

To that end, it is necessary that coaches are given permission to hold young performers to agreed standards. They must allow the young performer to be challenged and to be disciplined when they fail to meet the minimum standards agreed. Importantly, this will impact not only the athlete themselves but also those around them. Parents and coaches can work together to instil the importance of being a good team-mate (or training partner) and we can model high standards of conduct towards others, including opponents and officials. This is vital to maintaining an environment that allows performers to flourish.

Finally, both coach and parent are crucial in supporting and reinforcing a long-term perspective. It is vital that both coaches and parents do not fall under the thrall of chasing short-term wins, to the detriment of the long-term mission. Both parties share a great responsibility to be the grown-ups in the room.

Key Take-Home Messages

1. Parents play a vital role in enabling youth-sport participation, especially in the early years.

2. Excessive parental involvement or intervention can undermine autonomy, resilience, enjoyment and engagement

3. The appropriate level of parental input must change as the child matures.

4. Over-protection prevents children from developing coping skills and confidence through challenges.

5. Parents' behaviour at practices and competitions significantly influences the athlete's experience.

6. A strong parent-coach relationship built on respect, communication, and shared purpose benefits the child.

7. Intrinsic motivation must remain at the centre — the child should feel ownership of their sporting journey.

8. Parents should regularly reflect on their motivations and behaviours to ensure they remain athlete-centred.

Practical Tips

✓ Use the long-term horizon as your guide — prioritise growth and capability over short-term comfort.

✓ Ensure your support equips the child with tools to cope independently — not dependence on constant help.

✓ Step back progressively as the child gets older; allow them more decision-making and responsibility.

✓ Let children experience manageable setbacks — these are essential learning opportunities.

✓ Keep sideline conduct calm, positive, and aligned with the goals of enjoyment and development.

✓ Talk with your child about their goals and feelings — listen more than you direct.

✓ Prioritise attention and connection outside of sport as much as within it.

✓ Set boundaries with coaches respectfully and privately — avoid contradicting them in front of the athlete.

Action Items

» Undertake the sport parent self-audit (see Appendix).

» Promote autonomy and prompt the young athlete to contribute more to decision-making and take on additional responsibilities over time.

» Model self-regulation and peer accountability - Agree with another parent to hold each other accountable for sideline behaviour and emotional control.

» Maintain and protect parent-child relationship beyond sport.

» Invest in building the relationship with the coach — establish expectations, define boundaries and delineate roles and responsibilities at the start of each season.

» Agree protocols for communicating during competitions, practices, etc.

» Protect intrinsic motivation: Ensure the child knows participation is their choice and your relationship does not depend on performance.

Instilling Belief and Helping Kids to Find Their Aim

A recurring theme in the stories of young performers who go on to become successful is the presence of a central character who comes onto the scene and proves to be pivotal in how the tale unfolds. The dramatic influence that a single individual can have on the trajectory of a young performer is remarkable. Having a grown-up treat you like you could be exceptional is a tremendously powerful thing for a young performer. It only takes one person to demonstrate their belief in the performer's potential for them to conceive what might be possible.

NOBODY EVER ROSE TO LOW EXPECTATIONS...

When we see potential in somebody this tends to be reflected in how we treat them. Such expressions of belief can transform how the individual views themselves and dramatically alter their perception of what they might be able to achieve. When our actions indicate that we think they are capable of doing great things the performer tends to rise to that expectation.

Showing genuine belief in the promise of a developing performer serves as a self-fulfilling prophecy. A fun fact is that the belief shown in the young performer does not even need an objective basis. All that is important is that the other party genuinely believes in the performer.

In a classic study (dubbed *Pygmalion in the Classroom*), schoolteachers were given a fabricated set of test scores that rated an arbitrary selection of kids in the class as high in aptitude. Given the (false) information provided the teacher naturally expected much of these randomly selected individuals and treated them accordingly throughout the school year that followed. What was extraordinary is that the randomly selected kids in the study lived up to what the teacher expected of them by scoring top marks in a real test at the end of the school year [199]. The kids themselves were unaware of the ratings – they merely responded to how the teacher treated them.

What these findings suggest is that all it may take is another person to see promise in a young performer for them to dutifully live up to it! It is of course all the more powerful when the individual in questions holds a position of status or authority (teacher or coach), as this lends instant credibility to their assessment of the young performer, no matter how far-fetched it might seem at the time.

BELIEF IS CONTAGIOUS (AND TRANSFORMATIVE)...

Unshakeable self-belief and indomitable will are hallmarks of champion athletes [200]. Part of this is a matter of temperament and is innate. All the same the origins of such self-belief can often be traced back to an influential figure who saw something in the athlete when they were a junior. The stars at the pinnacle of sport can generally point to somebody who saw their potential at an earlier stage in their journey. Intuitively it makes sense that it would take somebody believing in them for an aspiring young athlete to start to believe in themselves. Even Michael Jordan who is famed for his extraordinary belief in his own outrageous ability arguably owed some of this belief to his father, who remained a central figure in Jordan's life once he became a professional player.

There is a style of leadership that is described as *transformational* and this concept has been applied to coaching and parenting, respectively. In each case, what makes it transformational is the combination of inspiration and motivation, such that a markedly positive and lasting influence is imparted through expressions of genuine belief in their protégé's potential. Importantly, these great expectations are reinforced by correspondingly high hopes and interactions are imbued with a general spirit of optimism about the ultimate outcome. Over time this can have a profound effect that allows the individual to do more and go further than they thought possible.

The story of tennis great Rafael Nadal exemplifies how the influence of a singular individual during the formative years can bring about an extraordinary transformation. Rafa's uncle Toni – who happens to be a tennis coach – recognised his nephew's potential from an early age (the tale goes that Uncle Toni first glimpsed his promise when watching 3-year old Rafa on court). Rafa is one of the greats of tennis, best known as a ferocious competitor and renowned for his relentless style of play and formidable 'raging bull' on court persona. Yet Rafa was a shy and timorous child – indeed even as an adult what he displays on court is at odds with his mild manner away from the court (the family joke is that he is still afraid of the dark). The competitive fire and unwavering determination that have been so central to his success were forged on the practice court in his junior years under the transformational leadership of Uncle Toni who expressed his great belief in his nephew by holding him to a higher standard.

The story of Rafael Nadal and his Uncle Toni illustrates how the conduct of an esteemed coach, parent or mentor towards a young performer can communicate confidence and assurance in a way that the performer becomes imbued with these qualities. Mental toughness can flourish under such stewardship, such that the performer becomes more resilient and better able to perform under challenging conditions simply due to the transformational influence of one significant individual [201].

WE UNDERESTIMATE KIDS AT OUR PERIL (AND THEIRS)...

There is a darker side to the *Pygmalion in the Classroom* phenomenon. It is common for schoolteachers to make snap judgements of individual pupils in each year's cohort and treat them according to their initial impression. Teachers' expectations tend to be self-fulfilling in both positive and negative ways: just as those they expect to be academic high-fliers tend to do well, those deemed to be no hopers tend to fare poorly.

"Kids... rise or fall to the level of the expectations of those around them, especially their parents and their teachers"

– Jaime Escalante

The biggest disservice we can do to a young performer is being casually dismissive. Those involved in sport should also have more humility and be more cautious about making pronouncements of young athletes who are still developing. Talent identification and selection processes employed at youth level does a notoriously poor job of discerning which performers will be successful at senior level. Whilst it is true that some coaches do have an uncanny ability to identify potential, for the most part coaches' evaluations are highly prone to error and even the best will admit to prominent cases where their unfavourable assessment of an athlete was proven wrong.

In a very real sense, each young person has untold promise in whatever domain we choose to look at (academic or athletic). It would serve everybody involved in youth sport to adopt the mindset that any individual within a group of young performers might go on to achieve notable success. A head coach I worked with during my time with a national programme made exactly this point during an exchange with his assistant coach about a young player. The assistant coach made a dismissive comment about the future prospects of the player in question and the head coach's retort was that none of us can know with any certainty what a youngster might be capable of – or indeed what experience or interaction might light the fire for their future success. This comment has stayed with me. Moreover, the turning point for any developing young performer could be a coach, teacher or family member showing belief in them.

IT TAKES TIME TO FIND THEIR NICHE...

Admittedly certain sports do require that performers have chosen their parents well. Genetics are a determinant of success at the highest level to a varying degree depending on the sport. At a towering 5'6" I was never going to play in the NBA (so I settled on rugby – a sport involving violent bodily contact with large humans, suggesting my grasp of physics developed much later on).

But even when it comes to physical characteristics, an athlete's potential might be late to reveal itself. There are a host of examples of athletes who flourished late in sports that are skewed towards size.

A great illustration is the back story of three of the starting five from the legendary multiple championship-winning Chicago Bulls team that are lauded by many as the greatest ever to play in the NBA. Early in his journey Michael Jordan (generally considered the best to ever play the game) originally failed to win selection for his high school varsity team! Scottie Pippin went to a college that didn't even play in the NCAA and he only got his spot on the college team by first volunteering as team manager. Dennis Rodman is perhaps the best example of all; until a very late growth spurt after finishing high school he was not on anybody's radar and he only got the opportunity to play college basketball thanks to the intervention of a family friend who convinced the coach to take a chance on him. These greats of the game excelled when they eventually earned their shot, but in all three cases it all began with somebody who saw great promise in them when others didn't.

WHAT ALL THIS MEANS FOR THE MISSION...

Perhaps the biggest conclusion to draw is that we should seek to surround an aspiring young performer with transformational teachers, inspirational coaches and aspirational mentors as far as possible! Certainly the young performer should walk away from any coach who does not appear to rate their chances. Some individuals are temperamentally inclined to use these negative experiences as fuel, such that they respond to being written off by redoubling their efforts to prove their doubters wrong (I speak from personal experience). All the same, it is best that this mission is pursued under the direction of somebody else rather than sticking with a doubting coach!

Naturally there is some danger that a prospective coach might just tell the young performer what they want to hear. It is crucial that the belief shown is genuine (even if it is based on spurious grounds like bogus test scores!). The other key ingredient is that the standards applied with the young performer should be commensurate with the high expectations. This is in fact central to how we communicate our confidence in the young performer's capabilities.

It is certainly true that the sport parent can play a prominent role. In keeping with the archetypal paternal role (to encourage and cajole), a father's input and support encourages striving in a way that fosters mental toughness, especially among young adolescent athletes [201]. That said, these roles are far from immutable and there are many prominent examples of mothers who assume this mantle. Returning to the sport of tennis, whilst Richard Williams might be best known for masterminding the ascent of Serena and Venus Williams, the formidable Judy Murray (mother of Andy and Jamie Murray) is equally one of the best examples of profoundly influential sport parent. That said, most often this role is best played from the backseat [202].

It is absolutely true that what a young athlete needs from their parent is to know that they believe in them. Our faith in them should never be in doubt.

Whether it is a coach, a family member or a peripheral figure, a prominent person can be an agent of change who has a profound impact on a young person's trajectory. Having a third party express belief in their potential grants them license to dream and prompts them to conceive what might be possible. As well as broadening their horizons, this opens the door to contemplating where their quest might take them.

THE PROFOUND EFFECTS OF HAVING AN END IN MIND…

I am fond of the phrase 'aspiring young performer', which of course implies that the individual has a particular aspiration. Unfortunately, too often the aim is not specified, kept extremely vague or is simply assumed. As the young performer matures their outlook and attitudes can change dramatically, so we may find that our assumptions are out of date. When kids are not engaged it is often because they are unclear on why they are there and what they are seeking from the experience.

It is worth taking the time and prompting young performers to look ahead and think about where they might want their youth sports journey to take them. Giving proper consideration to these questions will help them to make full use of the opportunities that are on offer and act in ways that serve the best interests of their future selves.

We often need to help young performers to create the space to look ahead, mull over where they might want to end up and consider where their present trajectory might be taking them. Kids are increasingly bombarded with inputs, not least from devices in their pockets, so unless they are unusually focussed and forward-looking it is unlikely that they will do this in any rigorous way without being prompted. We can facilitate the process by providing a template with relevant prompts to give the exercise some structure (more on that later).

Having an aspiration however loosely defined is enormously helpful, even if it is provisional and subject to change. Directing our gaze towards whatever summit we wish to conquer provides the impetus to begin and continued motivation for the pursuit.

DECIDING WHICH STAR TO AIM AT…

Given the constellation of stars we could aim at, settling on which one to set our sights on is not a straightforward proposition. Thinking about who they look up to, such as sports stars that they admire offers some helpful leads. Reflecting on who inspires them and noting what their sporting idols have in common provides a good indication of what they might aspire to achieve and what type of person we might want to be.

Great sporting feats that inspire awe serve as a guide to what we prize the most. That said, this process is imperfect – it is more a guide than a template! To give an example, as a youth my sporting hero was a rugby union player named Neil Back who played for the best professional club in England and the English national team. In an era of giant lumbering players Neil broke the mould, being shorter in stature and lighter than the heavyweights playing in his position, yet his athleticism, ball skills and dynamic playing style made him one of the best to ever play the game. Pundits nevertheless wrote him off as too small to play at the top level and for a long time he was overlooked by the England selectors, until the burgeoning weight of his outstanding performances season after season finally made it impossible not to pick him and he went only become a key figure in the World Cup winning England team. I closely followed his story and I not only admired how Neil played the game but I was also greatly inspired by his triumph over all the doubters. Sadly, as much as I wanted to be like Neil, when the opportunity finally came to play in his position in the forward pack I had the rude awakening that I was nowhere near big enough to do so – and my genes were such that I never would be!

I later came to realise that is it was the essence and the qualities that Neil embodied that I really admired. It also became apparent that I was far better suited to a different playing position – and in fact it turned out rugby league rather than rugby union was the best fit for me. So what I strove to emulate was Neil's tenacity, courage and commitment to being the best prepared player on the pitch.

ADMITTING TO AN AMBITION TAKES COURAGE...

Given the obvious upsides to having an end in mind, it is striking how often young performers do not feel ready to declare their sporting ambitions. Some of this reticence stems from being apprehensive about the reaction of their peers. In teenage society holding lofty ambitions is viewed with suspicion or even scorn and it is not cool to be seen to strive. In this context, admitting to dreaming of achieving great things carries some risk of inviting ridicule.

It is an act of courage for a young athlete to declare a lofty aim, as it means exposing themselves to scrutiny. To strive to achieve something exceptional is to stand apart from the herd and to do so publicly invites external pressures and expectations. There is another reason that declaring an aim is daunting: in doing so we specify the conditions for a successful outcome and in turn what constitutes failure. Fully committing to the endeavour likewise takes real bravery, as this removes the final excuse – that I didn't fail because I wasn't really trying.

What makes a proposition risky is also what makes it rewarding. Striving to reach a summit that is unattainable for most people and the slim odds of success are part of what makes it an adventure. If it was easy to achieve there would be no glory. These are the necessary preconditions for a hero's journey! As parents and coaches we must provide this perspective to young performers to rouse their spirit of adventure.

RUNNING SOME SIMULATIONS...

A major obstacle to engaging in planning and looking ahead into the distant future is that it can all seem very abstract. The first step towards operating on a longer timeline is to give some thought to what their desired future might look like. Running some simulations in their mind helps to make it all more tangible. Practically, this is best achieved through a structured exercise, such as the one presented at the end of this chapter, and ideally should be done in conjunction with the coach as well as the parent.

As they ponder some potential future scenarios, the young performer will likely come up with a best case or ideal future. In turn, we should prompt them to consider the alternatives should events take a different course, including the potential worst case scenario if things really do go awry. This allows the young performer to come up with their own conception of an ideal future that they are inspired to strive towards, as well as envisioning the prospective negative outcomes that they should seek to avoid. Understanding what they wish to go towards as well as what they want to go away from provides added impetus, essentially giving them a push from behind to accompany the pull from ahead.

Imagining an ideal future that they are inspired to work towards not only provides direction and drive but also allows them to be more systematic in how they approach the quest. Once they have specified their aim it becomes possible to reverse engineer the potential routes and landmark achievements that will get them to the desired destination. In other words, they can make a plan and identify some clear objectives for the multi-year pursuit. From these plans and interim objectives will follow a defined series of steps and set of actions. Importantly they can also gain some initial impetus by identifying the immediate action items that will help them take the next step towards achieving the ultimate aim.

These thought-experiments serve to paint a more vivid picture of the destination and journey ahead in a way that is helpful for engagement and commitment. What would life look like if they were successful? Conversely, what would it mean if things did not go as intended? How upset they would be (or not) if things did not turn out in their favour? Thinking about the different ways things might play out and what the diverging outcomes would mean to them is helpful to gauge how committed they are to the pursuit. Deciding to pursue a future aim means opting to invest their time engaging in certain activities (practice, training, competition, etc.) and this necessarily means foregoing others. Getting an honest appraisal of how important it is to them and where it ranks among their other priorities, such as school, social activities and other pursuits, is therefore important.

EMBARKING ON THE QUEST...

Notwithstanding the challenges, there comes a point in the youth sports journey when an aspiring young performer must look towards the future, declare their aims and commit themselves to achieving them. Early adolescence is a pivotal phase from this perspective as this marks the point when young athletes start to acquire the faculty and inclination to aspire and work purposefully towards a future goal. That said, certain sports that favour early specialisation may require this commitment to be made sooner. For other sports this may be deferred to a later date.

The pursuit begins in earnest when the young performer identifies a long-term aspiration and makes the decision to commit to it. Once we know what we are aiming for we can set about equipping ourselves to achieve that ultimate outcome. Importantly this also helps the performer to envision their future self, which is also useful as the performer can model themselves against this aspirational future self in the present. This imagined future self sets the bar and becomes the standard that they hold themselves to.

By extension, this affords the opportunity to examine what they are currently doing and assess whether it is congruent with their stated aim. In other words, it is serving the mission? The young performer should ponder these questions in looking at how they are spending their time and what choices they are making. Is this getting me closer to where I want to go? Is this getting in the way? Are the choices that I am currently making taking me in the wrong direction and harming my chances of attaining my ultimate aim?

To help overcome the natural reticence to commit themselves, we should be clear that this is all provisional and subject to revision. The specifics of the plan are not so important as the fact that there is one. Anything that orients us towards the future enables us to engage in purposeful action in the present, secure in the knowledge we can always update our final destination en route.

Young performers often choose their destiny by a process of elimination. It is typical that they will try out a few options before they find their true north star. It is likely that the young athlete will change course or switch track entirely. In any case there will be valuable lessons learned along the way. These discoveries and formative experiences are part of what makes the journey so rich and valuable.

A young person is by definition a work in progress and so it follows that the ultimate destination remains subject to change as they advance on their journey. Rather than a one-off exercise, this should be revisited periodically. Understanding that they can return to the exercise at any time and revise their aims later on helps to take the pressure off.

Key Take-Home Messages

1. A single adult who genuinely believes in a young performer can change the entire trajectory of their development.

2. Expectations act as a self-fulfilling prophecy: young people rise (or fall) to the level of belief shown in them.

3. Transformational coaching and parenting combine high expectations with inspiration and trust in potential.

4. Adults routinely underestimate young people — premature judgements and talent predictions are often wrong.

5. Having a clear aim fuels motivation, engagement, and willingness to work through challenges.

6. Declaring an ambition takes courage — it exposes a young person to scrutiny and external pressure.

7. Aspirations should be revisited regularly; kids change, and their goals should evolve with them.

8. Helping young people visualise their future self gives them a path to act with purpose in the present.

> **Practical Tips**
>
> ✓ Show belief through action — communicate confidence by holding the young performer to meaningful standards.
>
> ✓ Give permission to dream big and set audacious goals
>
> ✓ Use positive expectations deliberately
>
> ✓ Avoid dismissive judgments — refrain from predicting who will or won't "make it" at young ages.
>
> ✓ Create moments to dream — prompt reflection on what excites them, who they admire, and why.
>
> ✓ Normalise ambition — celebrate striving, effort, and vulnerability in pursuing goals.
>
> ✓ Allow freedom to trial different options but encourage them to commit fully each time, understanding they can always switch later.
>
> ✓ Stay open and adaptable — treat aims as provisional and revisit them as they grow.
>
> ✓ Set boundaries with coaches respectfully and privately — avoid contradicting them in front of the athlete.

Action Item – The Planning Exercise

During my tenure as coaching director for an athlete development academy in New Zealand that served school-age young performers in all sports across multiple sites I developed the exercise described below. We routinely implemented this with the kids once they graduated to the middle tier in the programme (coinciding with the developmental phase approaching and encompassing the adolescent growth spurt). The exercise begins with specifying an aim, and then breaks down things in a way that is differentiated at multiple levels according to the timeframe involved. Aside from sharpening their focus and bringing a higher level of resolution, this has proven to be a helpful discipline to encourage the performer to be systematic in their approach. Of course this is an exercise that should be revisited periodically, not least as it is all subject to change.

Step One: Begin by identifying a long-term aspiration. What is the highest aim you can conceive of that you might want to pursue? (e.g. 'I want to be an Olympian')*

Step Two: Identify the stepping-stones. Imagine you are at base camp – what are the major landmarks on the ascent towards the summit (defined as the ultimate aim in step one).

Step Three: Working back from step two, what changes and improvements will allow you to advance towards the interim checkpoints identified? Identify the priority areas to work on over the coming period (3-6 months) which will allow you to make the next big step.

Step Four: How will you triangulate where you are now, track your progress and navigate your way to the next stage on the journey?

Step Five: Finally, set an intention for the short-term ('this is what I will do this month, this week, today…'). Now get cracking!

*This can all be changed or updated down the line, so no need to feel daunted about specifying an aim!

Keeping the Fire Burning

The journey from youth sport to senior level is variously described in terms such as *talent development* and *long-term athlete development*. The way these concepts are presented and the various models and frameworks that are put forward often fail to resonate with those on the ground. On a practical level, what is often left unresolved is how best to provide the right level of challenge and support to create the conditions that young performers need to thrive. In this chapter we tackle a more fundamental question: how can we help to ensure that young performers have the motivational fuel to sustain an athletic journey that is likely to span many years?

STARTING WITH THE FIRE...

The fire within is a highly individual phenomenon. We have all come across people who bring a burning intensity to all they do and certainly this is a trait we associate with top performers. That said, there is no single archetype and athletes competing at the highest level vary a great deal in this regard. Usain Bolt is a great example of a superstar who liked to keep things light and fun, even prior to his races on the biggest stage. The fire within is manifested in different ways!

Irrespective of temperament and personality type, arguably the biggest challenge we face is how to achieve an equilibrium. If we dump on a load of accelerant there will be impressive pyrotechnics for a brief moment, but we will then soon find we are then left with singed eyebrows and dying embers! On the other hand, if we tamp things down too much, we deprive the fire of the oxygen it needs, so that it fizzles out before it even got going. In essence these are the scenarios we are seeking to avoid with young performers.

Understanding what drives an individual's desire to participate and compete is important. Clearly it is crucial that the young athlete is passionate about their involvement in the sport. Equally, we should delve a little deeper into the nature of this passion. The term 'harmonious passion' is used in the literature to describe a healthy expression, whereby sport and the competitive striving occupies a significant place in the individual's life without obliterating everything else (such that it is in harmony with other aspects of their life) [203]. We can contrast this to the considerably less healthy all-consuming obsessive passion that is often driven by an insatiable desire to fulfil some emotional need or fill a gap in their life. The latter scenario tends to end badly.

The grown-ups in the performer's life are an important influence in this regard. As coaches we must be responsible in what attitudes and behaviours we model. What parents communicate in their words and actions in different scenarios will likewise influence their child's motivation and what mindset they bring to their participation in sport.

To be sustainable, there needs to be a desire to take part in the sport for its own sake. The reasons for choosing to participate should revolve around the sport and the pleasure they derive from participating rather than extraneous factors. If sport becomes a vehicle to satisfy some other need or external obligation this becomes a highly precarious basis for their continuing engagement in sport over the longer term.

INTRINSIC DRIVE...

What constitutes *intrinsic motivation* is when we do something for the joy and satisfaction the experience provides. In other words, participating is rewarding in itself. The positive feelings we associate with the experience leads to an ongoing desire to engage in the activity for the simple pleasure of doing so.

In its purest form, sport is an inherently rewarding experience. Most performers gravitate towards a particular sport for the enjoyment and satisfaction they derive from taking part. A common scenario is that the young athlete discovers an affinity for the sport and becomes captivated by it. In many cases they find they have a natural aptitude and pick it up relatively quickly, which adds to the enjoyment.

Intrinsic drive is the purest source of the enthusiasm young athletes have for participating and performing. Crucially it is not dependent upon anybody or anything else and is readily accessible simply by engaging in the activity.

Intrinsic motivation also has ancillary benefits, as those who report higher intrinsic motivation are also more likely to engage in unsupervised practice of their own accord. This is a reciprocal relationship that can create a virtuous cycle: the more that young athletes engage in self-directed deliberate practice, the more they nourish their intrinsic drive to engage in this activity [178]. Given its self-sustaining nature, intrinsic motivation is what we need to foster and preserve in young performers as they advance on the youth sports journey.

ENJOYMENT DRIVES ENGAGEMENT AND ENTHUSIASM...

At a basic level, kids engage in activity because it is fun. If taking part was no fun early on, then it is highly unlikely they would persist with it. In turn, a lack of 'fun' is commonly cited as the reason why kids disengage and drop out from youth sport.

Enjoyment is clearly a key ingredient from an engagement and retention point of view. Clearly, we need to make sure that the experience of participating in youth sport remains enjoyable if we want kids to continue. However, there is some nuance involved, not least given the variety that exists in what different individuals find enjoyable. To give an example, what my friends who are endurance and ultra-endurance athletes enjoy doing is not my idea of fun!

What brings enjoyment may also change over time, according to the aspirations of the individual and their motivations for participating. For instance, adolescent athletes in elite talent development pathways report that enjoyment remains imperative but their primary motivation at this stage is improvement. In this context, they find enjoyment in practice and competition that helps them to become better [204].

The types of activities that prove so engrossing that we lose track of time are likewise many and varied. Whilst it may prove elusive, when we do find ourselves in such a state of *flow* it is inherently pleasurable. Hallmarks of being in a state of flow are that the individual is totally immersed in the activity and free from self-conscious or critical thoughts as they perform [205]. The experience of flow is uniquely enjoyable and rewarding, making it highly motivating for young athletes in a way that increases their desire to participate [206].

There are various ingredients for achieving flow, some of which differ to what we conventionally think of as enjoyable or associate with a good time. For instance, there needs to be a strong element of difficulty and challenge, such that the activity stretches the performer towards the limits of their skill and capability. What this also means is that young performers must first attain a level of skill and proficiency before they can access this state of flow.

OPERATIONALISING 'FUN'...

'Fun' is referred to incessantly by those who operate in youth sports and athlete development (both in the scientific literature and in marketing). Unfortunately, 'fun' is a vague term. If it is so important then we should operationalise 'fun' – but in order to do that we need a clear definition. Some attempts have been made to unpack what kids actually mean when they describe some aspect of their youth sport experience as 'fun'. One such study identified 11 distinct themes within four general tenets, comprising a dizzying 81 different determinants [207]. The most highly rated dimensions were 'positive team dynamics' (encompassing such aspects as playing well together as a team), 'trying hard' (trying your best) and 'positive coaching' (coaches treating players with respect and encouraging the team).

Ironically those who specialise in working with kids do not always have a very evolved notion of fun. Judging from social media, the most common interpretation seems to be limited to frivolous playground games and obstacle courses. In many cases, the adult supervision does not appear to include any guidance or feedback and the most hardcore proponents react with hostility to anything that resembles a structured learning environment or direct instruction. It is important to recall the education part of physical education. Those of us who work with young athletes need to be clear whether we are operating a talent development environment or a day care centre.

Reassuringly, parents' conceptualisations of the most important factors that make the youth sport experience fun seem to be much closer to the young athletes' [208]. It follows that parents have a big role to play in steering things in the right direction with their consumer choices and feedback.

Talking of fun, one of the fun parts about working with younger kids is that they have boundless enthusiasm. They will happily run around and play the sport, with or without a grown-up being present. Younger kids' attention spans and bandwidth for instruction tend to be quite limited, so the role of the coach at this stage is to provide enough structure and direction to ensure it is not complete chaos and some learning is actually taking place.

Over time we need to provide a little more direction and temper the exuberance with discipline to allow kids to continue to progress and keep them in one piece. The coach is the main source of direction albeit parents can help reinforce key messages, whereas instilling discipline is a shared endeavour between coach and parent. That said, we cannot ever lose the enthusiasm. In many ways, enthusiasm is our most direct fuel source.

"You want to keep enthusiasm because that's your fuel.
You have to balance discipline and enthusiasm.
Discipline is critical: you have to be able to show up.
But you have to enjoy it: enjoying it with discipline is key."

— Joe Rogan, former US Open taekwondo champion (also stand-up comedian and podcaster)

The locus of this direction and discipline will necessarily shift over time. As the young athlete learns and matures, they should be encouraged to assume greater control and ownership over these aspects. A growing emphasis on self-discipline, agency and self-direction are crucial to renew and maintain enthusiasm as the young performer advances on their journey. Within these constraints we can still keep things playful.

RENEWABLE ENERGY...

Mastery is a renewable source of energy and ongoing motivation. The pursuit of mastery has different facets: mastering skills, mastering the game and mastering ourselves. Pursuing each of these elements of mastery brings its own rewards; it is an ongoing journey of discovery that provides a sense of achievement that is not contingent upon external factors such as the outcome of competition. Happily, the quest to attain mastery is also a journey that has no endpoint – we can always find ways to develop and something we can improve upon. Progress is inherently rewarding. Striving towards mastery thus has the potential to provide endless fuel for our journey!

Every sport has an initial barrier to entry – the performer must attain a basic grasp of the fundamentals for the activity to become engaging and enjoyable. Thereafter, becoming more competent continues to bring its own rewards. As the performer becomes more adept, this expands and enriches the experience in a way that participating in the sport becomes more and more enjoyable and engaging. Performing newly acquired skills in itself makes for a pleasurable and satisfying experience. Moreover, as young athletes become more skilled, we open up the possibility of experiencing *flow*. All of this points to the importance of high quality coaching.

There are multiple layers to any complex competitive endeavour. Over time we gain a growing appreciation of the nuances and the intricacies of the sport. As young athletes progress, we peel back more layers and gain a deeper understanding. Even the most experienced athletes are still discovering new facets of the game within the game that they can strive to master.

Competitive sport is extremely rich in opportunities to challenge and develop mastery over ourselves. Practice and competition test a young athlete's command over their body and mind under fatigue and miscellaneous other challenges. Competition offers ample scope to stretch their ability to make the right decision under pressure, execute when it matters and keep going when pushed towards the limits of their endurance.

Challenge is an abundant source of fuel for the journey. Challenge can be presented in different ways according to what drives the individual. For instance, I have always been very easy to motivate - bright coaches (and colleagues) soon figured out they just needed to tell me they didn't think I could do something and I automatically redoubled my efforts to prove them wrong!

However, challenge does not always mean throwing down the gauntlet. Many of us enjoy challenging ourselves to solve a complex puzzle. Once again, sport and acquiring athletic skills offer an endless source of new puzzles to solve! This fascination is part of what makes sport so captivating and again this is something we need to emphasise and preserve when supporting young performers.

CHASING PERFECTION...

The best spend their athletic careers in the pursuit of the perfect game or perfect performance. At their best, a star performer might come tantalisingly close, but perfection will always remain out of reach. This elusive quality is actually part of what makes competitive sport so engaging. Whilst perfection might be unattainable, it remains a worthy aspiration. There is merit in striving to achieve the impossible. Striving for perfection provides the motivation for the relentless pursuit of better. The caveat is that the pursuit must be approached in a manner that can be sustained. There are costs and potential hazards that must be managed.

Perfectionism has typically been presented as a negative trait in the context of youth sport. There is an understandable fear that unrealistic or unattainable expectations might lead the young performer to be excessively hard on themselves in a way that diminishes enjoyment and satisfaction, such that it could conceivably contribute to burnout or even dropping out.

However, there are aspects of perfectionism that are functional and adaptive for aspiring high performers. Champion performers who go on to achieve extraordinary success at senior level commonly report perfectionist tendencies. Indeed, this is one of the features that distinguishes them from their similarly talented but ultimately unsuccessful peers [202].

Another striking finding is that those who score higher on perfectionist striving typically perform better [209]. This makes some sense, as these individuals accordingly invest more time in practice and training, which we would expect to result in better performance over time. Indeed, those performers who exhibit perfectionist striving also tend to be more proactive and systematic in their approach [210]. In other words, they put in more effort (both physical and mental) overall and are also more considered and diligent in how they direct their efforts.

The talent development literature increasingly recognises that perfectionism is not unidimensional and the positive elements are now more readily acknowledged. The mindset of continuous improvement has been described as exemplifying *healthy perfectionism* [211]. Rather than leading to burnout or dropping out, we find that those performers who exhibit the adaptive parts of perfectionism typically become more engaged over time [212]. Moreover, perfectionist striving makes individuals more inclined to stick to their lofty goals rather than settling for less.

In view of all these merits, we should differentiate between types or expressions of perfectionism. In particular, there is a crucial distinction between perfectionist strivings versus perfectionistic concerns. *Perfectionist striving* is associated with very high personal standards and an insatiable drive to become better. *Perfectionistic concerns* are more focussed on the implications of falling short and the prospect of negative evaluation [213]. The former is an intrinsic drive (the individual holds themselves to their own high standards), whereas the latter is more focussed on external factors (notably the judgement of others) and the consequences of a negative outcome.

What is clear is that certain aspects of perfectionism are useful and there are other facets which may be unhelpful or even detrimental. The functional and adaptive 'perfectionist striving' element may be accompanied by dysfunctional perfectionistic concerns in some individuals, but this is not necessarily the case [213]. Allowing for such distinctions gives us the option of keeping the good parts, whilst guarding against the less helpful aspects.

In a very real sense, perfection is an impossible standard. Whilst it has an aspirational quality, we need to avoid a situation where the individual is constantly beating themselves up for failing in this impossible task. We do not want to rob the experience of all its joy. It is vital that young performers are still able to enjoy themselves and find satisfaction in the small wins as they continue to strive upwards and seek ways to become better.

There is an inherent tension between striving versus satisfaction. Clearly we do not want to be too easily satisfied as this would remove any impetus to try harder or do better. Equally, when it comes to ever-striving young performers, we need to help them find peace with the idea that they might never be fully satisfied.

Practically, how the performer responds when they do not perform to their lofty (and perhaps unrealistic) expectations of themselves is likewise crucial. They must have faith in their ability to improve and rise to the challenge. When assessing where they are now, 'not there yet' is better than final or fatalistic judgements, such as 'I'm not good enough'. The framing can be the difference between motivating versus dispiriting.

Essentially, we can make it a game to see how close to perfection they can get. It then becomes a quest to discover how far they might go in the pursuit. An impossible standard is still worth striving towards, but recognising it as such fundamentally changes how they interpret the situation when they fall short and importantly makes them more forgiving in their judgements of themselves. When perfectionism becomes a game they choose to play rather than simply a judge that always finds them wanting this makes for a much healthier situation!

WHAT GETS IN THE WAY...

The motivational climate at practice and during competitions naturally has a major bearing on the young performer's mindset and experience. The coaches clearly play a big role here, given their stewardship over the practice environment and what tone they set with regards to attitudes towards competing. However, the coach is not the only agent involved. Interactions with team-mates and peers certainly affects the experience when practising and competing. For team sports particularly the conduct of team-mates towards each other (and opposing players) is a decisive factor. For instance, team-mates' prosocial and antisocial behaviour are demonstrated to have an emotional impact on young athletes and ratings of burnout [214]. Whilst individual sports are somewhat different, the manner in which training partners and even competitors engage with each other still has some bearing on what the experience delivers.

Naturally the grown-ups share some responsibility with regards to what behaviours we accept and tacitly encourage. Coaches need to uphold standards of conduct and parents play a vital part in supporting these efforts. It is important to deal with behaviour that negatively impacts the rest of the group in a swift and decisive manner; this does however rely upon the cooperation of parents, especially when it concerns their own child.

PERILS OF EXTERNAL VALIDATION AND OTHER EXTRINSIC REWARDS...

What does need to be protected is the young athlete's internal fire and intrinsic motivation to play, practice and participate. As young athletes proceed on their youth sports journey they face growing threats to this intrinsic drive. There are clear and present dangers of extinguishing intrinsic motivation, with the risk that they might ultimately drop out not only from that particular sport, but sport in general.

As young performers start to achieve success, inevitably they start to receive acclaim and attention from others as a result. Rewards and recognition can certainly make performers feel good about themselves; however, there are associated risks. Ironically, early success can be a threat to the young athlete's resolve and motivation for the journey ahead, as they become exposed to the accompanying extrinsic rewards, such as recognition, external validation and other prizes. External influences and concerns can easily infringe on the young athlete's participation and their behaviour can become motivated by rewards and recognition in a way that diminishes the intrinsic pleasure derived from the pursuit itself.

The digital age brings a whole new world of external validation. Social media status not only gives a false sense of achievement but the rewards of 'likes' can create a craving, which has the capacity to derail the entire journey. Extrinsic rewards and external validation are like accelerants which cause the fire to flame brightly initially but then burn out as the oxygen is rapidly exhausted. We can even see a bizarre scenario where the athlete starts to derive validation from the social media attention, rather than from actually achieving success in the sport in real life. Any intrinsic motivation to engage in the sport for its own sake has been long since extinguished at this point.

Rafael Nadal's long-time coach 'Uncle Toni' who we met in the last chapter, took a characteristically strong line in this regard. A telling story is that when young Rafa won the Spanish junior title Uncle Toni presented him with the names of winners over the previous 25 years – he recognised just two names on the list (the only two who had successfully gone on to professional careers at senior level), which brought him back down to earth as intended!

Many of the extrinsic sources of motivation have the opposite characteristics of the intrinsic drive we described earlier. There is some nuance here as there are extrinsic factors that are ancillary to the sport and do involve others but nonetheless add to the intrinsic motivation and enjoyment that comes from participating, such as hanging out with friends through the medium of sport. What we need to guard against are the many external rewards that are entirely in the hands of others and are also contingent on the outcome (that is, dependent upon a successful outcome) rather than the act of participating itself.

The latter type of extrinsic rewards and external validation can come to overshadow the pure positive feelings and simple pleasures derived from engaging in the activity itself. Not only can this extinguish an all-important energy source over time, but it also places the performer at the mercy of others and external factors that beyond their control.

Throughout the journey the performer must remain clear that they are not doing this to impress others. It is nice to get recognition but external validation and other rewards must not become a driver for their behaviour.

SEPARATING ENGAGEMENT FROM EGO...

If we want kids' engagement in sport to remain pure and untainted by extraneous concerns then it follows that we should seek to avoid dragging their ego into proceedings as far as possible.

From this perspective there is an important distinction to be made between participating with a focus on mastery versus engaging in practice and competition a way that is more 'ego-involved'. A mastery-oriented mindset keeps the focus on the pursuit and the process. As long as the endeavour is primarily concerned with mastery, the learner is motivated to embrace and actively pursue challenges as opportunities and they remain eager to solve the puzzle.

In contrast, an ego-involved motivational climate centres around the rewards associated with the outcome, such as praise, status and prestige. As this way of approaching participation primarily revolves around outcome, it is not congruent with or conducive to the desire to engage in the sport for its own sake. Engaging in practice and competing is stripped of any inherent meaning when it merely becomes a means to an end. Whereas mastery is about continuous improvement, such that progress is measured in relation to the learner themselves, ego is primarily concerned with effect on the individual's standing in relation to others. When the whole endeavour becomes about boosting and preserving social standing, this dramatically changes the equation with respect to perceived risk and reward.

'Comparison is the thief of joy'

– Anon

It is important that the grown-ups are mindful and remain vigilant to avoid dragging ego into proceedings. When performers start to become concerned about how others are judging them this naturally makes them more averse to taking risks and trying things. The more participation in sport becomes entwined with their ego, the more of a barrier this becomes. The endeavour can quickly become a continual exercise in protecting their precarious status in the minds of others. This can be particularly problematic during the teenage years, albeit grown-ups are also not immune!

What is often overlooked and certainly something that we need to recognise with developing performers is that ego and status must be carefully managed, especially during the adolescent years when individuals are highly sensitive to social judgement. We need to be very careful about conferring status upon a young performer. Publicly identifying kids as 'talented' can create its own problems. The mantle can hang heavy, adding unnecessary external pressure when performing under the scrutiny of onlookers. Another adverse consequence is that the more attached they become to their 'talented performer' status, the more they seek to preserve it, which creates an aversion to situations and scenarios that might imperil their standing in the eyes of others. Heightened sensitivity to potential threats to their status and self-image is often manifested in a tendency to engage only when the odds are in their favour.

When the athlete persona comes to define the young person's sense of self and their status among their peers, this raises the stakes inordinately. The perceived consequences when their athlete status comes under threat can start to seem catastrophic. Understandably, when faced with this scenario some young athletes respond by withdrawing. When athletes opt to not invest effort during practices or visibly stop trying when competing this can seem like an act of rebellion – and in some cases it is. However, it is equally possible that refusing to engage constitutes a defensive tactic to protect their ego in the face of a grave threat.

An extreme example of this is the phenomenon seen in sports such as tennis where talented players intentionally 'tank' matches. To the observer this might appear to be a bizarre act of self-sabotage or simply petulance; however, there is a perverse logic to it. Opting out of the contest serves a purpose, whether or not they are conscious of it at the time. Making a public show of not making any effort, intentionally losing points and effectively laying down arms permits them to tell themselves that they did not really lose as they were not trying. This spares them from confronting the possibility that they might not be as good as the outside world has been led to believe.

RECALLING THE YOUNG PERSON BEHIND THE ATHLETE PERSONA...

Identifying strongly as an athlete is not inherently positive or negative but is rather a question of balance. The young person's relationship with their *athlete identity* serves to shape how it affects them for good or ill. This also somewhat depends on the circumstances. For instance, whilst a strong athlete identity bolsters the young athlete it may add to the mental toll during periods out of action due to injury [215]. The scenario we need to avoid is that the athlete persona subsumes all other parts of their identity.

To avoid their involvement in sport becoming all-consuming it is crucial that young performers continue to invest in other areas and remain connected to other facets of life beyond the sporting domain. That way not everything is on the line every time the athlete competes. As coaches and parents we should be seeking to eliminate existential threats as far as possible!

As coaches we must remain mindful that we do not simply coach athletes, we coach humans who also happen to be athletes. Each athlete is an individual beyond the realm of sport: the child of a parent, perhaps a sibling, a friend to various others, a student in school, etc. Sport parents are not simply concerned with raising a young athlete; they raise humans with multiple dimensions who operate in a host of domains, one of which happens to be sport.

The individual's self-concept beyond the sporting arena and the degree to which they view themselves in a positive light when removed from the sport become increasingly critical to last the course. It follows that we need to help young athletes to cultivate a sense of self that is separate from their sporting identity. Maintaining a social circle and other interests that are entirely separate from sport are important from this perspective. The more assured they are in of their worth and status independent of sport, the more protected they become and the better able they are to face challenges within the sporting domain.

PRIMING...

Perception is hugely powerful in shaping experience and framing shapes perception in a way that affects motivation. The young athlete's experience varies dramatically based on what they perceive the stakes to be. How we prime performers to appraise an identical task prior to performing can have a profound impact, to the extent it has a measurable effect on their stress hormone response [216]! When the *goal-priming* that performers receive focuses on the task the experience is less stressful. Conversely, when the same task is presented in a way that emphases social evaluation and primes the expectation that they will be treated based on how they perform relative to the rest of the group (preferential treatment for those who perform best, neglect for those who perform worst) this naturally induces stress.

This has important implication for how we frame things within the practice environment and when competing. Coaches can unwittingly put the onus on outcomes and status when they show favour to the best performers in the group. We also reinforce this mindset when our treatment of athletes is contingent upon how well they are performing.

Parental conduct and communication likewise contribute to shaping how young athletes appraise their involvement in sport and their motivation towards participating [217]. As parents it is critical that we are consistent in how we treat kids regardless of how they fared in the competition arena.

Coaches and parents alike share a responsibility to encourage performers to consider both practice and competition as serving the quest for continuous improvement: every practice and competition presents an opportunity to become better. Being unduly concerned about the opinions of others (up to and including coaches and parents) is clearly not conducive to the mission. Moreover, the judgements of those who are external to the process also become somewhat irrelevant once we adopt this perspective.

More generally, the element of choice is something that is worth emphasising. For instance, we should encourage performers to acquire the habit of speaking in terms of choosing to do things – i.e. 'I choose to practise', 'I choose to go to training' and so on. When we can contrast this with framing things in terms of what I have to do, or where I have to go (I have to practise, I have to go to training, etc.), it quickly makes everything seem like a chore.

A sense of obligation is generally not conducive to feeling enthusiastic about the prospect of doing something. The reality is that some young performers do feel obliged to participate in sport out of a perceived sense of duty, perhaps towards their parents or other notable people in their life. This can create a sense that they are no longer engaging in the activity of their own free will, but rather to keep others happy or to justify the investment made in supporting their participation.

Feeling a sense of responsibility (such as towards their team-mates and those who helped them) is not inherently a bad thing. However, the performer must retain the sense that they would freely choose to participate of their own accord and for the intrinsic rewards they derive from doing so, irrespective of whatever responsibilities they might feel towards others.

Key Take-Home Messages

1. Young performers can burn out if overloaded or lose motivation if under-challenged. The goal is to maintain an equilibrium that keeps their fire alive.

2. Intrinsic motivation is the most powerful and renewable fuel. Enjoyment, satisfaction, curiosity, self-directed practice, and a love of the sport itself provide long-term energy. Intrinsic drive must be nurtured and protected at all stages.

3. Harmonious passion—sport complementing rather than consuming life—is linked to sustainability and wellbeing, whereas obsessive passion often leads to burnout and disengagement.

4. "Fun" is deeper than many adults assume. Kids value trying hard, positive coaching, good team dynamics, skill progress, and meaningful challenge—not simply entertainment. Enjoyment evolves as athletes mature.

5. Perfectionism can be positive if channelled well: perfectionist striving is adaptive and motivating; perfectionistic concerns are unhelpful and need to be mitigated.

6. The motivational climate matters enormously: prosocial environments created by peers, coaches, parents help motivation; antisocial behaviour contributes to burnout.

7. External validation threatens intrinsic drive – recognition, status, rankings, awards, and especially social media can pull attention away from the joy of the sport itself.

8. Ego involvement derails learning and risk-taking. When sport becomes tied to status or identity, athletes become risk-averse and overly concerned with judgement.

9. Mastery is an ongoing journey and endless source of renewable motivation. Mastery orientation—focusing on improvement—keeps engagement pure.

10. Their sporting identity should be only one facet of who they are: a balanced self-concept, including interests and relationships outside sport, protects wellbeing and reduces psychological risk when setbacks occur.

11. Language that emphasises growth and steers attention to the task rather than the outcome and potential consequences shifts perception and reduces stress.

Practical Tips

✓ Maintain dual focus on discipline and enthusiasm to help young athletes learn to show up consistently and enjoy the process.

✓ Encourage a mindset that every practice and competition represents a chance to become better.

✓ Seek environments that provide meaningful challenge with practices that stretch but do not overwhelm, so kids experience the satisfaction of becoming better.

✓ Building competence increases engagement and enjoyment.

✓ Work with the coach to keep the focus on continuous improvement: the ongoing imperative of getting better over time overrides short term outcomes

Keep young athletes grounded and keep things in proportion - do not allow kids to let successes in junior competition go to their heads or let losses weigh too heavy.

✓ Keep the focus on the young person behind the athlete persona.

✓ Reinforce the separation between the sporting domain and the many other facets of their life ('what happens in the arena stays in the arena')

✓ Keep focus on continuous improvement – progress is inherently rewarding.

Action Items

» Model balanced, healthy passion – show enthusiasm with perspective to demonstrate that sport is important, but not everything.

» Direct focus towards the task and solving the puzzle.

» Avoid labelling kids as 'talented' (or otherwise) as far as possible!

» Help performers to learn to leave their ego on the sidelines when they attend practice and compete (they are there to get better, not to impress anybody).

» Coach family and friends to avoid questions that focus on outcome or bring their ego into play (Did you win? Did you score?)

» Steer the focus towards process and mastery when communicating with kids after competition (Did you execute well? How was your game management?)

» Maintain equanimity – keep interactions consistent whether they win, lose or draw.

» Teach kids to give little weight to judgements from those external to the process

» Be vigilant to avoidant behaviours – that is, shying away from testing themselves or swerving contests where the odds are not in their favour

» Remind kids it is always a choice and not an obligation: "I choose to practise" vs. "I have to practise."

Challenges and Opportunities of Adolescence

The onset of adolescence marks the start of a pivotal phase in the young athlete's development. From my professional experience I can attest that the adolescent years present a unique and unparalleled opportunity to have a profound impact. The dramatic transformation we can observe over this period in young athletes' development surpasses anything we might see once they reach the senior ranks. This is a time of great possibility but there is also significant potential for things to go awry. In keeping with it being a time of great change, it is a highly challenging period to navigate – both for the athlete and the grown-ups!

Prominent authors in talent development and sports parenting differentiate the phase commencing around age 12 from the earlier foundation period spanning mid-late childhood (ages 8-11) [218]. It will not be a shock for parents to hear that puberty heralds a distinct developmental period. Practically, it all comes sooner for girls and there also is significant individual variation, as we saw in an earlier chapter.

In any case, adolescence is a crucial period that warrants investing significant attention for coaches and parents alike. This phase of the youth sports journey is the time when young athletes must take their destiny into their own hands. If coaches and parents fail to encourage and enable this transition (or worse deny the young performer the opportunity) we can expect that they will tune out. Many young performers disengage or walk away from organised sport entirely during this phase. Sometimes this is an act of teenage rebellion but in many cases it is because they have come to view participating as something they are doing for others rather than for themselves. Social pressures are another major factor, not least as their peers may be drifting away from sport during this phase.

EARLY ADOLESCENCE AS A KEY DEVELOPMENTAL WINDOW...

As many parents will have observed, there are fertile windows of development in the childhood years – for instance, young kids are a sponge for learning and acquiring language as well as cognitive and motor skills. What is less well recognised is that the transition from childhood to adolescence likewise heralds a distinct window of development that shapes young bodies and minds.

Puberty begins in the brain [219]. Along with the physical transformations that accompany puberty, adolescence is a critical developmental period for the brain. Changes in brain structure and function during this phase in turn prompt *neurobehavioural* changes in teens. There is a major reorientation in attention and motivation over this period. Notably, there is a newfound urge to venture out and explore the world that exists beyond the world of their childhood. Sport can be a great vehicle for satisfying these cravings, given the opportunities to travel and meet people from different communities and cultures.

These years are formative in establishing the young person's identity and figuring out their place in the world [220]. One of the overarching themes of this phase of development is learning how to navigate different social structures and interactions with others in various contexts. With the growth and maturation of key brain regions that constitute the *social brain* comes a growing propensity to develop *social cognitive skills*. The interplay between developmental and environmental factors leads to a growing capacity for social and emotional intelligence. Young adolescents become better able to intuit the emotional state of others, respond to social cues and to consider events from others' perspectives [221]. Organised youth sports are one of the more stable social environments where this learning and development can take place.

Along with the burgeoning sense of self and capacity for *social reasoning*, the individual's notion of moral behaviour is shaped during this phase of development with the aid of experience and socialisation. Youth sports can serve as a rich context where moral behaviours are learned from peers and modelled by the grown-ups [222]. This does underscore the importance of finding the right environment, including a good group of team-mates or training partners.

The profound changes that occur during this phase have important implications for the youth sports journey. In the last chapter we spoke about the need to keep the fire burning; this phase is often the time that the fire is ignited as young teens start to contemplate the future. Some of the most profound neurocognitive changes concern executive function, which is reflected in an increased capacity for long-term planning. The acquisition of *meta-abilities* supporting goal-directed action and self-regulation are manifested in a growing propensity to make sacrifices in the present in service of their future self.

Particularly with the right guidance and support, the young performer also becomes progressively better equipped to manage struggles and respond to setbacks as they advance through the teenage years. Emotion regulation and the ability to govern themselves amidst heightened emotions, such as during contests and interpersonal conflicts, are honed throughout this phase. Competitive sport provides a rich learning environment from this perspective, as most coaches and parents will attest!

PERILS OF THE TIME...

Whilst this phase of development offers great opportunity, it is a sensitive period in every sense and there are associated perils that we must be aware of. The most serious hazard is that adolescence is a time where young people are especially vulnerable to mental health issues [221]. As the rates of mental health problems among modern youth continue to climb (even prior to the pandemic) these issues constitute a mounting cause for concern.

The choices that young people make during this turbulent time can often exacerbate mental health struggles. One such example is that this phase coincides with a massive rate of kids dropping out of participation in organised youth sports. Survey data from youth sports in the United States indicate that 70% of kids drop out from participating in organised sports around age 13. This is especially unhelpful as it deprives them of the regular physical exercise and much needed in-person social interaction that youth sports provide. The positive association between youth sport participation and mental health in adolescence underlines the important role that organised youth sports play in this regard [64, 66].

One striking finding is that the rates of drop out are consistently reported to be most dramatic among females. For instance, data from Australia highlight that the participation rates for females aged 15-19 are less than half that recorded among girls aged 4-14 [223]. Adolescent females are the population most prone to mental health issues, so the fact that sports participation among females reaches its nadir during this period is something that requires urgent attention.

Sports organisations have a responsibility to do a better job of considering the unintentional negative impact of their policies and systems on young performers. The reticence of sporting organisations to recognise their own contribution to this problem remains a barrier.

For those who remain, the turbulent changes that occur during this time can start to influence how young performers approach training and how they appraise competition. This period can prove pivotal in the role that sport plays in the young performer's life. During adolescence when young people are striving to form their own identity it is unsurprising that many young performers latch onto their 'athlete' status.

The role of youth sport in relation to social identity is somewhat double-edged. On the one hand, identifying strongly and positively with the sport and the team that they are part of lends a sense of belonging and increases enjoyment, which adds to the motivation to continue participating [224]. On the other, when the athlete persona comes to define their standing among their peers and even within their family, sport can become the primary source of validation and the young person's sense of self-worth. In this light, aspects of the participating in the sport can take on a very different hue. Carol Dweck's work popularised the idea of fixed versus growth mindset. It is highly probable that the seeds of a fixed mindset (aversion to failing in front of others and avoidance of scenarios where that is a possibility) are sewn during this time.

In this phase when they are seeking to establish their social standing, adolescent performers become especially sensitive to social evaluation from their peers and this has been greatly compounded since the advent of social media. Social media has added a capricious new dimension to the social context of participating in youth sports. As an intrusive source of external recognition and validation, social media can be problematic even when things are going well.

The significant potential for harm with social media applications that involve sharing images has been highlighted for young females in particular. Young performers are especially vulnerable to negative interactions online when things are not going their way.

When things go awry social media can become a hugely malevolent influence. The one-to-many format of social media amplifies the reach and magnifies the impact of toxic and negative comments. The distance and anonymity on these platforms removes many of the constraints and indeed consequences for perpetrators and those who pile on, such that this can spiral into full-blown abuse and bullying. Even for mature adults it would take herculean self-assurance to shrug off this sort of unsolicited abuse, so the idea that children and adolescents might be exposed to it is a frightening proposition. The damage wrought by online abuse and bullying can be severe.

In view of this, the increasingly common tendency for enthusiastic sport parents to create social media accounts for their young performer as part of the effort to 'build their brand' is a troubling development. Whilst the intention of increasing their social media profile is to attract the attention of scouts, this is fraught with risk and the potential for harm is significant.

PEER INFLUENCE...

During childhood the ascendent role of parents as the primary caregivers means that our influence on our child's life is unrivalled. As kids transition to their teenage years, they come to cultivate their own social lives and start to spend increasing time interacting with peers rather than family. Friends and members of their peer group accordingly assume a greater role in their social and emotional life. The primacy of the parental role comes under increasing challenge over this period as we must vie for influence with their friends and other prominent figures in the young athlete's life beyond the home.

Adolescents are not only more susceptible to peer influence but also more sensitive to social isolation and the threat of rejection by their peers [221]. Teenagers are renowned for risk taking behaviour, yet they tend to be decidedly risk-averse when it comes to breaking social norms within teen society [225]. The need to belong is strong and this makes social risk taking decidedly unappealing.

Ironically teens can be remarkably compliant when it comes to the social expectations of their peers! Those in their social circle will inevitably have some influence over the choices that young people make. Teens are more likely to engage in risky and potential harmful behaviour when they are being egged on by their friends [221] – once again, this is more about conformity than rebellion on the part of the individual.

Social pressure is a decisive factor leading teens to opt out of participating in organised youth sport [226]. We need to recognise what courage it requires for young performers to resist the pull of their peers during this phase when the over-riding imperative is to fit in. This is often felt particularly strongly by young female athletes, as teenage girls tend to be especially sensitive to social concerns. Young female athletes who have friends who are supportive are accordingly more likely to continue to participate in organised youth sport [227].

Social groups in teenage society are notoriously unstable and navigating this capricious social world is one of the major stressors that adolescent performers face. One of the ways that teenagers manifest their insecurity is by belittling others out of envy and a desire to cut them down to size. Simply by achieving sporting success and recognition young performers can make themselves a target for this kind of jealousy and ill will. Once again, my experience is that this tendency to undermine and react negatively to others' success sadly seems to be more common among females. That said, whilst young male performers might be less likely to receive outright negative treatment from their peers, those identified as talented nevertheless commonly experience a sense of jealousy even among friends [204]. High-performing male and female adolescent athletes alike need to gird themselves against 'tall poppy syndrome'.

CURATING THE PEER ENVIRONMENT...

Along with attention and motivation, there is a tendency for major social reorientation during adolescence as young teens strive to find their tribe [219]. Given the extent to which they may be influenced by peer pressure, the peer group(s) that the young person surrounds themselves with becomes enormously important.

Peer influence is not necessarily bad: in the right group the social rewards act to incentivise and promote prosocial behaviours [221]. The quality of their friendships during the turbulent mid-teen years are a major factor in determining how resilient and able to cope they prove to be when faced with adversity [228]. Clearly young performers need to choose their friends well and do their best to cultivate these relationships so that peer influences exert an overall positive effect.

Once again, it is imperative to keep teens involved in youth sport, as this makes it less likely that they will fall in with the wrong crowd. To ensure this, the youth sport environment must provide for the all-important social element and sense of belonging that teens crave. A common reason that teens drift away from youth sports is the pull of wanting to hang out with friends. It follows that their involvement in youth sport needs to offer a viable (and attractive) alternative social community [226]. Team sports and group-based activities are advantageous from this perspective, as they naturally confer a sense of being part of the team or the member of a group. That said, individual sports can provide a sense of community and belonging, to the extent that the athlete feels that they are part of a training squad and identifies as a member of a club. The opportunity to interact with older athletes is also invaluable.

Importantly the friendships that are forged in sport are naturally more supportive and positive towards their sporting endeavours. The role of peers in supporting the mission becomes more important as young athletes progress along the youth sports journey. Whereas before we had the trinity of coach-parent-athlete, we now add peers as the fourth element in the support structure.

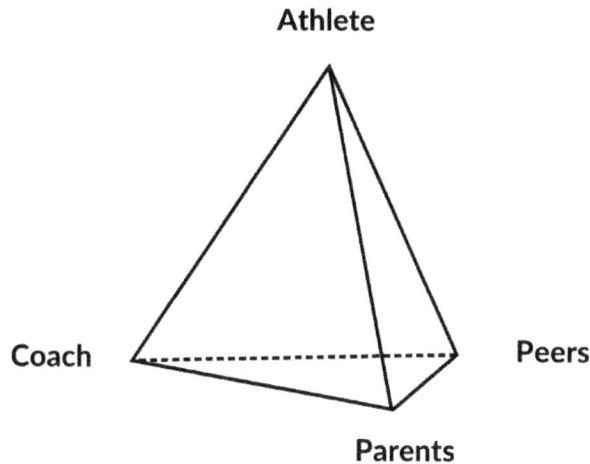

Those advising the young performer should therefore emphasise the importance of curating their peer group. It is important for youth athletes to cultivate a social life beyond the sporting arena and maintain friendships that are independent from their involvement in sport. Equally, there is the thornier issue of advising adolescent performers to surround themselves only with people who have their best interests at heart.

THE COUNTERBALANCING INFLUENCE OF THE GROWN-UPS...

As the young athlete matures later in adolescence they become better able to make good choices and resist peer pressure, but in the meantime there is a storm to be weathered. The initial period that follows the transition from childhood into adolescence presents new and exciting challenges for parents in particular!

Whilst the pull of their peers is strong, teens will nevertheless look to the grown-ups in their life for guidance and wisdom. Parental support and a family sport culture remain important factors in encouraging the continued participation in organised sport among adolescents [229]. Aside from parents, prominent figures in the lives of teenage performers will likely include teachers, coaches, other practitioners and even older performers. With echoes to a previous chapter, any one of these figures in the life of the young athlete can have a profound influence during this impressionable time. As well as providing a buffer and an oasis of calm during conflicts, we can counterbalance peer influence with alternative perspectives to mitigate the detrimental effects of social pressures.

Fundamentally, teens must be enthused enough about the prospect and potential rewards of taking a different path to overcome the default reticence to deviate from what everybody else is doing. It follows that we must make a compelling case for the alternative – and then do our best to ensure that it delivers. Happily, youth sport offers an exciting, testing and rewarding experience when handled properly.

Only the performers themselves have the power to choose to pursue a long-term aim and only they can decide how much of themselves they invest in the day-to-day process. We should however encourage young athletes to be bold in their aspirations. The virtues of forging their own path are likewise worth emphasising and we should appeal to the spirit of adventure that is undernourished in modern times. The hero's journey of striving to reach the highest level is a plentiful source of inspiration to feed their natural hunger for challenge and adventure.

The grown-ups also have a role in shaping social learning. It is vital that young warriors are schooled and socialised properly. Adolescence is a pivotal period in shaping values and moral behaviour [219]. Coaches have a hugely important role when it comes to instilling values of sportsmanship and codes of behaviour. This is especially key with young males, given their propensity for testosterone-fuelled risk-taking and status seeking behaviours during this phase. The sporting arena is a key forum for learning to regulate aggression. Our conduct as role models and what we communicate, both directly and in our stewardship of the environment thus become all the more important. Parents (notably fathers) likewise have a key role to play in this regard.

THE EVOLVING ROLES OF THE GROWN-UPS...

The onset of puberty marks a notoriously challenging time for parents. One of the major factors that alters the dynamics of the parent-child relationship is the growing imperative to assert their own independence and take greater command of their lives [220] – and for young performers this naturally includes their participation in youth sports. What young athletes are seeking from parents and coaches, respectively, begins to change as we enter early adolescence. Where previously they might have been content to let the grown-ups take the lead, with adolescence comes the desire to assume a more active role and make decisions for themselves.

Over the course of the adolescent years the respective roles of the grown-ups in the young athlete's life undergo an evolution. In broad terms, as young performers mature, they increasingly look to coaches and authority figures beyond the family. The coach is in the advantageous position of being a (hopefully) respected figure who is invested but retains the distance to offer somewhat impartial judgement and guidance. To illustrate this progression, a study of male youth soccer noted that the younger players cite their father as the most prominent figure, whereas players in the older age group (15-18 years) attribute the coach as having the greatest positive influence on their performance [201].

There is a common assumption that the involvement of parents should recede during this phase in the youth sports journey. In reality, parents often continue to play an integral role, not least from a logistical standpoint as the training and practice commitments tend to increase over this period. This is especially true of adolescent performers who are part of talent development pathways and aspire to compete at college level and beyond. Once again, it is more accurate to say that the role of the sport parent *evolves* during the adolescent years, rather than necessarily diminishing.

Parents thus remain a crucial partner in the endeavour. There has been a realisation that initiatives aimed at promoting engagement and addressing psychosocial elements within a talent development context are best undertaken in collaboration with parents [218]. This does however make it all the more important that parental input is congruent with the guidance that is being provided by the coaches. It is in the interests of all parties to ensure that there is alignment on messaging – it benefits nobody if the young athlete comes to disregard what their parents say because they perceive it to be at odds with what their coaches have told them. Parents should take steps to find out what has been conveyed by the coaches so that they are sufficiently informed to reinforce the key themes. In turn, the coach has a responsibility to enlist parents as partners, explain the salient parts of the technical and tactical direction provided to the athlete and ensure that they are kept up to date.

COACHING YOUTH...

One obvious and yet oddly overlooked aspect of the role of the coach from a retention standpoint is making sure kids develop the necessary technical and tactical skills so that they feel secure in their ability to perform. A common reason for dropping out from participating in organised youth sport among teens is a perceived lack of competence [230]. Being more aware of social evaluation naturally makes it more important for young teenage performers to feel confident that they are capable of performing in front of others without embarrassing themselves.

The changing motivations of adolescent athletes should also be reflected in how we coach them. Notably the inclinations towards exploration, novelty and sensation-seeking should be accounted for in how we design and deliver practices. Practically, this means permitting more scope to play with different ways of doing things during practices as well as providing more variety in activities.

The quality of the coach-athlete relationship is similarly critical for providing a much-needed sense of assurance. This is when the ability to coach humans rather than simply coach the sport comes to the fore. Performers within age-group competition are far from a homogenous group, so there must be a readiness on the part of the coach to engage with each member of the group as an individual. Working with young performers at this time presents a huge opportunity, but we must be attentive and attuned in order to harness the burgeoning potential and avoid thwarting their growing desire to assert their independence.

Whilst the coach might be the director, by this stage of the journey there must be growing acknowledgement that this is the young athlete's show. At times, how things operate in practice is at odds with the notion of being coach-led but athlete-centred. Unquestioning compliance is not real engagement. We should be encouraging them to be curious about the why behind what the coach is directing them to do. As coaches we should take it as a positive sign when athletes ask questions, rather than a challenge to our authority! It is certainly better for the relationship for young athletes to voice any concerns or questions in the proper forum rather than harbouring them in private, so parents should encourage them to do so (and hold coaches accountable for responding in the proper fashion).

CONNECTING WITH TEENAGE ATHLETES...

Each young performer is different, both in temperament and from a developmental perspective, so clearly it is important that we tailor our interactions accordingly. Some young performers are awkward and unsure of themselves at this time, whereas others act out and overcompensate. Fun times! Moreover, this is a time of great change, so there will also be a high degree of variability and even volatility in how they present on any given day. This requires us to be both vigilant and adaptable in our day-to-day interactions.

Effective communication begins with attending to the young athlete. It is evident that athletes do differentiate when it comes to the facets of their sports participation where they welcome parental support versus what they prefer parents to stay away from. We need to make a genuine and concerted commitment to listen to what they have to say, particularly in this regard.

A common theme is the preference for parents to refrain from unsolicited technical and tactical input [231]. Another wish that is commonly expressed by young athletes (aged 13-14) is to be given more space when competing and be left to socialise with team-mates unencumbered [232]. In contrast, commenting on effort and attitude is deemed to be fair game and practical advice is often welcomed [231]. For instance, interviews with young athletes indicated that they generally approve of parents taking a role in encouraging them to continue to participate for all the benefits that organised youth sport offers and helping them to make good choices in relation to their participation (such as balancing school commitments) [232].

These general patterns are however far from universally applicable. Notably, some young athletes value parental input and appreciate receiving feedback on their performance – this perspective may be more common among those who aspire to compete at the highest level [204]. As highly interested spectators, parents are often the ones paying the closest attention and those who are knowledgeable about the sport are accordingly in a position to provide valuable (if subjective) insights.

What input is welcomed and received in the spirit intended (albeit sometimes grudgingly) versus what is perceived by the performer as interfering or cramping their style is a variable feast. Ultimately this is not something that we can second-guess. From a parenting perspective this means taking our lead from the young performer themselves by inviting them to specify the conditions for parental involvement in their sports participation, including what input we provide (and when). This is a conversation that is worth revisiting periodically as we advance along the journey, especially at the major transition points.

That said, youth athletes generally respond to being treated like a young adult. Paradoxically, one of the common ways we get things wrong with young people is by asking too little of them. We should show them more respect. It also turns out there is some truth to the assertion that teens need a firm hand. As the grownups, if we are permissive with adolescents – that is, either too indulgent on the one hand or neglectful on the other – the outcomes are typically not positive [233]!

NAVIGATING THE TRANSITION...

The adolescent years mark a key transition point for young performers and it is during this phase in their development that they must take the reins. A key message to the young performer should be that they are the master of their own destiny. The best coaches inspire by appealing to the part of the individual that seeks the best for themselves. To that end, another key message is that they are not all they could be. This is the first step to casting their mind to what they might become if they were to diligently invest their efforts in the endeavour.

Whilst our role must evolve during this phase, the parent-child relationship remains hugely significant. The family environment can provide much needed stability and our input and involvement remain vitally important. Youth athletes generally respond best to an *authoritative* rather than authoritarian style of parenting [211] and much the same is true of coaching. Whilst both styles of parenting involve being firm, insisting upon high standards and enforcing discipline, there are crucial distinctions.

The author*itarian* style is highly controlling, rather cold and unresponsive to individual needs. Adolescents tend to respond very poorly to this style of coaching or parenting, either disengaging or rebelling as they strive to exert their independence. Given the perils and counterproductive effects of authoritarian coaching and parenting these are to be avoided – without lowering expectations and abandoning any attempt to maintain discipline.

An authorit*ative* style involves clear standards and discipline that is consistently applied and enforced, this is managed in a fashion that is not controlling but is rather based on informed consent such that the terms are agreed in advance by all parties. Authoritative coaches and parents display a high degree of warmth and the grownups engage in a way that is highly responsive to the young person [234]. The benefits associated with authoritative parenting during the adolescent years include helping to foster a sense of autonomy and a healthy attitude towards work [235].

In seeking to avoid being authoritarian, the trap that I argue that parents have fallen into over recent times is being too permissive. The distinction between *authoritarian* and *authoritative* is not commonly made. A shallow conception and lack of nuance have arguably contributed to the over-correction.

It is also a challenge to strike the right balance. Even when judged and managed perfectly there is inevitably some friction involved from time to time. In the face of pushback, some parents (and coaches) understandably opt to avoid conflict and cede the ground simply to keep the peace. Just as there are perils to being too strict and rigid, there are harms that come from letting teens just have their way. This is a dereliction of duty: teens are a work in progress and still figuring things out, meaning that they rely on us as the grown-ups to provide appropriate boundaries and direction. Being indulgent is fundamentally not in their best interests and it is accordingly demonstrated that this approach is associated with bad outcomes. Whilst it has strangely fallen out of favour in some quarters, the pursuit of excellence is worth preserving and youth athletes respond best when we place appropriate demands upon them. This applies especially with adolescents who have aspirations of achieving something. It is part of our duty of care to uphold standards and hold them accountable.

Naturally, we need to meet each young athlete where they are, not least as making the transition requires that their faculties are sufficiently developed to make the necessary commitment and investment. We must also align our own expectations with what each young person is actually seeking from sport so that our approach as coaches and parents reflects their own motivations for participating, understanding that this is also liable to change over time. Practically this needs to be navigated on a case-by-case basis, as the athlete's relative stage of neurocognitive development will serve to determine their current state of readiness. At times we need to temper our enthusiasm and be patient. A common scenario is that the young athlete does not feel ready but feels pressured by the expectations of others, including coaches and teammates [204]. Clearly this is something that we should strive to avoid as far as possible.

The youth development years are best navigated as a guided process that involves the active participation of coaches, parents and even older peers. The aim is that we are operating in the *zone of proximal development*, whereby what we are asking of them is just beyond their present capabilities but close enough that they can manage it with the assistance and support of others.

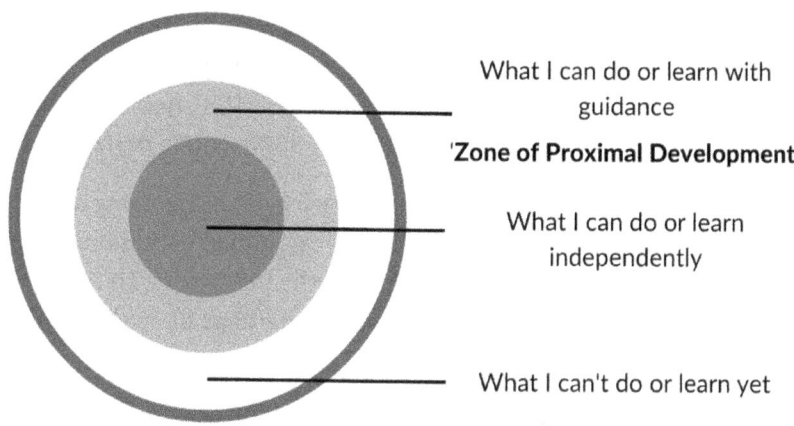

By extension, we need to be attentive and responsive to the growing capabilities of the young performer as they mature and make efforts to ensure that we permit increasing opportunities to fly solo. Through the course of this phase we should place progressively greater onus on the young performer and encourage them to take more initiative. This is a sign of respect and helps to affirm that we have confidence in them. Parents, coaches and teachers alike should seek to nurture and emphasise a sense of agency. Beyond emphasising the element of choice, we should encourage adolescent performers to assume their role as the principal actor in their own journey.

WISDOM OF THE ELDERS...

The grown-ups can share the benefit of their wisdom in helping adolescent athletes to deal with social pressures, expectations and relations with peers [204].

As neurocognitive faculties develop through the adolescent years, teens are continually honing their own *sensemaking* apparatus. However, with the advent of adolescence young athletes become increasingly self-conscious, so this is often an area where we can lend assistance in helping them make sense of things. Popularity and social status assume greater importance, so with the heightened awareness of the scrutiny on others, young performers become much more sensitive to what they do in public and how it might reflect on them. Aside from providing sage advice, lending the perspective of somebody who has the benefit of experience is helpful, not least to keep it all in proportion.

"What other people think of you is none of your business."

— Eleanor Roosevelt

A point worth emphasising is that very few are qualified to judge so the opinions of others should be given very little weight. Moreover, nobody is valid in judging an athlete based on a single performance (whether good, bad or indifferent) – this applies all the more so with junior competition and the development years – and certainly what happens in the arena does not define them. This should be the consistent message from coaches, parents and others in the young performers' circle.

It is also worth pointing out that those who spend their time disparaging others are typically not doing anything with their own life. Coming to this realisation is important in helping adolescent performers to pay less heed to the detractors. To that end, Theodore Roosevelt's *Man in the Arena* speech should perhaps be made compulsory reading for aspiring young athletes:

'…there are many who confine themselves to criticism of the way others do what they themselves dare not even attempt… It is not the critic who counts; not the man who points out how the strong man stumbles or where the doer of deeds could have done them better. The credit belongs to the man who is actually in the arena'

– Theodore Roosevelt

Negotiating the peculiarities of teen society is arguably the biggest challenge that comes with the transition to the adolescent years. In this regard, one of the more challenging aspects for adolescent athletes is adopting an appropriate and adaptive emotional response to discord with peers. Given their limited experience and the fact that their capabilities are still developing it is inevitable that they will make missteps over this period (most readers will be able to recall the mortifying feeling of making a *faux pas* in a social context as a teenager). It is vital that they ride out these occasional storms and stay in the game. To that end, we can help them deal with challenging events and emotional disturbances. On occasion we might need to talk them down but we can also assist with practical strategies to help them to keep things in proportion, including daily practices such as journaling, as we will explore in the next chapter.

Key Take-Home Messages

1. The adolescent years are a period of profound change. The potential for growth is enormous, but so is the risk of disengagement if young athletes are not supported appropriately.

2. Young athletes must take greater ownership of their journey - when participation is driven primarily by parents or coaches, disengagement becomes likely.

3. Organised sport can support wellbeing and social development; misaligned expectations or unhealthy environments can have the opposite effect.

4. Peer influence becomes central, social belonging, acceptance and conformity strongly shape behaviour, which can either support retention or dropout, depending.

5. Identity formation Identifying as an athlete can enhance motivation and belonging, but when self-worth becomes overly dependent on performance, young athletes become vulnerable to anxiety, fear of failure, and withdrawal.

6. Adolescents are hyper-aware of social evaluation – perceived lack of capability and feelings of insufficiency are common reasons for leaving sport, especially with girls.

7. Parental involvement does not end in adolescence; it changes. Support, guidance, and boundaries remain essential, but autonomy must be respected.

8. Adolescents need coaches who can coach people, not just sport—balancing high standards with empathy, flexibility, and individualised engagement.

9. Authoritative beats authoritarian or permissive, adolescents respond best to clear expectations, consistent standards; too much control or too little structure both undermine this.

10. Coaches should seek engagement, not obedience – the aim is helping young athletes to become capable, self-directed individuals who can make good decisions and take responsibility.

Practical Tips

✓ Be strategic and responsive to accommodate the changing dynamics of the parent-child relationship – both in general and as it relates to their participation in sport.

✓ Expect that roles and responsibilities will undergo revision during this phase as their relationship with parents and the world in general evolves.

✓ Teens need the structure and rich developmental environment that sport provides – so seek to avoid disengagement and drop out above all else.

✓ This is generally not a time to step back entirely: you still have a big role to play helping kids navigate challenges within sport and beyond.

✓ Aim for authoritative (warm and responsive but with clear standards of behaviour and appropriately demanding) rather than authoritarian in your sports parenting.

✓ Beware falling into the trap of being permissive – teenagers are looking to the grown-ups for clear and consistent boundaries, so be firm and hold your ground!

Action Items

» Negotiate (on a periodic basis) the parameters for parental involvement and agree rules of engagement.

» Afford more opportunities to assert independence within agreed constraints – allow them space when competing and freedom to socialise with team-mates

» Seek to be adaptable and responsive: allow young athlete to express their preferences for communication in relation to their participation (what, when, how)

» Together with coaches, provide the support and direction to allow adolescent performers operate in the zone of proximal development

» Refrain from giving unsolicited input on technical or tactical aspects as far as possible.

» Commenting on effort and attitude is always fair game!

» Request that the coaching staff keep you up to date so that you can provide a consistent message, support coaching initiatives and reinforce key themes

» Help kids to cultivate a relationship with the coaching staff that is based on mutual respect – encourage them to ask questions and voice concerns in the proper forum

» Strive to make peer influence work in the athlete's favour – enlist influential figures (senior performers, older peers) as the medium for key messages!

» Help to provide teens with an alternative social support network that gives them permission to be exceptional

Harnessing the Mind

In our efforts to prepare young performers we commonly fall into the trap of focussing on the body and overlooking the mind. The reality is that body and mind are inseparable. What goes on in the mind affects the body: our mental state and our inner-most thoughts have a profound effect on our physiological state. Making the best use of practice time is a matter of mindset and how well the young performer is able to harness and deploy their mental resources. We need to account for the mind even when engaging in something that is seemingly bodily focussed such as physical preparation. Equipping young performers for the journey also means helping them with strategies to harness their mind when performing and tools to handle the attendant struggles.

ATTENDING...

When it comes to attending practices, it not only matters that the athlete shows up but also how they show up. Being present in body is a necessary starting point but it is not sufficient. If the performer's mind is elsewhere then not much worthwhile will be achieved. How the athlete allocates and directs their attention are all-important.

Even the nature of the attention that a young athlete brings to bear profoundly affects what they perceive and how they experience things. The quality of our attention determines which parts of the brain we engage and how the world reveals itself to us as a result. Put more simply, how the performer attends to their practice shapes not only how they perceive it, but also affects how they engage with the task and in turn what learning takes place.

In the next chapter we will introduce the 5Cs approach that has been successfully applied in talent development environments such as professional (soccer)football youth academies [236]. One of the five Cs is *concentration*. Attention tends to drift so being able to notice when our mind wanders and then bring it back to the task at hand is an important discipline that we should seek to develop. One of the prompts that is employed simply involves asking the athlete whether they kept their eyes on the coach when he or she was speaking. In my own coaching practice when I am speaking to multiple athletes at once I am continually scanning the group to check that I have their attention and when I notice an athlete is looking away I will pause and pointedly wait for them to resume eye contact before proceeding.

Keeping their eyes on the coach is a good habit for a young athlete to improve their chances of taking in the instruction that is being provided. Another reason why this matters is that it will in turn affect how coaches engage with them. Coaches will tend to reciprocate and favour athletes who are attentive by giving them more time and individual attention in return.

Finally, what athletes attend to and where they direct their gaze when practising and competing matter a great deal. This is especially crucial in open skill sports (for example, team sports, racquet sports) to keep up with an environment that is constantly changing. How performers train their gaze and regulate these visual aspects of attention under pressure are vital. High stress tends to lead to a narrowing of attention – under duress we can become tunnel-visioned, so that we miss important stuff going on in the periphery. As well as game sense, what performers fixate on and for how long are also crucial for skill execution. Eye-tracking technology reveals that expert performers differ significantly in this regard when compared to those who are less skilled. Naturally this is especially crucial for aiming tasks (for example a golf put) and skills that involve intercepting an object or body in motion, such as striking or catching a ball, making a tackle, and so on. Coaches speak of keeping your eye on the ball for a reason!

MENTAL IMAGERY...

Part of coaching a skill is providing a young athlete with a mental representation of the task. Essentially, this involves painting mental pictures in the performer's mind using whatever analogies or descriptions best resonate for that individual. The objective is that the individual not only has a clear concept of the key features of the athletic skill, but also a sensory template of what the movement feels like when executed properly.

A related example of how we can harness the athlete's mind and their feel for the movement is by engaging in *mental imagery training*. Mental imagery goes beyond visualisation – some performers find mentally rehearsing the feeling of performing a skill is more useful than attempting to conjure the visual depiction in their mind.

In either case, imagining performing an action is highly effective in mobilising the same parts of our brain as when we physically perform the skilled movement with the body. For instance, we can employ this strategy of performing 'imaginary repetitions' during practice sessions by encouraging the young athlete to rehearse the movement in their minds before and after performing efforts in practice. This is a cool trick, as it allows us to log additional repetitions without physically performing the movement. Mental imagery practice also becomes hugely beneficial when athletes are not physically able to perform the movement with the body, such as when injured.

Another application of mental imagery training involves developing a pre-performance routine [237]. This works particularly with 'closed skill' tasks, where the athlete has time to mentally rehearse the movement before they execute it – an example is a free throw in basketball. With even a simple mental routine, we can effectively improve execution and the accuracy of the output.

BEING DELIBERATE...

Hours spent at practice are not equal. As far as possible we want to create the conditions for the young performer to be mindful and deliberate to get the most out of practices and workouts rather than going through the motions. What intention they bring to the activity and what mental effort they invest similarly have a marked impact on the response to training and the effects of practice.

Clearly the grown-ups who are directing practice and training have an important role to play in this regard. For instance, it is difficult to expect the young performer to be purposeful and deliberate in how they approach each practice and training session if it is not evident that the coach has a plan.

Taking the time to inform the young athlete of the reason and the context for the workout helps ensures that they have what they need to be deliberate in how they approach each training session. Parents and young performers should request that the coach explain their thinking and help the athlete to connect the dots so that they are clear the objective of the workout and the purpose of a particular exercise. At the risk of generalising, female athletes often have a particular wish to know the reasoning behind workouts and to understand what purpose it is designed to serve. This context is necessary in order to perform each repetition with intent.

Knowing what facets of the movement to concentrate on and understanding how it will help them to improve similarly helps young athletes to harness and direct their mind towards salient aspects during each repetition. Educating the young performer also helps to ensure that over time they become sufficiently informed to direct their own efforts so that they are less dependent on direct supervision.

Naturally, the performer also has an active role to play. One way to support young performers to be deliberate in their approach is encouraging them to keep a record of their workouts. The incremental gains and compounding effects are not readily noticeable in real time, in the form of a *training diary* helps to provide a tangible sense of progress over time. Being able to look back on all the work that they have invested also provides assurance that they are prepared as they enter the competition arena.

I routinely encourage the athletes I coach to download their thoughts and recollections after each practice session, including the 'teachable moments' that occur from time to time. It is helpful to have a repository where the young performer can download and reflect upon discoveries, challenges and coaching interactions as they arise. Maintaining a *practice journal* supports deliberate practice in that it helps the athlete to make the most of the day-to-day opportunities to learn and improve as they present themselves. The mind continues to work to solve the puzzle during the times in between practices, so as well as enabling the performer to download and reflect on what happened during the session, a practice journal can be helpful to capture the flashes of inspiration, 'aha!' moments and insights that come to mind at random moments.

THE MENTAL SKILLS ARMOURY – WHAT ARE THE DIFFERENCE-MAKERS?

Developing the *mental performance skills* that allow young performers to cope with challenge and execute under pressure is increasingly acknowledged as an integral part of the talent development process. If we are seeking to cultivate relevant psychological skills and associated traits, we should first consider what factors discriminate between those who successfully navigate the rocky road to the elite level versus those who fall by the wayside.

Helpfully, the talent development research has sought to identify the psychological characteristics that facilitate a successful journey to senior level [238, 239]. As well as possessing the relevant tools in their armoury, how strategically and successfully they are deployed at different stages in the journey also proves to be important [240].

Commitment is one factor that often differentiates those who achieve emerge as successful from those who come close but do not quite make it to the elite level [202]. Naturally this includes the depth of the desire and resolve to participate in the sport; however, high performers also demonstrate a commitment to the pursuit of excellence. Sadly, we cannot be committed on their behalf – as a coach and practitioner I can attest that it is not a viable proposition if I am more committed that the athlete is! The desire to participate and to strive must come from the young athlete themselves. Most athletes claim to be committed when asked – and typically they mean it at the time. Nonetheless, genuine commitment is manifested in action. It is absolutely fair game for parents and others to point it out when the behaviours we observe do not align with what the athlete has verbally committed to.

Another point of difference is the *reaction to challenge* and setbacks. High achievers seem to exhibit a more proactive approach to coping. This begins with a healthy attitude towards challenge, so part of the process is learning to regulate how they respond to cues and contexts that appear daunting or even threatening. In turn we can do our part to help cultivate the will and determination to dig deep and prevail under unfavourable or testing circumstances (more on that in a later chapter).

Those who excel possess an ability to *reflect* and get the most from experiences. Certain opportunities to learn and grow can be anticipated in advance (such as key contests), such that it is possible to help prime the performer to engage in the right spirit. Equally there are many cases where we stumble upon experiences that prove to be instructive. The propensity to exercise self-awareness and willingness to engage in critical self-analysis are key attributes. Often these are chastening experiences, so it requires honesty, humility and fortitude to take the salient lessons. We can help kids to develop the cognitive faculties involved by guiding them through the reflection process with regular debriefs. We can also equip them with certain tools to help make self-reflection part of their routine – the aforementioned practice journal is one such tool.

How young athletes handle *rewards* is another key factor [202]. As we noted in an earlier chapter, it is important that young athletes do not get carried away with successes achieved on the way and we need to avoid the perils of an inflated ego. Those around the young performer can certainly help them to keep their feet on the ground. A signature trait of those who succeed is that are always striving rather than lapsing into complacency. The best do not pay too much attention to their own press; they resist the notion that their work is done and are always seeking ways to challenge themselves and improve. That said, taking the small wins along the way is equally important!

Continuing the theme, *independence* is one of the key psychological characteristics for success on the talent development journey [238]. When coaches cite a lack of maturity among adolescent performers they often point to a lack of independence [241]. A key objective in the process of developing and preparing young performers is ensuring that they become self-sufficient, such that they are able to operate independently, rather than being reliant on others. The talent development literature accordingly emphasises the importance of coaches and parents creating an environment that supports autonomy.

Equally, it is worth emphasising that autonomy is the endpoint and it is a process to get there. We should make the distinction between athlete-*centred* and athlete-*led*. For instance, it is appropriate that the coach directs proceedings early on. During the early stages especially the role of the coach is to provide instruction and impart their knowledge to enable young performers to learn, acquire skills and better understand the intricacies and less intuitive aspects of the sport. Once the performer better understands what they are doing and they have attained a certain level of knowledge they should be afforded greater opportunity to self-regulate and exercise more choice in how they approach their development.

BRINGING SELF-REGULATED LEARNING TO SPORT PRACTICE...

Much like classes at school, organised youth sports practices and training sessions are generally conducted in a group format. Of course not every member of the group will learn or progress at the same rate. Not everybody is starting from the same point, plus the trajectories for motor learning and development related to growth and maturation are all highly individual. As in the classroom, there will be individuals who are struggling to pick things up, whereas others will be ready to forge ahead. Whilst the coach might do their best to accommodate the range of abilities and learning trajectories in the group, in practice this is very difficult, especially when dealing with a large and mixed cohort. Whether at school or in sport, in reality it falls to the individual to make sure they are making the most of the opportunity to learn and take steps to avoid being held back or left behind.

In earlier chapters we made the case that making multi-sports engagement viable – and balancing other commitments such as school – requires coaches and athletes to be more economical with practice time. Practically, this also requires the young athlete to be more proactive in how they approach their own skill development and athletic preparation. Applying the self-regulated learning framework can help kids to take more ownership over their learning process to ensure that they are progressing as they should be.

Kids who engage in youth sports are student-athletes by definition – they are in school as well as participating in sport and we want them to perform well in both arenas. Whether attending class or practice, an overlooked part of the endeavour is learning how to learn. In each context, we should prompt kids to take some responsibility for their own development rather than leaving this to chance or otherwise delegating all responsibility to the coach (or teacher). In other words, we should encourage them to assume their proper role as an active participant in the learning process rather than a passive recipient of instruction.

The overarching purpose of self-regulated learning is to enable kids to become better and more independent learners. Importantly, the approach also permits the learner to tailor their approach and accommodate whatever constraints they are operating under, including their own present limitations. This personalised and systematic approach provides the means to exploit their individual strengths as well as filling gaps in knowledge and skills and addressing any deficiencies that might impede their progress.

Sports practices and athletic preparation should lend themselves well to self-regulated learning as young performers typically find these activities inherently rewarding and worth engaging in for their own sake. In this way, youth sports have the potential to serve as a gateway to self-regulated learning. The experience of applying these methods in the domain of sport will equip kids with the relevant tools and enable them to transfer the approach to their schoolwork.

THE ELEMENTS OF SELF-REGULATED LEARNING...

The self-regulated learning process comprises three distinct elements: forethought, application and reflection [242]. The 'forethought' part of the process begins with having the student-athlete identify learning objectives or process goals for themselves, as a necessary first step to directing their efforts towards attaining those outcomes. The next task is to proactively come up with strategies and methods to assist them in the pursuit. The coach's perspective will be helpful, plus an ancillary benefit of taking the initiative in requesting the coach's input and assistance is that the young performer is likely to be rewarded with extra time and attention.

Putting these strategies into practice begins with the learner taking steps to curate and manage their own learning environment, as far as that is possible. Part of this is finding the most conducive time and place. The young performer should do what they can do to optimise the environment for engaging in independent practice outside of supervised sessions (much like creating the most conducive conditions for doing homework or independent study outside the classroom).

Time management is important, but it is also important to consider how they are allocating mental and physical resources. To help with regulating these resources, we can suggest that kids track how they are spending their time. Tracking critical aspects of student-athlete life such as sleep and nutrition likewise helps to ensure that they are supporting their ability to practice and learn.

The 'performance-control' phase of self-regulated learning comprises self-control and self-monitoring. In the context of sport practice, this includes the pre-performance routine, which typically includes composing themselves and mentally rehearsing the movement before each repetition. The other element is self-monitoring or self-observation as they execute the practice task.

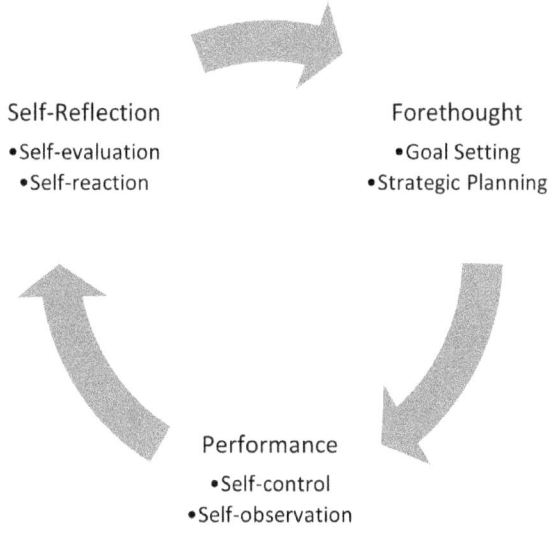

Cyclical Self-Regulated Learning Process

The final 'reflection' phase is a crucial part of the self-regulated learning process. The three phases together make up a cyclical process and the reflection phase is essential to the self-regulatory feedback loop [243]. In this way, it is integral to the iterative process of identifying what well wrong, refining the approach with each repetition and reviewing the outcome. One of the things that separates more accomplished athletes is that they are quicker to engage in self-evaluation [243]. They are also better at making the correct attributions when errors occur and in general respond in a more adaptive manner to failed attempts, such as seeking input, rather than becoming dejected.

The cyclical self-regulated learning process thus provides a means for problem-solving and troubleshooting, allowing the student-athlete to navigate roadblocks during the learning process and come up with a way forward. As performers acquire a more refined feel for the movement with practice, we should help them to hone their ability to detect errors and figure out how to fix them. Increasingly I ask the performer to describe what happened and what they thought went wrong, rather than simply telling them. If we want young athletes to become more proficient at correcting errors, then we must afford them the opportunity work through the problem and come up with a fix rather than simply giving them the solution.

What we are striving for is a scenario where the individual is able to do this increasingly independently of external input, so that they are less and less dependent on the coach. The ultimate objective of the coach should be to ensure that the athlete is able to operate independently such that they can cope when the coach is not there.

In addition to continually assessing how things are going and reviewing progress, the learner is prompted to critically evaluate their learning process periodically. They are asked to rate their success in implementing strategies and determine whether they are on track towards the learning outcomes that were originally outlined. Going through this self-reflection exercise helps kids to adapt and refine their process, such that they are better equipped to respond to setbacks or stalled progress in positive fashion.

One of the biggest benefits of self-regulated learning is that it promotes self-efficacy, as it fosters a genuine sense that their learning is in their own hands. Honing self-regulated learning skills helps student-athletes to adopt a more proactive approach to their own learning [242]. Implementing the self-directed learning process makes them make them more inclined to evaluate their progress against their own personal goals, rather than comparing themselves to their peers. All of this makes it more likely that kids will persist and persevere, rather than becoming discouraged.

FIGURING OUT HOW TO GET THE BEST OUT OF THEMSELVES...

Engaging in the self-regulated learning process helps kids to figure out how to motivate and apply themselves. Individual temperament inevitably comes into play here and certainly this might be a heavier lift for some. In particular, how highly they rate on the personality trait of conscientiousness will determine their natural predisposition and how inclined they are to apply themselves. All the same, whatever their starting position it is nevertheless possible to cultivate work ethic for each individual. What self-regulated learning does is provide the necessary structure to be more systematic in their approach, such that they are better able to exercise self-discipline.

The reflective element of self-regulated learning also encourages kids to become more self-aware. It is imperative that the athlete not only learns the game but also comes to understand themselves, such that they are able to fully exploit the plentiful opportunities to learn and adapt. Self-awareness is also the starting point to developing different facets of self-regulation such as self-discipline and impulse control. Cultivating the ability to better regulate emotions is another crucial aspect to allow the performer to manage themselves in the competition environment and beyond. Once again, the grownups have an important role to play here.

"We do not learn from experience... we learn from reflecting on experience."

— John Dewey

Reflecting on events and experiences requires being honest and clear-eyed about their own actions. The individual must strive to be detached and separate their ego during the after-action review process. The version of events that they tell themselves must reflect reality in order to be able to correctly attribute causes for successes and failures. An important realisation for the young person is that they must be unsparing when looking back if they are to learn from experience, take appropriate corrective action and avoid making the same mistakes in the future.

In the context of youth sports, early adolescence marks a key phase in development where we should seek to utilise the self-regulated learning approach in earnest. Prompting the young performer to consider what they are seeking from their participation and thinking about where they might want their youth sports journey to take them will set the stage for identifying specific objectives to help them progress towards that end, which is the first step in the self-regulated learning process.

Whilst it is vital that the young person takes ownership, what we can do is help with tools to support different aspects of their self-regulated learning. This might include providing a template for a training log where they can record workouts. We should also encourage young performers to keep a practice journal where they can capture key learning points, coaching input that resonated and any discoveries or lightbulb moments that come along the way. Similarly, we can help them to come up with methods to monitor their progress and a means to evaluate themselves periodically. The caveat here is that it should be made clear that these are simply tools that the young performer is encouraged to make use of on their own behalf, rather than something that is being led or imposed by the coach or parent.

Self-regulated learners are not only more engaged and more focused but also more coachable. From a coaching perspective, young performers who exhibit these traits are more rewarding to work with, so the experience becomes much more satisfying for everybody involved. This creates a virtuous cycle: through adopting this approach the young performer is also more likely to receive additional time and attention from the coach!

SELF-TALK...

As coaches and parents we take a great deal of care with what we say and how we communicate with young performers. Yet when I am coaching I am mindful that there are two voices (at least) that the athlete is attending to. In addition to whatever instructions or feedback I am giving, there is always the voice in the athlete's own head, which is arguably far more influential. Naturally we don't have access to a young performer's innermost thoughts, but sometimes they bubble up to the service. In sports psychology terms this is encapsulated as 'self-talk'. Self-talk encompasses how we talk to ourselves out loud as well as what we are telling ourselves in our own heads.

This topic has particular resonance for me. I vividly remember a school (soccer) football match when I was audibly berating myself on the pitch to such an extent that I could actually sense the disquiet I was causing among the opposing players who were unfortunate enough to find themselves within earshot. Many years later a young squash player who I had worked with took this a step further – after each loss he suffered on the professional circuit he would take to social media to publicly beat up on himself in front of an online audience.

Why we would turn on ourselves in such a way seems to defy logic. Yet, my experience is that aspiring young athletes who hold themselves to a high standard and strive to excel also have a tendency to beat up on themselves. Any virtue has a downside and a characteristic of high achievers in different domains is that they tend to be their own biggest and most scathing critic.

"Be careful how you are talking to yourself because you are listening."

— Lisa M. Hayes

Whilst public outbursts offer the most striking manifestation, we should recognise that this is simply the athlete verbalising out loud what they are telling themselves in the privacy of our heads. The self-talk that happens out in the open offers a glimpse into the chatter that goes on constantly between their ears. Such outbursts thus provide an opportunity for those in the athlete's corner to shine a torch on what and how they habitually communicate with themselves. In doing so we take the first step towards helping the young performer to harness their internal dialogue in a way that better serves them.

One of the most common triggers for a young athlete to berate themselves is when they commit an error. Aside from the fact that nobody sets out to make mistakes, depending on the nature and circumstances, mistakes are not necessarily something they should admonish themselves for. Errors are not only inevitable but also integral to the development process, especially when operating at the frontier of our present capabilities (which is where the growth happens). It is vital that performers give themselves some grace and do not punish themselves out of making the kinds of mistakes that are a necessary byproduct of striving to improve and develop.

More generally, berating somebody in public has negative consequences for the health of the relationship. This applies all the more when that person is ourselves. Toxic relationships are to be avoided, but when our tormentor resides in our head this poses something of a problem. Holding ourselves to a high standard is one thing, but when nothing is ever good enough the constant disapproval and even scorn from the person who in theory knows us best (i.e. ourselves) weighs heavy and is clearly not conducive from a performance health perspective.

This is akin to *Solomon's paradox*, whereby we tend to be wiser when advising others than when acting on our behalf. A handy workaround is to imagine we are counselling somebody we care about and then we tend to give ourselves better advice. In the same way, the best way I have found to help young athletes realise the folly of the 'friendly fire' they are directing towards themselves (including in the example I cited above) is to point out that they would never dream of speaking like that to anybody else. I ask them to imagine they were speaking to a team-mate or training partner. In this scenario, they immediately recognise that it would not only be wrong but also counterproductive to behave so contemptuously towards somebody who they rely upon daily and need to perform well in order to be successful. Of course, this equally applies to themselves! Directing abuse and scorn towards themselves clearly does not serve them or the mission. Once young performers acknowledge this they can resolve to address themselves as if they were speaking to somebody they relied upon, cared about and wanted the best for.

Anybody who has been around negative people can attest how draining it is to spend time in their company. Something to ponder is how much worse it is for the person themselves, given that they have no way to escape the constant stream of negativity within their own head. Aside from being counterproductive, wallowing in bitterness and resentment or ruminating on negative thoughts is debilitating. From a performance health perspective, this is something that young performers need to be mindful of. As the grown-ups who are supporting them, we can be of help in this regard.

Tuning in to monitor our internal chatter is important for other reasons. There is a more insidious form of internal dialogue that undermines our efforts in other ways. Within all of us there is an enabler who readily offers excuses and comes up with rationalisations to let ourselves off the hook when we are thinking of skipping practice or taking short-cuts. At these times it serves to pay attention to the still quiet voice inside us that sees what we are doing for what it is. In order to win these internal battles the young performer needs to attend to their internal dialogue and go with the part of themselves that wants the best for them.

Whilst it is necessary to have some compassion for themselves, not least when it comes to the tone of their internal chatter, it is equally important that aspiring young performers learn to hold themselves accountable. In our own minds we are continually constructing a narrative to explain and justify our role in events. It is important that young performers monitor their internal commentary and scrutinise the story they are telling themselves to make sure that they are not deceiving themselves or blaming others but rather taking responsibility and learning the lessons from each experience.

Finally, it is sometimes necessary to have a word with ourselves and on occasion tough love is called for. There are times we need to give ourselves a kick up the backside. But again, the love part of 'tough love' is important, so this should be done in the spirit of coaching and encouragement. Just as they might cajole a team-mate to wake up and get their head in the game when they can see that they have switched off, a young performer can play the role of trusted friend to themselves to keep them on task and hold themselves to the goals they have committed to.

THE ABILITY TO RISE TO THE OCCASION...

A sense of control is an important ingredient for *clutch performance*, which describes the ability to rise to the occasion and perform when it matters. This is a conscious process whereby performers 'make it happen' by redoubling their efforts (both physical and mental) and deliberately harnessing and directing all available attentional resources. The respective aspects that underpin clutch performance can be developed during practice and as part the training process for performers who choose to invest in this endeavour.

The best athletes have an aura that sets them apart and allows them to elevate their performance on the biggest stage. Athletes competing at the highest levels rate higher on measures of mental toughness than athletes at lower tiers of competition. Being mentally tough is clearly an important quality when operating in the crucible of major competition and also in rendering the athlete resilient to challenges and setbacks.

Once again, a performer's ability to exhibit mental toughness depends in large part on the quality of the coping strategies and tools at their disposal [244]. Three elements that underpin mental toughness are perceived agency and control over outcomes, constancy in how they approach challenge and unshakeable confidence in their own ability (i.e. self-belief). Agency and sense of control come from the athlete feeling they are steering the ship, rather than others dictating what happens and making choices on their behalf. Constancy in approaching challenge has an element of tenacity, but also encompasses the habit of appraising scenarios as a challenge to confront and an opportunity to discover something. Finally, self-belief in general and self-efficacy in specific contexts are developed through the experiences of having these abilities tested and successfully coming through these trials.

It follows that young athletes need to be regularly challenged and tested in order to hone these abilities and build their confidence. To facilitate this process, we also need to help young performers to come up with strategies when they are feeling out of their depth and there is a lack of clarity on how to proceed. Not only will this relieve stress and make the prospect less daunting, but it will also help them to successfully handle whatever the situation throws at them.

GETTING A GRIP...

In all likelihood, performers will experience setbacks that cause them to question themselves. These trials are a necessary part of the journey, but at times performers can get trapped in a negative head space. When we find ourselves in such disarray it typically is not our emotions that are the problem; rather it is the negative and self-defeating thoughts these feelings elicit and our tendency to ruminate upon them that causes the ongoing stress and anxiety. To reiterate, it is not what we feel, but our thoughts about what we feel that often lead to problems.

When we get into a negative head space there are some typical cognitive distortions at play that affect our perceptions, including our interpretation of the actions of others and how we appraise whatever situations we are facing. The path back from a negative space involves first confronting and delving into how we are feeling, unpacking our thoughts on how we are feeling and examining the stories we are telling ourselves. In doing we create the opportunity to interrogate the often flawed logic that may be distorting our impression of the situation at hand and how it reflects on us. The whole house of cards may simply collapse under the weight of its own illogic, allowing us to return to the task at hand.

PRACTICAL TOOLS AND COUNTERMEASURES...

We have described the merits of a keeping a training diary and journal to assist with the training process and we can encourage young athletes to take a similar approach to their life outside sport. Journaling is a very helpful practice for performers. Expressing things on paper (or electronic equivalent) is akin to having a dialogue with yourself and as such helps the individual to process whatever occurred, interpret what to make of it and perhaps make some sense of it all. This can be a first step towards coming up with a plan of action to resolve whatever issues they are encountering.

When young performers are feeling troubled, a necessary first step is to get negative feelings, appraisals and ruminations out of their head and expose them to daylight.

Importantly this practice provides a means to arrest the spiralling thoughts and feelings of dread, as once they are out in the open or onto the page we are able to critically examine the version of events we have constructed in our heads. A related practice that has been used successfully with competitive athletes involves a brief writing intervention in the aftermath of setbacks or disappointing performances to take the sting out of it and help the performer to move on [245].

Dialogue with another person is another great way to do this – not least as this also offers the benefits of a more neutral perspective. That said, kids are sometimes guarded about sharing their inner-most thoughts and feelings, so it is important that they are able to fall back on the alternative and complementary strategy of writing things down.

Key Take-Home Messages

1. Mind and body are inseparable. Mental state directly affects learning, physiological responses, skill execution, and performance under pressure.

2. Being present matters. Showing up physically to practice is not enough; how a young athlete directs their attention determines the quality of learning.

3. Attention is a trainable skill. Focus, gaze control, and awareness can be developed and significantly influence performance, especially in dynamic, open-skill sports.

4. Mental imagery enhances learning. Imagined rehearsal activates similar neural pathways as physical practice and can supplement or replace repetitions when physical practice is limited.

5. Not all practice hours are equal. Deliberate, mindful practice produces far greater returns than time spent going through the motions.

6. Reflection accelerates development. Journaling and structured reflection help athletes recognise progress, extract learning, and build confidence.

7. Psychological skills differentiate long-term success. Commitment, coping with challenge, independence, reflection, and self-belief differentiate those who excel.

8. Autonomy is the goal. The aim of coaching and parenting is to develop athletes who can self-regulate, problem-solve and direct their own development.

9. Self-regulated learning is foundational. Athletes who learn how to learn become more independent, adaptable, coachable and persistent.

10. Self-talk shapes outcomes. Internal dialogue can either support growth and performance or quietly undermine confidence and motivation.

11. Mental toughness is built through challenge, reflection, perceived control and effective coping strategies.

12. Negative headspaces are driven by thought patterns, so addressing distorted thinking is key to regaining control.

Practical Tips

✓ Teach kids that attending practice means being present in mind not just in body.

✓ Reinforce simple habits such as eye contact when receiving instruction.

✓ Ensure athletes understand the purpose of each session and drill.

✓ Three key elements we need to help kids to harness during practices and training: **attention**, **intention** and **directed mental effort**.

✓ Find coaches who coach in a way that accounts for these elements and provide the necessary information and help kids can connect the dots

✓ Together with the coaches, help kids to explore mental imagery training and rehearsal during practice and a pre-performance routine during competition

✓ Encourage the young performer to keep a training diary to log the work they put in..

...and a practice journal to get the most out of every practice, recording what they worked on, what they learned, what challenged them, any "lightbulb" moments.

✓ Kids' perceptions of the coach and how the plan, workouts and coaching input are presented matter – work with kids and coaches to optimise this as far as possible

✓ Hold kids accountable to the actions they have committed to (walk the talk).

✓ Help kids to regularly engage in self-reflection.

✓ Encourage kids to respond with curiosity when things do not go as expected

✓ Guide kids through a systematic and graduated approach to facing things that make them fearful or apprehensive – exposure therapy works (but needs to be voluntary)

✓ Educate young performers on the importance of getting concerns and anxieties out in the open to process events and empower them to move forwards.

✓ Journaling is a powerful practice to manage spiralling thoughts and mental turmoil.

✓ Help athletes to become aware of their internal dialogue – when beating up on themselves ask: "Would you speak like this to a teammate?"

✓ Encourage writing or talking after difficult performances to guard against rumination, unmask distorted thinking and exaggerated narratives.

Action Items

» Hold kids accountable to these three things to each practice or workout:
- did they keep their eyes on the coach when they were speaking (attention)?
- were they purposeful and clear on what they are trying to do (intention)?
- were they dialled-in during the practice or competition (directed mental effort)?

Considered Communication: Care, Caution and Candour

When dealing with children and animals we should be aware of our influence. Athletes are naturally sensitive to the opinions of the coach, which means that as coaches we need to be conscious of what messages we are sending, how we are expressing ourselves and the potential impact on the young performer. Parents of course face the additional challenge of balancing the role of parent with their sport parenting duties, to make sure they remain a parent first and a sport parent a distant second. Retaining some separation between sport and life outside sport is crucial, especially when it comes to the relationship between the performer and their parents.

As parents and coaches, we clearly have some standing, so we can expect our actions and interactions will condition kids' behaviour and shape how they think about the world. The implications of what we might be consciously or unconsciously communicating through our words and deeds are profound and extensive. It is worth pausing to think about what values we are instilling, what expectations we are creating, what behaviours we are incentivising and what beliefs we are reinforcing.

Given that our words and actions are liable to shape kids' attitudes and behaviours then we must strive to use this power for good. As coaches and parents we can wield our influence in a positive way by consciously striving to reinforce attitudes and behaviours that will serve them.

CONSIDERING MESSAGING…

In essence, we communicate our expectations through our words and actions. Our values are similarly expressed in how we react to different behaviours. In particular, kids are very attentive to what we praise and reward. It follows that we should be very considered in how we respond and intentional about what we praise and when.

To that end, it is worth taking a moment to define what is praiseworthy. A good starting point is to specify what virtues we want to promote and what behaviours we are seeking to reinforce. Compiling this list will require us to identify the attitudes and behaviours that will enable the individual to continue to learn and develop over time.

We should focus on things that are under the control of the individual or they have the power to influence. To that end, we should praise and reward things like effort and application. Importantly this instils a sense of agency. By communicating that these are the things we value, it also helps to engender these values in the young person. Individuals who apply themselves and give full attention and effort should be given the recognition and rewards that their efforts deserve, rather than showering attention on those who are blessed with innate talent or physical gifts bestowed via the genetic lottery.

Perhaps as a result of the positive parenting movement and related trends in coaching, there is a notion that it is good to be generous with praise and rewards. What this ignores is that how we dispense praise and rewards matters. Handing out gifts apropos nothing and irrespective of whether they are deserved often has a disruptive effect on kids' behaviour. Any parent who has observed how their kids respond to the largesse of a well-meaning relative (often a grand-parent) can attest to this!

We can expect that a scatter gun approach to dispensing rewards will similarly produce highly variable results. When we hand out gifts of praise and rewards for no particular reason, the young person will nevertheless be inclined to connect the dots and relate the reward to whatever event or behaviour was most recent. Any connection might be entirely spurious and purely coincidental. Clearly none of this is conducive to instilling particular values or reinforcing specific behaviours.

JUDICIOUS REWARDS...

Our approval should be conditional – and it should be conditioned on the right things. We should realise whenever we dispense rewards with our words or actions we are reinforcing something, whether it is a behaviour or a belief. Once we reckon with this reality, it follows that we need to be judicious with praise, rewards and other types of reinforcement. Positive reinforcement generally takes the form of rewards and praise. However, we can also influence future behaviour but choosing not to impose the expected penalties or withdrawing sanctions that have been imposed previously.

Praise and rewards are a prized commodity and should be treated as such if they are to retain their value. It follows that we must be careful and selective with our praise. We risk diminishing the value of rewards and praise when we dispense them too readily. This is especially true for coaches. We are not cheerleaders. I vividly recall watching a university basketball team going through their pre-game warm-up. The coaches were on the court and seemingly wanted to high-five every player after every shot, whether or not they made it. It made for uncomfortable viewing. The players were playing along but generally appeared bemused and many of these interactions looked very awkward, as if the players felt self-conscious and embarrassed on the coaches' behalf.

What, when and how are all important variables with praise and rewards. Offering praise and rewards for actions that take little effort or application sets the bar pretty low. We also need to be disciplined about withholding rewards until the specified preconditions are satisfied. Being too trigger happy and lax about the requirements weakens the incentive to meet the standards we have set out. This undermines the premise of the arrangement as well as our credibility as arbiters. Kids can reasonably conclude that there is no need to discipline themselves and meet the purported standard if the likelihood is that they will receive the reward in any case.

As for the 'when', in general, less is more. When rewards are received less frequently their impact tends to be greater and they are experienced as more meaningful. A variable reward schedule is famously much more potent as a means to reinforce behaviour. Constant praise, especially something vague and generic like 'good job', becomes noise that is barely registered.

Finally, how we give praise and rewards matters when it comes to reinforcing the right beliefs and behaviours. This includes how we articulate the reasons for rewards. Praise is most meaningful when it is specific. When offering praise, we should seek to call attention to precisely what they did that was praiseworthy. We should explain why it is important and how it will help them to be successful in the future.

Hopefully I have made the case for being discriminating, such that we reserve praise and rewards for instances when they are genuinely warranted. That said, it remains important that we notice when kids do things right. Often these are small or subtle things that are only discernible if we are paying close attention. It follows that we should be attentive. Indeed, attending to kids and giving recognition to the good things they do is reward in itself. Equally, we need to have a discerning eye. We should also take notice when young performers are inattentive, going through the motions or messing around.

It is said that the ultimate test of moral behaviour is what the individual does when nobody is watching. However, this is shaped by their experiences when somebody is watching. For young athletes, that somebody is the coach, their parents and hopefully their teachers.

STANDARDS SHAPE BEHAVIOUR...

In practice, our standards are defined by what we accept on a day-to-day basis. This is embodied not just in our actions but also our inaction. Failing to act or speak up constitutes tacit acceptance. There is a natural temptation to let things slide. In any given situation we can rationalise that it is not worth the hassle and decide to make an exception. There are costs to this. In every instance, we need to think about what message we are sending and how this will alter expectations moving forwards. Letting them get away with it effectively reinforces if not the behaviour itself then at the very least certain attitudes and beliefs regarding that behaviour. It implies that we are either not paying attention or it is not a big enough deal to comment on. Either way, the message is that it doesn't really matter.

If we are to reinforce the right behaviours – and uphold standards – then we need to consistently attend to behaviour and respond accordingly. Our duty as coaches is to exercise quality control, not only with technical execution but also practice behaviours in general. Just as we should encourage good habits, our disapproval should be evident when attention, effort, attitude and conduct are not up to standard. This does not necessarily mean handing out sanctions or punishment, but when they are sloppy, inattentive or otherwise misbehave during practice or competition it should at least be clear that it has been noticed. Kids are attentive to our reactions. A look or a raised eyebrow can send a clear message. Parents can support these efforts, as well keeping an eye on conduct away from athletic arena.

SUPPORTING KIDS' SENSE-MAKING...

The utility of an experience depends on the performer's ability to acknowledge and understand what occurred. As they reflect on events, the young athlete will need to parse the causal factors, attribute responsibility and identify the salient lessons. One of the ways we can serve performers is by lending some objectivity to their subjective experience. The conversations with those around them are an integral part of how the performer makes sense of events, think things through and elucidates what lessons to take.

The value derived from the trials that all young performers go through does depend upon the extent to which their perceptions and reflections after the event are grounded in reality. To that end, there is an onus on us to ensure that the performer maintains a healthy relationship with the truth and remains in touch with reality.

We should cultivate the habit of seeing the world as it is rather than how they might wish it to be. Confronting the present reality is a necessary first step to come up with viable solutions and find a way forwards. Being realistic about the present situation does not mean being pessimistic about the future. What we are aiming for is rational optimism rather than naïve optimism.

CANDOUR IS A SIGN OF CARE...

What we want to hear and what we need to hear do not always match up, and in some instances these are distinctly different things!

"A coach is someone who tells you what you don't want to hear, who has you see what you don't want to see, so you can be who you have always known you could be."

— Tom Landry

The terms *radical honesty* and *radical candour* have become popularised, which implies that honesty and candour are now deemed to be radical acts! The motivation for being less than truthful with another person is often to spare their feelings. Whilst this seems laudable on the surface, when we consider the longer-term consequences it becomes less so. It is also worth considering the possibility that another reason we choose to spare the other person from telling them the truth is that it is simply easier for us!

A vital and often overlooked aspect of tough love is the second part; it takes somebody who respects and cares about a person enough to tell them the truth. Sharing our honest opinion takes fortitude as it means accepting the risks and the blow-back that might ensue. Clearly it is far easier and poses much less personal cost to simply go along with what the other person is saying and play along even if we know it to be false or misguided.

Everybody involved needs to be clear that telling the performer truths that might be unwelcome or prompting them to confront the reality of the situation is a sign of respect and care, as opposed to being interpreted as being harsh or mean. Author Kim Scott describes a quadrant for feedback that has care for the other individual on one axis and on the other axis is willingness to challenge them [246]. What she terms 'radical candour' sits in the *high care* and *high willingness to challenge* quadrant. This is where coaches in particular should operate. Conversely, the trap that coaches and parents alike should avoid falling into is the *high care/low willingness to challenge* quadrant, which spares the performer's feeling in the short-term but ultimately does not serve them or help them achieve their sporting aspirations.

SHORT-TERM EASY; LONG-TERM HARD...

What seems expedient in the moment is often at odds with what will actually serve the long-term mission. There is always a temptation for the performer to go easy on themselves and ignore troubling facts.

"We optimise for short-term ego protection over long-term happiness"

— Shane Parrish

By extension, it is far easier to omit the truth to avoid the other person taking offence or becoming upset with us. Avoiding telling somebody an uncomfortable truth might spare ourselves from the awkwardness of doing so and perhaps the unpleasantness of their reaction but it certainly will not spare them from the eventual reckoning.

Ultimately, avoiding uncomfortable truths and choosing to overlook the reality of the situation only delays the inevitable. The longer the moment of reckoning is deferred, the more of a rude awakening it is likely to be. One of the things that makes competitive sport great but also uncomfortable at times is that it is unsparing. The young performer will be confronted with the reality when they step into the competitive arena, as any flaws and shortcomings will be ruthlessly exposed.

In this way, we are only setting them up for a bigger fall when the mighty wave that has been temporarily held back or steadfastly ignored comes crashing down. Rather than putting things off until to a point that it totally overwhelms them, it is far kinder and serves the performer far better to deal with reality in manageable doses on a regular basis.

PSYCHOLOGICAL SAFETY VERSUS 'SAFE SPACES'…

Psychological safety is an important concept for talent development and youth sports. Young performers should have a forum for expressing opinions, concerns and feedback to coaches and others without fear of reproach. However, somehow this concept has become misconstrued and has morphed into the idea of 'safe spaces', which bears very little resemblance to the original idea.

There is presently an odd preoccupation with subjectivity even when it comes to 'truth'. Such strange societal trends have led to a reticence to challenge or even question a person's beliefs on the grounds that 'their truth' is valid and beyond reproach. In this climate, 'safe spaces' describes a forum where the individual can be assured that whatever views they express will be accepted without challenge.

Whilst this might all be motivated by good intentions it is also entirely misguided. The policy of 'affirming' often amounts to reinforcing another person's delusion. Unfortunately, objective reality does exist and it cares little about our feelings or the particulars of the version of reality that exists in our own heads. As the grown-ups that performers look to for guidance we are failing in our duty of care when we allow the performer to delude themselves, or worse still participate in reinforcing the delusion.

To reiterate, psychological safety remains important such that young athletes feel able to give candid feedback to the grown-ups, with some confidence that it will be heard and assurance that there will not be any adverse consequences for doing so. Equally, this has to be a two-way commitment. Both parties need to voluntarily consent to giving and receiving candid and honest feedback, accepting that it might sometimes bruise their feelings.

Where the safe space idea does apply in talent development is creating and maintaining an environment where the performer has the freedom to try things, take risks and make errors. Equally even in this case they will nevertheless benefit from having their views challenged and being offered honest feedback.

TERMS OF REFERENCE…

From a development perspective clearly it is critical that both the performer and those who support them commit to prioritising long-term growth over short-term indulgence. Whatever we choose to share should be grounded in truth. If what we are telling them does not reflect reality then we are only setting them up for more pain down the road.

Earlier we underlined the importance of helping young performers to keep their ego in check; resisting the urge to protect fragile egos is an extension of this. Ego protection is arguably the biggest barrier to change and obstacle to future development. It is essential that not only the performer understands this; the grown-ups around them also need to have this realisation. A major tell that a performer or indeed a coach is heading for a fall is when they make public statements that indicate they are lying to themselves. This also suggests that those in the inner circle are failing to disabuse them of false notions, or else they are no longer paying attention to those around them.

The debrief that follows a competition and teachable moments in general should be conducted with frank honesty. We need to be able to specify the problem in order to set about solving it. Vague criticism is unhelpful from this perspective. Feedback must be specific in order to direct the performer towards what steps they need to take. Given the object of the exercise is to better equip the performer for future scenarios it follows we need to provide clarity on what specific actions and improvements are necessary.

Critical feedback is of course not easy to hear (albeit it does become easier with practice). It is however necessary if the performer wants to continue to develop and improve. It is also true that the hardest lessons have the most resonance and tend to prove pivotal in the performer's journey, albeit they need to be ready to heed them.

Success in this endeavour relies on clear expectations from the outset, which in turn requires explicit agreement from all parties with their fully informed consent. There need to be clear terms of reference for the mission and clear terms of engagement between each respective party (parent, coaches, performer) and each person needs to be comfortable that they have entered into this arrangement willingly (reserving the right to withdraw at a later date). A high degree of trust is required, which naturally takes time to develop.

COMMUNICATION STRATEGIES AND TACTICAL CONSIDERATIONS...

There has been some exploration of the public and private communication between parents and young performers surrounding their participation in organised youth sports. In addition to what parents yell from the side-lines, the content and quality of exchanges that occur outside the practice and competition arena are also highlighted, such as the car ride to and from competitions as well as debriefs and dinner table conversations at home.

Efforts to provide guidance and advice in this regard are somewhat thwarted by the fact that what is 'optimal' or most appropriate will naturally depend on a host of different variables, including individual temperament, the dynamics of the relationship and other situational factors. How kids interpret the verbal and non-verbal communication they receive varies markedly. Simply put, there are no 'one-size fits all' recommendations that are applicable with all individuals or appropriate in all situations.

What young performers are seeking will depend on their temperament and their attitude towards their own participation in sport. It is important that we take into account their aspirations in sport (as opposed to what aspirations we might have for them!). Clearly a young performer who is driven by the dream of competing at the highest level will have a very different perspective to one of their peers who is participating for enjoyment and social reasons.

Clearly it is crucial to allow for such individual differences; nevertheless, we can offer some general guidelines. Young performers do not appreciate parents being dismissive or derogatory about the opposition prior to the contest. Negative comments from the side-lines are likewise not generally welcomed by performers [231]. Critique that is given in the spirit of helping the young performer to become better trumps criticism that is framed in purely negative terms.

Most young athletes consider comments and feedback regarding effort and attitude to be appropriate parental input [231]. Words of encouragement and expressions of support from parents are naturally also generally well received. That said, it is most impactful to comment on specific actions relating to effort ('great hustle') and intention ('nice idea'), whereas vague and constant praise ('good job!!') can seem inauthentic such that it becomes white noise. Interviews with young performers indicate that whilst they do not want their parents to be haranguing them from the side-lines, they also do not want them to act like a crazed fan.

TIME AND PLACE...

It is important that we exercise judgement in what we choose to share and when, especially during times when the young performer is emotionally raw and more prone to being affected by a careless word or gesture. Clearly there is a time and a place.

Aside from being hugely significant figures in the young performer's life, parents are likewise often present during the emotionally charged moments before, during and after competition. We should be considered and selective in sharing only what might be useful or helpful for them to hear in the context of the situation. There are also frequent occasions where the best approach is to give the performer some space.

The 'when' also has a bearing on the 'what'. Time and place will determine what is most appropriate and best received [247]. For instance, when they are competing young performers are not generally looking for technical or tactical input from their parent [248]. Conversely, they might be amenable to hearing this type of advice or feedback in a different setting, depending on whether or not the young athlete views their parent as a credible authority who is qualified to be providing coaching input!

More generally, timing is key and it pays read the situation and find the most favourable moment. Tact and judgement are called for. At times performers are eager to talk (or vent), whereas in other instances it is best to give them some space.

Oftentimes we will find performers are more open to having in-depth discussion or receiving feedback later on, once they have had some time to decompress and process events. We should also respect that at times they simply might not want to talk about it. For instance, when performers are nervous prior to a big competition the event and sport in general might be the last thing they want to talk about. At such times it can be better to keep the conversation light and fun.

Parents are generally pretty good at reading their kids and being attuned to how they are feeling. All the same, if we are unsure about their preferences on these matters we should perhaps just ask them!

ON THE WAY TO AND FROM PRACTICES AND COMPETITION...

The day of the competition and the car rides to and from the venue are good examples of times when we need to give special consideration to how we interact and communicate with young athletes. Whilst it can be an opportunity to connect with athletes, the car journey has some particular challenges. The necessity of keeping our eyes on the road limits our ability to attend to non-verbal cues!

How we speak to young athletes at these times matters more than usual. A study observing parent-child interactions on the way to tournaments found questioning that was interpreted as the parent talking at the young athlete and telling them what they should do was typically met with resistance [249]. Young athletes tend to disengage when parents try to present themselves as an authority on matters relating to the sport. During these times we should consider whether kids want us acting in the role of self-appointed coach versus simply being their parent.

In terms of the 'how', it is typically best to avoid jumping in and telling them what we think. In general, it is better to begin by engaging the young performer in conversation and encouraging them to speak, not least so we can gauge how they are doing and get a better sense of what they need from us. Effectively this amounts to asking questions and giving them an opportunity to speak before we offer our own opinions.

How we ask questions is however important from this standpoint. To illustrate the point, a research investigation that employed video recordings of the car ride to and from competition found that the parents studied tended to default to closed questions with a simple yes/no answer, which often results in stilted, awkward and one-sided exchanges [250]. A better strategy to entice them into conversation is to use neutral open-ended questions that invite the young performer to share their thoughts and reflections.

Aside from being a more engaging way to get the conversation flowing, this treats the young athlete as an equal in the exchange [249]. Of course, this works best when these questions are asked in a genuine spirit of being interested in hearing what they have to say. One of the ways that overexuberant parents tend to trip up is by interjecting with their own thoughts before the young performer has finished expressing what they think.

As well as inviting the young perform to speak it pays to *offer* feedback, providing them the option to agree or decline to hear what we have to say. This is generally a good strategy, not least because the simple act of giving the green light automatically makes them more receptive to hearing what we have to say, as compared to simply being presented with unsolicited feedback.

MESSAGE AND MESSENGER...

There is room to be strategic not only with respect to the message we convey but also the messenger we employ to impart this information. A friend of mine was a master of using others as the conduit for communicating certain messages to his kids. Especially once they became teenagers Larry would regularly enlist somebody his kids held in high esteem to convey whatever advice or piece of wisdom that he wished them to hear, knowing it would be better received that way (or at least less likely to be dismissed).

In my own experience, what many of the parents of young athletes I work with most appreciate is that their kids trust and listen to me – and often what I am telling them is essentially repeating what their parents have tried to convey but met with resistance! Funnily enough, this scenario is particularly common with teenager performers. A coach, a mentor or even an older athlete that the young performer looks up to can be an effective conduit for communicating messages that the parents endorse. Naturally it is crucial that the coach or anybody else advising the young performer on matters of importance is doing so with parental approval. Beyond consent, for this collaborative approach to work to best effect it is likewise important that we establish clear expectations and defined boundaries from the outset.

Key Take-Home Messages

1. Words and actions condition behaviour. What parents and coaches say, reward, ignore, or tolerate shapes young athletes' beliefs, values, and expectations—often more powerfully than intended.

2. Praise and rewards reinforce something every time they are given; if poorly targeted, they reinforce the wrong things.

3. Constant, vague, or indiscriminate praise quickly loses value and credibility.

4. Standards are defined by what we accept. Inaction or silence is interpreted as approval and becomes the de facto standard.

5. Development depends on sound sense-making. Young athletes need help interpreting experiences accurately in order to learn from them.

6. Candour is a sign of care. Avoiding difficult truths may feel kind in the short term but ultimately undermines growth and resilience.

7. Psychological safety does not mean freedom from challenge. Supportive environments must still confront reality, challenge false beliefs, and encourage accountability.

8. Timing and delivery matter as much as content. Even true messages can be harmful or ineffective if delivered at the wrong time or in the wrong way.

9. Short-term comfort often conflicts with long-term development.

10. Growth requires resisting ego protection in favour of realistic, constructive feedback.

Practical Tips

✓ Be intentional with praise— consider what belief or behaviour you are reinforcing.

✓ Vague criticism is unhelpful – feedback must be specific in order to be actionable

✓ Treat praise and rewards as valuable currency—less frequent, well-earned praise has more impact.

✓ Notice and acknowledge small, often overlooked positive behaviours, not just standout moments.

✓ Help athletes reflect honestly by discussing what actually happened, why it happened, and what can be learned.

✓ Help kids to understand what psychological safety actually means – that is, the freedom to share honest feedback without fear of reproach

✓ Choose the right moment for feedback—avoid emotionally raw situations immediately before or after competition.

✓ Separate ego as far as possible but do not allow kids to let the urge to protect their ego to impede their progress

✓ Use open-ended questions to facilitate conversation and encourage sharing.

✓ Consider if a different messenger (coach, mentor, role model) would be more effective.

Action Items

» Audit your praise: Over the next week, note what you praise and ask whether it aligns with long-term development.

» Define your standards: Write down the behaviours you expect (effort, attention, conduct) and commit to consistently reinforcing them.

» Instil the principle 'do not lie', especially to themselves

» Enter into an agreement to serve as an 'accountability partner' for your child

» Normalise honest feedback: Make it clear that truthfulness is an expression of care, not criticism.

» Agree on terms of engagement: Establish shared expectations around feedback, honesty, and long-term priorities between parent, coach, and athlete.

» Respect time and place: Defer feedback when emotions are high and revisit when the athlete is more ready to hear it.

» Strive to operate in the high care/high readiness to challenge quadrant!

A Tool for Parents: The 5 C's Framework to Guide Conduct and Communication

Perhaps the most practically useful tool to guide sport parents' interactions with young athletes presented to date is Chris Harwood's *5 C's framework* [251]. This was originally developed for coaches and subsequently field-tested, notably in the applied setting of an elite (soccer) football academy [236], with the involvement of both parents and coaches.

The framework provides five foci for parents to help direct their communication and conduct towards their child in relation to their participation in youth sport, with the intention of reinforcing key behaviours:

Commitment – diligence, effort and time invested in their own participation in sport and other priorities (notably schoolwork)

Communication – giving attention to the quality of their interaction with fellow athletes (notably team-mates), coaches and parents

Concentration – being dialled in when receiving instruction, during practice, when performing

Confidence – willingness to express themselves, courage to try things and not withdraw when things are not going their way

Control – self-discipline, regulating emotions and behaviour under challenging conditions

Equipping the Performer for the Journey

Cultivating Courage, Grit and Resiliency in Young Performers

Virtues and assets like courage, perseverance and resilience are developed through action. The idea that courage is something that can be developed may be a revelation to many kids and perhaps even some parents! Perseverance is also as much a matter of inclination and choice as anything else. Resilience is also not simply an innate quality but is rather a property that emerges as a result of successfully weathering difficulties and coming through trials. It follows that we can and should help young athletes to purposefully cultivate these qualities as they progress on their youth sports journey.

WHAT BRAVERY IS...

For coaches and parents seeking to teach kids to practice bravery, a necessary starting point is to help them to understand what courage is. Kids often imagine that those who are brave are fearless or free from doubt. This is not the case. Real bravery is experiencing fear, doubt and even dread but nevertheless opting to proceed. We cannot extinguish fear or doubt. But through our actions we can become braver.

'I learned that courage was not the absence of fear, but the triumph over it. The brave man is not he who does not feel afraid, but he who conquers that fear.'

– Nelson Mandela

The process by which we cultivate courage is counterintuitive. On the face of it, things that make us apprehensive or appear threatening would seem to be best avoided. Where dragons roam the sensible option would seem to be to hide away somewhere safe and hope that the danger passes us by. But of course, fortune favours the brave. Rather than cowering, it is the courageous individual who opts to go forth and seek out the dragon in its lair who wins out. Such acts of courage are rewarded, if not with treasure then in other ways, not least helping the protagonist to become more assured and powerful.

Moral virtues such as courage are a matter of habit or persistent patterns of behaviour. What this means is that courage can be cultivated through our actions. If we act with courage on a consistent basis we can make ourselves more courageous as a result. Moreover, regular practice of courage turns out to transfer to other realms. To use a specific example, acting with courage in the realm of sport can help kids to become more courageous in other aspects of their lives.

BEING A HERO...

Children have a natural affinity for tales of heroes – our four-year old son is obsessed with the Marvel universe. As kids become older, we should encourage them to assume the role of hero in their own story. The youth sports journey can serve as their adventure or heroic quest. Initially this can seem a stretch, as they may not perceive themselves to be heroic or courageous. What we should point out is that any hero's story is a tale of transformation. The hero does not start out as a hero but becomes one by the end of the story as a result of the trials he or she goes through on their quest and the acts of courage they perform along the way.

It is widely recognised that sport helps kids to build confidence. What is often overlooked is this applies especially in adolescence. This is the time in our lives when we are at our most self-conscious and sensitive to social judgement. One of the reasons Spiderman resonates so much is that he is an improbable hero, being a scrawny kid who is largely rejected by high school society. It is worth pointing out that many of sports stars were similarly unassuming figures in their youth.

Whilst they might not be battling super villains, youth sports journey provides ample exposure to trials and tribulations. As such, it also offers abundant opportunities to become braver. When they opt to take these opportunities, kids develop a more favourable impression of themselves.

As an aside, this is the way to cultivate genuine self-esteem. If we want kids to have a robust sense of self-worth, they should seek to become an admirable person and act accordingly. In other words, we should encourage them to venture forth and valiantly strive to achieve their highest aspirations. Simply put, genuine self-regard comes from attempting things that would make them worthy of esteem in their own eyes and in the eyes of others.

Competitive sport demands a degree of bravery, even (or perhaps especially) at youth level. We should acknowledge the courage it takes to engage in competition. Depending on the sport there can be an element of physical courage but arguably more notable is the courage required to confront fears and grapple with insecurities. For a start, entering into the contest means accepting the possibility of losing. Even school competition and low stakes junior tournaments involve putting fledgling egos on the line, as young performers subject themselves to the scrutiny of onlookers and social judgement.

Rather than focussing on the outcome of the contest or how they performed on the day, we should celebrate kids simply for volunteering to participate in the contest. Whether they win or lose, the act of stepping into the arena in itself elevates them above those on the sidelines.

It is important that parents and youth sport coaches likewise acknowledge and incentivise courageous behaviour within the arena. We should encourage young performers to be the person who puts their hand up during the decisive moments in the contest rather than shrinking into the background. We should also praise kids for having the courage to try things and take the game to the opposition rather than playing it safe. Whether it comes off or not, the willingness to be inventive, to be bold and express themselves are courageous traits that are worth reinforcing.

INTO THE UNKNOWN...

The journey requires the young performer and those who support them to navigate the unknown and the unexpected. Reaching the highest level (and remaining there) demands initiative, problem solving skills, judgement, decision-making and reflection to support adaptive behaviour. In effect we should be seeking to prepare young athletes to be adaptable and unfazed when faced with the unexpected.

On an individual level a performer's level of comfort with uncertainty depends on several factors, including their temperament. No performer is entirely immune from feeling apprehensive. It is somewhat discomfiting when there are so many unknowns and questions that remain unresolved as they prepare. It is quite natural for there to be some apprehension as they contemplate stepping into the arena. What we want to avoid as far as possible is a situation where the performer feels entirely overwhelmed. Once again, the best way to do this is to cultivate a sense that they are equipped and prepared to cope with whatever the situation might throw at them.

When unexpected outcomes occur, we need to help performers foster the habit of being intrigued about what they might discover and curious about how they might go about solving the problem, rather than reflexively responding with disappointment or frustration. The scenario should pique our interest and inspire fascination. The challenge of a puzzle to solve is motivating.

FRAMING MATTERS...

With kids in general and aspiring young performers in particular there is often a need to change how they view things that make them apprehensive or fearful. When the prospect of doing something seems daunting it is a good sign that it is a worthy challenge. It is the very things that test our mettle that prove to be worth pursuing and bring the greatest benefits. Scenarios that young performers might otherwise perceive to be threatening or anxiety-inducing can be represented as challenges and opportunities that might bring rewards and advance them along their journey.

The ability to reappraise scenarios that might provoke anxiety and learn to reframe them in a way that better serves, also changes how they are able to engage. Trials that stretch the limits of their abilities can start to be perceived as (positively) challenging rather than cause for trepidation.

We can also help kids to reframe how they relate to conditions of pressure. What thoughts and emotions are elicited depend not only on our interpretation of the situation but also how we choose to approach it. Returning to the dragon example, when we choose to go towards the threat and seek out the thing that frightens us of our own accord, this changes everything (even down to the physiological response that is elicited). By choosing to voluntarily engage on our own terms we have the power to transform the situation into a challenge that beckons rather than threat that looms. We can take this a step further and encourage aspiring young performers to actively seek out scenarios that make them apprehensive and purposely use them for sparring practice.

EXPOSURE THERAPY…

Exposure therapy is the practice of providing opportunities for an individual to face their fears in a graduated and systematic fashion – for instance, somebody who is scared of spiders might first be shown a picture of a spider and over time progress to actually handling a live spider. The important part is that this is done voluntarily. The individual remains in control: they not only choose to participate, but they are also able to set the terms, such that they proceed of their own volition and at their own pace.

In the context of sport this would begin with exposure to conditions of uncertainty and pressure during practice. Whilst we can and should attempt to recreate the competition experience in a practice environment, the best way to prepare the performer to manage the stressors encountered in the competition arena is by competing. To that end, we can intentionally use minor competitions for specific competition preparation. The objective of these lesser trials is to inoculate the athlete against negative aspects of stress by intentionally exposing them to challenge and stressful situations under lower stakes conditions.

Exposure therapy does not necessarily make people less afraid, but what it does do is make them braver. Nevertheless, the prospect of doing something is also typically far more daunting than the reality. To use a metaphor, it is better to seek out the dragon in its lair and engage it on our own terms than to wait for it to come for us. Choosing to confront a situation that induces fear and anxiety robs it of much of is power. Indeed, even if the worst-case scenario does come to pass, at the very least the performer will discover that the sky has not fallen in and the sun still rises the next day, teaching them the important lesson that most experiences are survivable! Over time performers may come to relish these experiences for the opportunities they afford to test themselves and become better prepared for whatever they might face in the future.

Once again, all of this needs to be done with the full consent and approval of the performer; it needs to be something they need to enter into willingly. The first step towards mastery is choosing to confront the situation. The key ingredient in this alchemy is that they must do so voluntarily.

SHIFTING PERCEPTIONS ABOUT NERVES PRIOR TO PERFORMING...

Learning how to handle nerves and deal with anxiety when performing is an important capability for any performer. The ability to perform on the big stage and execute under pressure naturally becomes more important as a young athlete advances and moves up to higher levels of competition.

Anxiety is a natural and somewhat necessary part of being an elite athlete and indeed for athletes who seek to excel at any level. By definition there is uncertainty in the outcome; but of course, if the outcome was certain, this would rob the endeavour of its meaning. Similarly, athletes care deeply about performing well, and the prospect of failing to do so naturally causes disquiet. Once again, this is an integral part of striving to excel. If the outcome didn't matter to us, and there was nothing on the line, there would be very little drive to engage in competitive sport.

So we have established that being anxious to perform and mindful of the stakes involved is part of striving to excel in sport! It is important for aspiring performers to realise and accept that this is the case. Indeed, the message that it is normal and natural to experience nerves is reassuring to many athletes.

We often have a perception that elite athletes are not affected by anxiety, and this is a fallacy. Those who appear at ease on the big occasion and successfully perform under pressure have simply learned to manage what is an integral part of competing as an athlete. To paraphrase Mark Twain, courage is not the absence of fear but mastery over it.

GRACE UNDER PRESSURE...

With the increasing spotlight on mental health among high profile athletes, it has been proposed that we should attempt to ameliorate stress with various accommodations. Often this amounts to trying to downplay the importance of the event or suggesting that the outcome does not really matter. I would argue that this is entirely the wrong approach. We should rather acknowledge the crucible of competition for what it is – something that exists to test the mettle of the athlete. In doing so, we can encourage young athletes to relish the competitive aspect of sport for the opportunity it presents to challenge themselves.

'Get the butterflies in your stomach flying in formation'

– Attributed to golfing great Jack Nicklaus

How we appraise whatever situation we face has a huge bearing on how we experience it and what feelings of stress are elicited. What perspective we adopt shapes what emotions and mental turmoil (or lack of) we feel as a result. For example, we can either appraise a situation as a threat, as a challenge, or as an opportunity. The thought processes and emotions we feel as we anticipate and go through an experience will be very different in each scenario, simply as a result of how we perceive what is an identical situation.

Given how malleable our perception is, it is possible to hack the process simply by reframing both how we view prospective events and how we interpret the sensations we feel in our body. The same physical 'symptoms' can be experienced as either anxiety or excitement, depending on our internal narrative and what interpretation we choose to apply.

We can seek to equip performers to regulate themselves so that they can harness this nervous energy, so that it no longer distracts or detracts from performing. Most of these tools likewise come into play away from the competition arena, not least during the days and weeks prior to a big event as young performers contemplate the prospect.

All that said, the likelihood of perceiving a situation as a challenge rather than a threat often comes down to whether the performers feels that they are up to the challenge. *Coping self-efficacy* is the term used to describe the performer's sense that they are equipped to handle whatever challenges they might face in the sporting realm [252]. If the performer feels that they have the resources to cope they are more likely to feel positively about the prospect.

Finally, one of most effective ways to foster the habit of acting with courage is to surround yourself with courageous people. Here again, youth sport offers kids a rich environment where they can associate with other courageous individuals who choose to step into the arena rather than being part of the crowd who opt to stay on the sidelines.

IN FOR THE LONG HAUL...

The journey is long, particularly for those who aspire to reach the elite level. The capacity to stay the course and the ability to bounce back after setbacks are accordingly crucial. Over recent years talent identification in sport has begun to acknowledge and account for the importance of determination and ability to persist in the face of challenges [253]. The merits of 'grit' are increasingly championed and a common debate is how we might develop resiliency and mental fortitude in young performers.

Grit is described as the ability to persevere through difficulties and continue striving towards the ultimate aim. Beyond talent, achieving excellence in any domain requires persistence in interest and effort [254]. Along with the ability to persevere, it is also crucial that performers are able to resist the allure of short-term rewards or succumb to other influences that might divert them from their ultimate aim. In the digital era this has become perhaps the biggest obstacle.

The concept of *grit* captures each of these elements. Of the three factors used to define character (intellectual, inter-personal and intra-personal), grit relates to the *intra-personal* element. Grit concerns the internal dialogue we have with ourselves and our internal decision-making process that steers our behaviours, including what we choose to act on and how much of ourselves we choose to invest in the endeavour.

More specifically, grit is a personality trait that leads an individual to invest in hard work and pursue long-term goals with sustained zeal. Ratings of grit are accordingly predictive of long-term success in different domains, notably sport. The underpinning elements of grit include motivation and the meaning that we ascribe to our chosen quest. A deeper sense of meaning not only fuels motivation but also alters how young performers respond to challenge and difficulty.

The talent development journey is a prime example of delayed gratification – by definition, the reward of fulfilling a long-term aspiration will only arrive an unspecified number of years in the future. Moreover, if the aspiration is ambitious enough then success is far from assured, meaning there is a chance that the reward may not come at all. Crucially grit encompasses the drive to selectively engage and invest effort in purposeful actions oriented towards long-term outcomes, in preference to whatever other opportunities for instant gratification that might be on offer. Once again, it is immediately obvious how this might be useful for young performers!

THE VALUE OF RESILIENCY...

"Fall down seven times, stand up eight"

– Japanese proverb

Sports are a metaphor for life. I do not subscribe to the view that every kid should receive a participation medal and that we should not keep score in games. Rather we should recognise the benefits of sports for the rich emotional experience they provide for learning important life lessons and acquiring key coping skills. The virtue of perseverance is one of the higher values that kids can take from sport, albeit parents have a role in helping them to learn this.

Clearly it is important that aspiring performers are not easily put off, so that short-term failures or disappointments do not derail their progress and lead them to become demotivated and dispirited. When we speak of resiliency, what we are specifically talking about is the ability to respond positively and the fortitude to bounce back following setbacks.

A great perspective shared by Justin Langer (former head coach for the Australian men's cricket team) is that when he looks back on the darkest periods of his playing and coaching career he does so fondly, as these times proved invaluable and had the biggest impact in making him a better player and coach, respectively. What these insights reveal is that the trials and setbacks experienced by young performers are an essential and highly valuable part of the journey. More specifically, these obstacles and challenges afford the opportunity to acquire and develop resiliency.

Under the right conditions, a young person's participation in organised youth sports can provide a rich context for developing resilience. The trials and struggles that are part of the journey teach young athletes to anticipate challenges and prepare accordingly, as well as learning to be adaptable and respond appropriately in the face of unforeseen difficulties. The motivational climate that surrounds the young performer's participation and the behaviour modelled by coaches, parents, and peers help to shape these lessons.

Of course it is not quite this simple. It is important to realise that it is not sufficient to simply go through hard times. The events themselves are neutral; it all depends on how the individual chooses to respond. The enduring effects of these experiences on the performer might be positive but they can equally be negative. Clearly a decisive factor in determining how we look back on events is whether we ultimately prevail!

Parents are an important source of support and direction when the young athlete inevitably experiences setbacks and makes mistakes. With appropriate guidance we can help young performers take advantage of the opportunities to develop resiliency that come from experiencing failure in the sports realm. The intense emotions that are elicited similarly creates a great learning environment for developing the various facets of emotional intelligence. What can make the difference between positive adaptive responses and unfavourable aversive responses is how the athlete learns to anticipate and interpret what are emotionally charged but also very rich experiences. Once again, this is something that parents and coaches can help with.

RATIONAL OPTIMISM...

"Nothing in life was set in stone and nothing in life is promised us..."

— Faith Hunter

It is important that expectations reflect life's realities. Some wisdom that my dad passed down to me was along the lines 'nobody said life was fair'. It is also true that unfairness is not always evenly distributed.

It would serve aspiring performers well to cultivate some stoicism when contemplating setbacks. It is important to realise that there is no cosmic conspiracy against them. When things don't go their way this is no cause to feel picked on.

Feeling aggrieved or having a chip on their shoulder certainly won't serve them moving forwards.

A trap that some fall into is to view life as something that happens to them. The notion that we are at the mercy of fate or external forces beyond our control is not only disempowering but also absolves the individual of any responsibility. None of which is helpful if we wish to turn our present situation around or indeed achieve anything in the future.

Accepting that life is not always fair and the possibility that misfortunes will befall them from time to time does not mean that they cannot be optimistic about the future. A big part of this is feeling assured in their ability to cope with whatever life might throw at them. To come full circle, this assurance is acquired through the experience of doing hard things and going through difficult times.

The journey to achieving any long-term goal comprises a long series of choices. This is a good definition of achievement: the cumulative result of the choices made and actions taken over an extended period. More fundamentally, any young person is in the process of becoming and their choices and actions change them.

"The best way out is always through."

— Robert Frost

Certain situations are more formative than others and how they choose to act at these moments will prove decisive. Such instances include how they choose to proceed when faced with a daunting prospect, whether they choose to withdraw or tackle problems head on, how they choose to respond following setbacks. In each scenario, they will emerge as a different person according to what path they choose. With our guidance they can become braver, more tenacious and more resilient through their actions over time.

Key Take-Home Messages

1. Courage is not the absence of fear; it is choosing to act despite fear, doubt, or uncertainty.

2. Courage is a habit that can be cultivated through repeated action, not a fixed personality trait.

3. Sport provides a powerful training ground for courage, particularly during adolescence when self-consciousness and sensitivity to judgement are highest.

4. Stepping into the arena matters more than the outcome; participation itself is a courageous act worthy of recognition.

5. How pressure is framed shapes how it is experienced — threat, challenge, or opportunity lead to very different responses.

6. Voluntary exposure to difficulty builds bravery; avoidance strengthens fear, while chosen engagement weakens it.

7. Nerves and anxiety are normal and necessary when striving to perform well; elite performers manage them rather than eliminate them.

8. Grit reflects sustained commitment to long-term goals, combining sustained effort, persistence of interest, and resistance to short-term distractions.

9. Resilience is built through setbacks, provided young athletes are supported to interpret and respond to them constructively.

10. Parents and coaches strongly shape meaning-making. Their reactions influence whether difficulty becomes growth-producing or discouraging.

11. Character is formed through the cumulative effect of choices made and actions taken, especially the choices and actions taken under challenging conditions.

Practical Tips

✓ Praise acts of bravery (e.g. trying something new, putting themselves forward).

✓ Reinforce the idea that courage grows through action, not confidence first.

✓ Help athletes reframe pressure as a challenge or opportunity rather than a threat.

✓ Normalise nerves by explaining that even elite performers experience anxiety.

✓ Teach athletes to interpret physical sensations (butterflies, tension) as readiness or excitement.

✓ Create graduated exposure to pressure in training (e.g. small competitions, constraints, decision-making under fatigue).

✓ Ensure exposure is voluntary with performers retaining a sense of control.

✓ Emphasise long-term goals over short-term results.

✓ Help young performers reflect on setbacks as learning opportunities, not personal failures.

✓ Avoid rescuing athletes too quickly from disappointment; allow space for emotional processing.

Action Items

» Educate kids on what courage is, explaining that bravery means acting despite fear, not feeling fearless.

» Model courage by showing calm, constructive responses to uncertainty, mistakes and setbacks.

» Help kids to cultivate pride in their ability to pick themselves up and bounce back after setbacks – 'Fall down seven times, stand up eight'.

» Enlist the coaches in a shared commitment to cultivate courage and persistence, ensuring these behaviours are consistently reinforced.

Getting Things Wrong: Making New and Better Mistakes

Much of what I do as a coach involves helping individuals to acquire new skills and coaching them to move in ways that differ to what they are accustomed to. When we attempt something new or try out a different way of doing things we naturally do not get it right first time or every time. Learning, relearning or refining skills means having a go – and in turn getting it wrong with some regularity! Not everybody enjoys going through these trials but they are nevertheless a feature of the process.

Full disclosure: during my younger days playing sport I was more prone than most to losing the plot when I wasn't performing to my own expectations or picking things up as quickly as I felt I should be. It is fair to say I would fairly regularly throw my toys out of the pram and spit out my dummy. Whilst I have acquired wisdom along the way (and I do a better job since becoming a coach), I very much identify with performers who struggle with being Zen as they intently strive to meet their own high standards in their quest to develop and improve.

DARING GREATLY AND ACCEPTING THE POSSIBILITY OF FALLING SHORT...

Growth requires a willingness to put oneself in situations that have a significant probability of failure. For young athletes to develop there needs to be a readiness to step up to higher level competition and be exposed to environments with more accomplished athletes, which inevitably means feeling a little out of their depth. In these scenarios it is reasonable to expect that the young performer's limitations might be exposed – indeed this is the point of the exercise. Likewise, when they enter a contest with a stronger opponent, there is the distinct possibility that they might lose. Whilst these might be chastening experiences, it is the cost of doing business and young performer must accept these terms if they are to derive the benefits.

Even under more routine conditions sometimes things do not go as expected. This is the nature of competitive sport. Any loss tends to sting and having their faults exposed will tend to bruise young egos, especially when they were expecting to win. All the same, this should not be cause for consternation. Rather than feeling discouraged or despondent, the appropriate response is to be intrigued about what insights this offers. When events unfold in a way that is contrary to our expectations this reveals a gap in our understanding and provides valuable information. Unpalatable as they might be, these surprises are gifts that allow the young athlete to become aware of vulnerabilities and shortcomings, such that they can equip themselves and avoid being blindsided at a later date when it might prove more consequential.

"Only those who dare to fail greatly can ever achieve greatly."

— Robert F. Kennedy

Beyond a readiness to try and fail on a day-to-day basis, we need to accept that the bigger our ultimate aspiration might be, the higher the odds that we might not be successful in the endeavour. The magnitude of the challenge and the probability of falling short are to be emphasised rather than glossed over; this is what makes the quest aspirational! If the goal was easy to attain and success is assured, the endeavour would lack any real meaning. Naturally, we venture forth and persist through setbacks in the hope is that we will ultimately prevail, but this is far from guaranteed – that is the source of the appeal.

GETTING IT WRONG IS INTEGRAL TO THE PROCESS OF RAISING OUR GAME…

Getting it wrong is an inevitability when pushing towards the limits of our present capabilities. Conversely, if we find we are getting everything right every time, the odds are we are operating so far within our limits that very little growth can be expected. Pushing the envelope or adding to our repertoire of skills means getting out of our comfort zone and spending time doing things that challenge us. As we push the boundaries of our present capabilities, naturally we will fail at various points in the process. The model for improvement is this: try; fail; fail better, again and again until we ultimately succeed. Then we promptly move onto the next height and repeat the process.

If a young athlete aspires to perform at the highest level, they must be ready to extend themselves and expand their capabilities, which inevitably means failed attempts and imperfect execution as they struggle to get to grips with things. In fact, this also applies when a young performer is simply seeking improve upon their personal best, whatever their present competitive level or sporting aspirations.

Part of what separates the best performers is that they have different practice habits to the rest. Whilst mediocre athletes choose to practise what they are already good at, the best opt to spend that time working on weaknesses [255], meaning that they are likely to commit more errors during practice rather than less.

In other words, continual improvement means getting it wrong to varying degrees on an ongoing basis! Naturally, this can be particularly hard for driven individuals who set high standards for themselves. Nevertheless, achieving those high aspirations means pushing into territory where will get it wrong more often and pushing ourselves to practise what we are not good at.

All of this can present a problem if we are not able to get our mind around it. For some the experience can elicit negative emotions, to such a level that they abort the learning process or even give up participating entirely. Clearly we need to revise our thinking in how we relate to errors and make our peace with getting it wrong.

NO PROGRESS WITHOUT FAILURE…

As the saying goes, there is no success without struggle. The fear of making mistakes can become disabling, particularly if our aim is to try something new or different. It follows that we need to reframe how we think about making errors so that learning and development are not constrained by the desire to not get it wrong.

"The greatest mistake we make is living in constant fear that we will make one"

— John C. Maxwell

The road to learning and improving is littered with mistakes and failed attempts. Our early attempts as we embark on the learning process will inevitably be imperfect. Even once we become proficient, every attempt is far from perfect. Whilst we might see the feats of athleticism and skill that stars of the sport execute on the big stage, what we don't see are all the failed attempts in practice on their way to achieving those heights.

Even the most accomplished of performers still struggle at times. This is the case particularly during the early stages of learning or transitioning to a new way of doing things. As I am fond of telling athletes I work with for any length of time, even when you become a pro or an Olympian I will always be able to pick out something that can be improved!

The sport of high jump (likewise pole vault) is notable in that whatever the competition ultimately every competitor in the field fails. The winner is simply the person who fails at the highest height. There are lessons here that apply beyond track and field athletics.

EXPLORING PROBLEMS AND SOLUTIONS...

Mistakes have a bad rap. We learn nothing without errors. Trial and error are fundamental to our discovery process. From this perspective, mistakes are nothing but data points that help to inform our approach moving forwards. For anybody familiar with the game battleships, the misses just tell us where the other players ships are not located.

Trial and error is both a route to solutions and part of the discovery process where we establish the limits and explore the problem-solving space we are working in. Making errors is how we find out about the world; it is also how we learn about whatever puzzle we are trying to solve.

Trial and error-based exploration yields information on the constraints and boundaries of the problem space we are operating in. As we stray into uncharted territory mistakes are inevitable; then again, these same mistakes reveal information that was previously unknown to us. In this context mistakes represent discoveries.

"I have not failed. I've just found ten thousand ways that won't work"

— Thomas A. Edison

Making errors is also part of how we trial potential solutions. Attempting anything new or different carries the attendant possibility that we might fail in the attempt. The quest to be creative and innovative in our problem solving likewise necessitates the freedom and willingness to try new and different things. If we stay within the narrow confines of what we already know we will never find out what is (and what isn't) possible.

Creators and innovators speak of *failing forwards*. This principle applies whether we are seeking to explore new questions or find different solutions to existing problems. When stepping into the unknown and trying new things it is inevitable that we will make mistakes. In fact, making mistakes is an integral part of the process.

FIGURING IT OUT TO ALTER OUR DEFAULT RESPONSE...

From a coach's perspective it is always interesting and quite informative how different individuals respond to making mistakes. At times it is a struggle and on occasion this can be source of frustration. I have found this to be universal with any athlete, regardless of sport, age, or competition level. When things go awry, our default response can be either positive (and adaptive) or negative. The latter obstructs the overall mission of improving and developing. Rather than responding to mistakes negatively we should rather seek to use them.

There is often a need to manage and reframe expectations – particularly for those who have a tendency towards perfectionism. We are not looking for flawless; this is not something we should be aspiring to. Striving to improve and push the boundaries of our present capabilities means things will get messy. Flawless preparation generally means underwhelming performance in competition. We might be aiming for flawless execution when it matters (at the pinnacle event) – but practice remains the time and place where we can and should be trying things and making mistakes.

In recent times the fixed versus growth mindset idea has become somewhat laboured. However, a useful and important take away from Carol Dweck's work is how individuals classed as having a 'growth mindset' differ in how they entertain errors and how they respond [256]. Having faith that ability is not fixed, such that there is scope to become better, is a prerequisite. These fundamental beliefs determine the individual's default response and affect the likelihood that they will persevere and remain engaged with figuring out the puzzle, versus becoming dejected and giving up. It follows that we should start here and make sure that kids are not labouring under faulty assumptions and self-limiting beliefs.

Fear of getting it wrong is the other major barrier we need to overcome. Changing their interpretation is key to altering the young performer's perception, so they can engage in a more beneficial way. A mistake should not be taken as a reflection on the individual (or at least not a negative one). There is no good reason why a failed attempt should elicit negative emotions. It should certainly not be cause for the athlete to beat themselves up. As long as it was made in a genuine effort, an error or failed attempt is simply a piece of information that helps in the pursuit.

Essentially, the young athlete just needs to divine what each mistake is telling them. The wrong interpretation is to assume that it means they are inadequate. On the contrary, it simply means that they have not figured it out yet. Getting it wrong or not achieving the desired outcome should simply prompt them to reflect and figure out why. The first step is to review and get some clarity on what just happened, as this information will indicate the possible causes for the error.

Sometimes a mistake is merely an indication that they are not fully dialled-in, so they may just need to refocus for the next attempt and pay more attention on the next attempt! Alternatively, we might have just pushed beyond their young athlete's present limits, in which case we have just discovered where the present boundaries are. Most often we simply need to help the athlete to revise their approach slightly, make the necessary adjustments and try again.

MISTAKES ARE NOT CREATED EQUAL…

Making mistakes on a regular basis is not necessarily a problem, as long as it is serving a purpose. All the same, errors are not created equal. Some mistakes are acceptable at a given time and space, others less so.

Mistakes come in different forms and fall into various categories. For instance, there are process errors, execution errors and judgement errors. To some extent, there is a time and a place for each of these respective errors. The degree to which we should tolerate the different types of errors committed by ourselves and others is however situation dependent. Intent also matters a great deal.

For instance, in sports such as tennis commentators make the distinction between forced versus unforced errors. The more enlightened professional sports teams similarly differentiate between errors of execution and errors that are attributable to poor work rate when analysing players' performances. Errors of execution might be acceptable, depending on the intent and context (for instance, rolling the dice on a low probability play to break the deadlock or salvage the contest), whereas errors of work-rate are not.

"Make mistakes of ambition and not mistakes of sloth".

— Machiavelli

These are important distinctions. We need to be discriminating in how we entertain errors and what level of tolerance we apply, based upon the type of error and the circumstances. For instance, in the context of elite sport any error caused by a lack of effort or attention is not acceptable; these errors can be costly, yet they are easily preventable and do not serve any positive purpose.

At the youth level clearly much lower stakes are involved and we are generally more concerned with learning and long-term development rather than the outcome of any given contest, which affords greater allowance for making mistakes.

MAKING USE OF MISTAKES...

Whatever the nature of the mistake, errors only serve us if we learn from them and change our future behaviour in response. Accepting the premise that errors are information, by extension an error must be acknowledged before it can serve any positive function.

No lesson can be taken if the learner does not attend to the error and the information contained within. This has important implications for those guiding the young athlete. Letting a mistake go unacknowledged serves nobody. An error needs to be brought to the attention of the learner in a timely manner if they are to learn from it.

By extension, the individual involved needs to own that they have made an error. Another thing that differentiates the practice habits of better athletes is a readiness to acknowledge when they have made an error [255]. Conversely, blaming others or making excuses should be seen as a red flag, as this will impede learning. Taking ownership for an error also means being accountable for putting it right. It should therefore be an expectation that the individual immediately takes any necessary steps to put a fix in place and make their error right as far as possible.

Finally, once the young athlete has reflected on the decisions and actions involved in their mistake and taken the lessons, it is essential that they move on. Coaches, parents and athletes need to acknowledge the uncertainty inherent in the space we are operating in, appreciate that the information we are working with is always incomplete and allow that mistakes will happen. Continually beating ourselves up for past mistakes is futile and serves nobody. As the grown-ups we can model this by not dwelling on mistakes and we can encourage young performers to do the same.

"To make no mistakes is not in the power of man; but from their errors and mistakes the wise and good learn wisdom for the future".

— Plutarch

MAKE NEW MISTAKES...

To paraphrase Einstein, trying the same thing and expecting a different outcome is lunacy. If we are going to make progress, then it is important that the young athlete makes mistakes in new and exciting ways. In turn, we should ensure that they learn from each mistake, in order that they can make different and better mistakes as they proceed.

Coaches and parents should help the young performer to make sure that they are making a new mistake each time (or at least new a variation on a previous mistake!). A new or different mistake reveals new information. Committing the same error reveals nothing new, although it does have implications for the person making the mistake.

"A mistake repeated more than once is a decision".

— Paulo Coelho

The same mistake made over and over again demonstrates a lack of learning. If the young athlete is repeating a given mistake on a regular or even a periodic basis, this shows they either failed to learn the lesson or they are not paying attention. To some degree making the same mistake is a choice, in the sense that it is in their power to avoid doing so.

IN CLOSING: GIVE IT TIME TO WORK...

New and better does not necessarily immediate yield superior results. It is important to recognise that the new way may not outperform the old way in the short term. Equally, there is very little growth that comes from sticking with the default option, particularly if seeking nonlinear returns or great leaps forwards. As the old axiom goes, doing what we have always done will get us what we have always got.

If progress has slowed or plateaued entirely it makes sense to not only try something different, but also stick with it long enough to refine our new approach, make necessary tweaks and consolidate any changes to fully establish the efficacy of our new approach.

Key Take-Home Messages

1. Getting things wrong is not a flaw in the learning process; it is the learning process.

2. Progress requires a willingness to step outside comfort zones and accept a real possibility of failure.

3. If you are never making mistakes, you are probably not stretching yourself or developing new capabilities.

4. Fear of making mistakes can stall development, reduce engagement, and lead to avoidance or dropout.

5. The best performers practise what they are not good at, accepting frequent errors as the price of improvement.

6. Not all mistakes are equal; errors of effort and attention are different from errors made in pursuit of growth.

7. Learning depends on recognising, owning, and responding constructively to mistakes.

8. Repeating the same mistake reveals a lack of learning; new mistakes reveal new information.

9. Meaningful improvement takes time—new approaches may not deliver immediate results, but are essential for long-term progress.

Practical Tips

✓ Expect learning to feel messy, uncomfortable, and imperfect—this is a sign you are doing it right.

✓ Reframe mistakes as data points that help guide your next attempt rather than as failures to be avoided.

✓ Encourage curiosity when things don't go to plan: What did this attempt reveal?

✓ Separate self-worth from performance; a mistake says nothing negative about who you are.

✓ Distinguish between: Acceptable mistakes (errors of execution or judgement while learning), and Unacceptable mistakes (errors caused by lack of effort, focus, or care).

✓ Mistakes made in a genuine attempt to do something creative or push their limits are often worthy of praise

✓ Use practice environments as the lab to experiment, explore and take risks.

✓ Manage expectations for those with perfectionist tendencies—aim for progress, not flawlessness.

✓ After an error, help kids to reflect, adjust and move on rather than dwelling or self-criticising.

✓ When progress stalls, deliberately try something different instead of repeating the same approach

Action Items

» Educate kids to view an error as a data point; the act of making an error provides the information that enables learning

» Teach kids to fix, adjust and iterate, identifying one small change to apply on the next attempt.

» Promote the principle of making new and better mistakes.

» Instil in kids the discipline to acknowledge and own their mistakes and take responsibility for putting them right

» Adopt the position that the same mistake repeated means it is a choice or they are not paying enough attention – this needs to be remedied in either case

» Help kids to learn from mistakes and move on – beyond taking the lesson, ruminating and beating themselves up is unhelpful!

» Commit to patience: Give new approaches time to work before judging their effectiveness.

Strategies to Deal with Distraction

Distraction is a constant feature of modern life. The younger generation are growing up as digital natives and the allure of technology is ever-present in most environments. Clearly the genie is not going back in the bottle, so it is up to us to take steps to equip young performers with strategies to take back control and better deal with distractions of all kinds. This starts with becoming more mindful in our own use of digital technology so that we can model the right behaviours!

The capability to marshal the mind and resist becoming side-tracked is arguably the new superpower. Being able to conserve precious mental resources and stay on task amidst all the distraction not only confers a competitive advantage but represents the key to unlocking new possibilities for long term achievement in sport and beyond.

One of the remarkable things about sport is its power to captivate. When a young performer finds their sport, it has a fascination that can hold their attention indefinitely. Being immersed in purposeful activity – the state of *flow* – is inherently pleasurable and provides a sense of meaning. The inability to harness our attention and being in a state of constant distraction is the opposite – it is inherently unsatisfying and does not make us feel good. To remain engaged and realise the rewards, performers must resist the distractions and avoid being diverted from their path.

MANAGING FINITE MENTAL RESOURCES...

As we identified in an earlier chapter, intention, attention and directed mental effort are three elements that we must invest carefully if we are to sustain development and be successful over time. Like time and money, attention is a scarce resource and we need to prize and protect it as such. Student-athletes must learn to manage their time and deploy their mental resources in the most productive way, given the need to satisfy the competing demands of pursuing success in their chosen sport(s) and academic achievement.

We hear sportspeople talk a lot about focus. In part, focus depends upon the performer's ability to tune out extraneous noise and distractions within the environment. What is less talked about (perhaps because it is not visible to the outside observer) is that another part of focus is dealing with the distractions of internal noise and interference within our own mind. Feelings, self-talk and distracting thoughts are elements that every performer must learn to manage.

Failing to manage mental resources and handle distractions effectively is detrimental to the individual. The distraction of technology has become an insidious problem in all areas of human performance. It is increasingly evident that mobile digital technology imposes a significant cost on our mental resources. Even having a smartphone in the room impairs cognitive capacity and impairs task performance [257]. Digital distractions also impair concentration and working memory, which should be especially worrying for young athletes as it interferes with the ability to learn [258]

Reports of digital distraction among sportspeople include the tale of a college coach who felt compelled to introduce cell phone breaks within team practice sessions to allow the players to satisfy their apparently overwhelming cravings to check their phones. Late night use of smartphones and social media among professional players are also documented as resulting in measurable determinant effects on their performance statistics in games the following day [259].

THE OTHER KPI: KEY PERFORMANCE (AND DEVELOPMENT) INHIBITORS…

One of the most crucial aspects of the talent development process for the young performer is getting to grips with what goes on between their own ears, especially as it relates to their ability to learn and perform. Managing the effects of extraneous influences on their mental processes and behaviours is an integral part of this. Oddly, talent development pathways and youth sports in general have been slow to equip performers with strategies or countermeasures to deal with outside pressures and influences that may detract or distract from the mission. This seems a glaring omission, especially when we consider that the task faced by impressionable young performers has never been more challenging since the introduction of social media with all its pervasive influence.

One of the most important ways in which parents can support the mission is by helping to ensure the young performer's actions beyond the practice and competition environment are helping or at least not hindering. Naturally this includes healthy eating and sleeping habits but it also extends to other 'athlete health' behaviours relating to the consumption of digital media, such as regulating screen time and social media use.

Arguably the most troublesome aspect of digital technology in general and the smartphone in particular is that it serves as a portal to social media applications, which can be kryptonite to the young performer in a number of different ways. Social media applications on phones and smart devices are engineered to hijack the dopamine system, providing reward signals that feed compulsive use, and in the developing adolescent brain they find a particularly receptive target. The sense of social validation and acceptance that teens derive from their social media accounts adds to the impulse to constantly check in on their smartphone [260].

"Are you here to tweet, or are you here to compete?"

— Peter Haberl

Smartphones and social media increasingly infringe on young athletes' participation in sport, becoming a distraction during practices and even competition. The time spent taking photos for their social media channels is only one small part and is far exceeded by the endless hours spent checking for 'likes' and comments as well as mindlessly scrolling their social media feed. As well as being a time suck this also drains cognitive resources.

GETTING TO THE HEART OF THE ISSUE (UNCOVERING THE SOURCE)…

There are a growing number who have sounded the alarm that we have become prisoners or slaves to technology specifically engineered to hijack our and exploit psychological triggers to manipulate our behaviour. Certainly some elements of this narrative are factual (yes big tech does design and engineer software and product features to hook and hold our attention); however, it is not the whole truth. This version of events absolves us of any responsibility, but the bigger problem is that it robs us of our agency and denies us the possibility of taking steps to change the situation, short of abstaining from using technology entirely (which for most of us is not a practical solution).

It is true that indulging the urge for distraction has never been easier. It is also true that once we engage with technological distraction there a number of inbuilt hooks and tricks that keep us distracted for longer. However, none of this changes the fact that the urge for distraction comes from somewhere. Often our urge to indulge in distraction originates from within us. The trigger is not always external or passive. If we observe our own behaviour, we find that we frequently seek out distraction by actively reaching for our devices. Breaking the cycle requires us to recognise this, and in turn take steps to deal with the causes of our cravings for distraction so we can come up with some strategies and practices to take back the reins.

CREATING SPACE…

"Between stimulus and response there is a space. In that space is our power to choose our response. In our response lies our growth and our freedom."

— Viktor Frankl

When we lapse into mindless conditioned behaviour our actions are prompted by a trigger or urge without any conscious thought or intention in between. Intrusive alerts (what author Nir Eyal describes as the 'pings, dings and rings' of mobile technology) are certainly a factor, but the urge and cognitive interference remains even when devices are in 'silent' mode [261].

By inserting a buffer we can create the necessary gap between the stimulus (trigger) and indulging the urge (response). We can then employ this time to gain some awareness of the trigger and allow discomfiting thoughts or feelings to subside. This simple practice provides young performers with an opportunity to unmask the underlying issues, be more aware of compulsive behaviours and cultivate better habits.

Giving ourselves permission to indulge the urge once the time delay has lapsed (if we still wish to do so) robs it of some of its power (the sense of relief that comes when we give in). Inserting this fire break also brings immediately benefits as the young performer will often find the urge for distraction has passed once the buffer period is over. Having 'surfed the urge' they are able to return to what they were doing originally.

CURATING THE ENVIRONMENT...

Certain distractions cannot be removed entirely but they can be better managed. Knowing that there are external triggers which have the power to hook and hold our attention, we can take steps to curate the space around us to manage and mitigate their effects on us.

Aside from keeping devices beyond arm's reach (or better still in another room) we can hack back triggers and visual cues when we do have these devices in our possession. Turning off intrusive alerts and notifications eliminates much of the interruption. We can rearrange the icons that appear on the home screen to lessen the temptation. Better yet is to delete social media applications on the smartphone entirely and restrict ourselves to accessing them on other devices. Other related practical steps include getting a watch to escape the tendency for attention to be captured when we check the time on our smartphone.

Whilst parents and coaches can certainly take a lead and propose these strategies, agency remains paramount if the performer is to effect any lasting changes in their own behaviour. Having an accountability partner is helpful but each individual must make the choice to take action and voluntarily commit themselves to adopting these practices.

Once they have chosen to take action, the young performer should pledge to undertake certain steps or opting to commit to specified rules (e.g. no smartphone when studying). Publicly entering into an agreement with another person (of their own free will) can help to hold themselves accountable, particularly if there is some cost involved! Choosing to sign up to terms such as a financial penalty or forfeit can add teeth to the commitment as they now have 'skin in the game', helping to boost motivation during times of weakness! A helpful contraption to compliment this approach is a time-lock mini kitchen safe – place the device in there, set the timer and the phone is beyond reach of temptation until the time is up!

IN CLOSING: CREATING CONDITIONS FOR SUCCESS...

As well as regulating their digital media consumption, doubling down on sleep and maintaining a regular exercise regimen is crucial for young performers who wish to maximise their mental resources and become better at how they manage them. The latter is usually a given, whereas many student athletes need to take steps to improve their sleep habits. To come full circle, being disciplined with using technology in the evenings and eliminating devices from the bedroom is part of this practice.

The final key that unlocks so much is when young performers adopt the practice of relieving psychological discomfort by reaching out to real people when something is on their mind and talking through whatever is bothering them rather than seeking to distract themselves from troubling thoughts and feelings of disquiet. This begins with acknowledging that distraction at best turns down the volume temporarily but otherwise just defers confronting the problem, compounds the drain on mental resources from nagging concerns and often makes the problem loom larger.

Key Take-Home Messages

1. Distraction is now a defining challenge for young performers growing up in a digitally saturated world.

2. Attention is a finite and valuable resource; it must be protected and invested wisely.

3. The ability to manage attention and mental resources is a critical performance skill and a life skill.

4. Distraction undermines learning, development and performance by draining cognitive capacity and working memory.

5. Focus is not only about blocking out external distractions, but also about managing internal noise such as thoughts, emotions, and self-talk.

6. Smartphones and social media impose a measurable cost on mental performance—even when not actively in use.

7. Social media platforms are deliberately designed to hijack reward systems, making them especially powerful distractors for adolescents.

8. Blaming technology alone is insufficient; the urge for distraction often originates internally as a way to avoid discomfort.

7. Developing awareness of distraction triggers restores personal agency and control.

8. Creating a pause between stimulus and response allows performers to choose rather than react.

9. Curating the environment is one of the most effective ways to protect attention and reduce temptation.

10. Lasting change requires voluntary commitment by the performer; imposed rules rarely lead to sustainable habits.

11. Learning to tolerate discomfort and seek human connection is a healthier alternative to habitual distraction.

Practical Tips

✓ Treat attention as a precious resource that deserves protection.

✓ Recognise that distraction can be external (environment, devices) or internal (thoughts, feelings).

✓ Helps kids to become aware of triggers that lead to distraction rather than reacting mindlessly.

✓ Teach kids to 'surf the urge', inserting a buffer period when they get the urge to check a device rather than immediately giving into distraction.

✓ Stress the need to keep smartphones and other mobile technology out of reach (ideally in another room) and out of view when studying

✓ Use practical tools such as watches to avoid unnecessary phone checks.

✓ Improve sleep by removing devices from bedrooms and limiting evening screen use.

✓ Rather than turning to digital distraction, encourage kids to confide in a real human when they are troubled or anxious.

Action Items

» Educate kids that regulating consumption of digital media is an essential student-athlete life skill.

» Instil the principle that the ability to focus is a superpower that offers a competitive edge, whereas being distractable is a key performance inhibitor

» Consider a 'dumbphone' and keep kids off social media as long as possible.

» If using a smartphone turn off intrusive alerts, prune the apps on the device and delete social media apps.

» Establish clear rules (e.g. "no phone when studying").

» Model mindful use of digital devices – get the whole family to commit to protocols for device use, including device-free zones and protected times, such as meal times.

» Encourage kids to agree terms for regulating screen time and smartphone use – include penalties or other forfeits when they break their pledges!

» Experiment with commitment devices (e.g. time-lock phone safes).

» Register improvements in focus, learning, sleep and mood as well as tracking reductions in screen time.

Agency and Accountability

> "If it is to be, it is up to me."
>
> – William Johnsen

Autonomy is a crucial objective in the talent development process, which naturally places increasing onus on the performer as they proceed on their journey. One of the most important ways that coaches and parents can assist the young performer is by helping them to assume greater independence as they progress on their youth sports journey. Cultivating a sense of agency is integral to promoting autonomy. Equally, another important principle to instil is that the power to choose and decide for themselves comes with certain obligations. Agency has wider implications, as it means holding themselves accountable for the choices they make in the sporting arena and beyond.

Whilst coaches (and some parents) might strive to impose their will, something we need to recognise and respect that the power lies with the athlete. Athletes have free will, and as such it is always a choice. The athlete chooses how much of themselves they invest in the process from moment to moment. This underlines why it is so important that the individual takes some ownership over the process (after all it is all down to them).

From a coaching perspective, the best way to promote agency and autonomy is to be *authoritative* (and avoid being authoritarian) and much the same applies with parenting. Rather than being too directive, the young athlete should be invited to assume their proper role and they should be afforded the opportunity to make their own decisions. We need to enlist the athlete as a partner and engage them in the process early on, such that it becomes a shared endeavour, to which the athlete is expected to contribute a great deal.

Young athletes typically welcome the notion of agency. What is overlooked and merits highlighting is that with agency comes accountability. Each individual is accountable for their choices and the consequences that ensue. This is the part that parents and coaches should continually emphasise.

THE OBLIGATIONS THAT COME WITH ATHLETIC ABILITY...

Natural talent and work ethic do not necessarily go together. Many will be familiar with the scenario of a talented performer relying on his or her athletic gifts and being lackadaisical in their approach. A sign of how often this phenomenon is observed is that it has given rise to the adage 'hard work beats talent when talent doesn't work hard'. Delving deeper, we could conclude that there is something about the situation faced by precocious talents that is somehow at odds with developing the skills and habits that are required to cultivate their extraordinary abilities.

When things come easily it is easy to be casually dismissive about the value of practice and hard work. During the course of their youth sports journey kids generally learn through experience that progress comes from diligent practice and consistent application of effort. This lesson can prove more elusive for the talented young performer, as the connection between hard work and success is not so apparent when they already enjoy significant rewards and recognition without having to try too hard.

Naturally, if a young performer is able to get by with minimal effort there is less imperative to work any harder than they need to. The fact that a precocious young performer is able to rely on their natural gifts can lead to complacency and a tendency to coast if left unchecked.

Of course, the reality is that there is always somebody out there who is more talented. Precocious talents who are able to dominate in junior competition without applying themselves inevitably face a reckoning at some point. When the time comes that the standard of competition no longer allows them to get by on talent alone, formerly successful juniors often find themselves entirely unprepared to meet this challenge. It is at this point that many heralded young talents fall by the wayside.

On one hand, natural gifts are clearly an asset – they confer a competitive advantage. On the other, they can also prove to be a liability. Advantages must be managed if we are to avoid them becoming an impediment to acquiring the skills and habits that permit young performers to develop over time. This starts with adopting the proper attitude and relating to their advantages in a way that serves them. Arrogance and complacency are not only unlikely to win them friends – and irrespective of talent it takes a village to reach the highest level – but also retard their development.

"To whom much is given, much will be required"

Luke 12:48

A critical message is that such gifts come with certain obligations. For readers who are uneasy about quoting scripture, there is the oft-quoted line from Spiderman that with great power comes great responsibility. They have been presented with a rare and much sought after opportunity. They have a duty not to waste it, not least out of respect for the many others who would give a great deal to have such a privilege. As well as being grateful, they should realise that they have an obligation to make the best use of their talents in service of themselves, their team-mates and those who support them.

For coaches at the youth level, the appropriate response when we encounter a rare talent is to adjust our expectations accordingly and raise the bar. Celebrating the individual before they have achieved anything is counterproductive as it implies that nothing further is required of them. Returning to the earlier quote, the opposite is true: the more gifted they are, the more should be expected of them. To that end, we must be careful about giving talented individuals special treatment.

Neither should we indulge those who are gifted. Everybody should be subject to the same standards when it comes to conduct and discipline. There should be an explicit expectation that the most talented athlete in the group should work at least as hard as other committed athletes in the squad. Indeed, recognising that their talent grants them status among their peers, as they mature the outstanding young performer should be held to a higher standard given how their example is likely to influence the group. Whilst it might seem harsh to single them out in this way, such an approach ultimately better serves the young performer as it promotes and reinforces the habits and behaviours that will enable them to continue to develop.

To bring it all together, our words and actions should reward effort and application - that is, the things that are under their control, rather than simply rewarding the talents they have been endowed with. This emphasises their agency over the development process and underscores that their contribution matters.

BECOMING ACCOUNTABLE...

A recurring theme of the preceding chapters and a consistent message for young performers is that their participation in the pursuit and sport in general is a choice that they make of their own accord. The kicker to this emphasis on agency is that the performer is accountable for the choices they make. After all, the power to choose comes with the responsibility of dealing with the consequences of those choices.

One of the more important choices that a young athlete must make is assuming the duties and responsibilities that go along with along with pursuing their sporting ambitions. For instance, the young athlete is accountable for how they show up to practice. It is up to them to make the right choices in advance to ensure that they are well rested, properly fuelled and ready to train. It makes no sense to defer to others and delegate these responsibilities.

Fully committing and investing all their efforts in the pursuit is a necessary step, especially for those who have aspirations of competing at the highest level. This is understandably a daunting proposition as it means becoming accountable for the outcome, leaving little room for excuses if they fall short.

"Sometimes we're responsible for things not because they're our fault, but because we're the only ones who can change them"

– Lisa Feldman Barrett

The other implication of being in command of our own destiny is that it is up to us to put things right even if the events that befall us are not of our own doing. There is much that it is within the power of the individual young performer. In turn, they are responsible for doing all that is within their power to remedy whatever situation they find themselves in.

PERSONAL ADMIN AND CATERING FOR THEIR OWN NEEDS...

In an earlier chapter we highlighted the perils of parents and coaches doing for a young performer what they are capable of doing for themselves. Clearly this does however require that the young performer steps up in return. At the most basic level, assuming ownership begins with taking responsibility for organising themselves. Personal admin is often not a strong point for a young performer, so this seems like a good place to start!

The highly successful New Zealand All Blacks rugby team are renowned for the fact that upon arriving at the venue on match day it is the coaches and players themselves who roll their sleeves up and together unload their bags and equipment from the team bus. This is indicative of the team culture that places high importance on humility and taking care of themselves so that others do not have to. A related All Blacks mantra is 'sweep the sheds'; the players themselves take responsibility for tidying up after themselves (including quite literally sweeping the changing room before they depart).

As they seek to emulate the mighty All Blacks, the first concern for a young performer is to make sure they arrive at practice and competition on time, with the right kit and their equipment in good working condition. Equally, what they should not overlook is the importance of becoming self-sufficient when it comes to looking after themselves during the times in between.

Sleep and nutrition are two of the most important pillars of physical preparation. Both of these aspects rely on the individual organising themselves and catering for their own needs (quite literally). Beyond personal admin and self-discipline, basic domestic and culinary skills are critical capabilities that young performers should seek to develop during their high school years.

Home comforts are not necessarily conducive to developing these athlete life skills. It is sadly a reality that student-athletes (and students in general) are arriving at college so ill-equipped to take care of themselves that some colleges in the United States now provide crash courses in basic cooking and how to use a washing machine. That there is a need for these courses at all is a bit mind-blowing, but the fact that these courses are over-subscribed speaks to the extent of the problem.

ATTRIBUTING CREDIT AND BLAME ...

It is said that experience is the best teacher. However, this is only true to the extent that we are able to connect the dots and heed the lessons. All of us are prone to *attribution bias*. We are generally quicker to recognise and highlight our role when the outcome is positive. Yet whilst we are happy to take the credit when it goes right, we are often far less quick to acknowledge our part and accept our share of the blame when things go wrong. Whilst this might be human nature, it is nevertheless a major impediment to taking the salient lessons from the experiences we encounter on the journey.

Just as being accountable means taking responsibility for the process, failing to accept accountability begins with a refusal to acknowledge that their own choices and actions contributed to the outcome. A hallmark of this is a tendency to blame others.

Young athletes are often quick to point fingers and bemoan external forces and events that were beyond their control. In doing so, they fail to reckon with all that was within their power to control. A key question to reflect on after the event regardless of the outcome is always 'did you do everything you could to the highest of your ability?'.

In a later chapter we will describe 'the circles' (circle of control, circle of influence, circle of concern). As well as separating and letting go of what we cannot control it is imperative that we remember to do the work to address all that is within our power to control and influence. When we look back there are often instances where had we taken responsibility and acted to 'control all the controllables', our actions might have averted whatever situation befell us.

Often the situation is complicated by the fact that they might have a legitimate claim: unforeseen events do occur and at times performers will be let down by those they were relying on. Even so, this should not necessarily change the conversation in the debrief. It is still critical to direct the performer's attention inwards and examine their own role. There is always merit in rigorously evaluating whether they did all they could to positively influence the outcome, regardless of what other external factors were at play. Taking responsibility and owning their part in what happened is necessary in order for the performer to take the relevant lessons from the experience.

ACCEPTING OUR ROLE IN ADVERSE OUTCOMES…

Clearly not everything is within our control, but individual agency is something that we nevertheless need to continually emphasise with young performers. It is critical for them to appreciate that they have the power to choose and exercise their own free will; and through those choices and actions they are able to change their situation and influence the world around them.

Part of growing up is accepting things won't always go our way. Depicting ourselves as a victim of circumstance when things happen is disempowering and clearly not conducive to responding in a positive and productive manner. The urge to complain is quite natural and of course there will also be times when there is a genuine cause to feel aggrieved. Equally, complaining about what is beyond our influence does not serve any useful purpose. Reclaiming a sense of agency is necessary if we are to switch modes from feeling aggrieved to realising the possibilities presented by the situation and assuming responsibility for putting things right.

Moreover, holding onto grievances and harbouring resentment is toxic to the individual. These are not indulgences that we can afford if we want to achieve great things. Beyond accepting life's realities, the appropriate response is to set about making the best choices and taking appropriate actions to move forwards. The next step from acceptance is owning whatever occurs or the circumstances we find ourselves in. If it is always somebody else's fault or we are constantly claiming to be at the mercy of unforeseen outside events through no fault of our own then clearly there is not much learning going on.

RESISTING THE ALLURE OF PLAYING THE VICTIM...

Given that a victim mentality is so unhelpful then we might wonder why so many seem to fall into this mindset. After all, if they are so convinced that the game is rigged against them then what is the point of trying? This is likely the source of the allure. It is an ingenious way of avoiding taking responsibility.

If the universe is conspiring against us and the game is rigged in a way that prevents us from succeeding, there is no fault on our part if we fail. This framing gifts an abundance of excuses and absolves us of any blame or responsibility for putting things right.

As parents and coaches, we must be mindful of the potential for our own conduct to reinforce these tendencies. Allowing young performers to make excuses and rail against perceived injustices is generally unhelpful especially if we allow them to gloss over their own contribution. Armed with this awareness we can exercise discretion and try to model the behaviours that we are seeking and direct their focus back to what they can do to change the outcome.

IN CLOSING...

As the grown-ups (in our miscellaneous roles as coach, parent, wise counsel, mentor, etc.) it is our job to encourage the young performers to step up and take charge of their own destiny. A greater emphasis on individual agency and accountability at times means letting them fail – after all, if the young performer comes to expect that we will bail them out then they will never fully take the reins.

Experience might be the best teacher in theory, but for this to work in practice the young performer needs to connect the dots and heed the lessons. After the event, whether the outcome was positive or negative, part of our role is to help them objectively evaluate how their choices contributed to the outcome and take the salient lessons moving forwards.

The final and perhaps most important take home message is that they are accountable for their choices and decisions beyond the practice and competition arena. Young performers are accountable for how they show up to practice, so they must take ownership of their personal admin, including nutrition and sleep. Culinary and domestic skills are crucial athlete life skills for them to develop during the teenage years!

Key Take-Home Messages

1. Young performers must increasingly take ownership of their sporting journey, especially once they enter their teens.

2. With choice comes the responsibility for effort, preparation, outcomes and putting things right.

3. Natural ability is a gift, not an achievement – we should coach young athletes to acknowledge their good fortune and the obligations that come with these gifts.

4. Effort and application matter more than talent – continuing development depends on habits, work ethic and application.

5. Parents and coaches play a critical role inculcating values, setting expectations, modelling accountability and avoiding indulging young talents.

6. Self-sufficiency is a key pillar of student-athlete life – personal admin, sleep, nutrition are essential components of athlete development.

7. Accountability enables learning. Growth depends on honest reflection, accepting responsibility and focusing on what is within one's control.

8. Victimhood and excuses are disempowering – blaming others or circumstances undermines agency and impedes meaningful progress.

9. Agency means accepting consequences for actions – shielding kids from this delays maturity and ownership.

10. Responsibilities of student-athlete life extend beyond the field – key accountabilities include daily habits away from the practice and competition arena.

Practical Tips

✓ Emphasise effort, preparation, and application rather than talent or outcomes.

✓ Be authoritative, not authoritarian: involve the athlete as an active partner rather than a passive recipient.

✓ Reinforce the duties and obligations that come with athletic gifts and the responsibility that come with the opportunities granted to them.

✓ Direct kids' focus to what is under their control and what they can influence and help them disregard the rest.

✓ Help kids to accept setbacks without blaming others and commit to constructive next steps.

✓ Resist the urge to intervene, excuse, or explain away poor outcomes.

✓ Allow young performers to experience consequences when appropriate, rather than coming to their rescue.

✓ Emphasise that being a high performer means taking responsibility for what they do in between practices, including what they consume and what time they go to bed

Action Items

» Urge kids to accept responsibility for arriving prepared: on time, with correct kit and equipment.

» Model personal responsibility in your own behaviour and language.

» Help kids learn to cook, how to do the laundry and make sure they practice these culinary and laundry skills, recognising these are crucial student-athlete life skills.

» With the young athlete, write up a student-athlete contract that specifies the duties and obligations that both parties are committing to.

» Teach kids to take responsibility not because it is necessarily their fault but because it is in their power to put things right

» Offer to become an accountability partner to the young athlete to make sure they maintain good habits during regular practices.

» Implement routine reflective practice 'What was within your control?', 'Did you do everything you could to the best of your ability?'.

» With the coaches, facilitate post-competition debriefs that help kids to be objective and take the salient lessons: 'what might you do better next time?'.

» Create space for the kids to reflect and problem-solve themselves before stepping in with suggestions or solutions.

Feeling Privileged and Practising Gratitude

Coaches and parents share a responsibility to help the young performer to relate to their own gifts in a way that best serves them and others. Arrogance is not only unbecoming but also inappropriate when it comes to gifts and advantages that were not earned but rather bestowed. The proper attitude towards such gifts of birth and circumstance is gratitude. A young athlete who has the ability and support to pursue their sporting aspirations is in a privileged position and it is important that they recognise and appreciate their good fortune. Equally, there is no need to apologise or feel shame about their natural assets or the benefits they enjoy.

The notion of privilege has taken on strange and somewhat dark connotations in recent times. This strikes me as a little odd. As a coach I feel privileged to work with performers who are committed to their craft. I am quick to acknowledge that it is a privilege to coach these individuals and to have them place their faith in my expertise. I feel grateful for my good fortune. I also feel a profound sense of responsibility to hold such a privileged position and a duty to do great work in return. Perhaps it is time to adopt a healthier attitude towards the advantages we enjoy. By reframing how we think about these things we can perhaps respond in ways that better serve the performer and those supporting them.

A HAPPY ACCIDENT...

Certain advantages are a happy accident of birth and the circumstances we find ourselves in. Due to forces and factors that are beyond the control of the individual many young athletes find themselves with privileged access to resources and opportunities. Of course much of this is pure luck; the role of the young athlete themselves is often largely incidental. What is up to them is what they do with these advantages.

Humility should therefore be central to how we think about advantages and what feelings we have in response. It is important that we acknowledge our good fortune when we find ourselves in such situations. In my case and for most people reading this, we can be grateful to have been born in a prosperous part of the world and in an era of relative peace and ever-improving living standards. There are other facets to the good fortune and happy accidents of birth and circumstances that young performers enjoy: they were born into a certain body; they were raised in a certain family and social circumstances.

Clearly we don't have any choice over the circumstances of our birth. Our role in the situation we find ourselves in as kids and the manner in which we are raised is also minimal at best. Much of it we have no direct control over and little to no influence in proceedings. Whether we find ourselves a position of advantage or disadvantage, our power resides in how we appraise our situation and how we respond to it. To that end, we might point out that these are gifts bestowed upon them from birth: these assets were not earned and they cannot take too much credit.

CREDIT AND BLAME...

Given the lack of control or influence over proceedings then naturally we should be delighted when it all works out in our favour. If we won the genetic lottery we should be especially stoked! Clearly we cannot claim any credit either – we didn't choose our parents or the circumstances into which we were born. On that basis, whilst a gifted young athlete might celebrate their good fortune, the appropriate attitude is gratitude. Humility is the proper response – it is important to both acknowledge our good fortune and be grateful for it.

Oddly, rather than humility and gratitude, the default response to any form of privilege in the recent period seems to have become scorn and shame. Aside from being irrational, this is also nonsensical. Just as we cannot claim any credit for our circumstances or privileged access to opportunity due to forces we had no influence over, then it also follows that we cannot be blamed for these things!

Yes, it is important to acknowledge and recognise all the ways we have been blessed by good fortune. But being made to feel shame for it is ridiculous. Feeling a sense of shame is entirely unjustified and also means that we fail to appreciate the gifts that have been bestowed upon us. Similarly, seeking to deny or even relinquish our privilege to somehow make up for this cosmic offence is also a bizarre and absurd response. It serves everybody better when we recognise these gifts and endeavour to do something useful with them.

Scorn, antipathy and resentment towards others on the basis of their perceived privilege or advantages is equally ridiculous and serves nobody. Hardship is also relative. When feeling aggrieved about our lot relative to those around us, it is worth considering the enormous number of people around the world who would happily switch places with us.

ADVANTAGES MUST BE MANAGED...

Advantageous circumstances and all the comforts these afford can pose their own problems. Paradoxically, privilege and being provided with advantages that are given rather than earned can reduce the impetus to strive. Ready access to the easy option can make us less inclined to do the hard yards that are required to achieve something meaningful in the long-term. Likewise, being untouched by adversity naturally makes us ill-prepared when unforeseen adverse events do occur and less equipped to struggle through hard times.

As we noted earlier, expressing pride for our gifts or displaying arrogance due to our privileged status are equally ridiculous. These things were given, not earned. Neither are they something performers should feel they need to hide or minimise. I can recall many instances of physically gifted young humans attempting to shrink themselves and stoop to placate those around them, especially with the Amazonian-like female athletes I have been fortunate to work with. In each instance, my instructions to them were to stand at your full height and let the rest of us gaze up at you!

Those performers who have won the genetic lottery must be granted the assurance to stand tall and express their gifts to their fullest extent and without apology. The only obligation they should feel is to acknowledge all the ways in which they have been blessed, be grateful for these gifts and their good fortune and recognise the attendant responsibility to use their powers for good.

GRATITUDE IS APPROPRIATE AND POWERFUL…

It is worthwhile to pause and acknowledge all the ways they are fortunate and be thankful. Gratitude plays an important yet often overlooked role for high performers and is highly relevant to the youth sports journey. The question is how we might help aspiring young performers to learn to appreciate the good stuff and leverage all the benefits that come with being more grateful.

Those who count their blessings and adopt a spirit of gratitude coincidentally also rate higher on measures of happiness and general wellbeing. As we study this phenomenon it becomes clear that this is no mere coincidence.

"Gratitude is not only the greatest of virtues, but the parent of all the others."

– Cicero

Gratitude is uniquely and causally linked to improved physical, psychological and emotional health and wellbeing [262]. The power of gratitude is such that clinicians and others have sought to devise interventions and practices aimed at fostering a sense of gratitude as a tool to promote better wellbeing in different populations, including those undergoing physical and mental health challenges. The positive effects observed have prompted high performers in different domains to attempt to hack the process to enjoy the benefits associated with gratitude in their everyday lives.

"Gratitude is the antidote to bitterness and resentment"

– M.J. Ryan

Gratitude is a shield against toxic emotions, such as envy and resentment. It is also a gateway to a more positive outlook on life. Something about being grateful on a regular basis seems to predispose us to having a more positive attitude towards ourselves, our present situation and our future prospects. Gratitude has a reciprocal effect on life satisfaction: feeling gratitude serves to make us more content with our lives, which in turn leads us to feel more grateful [263]!

The importance of socialising kids to feel and to express gratitude has been highlighted for raising happy and healthy young people [264]. The power of gratitude is particularly pertinent to young athletes and indeed anybody who has committed themselves to a long and arduous journey. The ability to deal with setbacks and remain optimistic about the outcome goes a long way to determining which individuals are able to stay the course and ultimately prevail. Being mindful and appreciative of the good stuff is an important part of staying positive and remaining steadfast, particularly during challenging times.

RECOGNISING THE GOOD STUFF...

It is in our nature to become habituated to even the most extraordinary things once they become part of our everyday reality. The extreme version of this is the *hedonic treadmill*. It is easy to fall into the trap of craving shiny and new things, only to find that once we possess the new item the allure soon fades, leading us to soon discard it to chase the next object of our desires, so that the cycle repeats and escalates without us being satisfied beyond increasingly fleeting moments. Clearly this is an extreme example, but most of us stand to benefit from paying more attention to the good stuff. It serves us well to periodically take an inventory of all we have to be grateful for and reflect on everyday wonders.

"Don't it always seem to go, that you don't know what you've got till it's gone"

— Joni Mitchell

What is striking is that there are so many good things that we have become so accustomed to that we no longer recognise their value. There are many miraculous things (our health being a prime example) that we tend to take for granted until they start to fail. Sadly, it is often only once we have been deprived of something that we come to realise how important it is to our lives.

Our environment provides our frame of reference and is natural to evaluate our present circumstances in relation to those around us. Inevitably this affects our ability to appreciate all that we do have, not least compared to so many in other parts of the world. A change in our circumstances or environment can thus give us a new appreciation of the things in our lives we otherwise take for granted.

Let me use the example of camping outdoors. I am from London (the one in England), so I am frankly baffled by the idea that people would sleep outside in a tent by choice and for pleasure. That apart, I do recognise the value of camping as a lifestyle intervention. Upon returning home from a camping trip I certainly have a newfound appreciation of everyday things such as indoor plumbing and sleeping on a mattress under a roof and with walls separating me from others. It turns out living indoors is pretty epic.

Periods of disruption quickly bring into focus all the good things that we normally overlook. What can appear mundane in our everyday lives are miraculous and life-changing under different circumstances. How about the fact that we have clean drinking water readily available at the turn of a tap?

If we can find ways to arrive at this realisation some other way then hopefully it won't always require extreme events to befall us before we appreciate what we have. With awareness we have the possibility to harness the power of everyday things. Perhaps we just need the right prompt to shine the torch on these riches, so they do not fade into the background or get overlooked entirely.

GRATITUDE AS PRACTICE...

Practising gratitude has two parts. We can say gratitude is a practice, in the sense it is something that we actively engage in. In other words, it takes us being mindful of what we have to be grateful for in order to feel grateful. But gratitude is also something we can *practise*, with the objective of getting better at it.

So how can we operationalise appreciation? One tool that more enlightened coaches encourage their athletes to utilise is a *gratitude journal* (legendary track and field coach Dan Pfaff is a proponent of this approach). Keeping a diary or daily log of the good things allows athletes to write down whatever events, people and miscellaneous other things they encounter each day that they feel grateful for. A related daily practice is to enlist a buddy and commit to asking each other at the culmination of each day what positive things happened. This serves as a prompt to reflect on the day's events, recall the positive stuff and express our appreciation.

Taking note of the good stuff and recalling what we have to feel grateful for represents a simple but powerful practice. Such tools are particularly valuable when we are struggling through hard times. Even in the darkest times there is nonetheless much that we can find to be grateful for, albeit we do need to prompt ourselves to look. A related practice when kids are feeling disheartened is to look back and recall times when they successfully negotiated challenges.

"Make it a habit to tell people thank you... express your appreciation, sincerely and without the expectation of anything in return. Truly appreciate those around you, and you'll soon find many others around you. Truly appreciate life, and you'll find that you have more of it."

– Ralph Marston

Whilst feeling grateful benefits the individual, expressing gratitude brings further value to all parties. During the youth sports journey much relies upon the goodwill of others – notably volunteer coaches who give up their time to help young performers and of course parents who do so much to support them and make it all possible. Sometimes this can seem like a thankless task. Acknowledging the contribution of all those who make it all possible (coaches, teachers, parents, officials) and expressing sincere thanks is not only the right thing to do but also makes it more likely that they will continue! Giving somebody a token of appreciation like a note or some small gift not only brightens the day of the person receiving, but also rewards and benefits the giver at least as much.

Key Take-Home Messages

1. Many of the advantages young performers enjoy are the result of luck and circumstance.

2. Because privilege is unearned, it should not be a source of pride or arrogance...

...equally it should not be cause for shame or guilt!

3. The most appropriate responses to advantage are humility, gratitude and responsibility.

4. Advantages can paradoxically hinder development by reducing motivation to strive and limiting exposure to adversity.

5. Gifted young athletes should not hide or minimise their strengths to appease others; they should express their gifts fully and without apology.

6. Gratitude is not passive—it is a powerful psychological resource that supports wellbeing, resilience and long-term commitment.

7. Practising gratitude is linked to improved emotional health, optimism and life satisfaction.

8. Gratitude acts as a buffer against toxic emotions such as envy, resentment and bitterness.

9. Young athletes often take everyday benefits for granted due to habituation; deliberate awareness is required to recognise the "good stuff."

10. Gratitude can be cultivated deliberately through simple, repeatable practices.

11. Expressing gratitude strengthens relationships and sustains the goodwill that youth sport depends upon.

12. Using one's advantages responsibly is a better response than denying, hiding or feeling ashamed of them.

Practical Tips

✓ Encourage young athletes to acknowledge their advantages honestly, without embarrassment or arrogance.

✓ Instil the principle that they should reject the idea that they need to apologise for the gifts that they were endowed with or other privileges that were granted to them.

✓ Encourage young performers to stand tall and always express their abilities to the fullest extent and emphasise the imperative to use their powers for good!

✓ Prompt young athletes to regularly notice positive aspects of their lives, including the opportunities they have to play sport and the fact they are fit and healthy.

✓ Use disruption or contrast (e.g. travel, change of environment) as opportunities to reflect on everyday benefits.

✓ Model gratitude by expressing appreciation and giving thanks— children learn it by observing it.

✓ Gratitude does not diminish ambition, as long as it is paired with recognising the obligation to cultivate their gifts and express them to the fullest extent possible.

Action Items

» Help young performers to understand the benefits of being appreciative and expressing gratitude and how it supports the mission!

» Periodically give kids the exercise of taking an inventory of all they have to be grateful for; this is especially powerful when they are feeling unhappy or aggrieved.

» Introduce a gratitude journal, where athletes write down daily or weekly things they are thankful for.

» As a family practice a simple daily or weekly habit of asking:

"What went well today?"

"What are you grateful for right now?"

» Suggest that kids enlist a gratitude buddy and make it part of their routine to ask each other what made them happy that day and what they were grateful for.

» Cultivate the habit of expressing sincere thanks to those who lend them their time and support, not least to improve the likelihood that they continue to do so!

» Make gratitude a tangible part of the training or family culture, not an afterthought.

» Schedule regular thanksgiving to reflect on how circumstances and contributions of others enable and enrich their sporting participation and life in general.

» Instil the principle that feeling grateful for another person comes with the obligation to tell them so.

Negotiating Obstacles Along the Way
Navigating Talent ID and Selection in Youth Sports

"Success is not final, failure is not fatal: it is the courage to continue that counts."

— Winston Churchill

Being subject to the whims of selectors is an inescapable part of youth sports. The vagaries of talent identification and selection are among the common travails that young performers face on their journey. Even the most successful athletes often recall disappointments at not being selected for teams during their early years competing at high school and junior level. To help parents and the young performers themselves deal with these trials it is helpful to understand the factors at play. In doing so, we can devise some strategies to deal with selection decisions and mitigate the negative impact.

Part of the difficulty when trying to make sense of why one individual is favoured over another is that selection policies are often opaque (sometimes by design) and even somewhat arbitrary. Sports vary widely in the degree of subjectivity involved. For sports where performance is measured in centimetres, grams or seconds, it is relatively straightforward to evaluate capabilities from competition results. However, for most sports the objective physical performance metrics that we are able to capture during testing are only part of the equation. Inevitably there is some judgement involved in selection. Sadly, this introduces an element of bias in selection decisions, even though it may be unconscious.

Limitations aside, most youth sports incorporate tests of physical performance as part of selection. Selection pathways and the standardised tests employed may differ according to the sport, but in general test scores are used to help identify potential in young performers. The criteria employed might be as simple as height, weight and wingspan, but particular tests of fitness and physical performance are typically also part of the basis for selecting athletes. National and provincial sport organisations similarly use test scores as part of the selection funnel for athlete development pathways.

AGE AND STAGE BIAS SELECTION...

There is a great deal of variation and individuality in growth and development, such that kids of the same chronological age can vary widely in their biological age and relative stage in their development. Relative age and maturation have a major bearing on physical attributes and performance test scores during the teenage years. It is not immediately obvious whether a disparity in scores is a true indication of potential or just reflects that one individual is relatively further along on their growth curve at that point in time. Clearly this poses a major challenge for talent identification and it also has implications for selection.

In general, early maturing athletes have a clear, albeit temporary, advantage in junior competition, especially in sports where size and physicality are major assets. This effect is particularly marked for boys given the dramatic changes in size and lean mass and free gains in strength and speed that coincide with reaching puberty in young males. As a result, early maturing athletes are heavily favoured in selection for age-grade competition.

As we learned in an earlier chapter, the 'relative age effect' skews selection for age-grade teams, simply due to where a young performer's birth date happens to fall in relation the dates used to determine eligibility. Overall those with a birthday that is just after the start of the eligibility period typically have an advantage by being close to a year older than one of their peers whose birthday falls just before the cut-off date. Despite being aware of this phenomenon, the relative age effect is still evident in selection for youth teams. Those who have a birth date that falls early in the eligibility period for the sport continue to be over-represented in age-group squads and professional academy squads [265].

Relative age and maturation are consistently found to bias selection at junior level across different sports, from track and field athletics [266] to team sports, including Australian rules football [267], (soccer)football [142] and ice hockey [144]. This phenomenon has been described as a 'tale of two selection biases' [143].

IS THERE ANY GOOD NEWS?

So far we have painted a bit of a gloomy picture for late maturing kids and those who are not favoured in the birth date lottery. However, whilst there might be disadvantages in the short term, some good news is that despite the early advantages, being highly rated as a junior is not necessarily predictive of later success at the senior level [138].

Talent ID and selection across the board is notoriously bad at picking out those who will succeed. A number of large-scale investigations point to the same conclusion: we cannot extrapolate future performance and predict success based on junior results and rankings. In other words, the approaches commonly employed in talent identification are entirely unreliable for identifying real future potential. Authorities in the area advocate against early talent identification and selection on the grounds that it is ineffectual, harms young performers and is generally costly for sporting organisations, not least in the waste of genuine talent and misdirected resources [268].

Given all the flaws, clearly we should not assign too much weight to these policies and decisions! All of this means that there is good reason for young performers to not feel too disheartened if they are overlooked or not rated highly in junior competition. Early success is not a prerequisite for success at senior level, even in sports where you would expect this to be the case. Irrespective of early disappointments, the chances that they will shine later in high school, in college and at senior level remain undiminished.

By extension, de-selection or demotion is not the end of the journey for athletes who are initially included in talent development pathways or junior squads. Selection decisions are provisional. A study of selection and de-selection practices in the professional academy systems in European football reported nearly 30% turnover in player selection/deselection each year [269]. Given this is the norm, the most common path for those who go on to play at the professional level is a sequence of selection and deselection during the academy years, rather than a continuous unbroken involvement in the talent development pipeline from junior to senior professional level [270]. What this means is that there is still a path for those who are deselected and doors remains open to them if they can persist and respond positively.

Moreover, the conversion from top performing junior to elite senior is remarkably low, to the extent that top performing juniors and elite senior athletes are largely separate populations. This is more good news, as it suggests that there will still be chances to break through later on if young performers can hang in there.

START SLOW, FINISH STRONG…

All of this should also serve as a wake-up call for those young performers who do enjoy early success and natural advantages. Being marked out as 'talented' as a junior does not necessarily help kids to achieve success later on. This is all the more striking given that those who emerge early on are likely to be given preferential access and additional support as part a talent development pathway.

Paradoxically the unfavourable conditions experienced by late-maturing young performers can ultimately work to their advantage. Continually coming up against bigger and more physically developed opponents forces kids to develop technical and tactical skills in order to compete. These young performers also tend to be more resilient and mentally tough by virtue of coming through these trials.

Thus, despite all the disadvantages, late-maturers end up being over-represented in elite and professional sport at senior level. Moreover, late-maturers tend to enjoy prominent success at the senior level having come through these trials.

COUNTERMEASURES…

Despite the flaws in these approaches, selection and talent ID processes remain a reality that young performers must deal with. Aside from accepting the unfairness and using adversity as fuel, there are some practical strategies that can help young performers in navigating these trials. For instance, investing in physical preparation –

particularly strength training – can help to equalise things and offset the natural advantages that their peers might be enjoying at that time.

Where physical performance tests are used for selection, there is also the option of gaming the system a little by specifically seeking to get better at those tests. A good example is the 'combine' that is used for selection to the NFL and the equivalent test batteries employed in other professional sports in North America. A micro-industry has grown out of this, with a host of facilities and programmes delivering 'combine preparation' as a service. At these places aspiring players go to receive coaching and training specifically for the purposes of improving their numbers on the physical tests employed.

Whilst I do not necessarily recommend these programmes, enlisting a coach to help develop a young performer's athletic abilities and in turn their ability to jump high, run fast and go far is certainly beneficial when it comes to selection (and more generally their ability to perform in the sport). Parents should however choose wisely, as the expertise to successfully deliver this support remains rather uncommon.

Parents and young performers would also do well to better understand the factors that are linked to future success and adopt these lessons. Disregarding performance and physical tests for a moment, elements of character (tenacity, resilience) that do show an association with future success in sport and beyond are worth cultivating. Adopting and maintaining a growth mindset is important, which means a commitment to continually striving to improve and remaining willing to persevere, irrespective of early success or recognition from selectors.

Key Take-Home Messages

1. Talent identification and selection processes are influenced by subjectivity, bias, and incomplete information. They are far less reliable than most people assume.

2. Differences in maturation and relative age strongly influence physical performance, test scores, and selection decisions, particularly during the teenage years.

3. Junior rankings and early selection do not reliably predict who will succeed at senior or professional level. Many elite athletes were overlooked or deselected earlier in their development.

4. De-selection is common and rarely terminal. Most successful athletes experience non-linear pathways involving rejection, deselection, and re-selection. Continuous progression through talent pathways is the exception, not the norm.

5. Late-maturing athletes are not doomed—often the opposite. While disadvantaged in the short term, late maturers frequently develop superior technical, tactical, and psychological skills that confer long-term success.

6. Talent development and selection are better at picking out who is currently advanced than who will ultimately excel, leading to wasted talent and misdirected resources.

7. Mindset and how athletes respond to setbacks and disappointments make the biggest difference to the ultimate outcome.

Practical Tips

✓ Do not over-interpret selection decisions, as they do not necessarily reflect ability or potential.

✓ Help young athletes understand that setbacks are common and early disappointments are a feature of most sporting journeys that end in success.

✓ Focus on controllables. Emphasise effort, skill development, learning, and attitude rather than outcomes that sit outside the athlete's control.

✓ Avoid using the 'talented athlete' label as far as possible, recognising that being marked out as talented early on can impede progress.

✓ Early recognition can create false confidence, pressure or complacency, while early rejection can foster resilience and adaptability.

✓ Reinforce the message that selection decisions and judgements from those who are external to the process are not defining and should not limit their horizons.

Action Items

» Teach kids to not assign too much weight to talent identification assessments – including not getting carried away or getting complacent when selected.

» Respond, do not react - avoid making decisions (e.g. quitting) based on selection decisions.

» Invest in dedicated physical preparation and athletic development to help offset the temporary advantages enjoyed by early maturing peers.

» Encourage young athletes to keep showing up and improving, regardless of selection status.

» Prepare kids for testing with coaching and practice for the elements of the tests employed to give them the best chance of maximising their scores.

» Encouraged kids to hang in there and emphasise that how they perform later on is what will ultimately matter for success at college level and beyond

» Treat selection decisions as provisional and reversible.

Separating the Circles

> 'Grant me the serenity to accept the things I cannot change,
> the courage to change the things I can,
> and the wisdom to know the difference.'
>
> – Reinhold Niebuhr

In an uncertain world we are frequently required to act with incomplete information. There is much that is not only beyond our control but also beyond our ability to know. To some degree we all crave certainty; we all want to feel that we on sure footing and have a sense that we know how to proceed. The reality is any competitive endeavour (and life in general) is inherently unpredictable. This is especially applicable to the youth sports journey. Young athletes who are finding our way in the world are often thrown into scenarios where they are not entirely sure what is going on! In life as in competition, there are typically 'known unknowns' that the performer will need to respond to as the situation evolves – plus likely a few 'unknown unknowns' that are not on the performer's radar at all going in.

It is disconcerting to find ourselves in a situation where much is beyond our ability to know and outside of our control; on occasion it can seem unbearable. Once again, the recent pandemic provides many vivid examples! So many performers in different parts of the world were confronted with a scenario where they had to continue their preparations without knowing when or even if events would go ahead. In numerous instances it is unclear precisely what challenges we might face as we step into the breach. The complexity of sport and life is such that we are often faced with challenging situations where there are many moving parts. It is not uncommon for athletes to find they have multiple curve balls and grenades thrown at them at once! In such circumstance it is easy for young performers to become overwhelmed.

In the performance realm we often speak of controlling the controllables. The first step is differentiating what is under our control and what is not. We cannot control everything. Attempting to control or influence things that we have no agency over is the source of much of our trouble. Regaining a sense of control starts with having the humility to recognise that there is much that is beyond our power to influence.

ONTO THE CIRCLES...

Picture an archery target formed of three circles. The target as a whole comprises everything we consider to be relevant to our lives – we will call it our *circle of concern* (all that is in the background we effectively overlook as irrelevant). Inside is a smaller circle representing what we have some degree of influence over, so let's call it our *circle of influence*. In the centre – the bull's eye on the target – is the smallest circle yet and constitutes what we have direct control over. The area within the bull's eye is our *circle of control*.

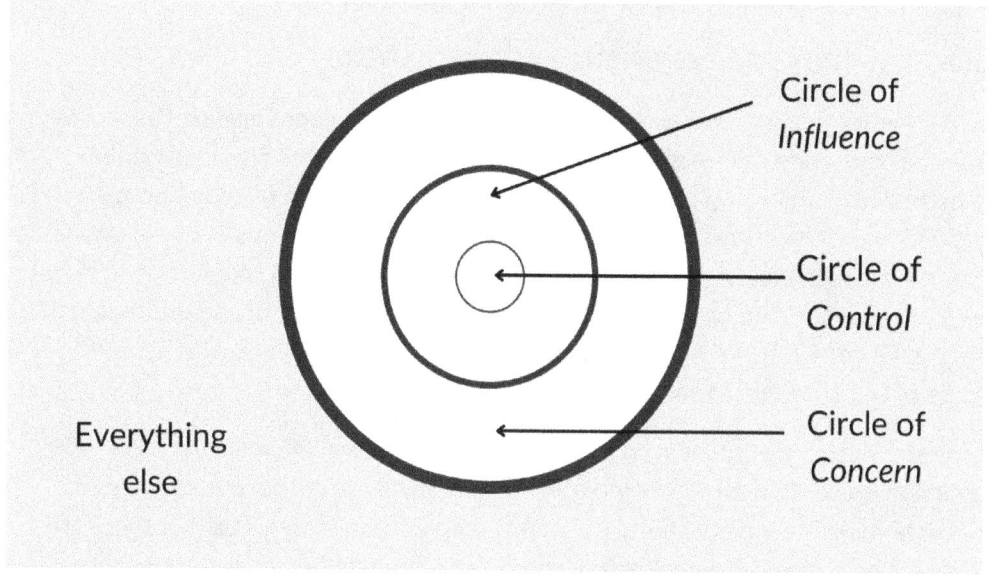

"Keep your world small"

– Andy Stumpf, decorated former Navy Seal and world record-breaking wingsuit flier

When we are feeling overwhelmed it helps to evaluate where we are allocating attention and expending other scarce resources. What is monopolising our attention are often legitimate concerns and may be genuinely concerning. Nevertheless, these are things that we have little or no control over or power to influence. The mantra 'keep your world small' is a call to selectively focus on the centre of the target. In other words, seek to attend first to what we can control and disregard other concerns that are beyond our influence.

A useful exercise under challenging conditions (the pandemic being a good example) is to break the situation down and methodically work out which elements fall within each respective sphere. We can then direct our attention, allocate resources and channel our efforts accordingly.

Aside from acknowledging what is beyond our influence and giving ourselves license to stop fretting about it, it is instructive and empowering to consider all that we do actually have control and influence over. There is much that is within our control, whatever the circumstances, and this applies even in the extreme case of the pandemic. In any event, disciplined action is the best remedy, which calls for being selective and investing our efforts only where we can have a direct impact.

Moving outwards, we should certainly seek to exercise what influence we have to our best advantage. Being realistic and acknowledging the limits of our influence also brings much needed clarity and perhaps a sense of equanimity.

CALIBRATING THE PERFORMER'S LENS ON THE SITUATION...

Whilst zooming in and narrowing our focus is helpful, so is zooming out! Pausing to remember the world that exists beyond our individual concerns also lends some much-needed perspective! In times of crisis performers benefit from temporarily removing themselves from the situation and those who are directly involved. Stepping out of the goldfish bowl of the situation and the sport in general often helps to refresh their view on what is going on. High profile performers at the elite and professional level greatly benefit from maintaining relationships and friendships with people outside of sport for these reasons.

Escaping the bubble of social media and getting back to real life and in-person interaction is excellent advice in general, but is particularly crucial during stressful times. Rejoining the outside world for a while also quickly reminds us that there are several billion people who are blissfully unaware of our travails and continuing to go about their daily business! However important or all-encompassing whatever we are facing may seem, it is always instructive to realise that the world will keep turning and the sun will rise tomorrow irrespective of the outcome.

We can also take steps to manage whatever might be distorting our perception of the situation. The act of writing things down in itself helps get our swirling thoughts out of our heads and onto the page so that we can appraise the situation in a way that is more rational, or at least less irrational. As with the original exercise involving the circles, this permits us to be clearer and more coherent in our thinking.

Situational awareness is important; however, beyond awareness of the situation, for full clarity we also need to be aware of our own state and how it might be colouring our perception. Naturally when we are stressed or agitated this is likely influencing whatever judgements we are presently making about the situation. It therefore pays tune into how we are feeling first and make the necessary allowances before proceeding.

CHANGING STATE...

Often when feeling overwhelmed it pays to pause and collect ourselves. There are a few practices and routines that can help us to reset and change our state to something that is more conducive to tackling the problem.

Simple breathing exercises can serve to alter the state of our autonomic nervous system. It remains sound advice to take a deep breath when feeling frustrated or overwhelmed! Slow, deliberate deep breaths help to slow our heart rate, reduce tension in the body and in turn help calm the mind. What the breathing example illustrates is that the mind-body connection is two-way (and our breathing apparatus serves as an intermediary between the two).

The reason why mind-body practices have become popular is that the actions we perform with our body influence what is going on within our mind. Training, and physical activity in general, is therefore not just a means to an end; in this context it can also serve as an outlet to relieve stress. The training facility can be a sanctuary during turbulent times.

Physical exercise can also be meditative. If we approach it correctly, exercising our body can do good things for our head space, both during the workout and afterwards. Much like sleeping on a problem, exercise can also help stimulate our thoughts and creative problem-solving. Getting out to exercise in nature offers additional benefits, refreshing our mind and boosting our sense of wellbeing, while our mind continues to grapple with the problem in the background. It is not a coincidence that many writers regularly take long walks!

Immersing ourselves in a familiar and absorbing activity can do wonders for our mental wellbeing and can also help us to shift our state. Well-rehearsed routines that are performed on a regular basis, such as a mobility series or a warm up, can attain the power of ritual. This is especially the case with the routine and warm up that is employed prior to competing – the activity provides something for the performer to focus on, which helps to mitigate pre-competition nerves, and going through these familiar steps serves to shift the mind into competition mode.

Other relatively mundane activities can also serve as a mind-body practice. Occupying ourselves in a task can provide mental refreshment and respite from nagging thoughts. In this way, everyday activities like preparing a meal can serve as a meditation.

Calming our minds by performing a sequence of familiar movements is similarly the basis of yoga, tai chi, and other related mind-body practices. They key point here is that many different activities can be meditative and serve as mind-body practice. The labels and connotations that come with what we generally think of when we hear 'mindfulness practice' or 'meditation' are entirely optional and do not need to become a barrier to participating and experiencing the benefits.

Key Take-Home Messages

1. Uncertainty is an unavoidable feature of sport and life; clarity does not come from controlling outcomes, but from controlling responses.

2. Feeling overwhelmed often stems from wasting attention and emotional energy on things that are beyond their control.

3. Separating concerns into what we control, what we can influence, and what we cannot change restores agency and confidence.

4. Progress and calm come from disciplined action, not from worrying or attempting to solve everything at once.

5. Narrowing focus ("keeping your world small") is as important as occasionally stepping back to regain perspective.

6. Mental clarity depends not only on understanding the situation, but also on recognising how stress and emotional state distort perception.

7. Simple, embodied practices—breathing, movement, routines—are powerful tools for resetting state and improving decision-making.

8. Mindfulness meditation does not require formal practice; many everyday activities can provide the same meditative grounding effect when approached deliberately.

Practical Tips

✓ When feeling overwhelmed, prompt them to pause and ask: Is this within my control? Under my influence? Neither?

✓ Help kids to give themselves permission to stop worrying about things that lie outside your influence.

✓ Help young student-athletes to focus daily effort on a small number of actions rather than trying to control and manage everything.

✓ Teach kids the power of simple breathing exercises to change their state when feeling overwhelmed or frustrated so they can think more clearly.

✓ Help kids to recognise that exercise is a tool for mental reset and refreshment, not just physical preparation.

✓ Encourage kids to get outside and walk in nature when grappling with a problem.

✓ Help kids understand the benefits of adopting a regular mind-body practice.

Action Items

» Instil the mantra 'keep your world small': selectively focus on what is within their control and disregard everything that is not under their power to influence.

» Teach kids about the circles! Walk them through the process of methodically breaking the situation down and figuring out which category the different elements fall into.

» Define daily controllables: Identify 2–4 actions each day that sit firmly within their circle of control and commit to executing them well.

» With the young athlete audit where they are allocating attention as a first step to better deploy mental resources and direct efforts towards what is under their control.

» Change state before tackling problems: Use breathing, movement, or a familiar routine before attempting to analyse or make decisions.

» Expose thoughts to sunlight Write things down to move them out of your head and onto the page, allowing them to appraise the situation in a more rational way.

» Make sure kids take scheduled breaks from the sport and study environment to regain perspective.

» Educate kids to proactively employ practices such as journalling, dialogue and social activity to get out of their head and regain perspective!

» Educate kids that attending to a familiar routine of movements such as a warm up has the power of ritual and offers a potent tool to handle nerves when competing

» Reframe uncertainty as a constant feature rather than a threat, and focus on responding well rather than second-guessing what might happen.

Purpose and Meaning

"Don't count the days; make the days count."

— Muhammad Ali

In an earlier chapter we walked through the process of delineating aims, objectives and goals. Whilst these frameworks are important to guide the pursuit and direct the young performer's efforts, from time to time it is helpful for everybody involved to take a step back and reflect on the deeper purpose behind the journey. This is especially important when setbacks inevitably occur, not least to deal with the anxiety of having their progress impeded. At these times it serves the young athlete to zoom out from the myopic focus on whatever goal they set themselves to remind themselves what it was that originally drew them to embark on the quest in the first place. Somewhere along the way this involves a realisation of what it all means to them on a deeper personal level.

RETURNING TO THE ORIGINAL AND DEEPER 'WHY'...

The learning process is not linear. This is especially the case for young athletes who are still growing and developing, which adds further volatility and fluctuations in performance. Kids not only progress in fits and starts, but it is also quite common to regress before they make the next leap forwards. Sometimes we have to take a step back to take two steps forwards. There will also be periods where things just do not go our way. This is something that young athletes who aspire to compete at the highest level will have to get used to – even the biggest stars experience periodic slumps in form at different times in their career.

During these lean times it becomes important that the young performer is able to draw on something else to sustain them. It is imperative that the pursuit itself offers some intrinsic value that is not reliant upon short term outcomes. The quest should provide a source of personal meaning, beyond the externalities and sense of gratification that comes from making unimpeded progress.

"He who has a why... can bear almost any how."

— Friedrich Nietzsche

The young athlete may however need some help to tap into the well of purpose and meaning, especially if they are not used to experiencing setbacks. One of the biggest ways that the grown-ups in the inner circle can assist is by prompting them to think back to what it was that originally motivated them to embark on the quest and drill down to the deeper 'why'. Such moments are instructive and offer an opportunity for us to reflect and remind ourselves of the overarching purpose behind what we are doing, beyond simply chasing whatever goals we have set ourselves.

HOW GOALS RELATE TO PURPOSE...

In theory, goals are an extension of purpose. The original 'why' that prompted us to engage in the sport or athletic pursuit, and the primary sense of purpose this provided, would naturally be our starting point. It follows that our involvement, and our desire to improve and develop, subsequently leads us to set short term goals and aspire towards a long-term objective.

Equally it is important to emphasise the separation. The goals were not the reason or original purpose for participating, but rather an offshoot of our participation. The reason this distinction is important is that when we set our sights on a particular objective, we can fall into a scenario where all other concerns become relegated to achieving this particular outcome. Rather than being an extension of the original purpose, when we become too immersed in the goal itself we can easily lose sight of our original 'why'. In effect the goal can displace the purpose – in effect becoming the reason why we do things. The pursuit itself can easily be reduced to simply becoming a means to an end.

I was recently prompted to ask somebody who requested my coaching services (a recreational runner) what their motivation was for running. He seemed confused by the question, so I asked whether the sole motivation for running was to achieve the 10k race time he had set himself, or whether there was any deeper meaning or wider value that running provided to his life. The question gave him pause. In this era of wearable technology and websites such as Strava where runners upload and share their workouts with an online community it is beguilingly easy for these ancillary concerns to become the focus. Not only is our attention is constantly drawn to the numbers displayed on our wrist, the motivation for running workouts can become at least in part about keeping up with the faceless horde online. There are potential benefits to this from an accountability perspective, but there are also clear downsides.

FINDING MEANING AND VALUE IN THE JOURNEY...

The satisfaction of attaining the summit is momentary and fleeting. In some ways, the successful culmination of the pursuit simply creates a new problem – what do we strive towards next! This is a common experience that many high performers grapple with: having dreamed of something for so long it can often like a let-down when they finally achieve it. Upon reflection what many come to realise is that the pursuit and the journey itself was the most rewarding part of the experience.

'Success is a journey, not a destination. The doing is often more important than the outcome.'

– Arthur Ashe

Striving purposefully towards some specified aim is a fundamental part of what lends meaning to our lives. The feeling of purpose and satisfaction that we derive from the quest is however available to us regardless of the final outcome. When professional athletes reflect on their career, it is often the friendships and memorable experiences away from the spotlight that are what they cherish most. Beyond the crowning achievement, the small victories and the challenges that engage us along the way are the essence of what makes the hero's journey special. A good analogy is the experience of doing a jigsaw puzzle: putting in the final piece is the least compelling part of the process – as soon as we have completed the puzzle, we very quickly lose interest. What captivates our attention and keeps us engaged for hour upon hour is contemplating the jumble of pieces and gradually piecing together the parts that make up the big picture in fits and starts, with the occasional frisson of excitement when we find a piece that fits.

To be clear, having an aim, clear objectives and goals are all important (hence we dedicated a chapter to them!). Aspiring to do great things is the first step to being a high performer and setting out our objectives and goals serves an important function. The point is that the quest can and should be rewarding in itself, in a way that is separate from and ultimately independent of the outcome.

Training must not be reduced to a grind. We must preserve the sense of meaning in the pursuit, not least to ensure that we continue to derive enjoyment and satisfaction along the way. Staying dialled into the purpose that underpins the goals we set also means we experience value and meaning in a way that is not contingent on anything else. Our intention of course remains achieving and surpassing the goals we set; but this should be in addition to the satisfaction we derive from investing ourselves in the pursuit, not in place of it.

Key Take-Home Messages

1. During difficult periods, goals alone are not enough to sustain motivation. Athletes need a deeper sense of purpose and meaning.

2. Purpose comes from reconnecting with the original "why"—what drew the young athlete to the sport in the first place and what it represents to them personally.

3. Goals should extend from purpose, not replace it. When goals become the sole focus, the pursuit risks becoming a joyless means to an end.

4. Short-term outcomes and external validation (times, rankings, data, social comparison) can distort motivation and crowd out intrinsic enjoyment.

5. The most meaningful aspects of sport are often found in the journey, not the destination—relationships, learning, shared experiences, and small victories.

6. Sustaining long-term engagement requires preserving meaning, enjoyment, and intrinsic value, alongside ambition and aspiration.

7. Training and striving should feel purposeful; it should not be a grind – even days when it feels like a struggle should be meaningful.

Practical Tips

✓ Encourage kids to zoom out from whatever goals they have set to remind themselves of the deeper 'why' behind the quest.

✓ Reframe stalls, slumps and setbacks as parts of the development process and an opportunity to reflect, reset, regroup and reconnect to the deeper why behind it all.

✓ Keep goals in perspective: Remind athletes that goals are tools, not the reason for participation.

✓ Watch for motivation drift: Be alert to signs that data, rankings, or social comparison are overshadowing what the original reason they go involved.

✓ Strongly discourage kids from thinking of training and practice as a grind or merely a means to an end!

✓ Help kids to cherish the experiences and friendships they enjoy through participating in sport – these are likely to be what they will look back on most fondly

✓ Along with the coaches, help kids to find purpose in the process and meaning in the pursuit

✓ Celebrate the process and appreciate the journey.

✓ Model perspective: Demonstrate through your own behaviour that meaning comes from engagement and growth, not just achievements and ticking off goals.

Action Items

» Have a "why" conversation under calm, low-pressure conditions to prompt the athlete to reflect on: Why they started the sport, What do they value most about participating, What parts are most meaningful for them now?

» Audit current goals - Review existing goals and ask: Do they still align with the athlete's deeper purpose? Have any goals begun to overshadow enjoyment or wellbeing?

» Create a purpose reminder routine or ritual: Help the athlete write down or articulate a short personal statement capturing what the journey means to them, to revisit during challenging periods.

» Reduce over-reliance on metrics, regularly train or compete without tracking data to reconnect with the feel of the activity itself and heighten the experience.

» Reframe success - After events or milestones, ask: What did you enjoy most? What did you learn? What moments mattered, regardless of outcome? What will remember?

» Educate kids that the journey delivers much more than simply reaching the destination – some of the most meaningful and satisfying moments are to be found along the way.

Adversity as Opportunity

"Smooth seas do not make skilful sailors."

— Proverb

What originally inspired me to write this chapter was a parent of a young field hockey player I had the privilege of working with, who greatly impressed me with how they chose to respond to a setback. Having been provisionally selected for the provincial squad for the coming season, her daughter had been de-selected because she failed to meet the standard specified by the selectors for a shuttle run fitness assessment at a recent preseason testing camp. There were various mitigating circumstances – she had endured many months out of action due to a recurring injury, which was the reason I had been called in to assist. The young athlete had made great progress and was rapidly returning to match fitness, so I offered to speak with the selectors and provide my assurances that she would make the standard if they would grant her special dispensation to repeat the assessment before the squad assembled to prove her fitness. Her mother graciously refused my offer to intervene on her daughter's behalf, asserting that this was something that her daughter should take on the chin. This particular sport parent had the wisdom to recognise that whilst it would be painful in the short term, her daughter would grow from the experience and it would fuel her to redouble her efforts and strive for greater heights in the future.

We generally think of times of adversity and setbacks as something to be endured, typically under duress. Our natural inclination is to steer clear of difficulties and we feel a strong urge is to shield those we care about from potential upset (and I can attest that certainly this hits much harder when it is your child). However, as the parent in question intuitively understood, whilst it might be hard to watch, going through these difficult experiences is vital. Naturally this becomes all the more crucial when our mission is to develop the talents of young performers in a way that sets them up to be successful at senior level.

The hard lessons often prove to be the most valuable. Setbacks provide the chance to see what we are made of and these trials test us in ways that will serve us down the road. After all, if our mettle has never been tested how much faith can we have in our ability to overcome when we face the ultimate test?

CRITICAL LIFE EVENTS...

If you look into the back story of any successful performer the odds are you will find tales of adversity. Some of the leading authors on the topic consider the bumps in the road to be so vital that we should intentionally seek to put them in the young performers' path [271].

What are termed *critical life events* are an integral and even essential part of the talent development pathway in sport and other domains concerned with mastery and excellence, such as music [272]. For clarity, what constitutes a critical life event is something out of the ordinary that derails the performer and causes disarray. Generally, this is not a pleasant experience, as such events temporarily cast us into chaos until we are able to get our bearings and plot a path forwards. Nevertheless, if navigated correctly, these experiences forge the performer and equip them for future success.

Given the attempts to eliminate potential or perceived harm within education and other parts of society, it becomes all the more crucial that we provide the necessary opportunities to face adversity in the context of sport. Beyond the desire to create resilient, capable and confident young adults, it is vital that the journey prepares the athlete to cope with the crucible of competition and the miscellaneous challenges they will inevitably encounter along the way.

STRESS TESTING...

As the saying goes, there is no success without struggle. One of the implications is that we will inevitably encounter obstacles and experience setbacks on the journey, especially if we are striving to do something exceptional. However, another equally important point that is often missed is that the struggle itself is a fundamental part of what ultimately leads to us becoming successful in our quest. The archetypal plot of any hero story is that some calamity befalls our hero, they struggle through hardship and through courage and perseverance they overcome and emerge victorious. A central theme is that calamity, hardship and struggle are integral to the transformation that the hero undergoes that allows them to prevail.

Character is forged in adversity. *Tempering* is a process that brings out the intrinsic toughness of a material and in much the same way it is with exposure to tough conditions that we express our intrinsic strength and become more durable as a result. Stress is thus necessary for flourishing; indeed a stressor is simply the stimulus that triggers us to adapt and increase our capacities to cope with future challenges. Resilience is an *emergent property* – that is, it emerges over time with exposure to conditions that test our mettle. This applies whether we are talking in terms of physical or mental strength. We should help kids to bear this in mind as they encounter challenging times and experience setbacks.

TIMES OF ADVERSITY BRING CLARITY...

Going through hard times is highly revealing. Not only do we discover who is really in our corner, but it is when we experience that we really find out about ourselves. Times of hardship reveal what strength the young performer has within them and what reserves they can call upon.

When the going is easy and things are a bit too comfortable it is hard for aspiring young athletes to truly appreciate the real significance of what they are striving towards. Under such conditions and amid the daily distractions, they can lose touch with the underlying motivation and deeper meaning of the quest. Often it is only when a young performer faces difficulty or suffers disappointment that they are able to appreciate what it means to them and realise why it is important.

Without being exposed to challenge and adversity a young person cannot really gauge what their present limits might be. Until they are tested, they have no real way of knowing what they might be able to handle. In much the same way, the depth of their drive and will to succeed is revealed to them only when they are put to the test.

DIFFICULTY IS DESIRABLE...

Performers need to experience challenge and disappointment. It is when confronted with obstacles that we are prompted to show what we are capable of. The hard times become the source of strength and confidence: emerging from these trials the performer is not only stronger but also more confident in their ability to face future challenges. Following this logic we get the concept of *desirable difficulty*.

"If you find a path with no obstacles it probably doesn't lead anywhere"

— Frank A. Clark

A coach shared with me that ironically one of the problems he faces with the kids in his programme is that being from affluent and supportive families their lives beyond the sport are relatively free from significant hardships. This seems like a nice problem to have. However, whilst it might not be intuitive, the reality is that when kids are shielded from adversity and conflict this renders them less well prepared to navigate threat [193].

Paradoxically, kids who are shielded from threats and hardship also tend to be more anxious as a consequence. There is some logic to this. Without having faced difficult times a person has no way of knowing how they might cope, so it is understandable that this might be cause to feel anxious, especially when contemplating the prospect of going out into the world on their own.

Building strength of character and resilience are essential parts of the talent development process. If the path has been too easy then they are unproven and thus ill-prepared for what is to come. Happily, sport offers ample opportunities to be exposed to challenge, difficulty and disappointment! It is important that the grown-ups understand the need and the benefit, not only so we can resist the urge to intervene unnecessarily but also to educate the young performer to embrace it.

SEEING THE OPPORTUNITY IN THE OBSTACLE...

To illustrate the power of perspective, one athlete I worked with during the early part of my career was a great role model for how young performers should handle adversity. I was working in professional rugby union at the time, and injuries are not uncommon for professional rugby players given that it is a sport that involves high impact bodily contact with other large humans. Even so the player in question had a phenomenal attitude when faced with periods on the sidelines due to injury and his perspective on coming back from injuries was quite extraordinary. Kieron not only quickly overcame any disappointment at the setback he had suffered, but then adopted the mindset of relishing the opportunity it presented to come back fitter, faster and stronger. This made a huge impression on me at the time, and it has stayed with me. As an aside, this attitude clearly served Kieron well. Despite suffering significant injuries along the way he nevertheless had a long and distinguished playing career, finally retiring in 2009 after 13 seasons playing at the highest level for club and country.

Navigating problems is how we learn and develop our capabilities. A problem is an exercise, a puzzle to figure out and lead us towards a solution. An obstacle that tests us can properly be viewed a stepping-stone that allows us to progress towards where we desire to go. Shifting our perspective helps us appraise difficulties in terms of the challenge and opportunity they represent, rather than a hardship we just have to suffer through. Adopting this framing alters how we anticipate and engage with the trials we face, allowing us to take more from the experience.

RESPONDING APPROPRIATELY...

The moments in the journey of a young performer that prove to be defining typically comprise setbacks and struggles. Returning to the archetypal hero's tale, these momentous life events which prove so pivotal commonly come in the form of crises. The most extreme case is when calamity strikes, such as a serious injury or some other misfortune, either in sport or in the performer's life beyond sport. Given their seriousness it is tempting to describe such instances as 'traumatic' and a prominent group has highlighted the role of 'trauma' in the talent development process.

It is worth highlighting that we have become very casual in what we label 'trauma'. In the popular culture references to trauma are becoming ubiquitous and even post-traumatic stress disorder (PTSD) is invoked for relatively minor everyday misfortunes. Such careless use of these terms is not just a matter of semantics; it has real consequences. We can see this in the trends in the data for anxiety and mental health struggles reported by young people in the United States over past decades [273]. What is striking about the steady decline in self-reported wellbeing among high school and college students with each successive generation is that standards of living have continually improved over this period. The fact that youth are more troubled and more negative in their outlook than ever despite the fact that life is objectively easier and better than previous generations is telling. What it demonstrates is the profound influence of the popular culture. In other words, part of the disconnect between subjective feelings and objective reality comes down to how each generation interprets the world and in turn how they perceive whatever challenges they encounter.

"I am not what happened to me; I am what I choose to become"

– Carl Jung

A critical juncture or single momentous event can be make or break for a young performer. For some it proves to be the making of them, whereas others fall by the wayside. More often it is more incremental, such that the single event that appears to be defining is in effect the culmination of many other smaller events that led up to it. All the same, how an individual appraises setbacks and periods of adversity sets the scene for how they choose to respond. In this way the framing and interpretation of a significant event has a profound effect in shaping which of these scenarios (make versus break) plays out.

Those of us in the athlete's corner need to be careful with the language we use, as it can matter a great deal to the outcome. There is a crucial distinction to be made between 'traumatic' and 'potentially traumatic'. The reason even the most calamitous event is only *potentially traumatic* is that what ensues has two very distinct and opposing outcomes in individuals within a group [274]. Very different scenarios can unfold following tragedy: one potential outcome is negative and dysfunctional, with lasting debilitating effects; the alternative outcome is positive and marked by a healthy response, such that the individual emerges from the experience transformed and more resilient as a result. Happily, the resilience trajectory is the more common of the two. In part the course that things take comes down to temperament, but it is also possible to shift our mindset, such that we appraise and respond to events in a way that better serves us. Clearly as coaches and parents we should seek to do our part to tip the balance in the young performer's favour.

So it is true that there is conceivably benefit to intentionally putting bumps in the road for young performers as they proceed along their journey. However, ensuring young performers encounter challenge and experience adversity is only part of the equation; we must also guide and support them to appraise obstacles and respond to setbacks in a way that is to their benefit. Being 'pivotal', things can go either way! The grown-ups in the athlete's corner are in a position to influence things such that the experience proves to be transformative in a way that is positive and renders them better equipped for whatever travails they might face in the future.

PREPARED...

Parents and coaches share a duty of care to prepare young performers to cope with whatever threats and challenges they might encounter in the competition arena and beyond. A big part of preparing young performers (and young people in general) concerns learning how to *approach*, *appraise* and *respond* to whatever events, challenges and mishaps might befall them.

The central theme of *approach* is learning to go towards the challenge rather than avoiding it. We must teach young performers to recognise the potential opportunities – the more daunting the situation the more it is likely to offer. Coming through trials and testing conditions is the route to developing resilience. Equally, having done so, our task is not done. Remaining resilient to some extent follows the principle 'use it or lose it'. When deprived of shocks or stressors we become more fragile over time and in turn less equipped to cope. It follows that it is appropriate that young athletes should learn to embrace the challenges that they encounter.

How we *appraise* a situation and the mindset we adopt is similarly powerful. What meaning we attach and what causes we attribute to events profoundly affects how we experience them. Part of this is managing our own expectations. It is important that performers retain an optimistic outlook, but it helps to temper this with pragmatism and a realisation that mishaps will occur on the way. Accepting that they might sometimes suffer misfortune makes it easier to quickly get past feeling sorry for themselves so that we can get onto tackling the situation.

Whilst there is much that is beyond our control, how we *respond* to events remains firmly in our power. This applies both in the moment and after the event. Win or lose, the intention should be to make the most of the lessons on offer. Always the objective is to emerge from the experience better equipped to navigate future challenges. Competitive sport is rich in opportunities to cultivate a healthy relationship with stress and we should help kids to regard stressful situations as stepping stones rather than landmines.

IN CLOSING...

Kids should be encouraged to embrace the challenges and obstacles that are a feature of the talent development pathway and the youth sports experience. In view of the merits, perhaps we should even seek out these challenges. Whilst it is not necessarily intuitive, a crucial part of the talent development process is incorporating obstacles and challenges. These experiences can be transformative and equip the performer with coping skills.

Arguably this is most important for young performers who enjoy parental support, the comforts of affluence and other advantages. Paradoxically these fortunate performers are most in need of opportunities to experience discomfort and difficulty. The revelatory idea of intentionally exposing young performers to adversity and challenge in a systematic and regulated fashion in service of their long-term development is something that is worth noting. An important caveat is that the young performer must also consent to this, such that they are a willing participant!

One thing that is clear is that we should certainly not fear or seek to avoid setbacks. Rather than feeling aggrieved and looking for a way out when we experience difficulty, performers should rather recognise the gift that they have been presented with. By adopting this perspective we can more fully leverage the opportunities afforded by these events and experiences.

Key Take-Home Messages

1. Adversity and setbacks are not interruptions to development; they are a fundamental part of it.

2. Many successful performers experience critical life events that temporarily derail them but ultimately strengthen their resolve and make them more capable and resilient.

3. Stress, challenge and struggle are necessary stimuli for growth and building resilience.

4. Shielding young performers from difficulty may provide short-term comfort but is likely to make them more anxious over time as they are unprepared for future challenges.

5. How adversity is appraised and framed shapes both how it is experienced and what long-term impact it has.

6. Perspective matters: obstacles can be experienced as threats or reframed as opportunities for learning and growth.

7. Negative events at most are potentially traumatic, with outcomes shaped by mindset, language, and support.

8. Parents and coaches play a pivotal role at moments of setback through the words they use, the behaviours they model, and the restraint they show.

9. Sport provides a uniquely rich environment to experience "desirable difficulty".

10. True preparation for sport and life includes learning how to approach, respond to and learn from adversity rather than avoiding it.

Practical Tips

✓ Be intentional with language: avoid labelling ordinary setbacks as "trauma" and instead frame them as challenges that may serve the mission long-term.

✓ Help young performers zoom out and see the longer-term developmental value of short-term disappointment.

✓ Encourage a mindset of "What can I learn from this?" rather than "Why did this happen to me?"

✓ Normalise struggle by reinforcing that difficulty is expected on any meaningful developmental journey.

✓ Model calm, constructive responses to adversity through your own behaviour.

✓ Resist the urge to intervene unnecessarily and help kids to leverage the opportunity these experiences offer to grow and equip themselves for future challenges.

✓ Be careful with language – avoid labelling experiences as 'traumatic' and emphasise that even calamity offers tremendous potential for growth.

✓ Help kids to recognise the opportunities presented when they encounter obstacles and help guide them to get the most they can out of the experience.

✓ Balance optimism with realism: setbacks and misfortune are part of life and sport.

✓ Use sport as a training ground for coping with stress, pressure, and uncertainty.

Action Items

» Use the biographies of stars of the sport to illustrate how going through struggles including critical life events ultimately proved to be the making of them.

» Emphasise agency: outside events and external factors might be beyond their control but how they respond is always up to them.

» Educate young performers on how they should approach, appraise and respond to times of adversity:

- Be brave and go towards the challenge rather than shirking from it – the more daunting it is, the more it is likely to offer.
- Accept that misfortune will strike from time to time, strive to view it in terms of opportunity and embrace the challenge in a spirit of optimism.
- Realise that their response will shape how the emerge from the experience and how well they are able to use it as a stepping stone to greater things.

Finding a Way

"Do what you can, with what you have, where you are."

— Theodore Roosevelt

Athletes who are successful over time are typically highly resourceful and adaptable. One of the reasons that early access to talent development pathways can hinder development is that young athletes become accustomed to having access to the best facilities and extensive support, such that they struggle when these things are not available. The pandemic affected athletes at all levels, up to and including professional and elite, as they found competition was suspended and for a time were unable to access their usual training facilities. This might have been a rare and unprecedented event, but young athletes will encounter less extreme periods of disruption on a regular basis, not least when competing away from home or overseas. The initiative to find a way to train remotely, navigate travel and compete amidst disruption, constraints and restrictions will come to the fore at these times, so we should make sure they are equipped to rise to the challenge.

A MATTER OF PERSPECTIVE...

To continue the theme of the last chapter, times of adversity are illuminating. As Joni Mitchell noted, it is often only once something is taken away that we come to appreciate how much we rely on it. On the other hand, we are also afforded the opportunity to discover new and alternative ways of doing things. Necessity is the mother of invention, and these experiences can ultimately work in our favour, rendering the young athlete more adaptable and less reliant. In this way, such times when young athletes are deprived of their usual facilities and support can be illuminating in ways that prove to be beneficial!

From a coaching perspective, it is also revealing how athletes respond at times such as these. Does the athlete simply accept the (somewhat valid) excuse that they are unable to train as normal and so opt to sit back and wait for things to change? Or do they set about finding ways to get it done using whatever tools and facilities that are available to them?

FOCUSSING ON WHAT WE CAN DO...

As a general rule it is more helpful to focus on what we can do, rather than lamenting the options that are temporarily unavailable. In various scenarios it pays to shift our thinking to what possibilities exist and how we might utilise whatever resources we have at our disposal. With some initiative and a bit of creative thinking we can do a lot with a little. This even applies when the young athlete is incapacitated in some way.

Periods of injury are a prime example of a situation where it pays to turn our attention to what we can do, rather than obsessing about what we cannot. A big part of my role when helping athletes with their injury rehabilitation is to open their mind (and also the practitioners involved) to what the athlete is still capable of doing. Naturally any injury imposes constraints, especially in the case of more severe sports injuries, and this tends to be the theme for what is communicated to the athlete during this time. It is liberating to switch our perspective and be curious (and courageous) in exploring what they are able to do without adverse effects. In spite of the restrictions, injured athletes often surprise themselves as they discover what they are still capable of.

FLYING SOLO...

When athletes are temporarily without their pit crew (if they have one), then the task of maintaining their own hardware falls squarely on their shoulders. As we noted in an earlier chapter, the most important equipment we need to invest in and take care of is our own body. Athletes will frequently have to find ways to train and keep their body in one piece when on the road or unable to access providers, so any opportunity to become better at self-management will serve them well down the road.

Using a motor sports analogy, it is routine practice for the engineers in the pit crew to run a full systems check before the race car goes out onto the track. The equivalent for athletes is to employ a daily routine comprising a series of mobility exercises that serves as a self-screen and systems check. This allows them to assess how everything is functioning and evaluate how the different components are moving. I recommend athletes make this self-diagnostic and daily calibration process part of their normal routine in any case, but it assumes greater importance when they are not able to access their usual training environment and support team.

Another routine part of the support I provide to athletes, regardless of age, stage, and level of competition, is to equip them with tools and knowledge to better manage their own body. For instance, there are various low cost, readily available and easily accessible tools that athletes can use for self-directed manual therapy. Under normal circumstances these provide a helpful adjunct for routine daily maintenance to complement whatever manual therapy input provided by other practitioners. At times when access to therapy provision may not be available, utilising these tools becomes all the more important.

ALTERNATIVE TRAINING ENVIRONMENTS...

There are naturally times, such as when on the road, when athletes are temporarily unable to access their normal training environment and they have to make do with whatever facilities are available. The ability to improvise is an important skill for athletes to come up with plan B workouts that provide what they need.

Whilst we are likely to be more restricted in terms of the training tools that are available, we can get a lot done with options that require minimal equipment. Simply exploiting gravity and using different terrain and urban architecture in creative ways can provide a good training stimulus. There are numerous workout options that involve only body weight resistance, including an extensive array of strength and mobility exercises ('calisthenics'), jump and plyometric training, drills and track-type workouts for acceleration and speed development, plus a host of conditioning activities. In combination with judicious use of hills, stairs, and other features of the local outdoor environments, a resourceful athlete can find a way to get what they need.

Key Take-Home Messages

1. Adaptability is a characteristic of successful athletes – those who thrive over time prove able to adjust, improvise and continue progressing under suboptimal conditions.

2. Over-reliance on facilities and support impedes development. Constant access to high-quality environments may limit an athlete's ability to cope when those supports are absent due to travel or unforeseen circumstances.

3. Periods of deprivation and disruption provide impetus and opportunity to develop coping skills – operating under constraints promotes initiative and problem-solving.

4. Focusing on what is possible, rather than what is unavailable, opens the door to creative solutions and continued progress.

5. Suspending access to facilities and support can accelerate learning – when athletes are forced to manage their own bodies and figure out solutions, they develop greater awareness, ownership and confidence.

6. The ability to adapt is a skill to be honed: resourcefulness and self-reliance can be taught, practised, and reinforced over time.

Practical Tips

✓ Encourage athletes to see breaks in routine as chances to explore new training methods, environments, and habits.

✓ Shift the question to "What can I do?" to promote agency and problem-solving during disruption or restricted access to facilities.

✓ Build self-management into everyday routines. Teach athletes to take responsibility for recovery and everyday maintenance, rather than relying on external support.

✓ Implement a daily mobility routine as a self-diagnostic tool to help athletes assess how their body is functioning and make necessary adjustments.

✓ Reward initiative and educate kids on the importance of cultivating the will and ability to find a way rather than being a victim of circumstances.

✓ Practise training without facilities – calisthenics, running drills, hills, stairs, and varied terrain can provide effective training when equipment is limited.

Action Items

» Intentionally create low-support situations, removing or restricting facilities, equipment or guidance to help athletes practise independence and adaptability.

» Ask reflective questions after disruption. For example: What did you learn about yourself? What worked? What would you do differently next time?

» Teach athletes basic self-care skills early. Include mobility routines, recovery strategies, and simple self-treatment tools as part of normal development.

» Ask the coaching staff to provide ideas and guidance for plan B, plan C, plan D workout options.

» Instil the mindset of focussing on what they can do and help them realise the possibilities.

» Along with the coaching staff, challenge kids to find ways to be creative and adaptable.

» Work with the coaches and other practitioners to equip young athletes with low-cost self-therapy tools for their kit bag.

» Work with young athletes to utilise whatever they have at their disposal to continue to train when away from their normal environment, such as during vacations.

» Encourage ownership during injury rehabilitation – help athletes explore options for modified training and adapted activity rather than defaulting to inactivity.

Concluding Comments

As we opened with, the sport parent comes in many guises, depending in part on which aspects of the youth sports experience they most value for their child. Kids similarly range widely in what they are seeking from sport – and indeed, this often changes over time. Accordingly, there is no blueprint to follow when it comes to guiding kids in their youth sports participation – much like with other aspects of being a parent!

Nevertheless, I hope this book provides something of a scaffolding and that you feel on firmer ground as you seek to support your child through their own journey. By illuminating the considerations that you will need to take into account, the preceding chapters hopefully help inform how you approach whatever tasks you are faced with in your role as sport parent and help you to handle the transitions as that role evolves. My intention is that the principles outlined can be readily adapted for your own purposes to allow you to apply the relevant information to your own context. Likewise, I hope the practical tips help you to guide your young performer through whatever scenarios you encounter. Above all, I hope the book has given you a newfound appreciation of why it is important that we keep kids in the game for as long as we are able.

Many parents of aspiring young performers have found community among the parents of other kids in the academy team or talent development programmes their child is part of. I encourage readers to build a community with other sport parents, both locally and perhaps further afield. This offers a great way to pool resources, share recommendations and create a peer support network. As well as lending a sense of community and a source of emotional support, doing so will allow you the opportunity to tap into the hive mind when faced with dilemmas! To take the first step, consider reaching out to other parents to share whatever information or guidance you have found valuable. Perhaps we will be able to grow an online community from those who have this book – the *Athlete Generation* substack exists for just this purpose!

To close, my sincere thanks for taking the time to read this book. I embarked on the project in an appropriate spirit of seriousness. Throughout the process I was acutely aware of the gravity of the topic and the fact that I am aiming to reach a vitally important yet under-served audience. It was fitting that the period of writing and editing the book spanned the birth of my son and his first few months in the world. Likewise, the writing and editing process for this revised edition coincided with Leo's fourth birthday. Contemplating Leo embarking on his own youth sports journey strengthened my resolve to do the topic justice and prompted me to revisit the book with a revised edition. I hope the renewed effort to reach and serve the audience proves successful.

Appendix

The Sport Parent Self Audit

Despite our lofty goals, we can unwittingly overstep. Our input is not always well received and our intervention does not always have the intended effect. It is also easy to get carried away in the moment. In various ways our conduct can become a source of friction with coaches and a stressor for the young athlete.

The best strategy to avoid such unintended consequences is to engage in regular self-reflection. Periodically, it serves everybody well to ask ourselves the hard questions and do our best to answer them honestly.

Before we begin, let us state at the outset that this is written with the intention of being challenging and even provocative. However, it is not meant to be accusatory - I am highly aware that parents are often maligned unfairly and that is not my intention. The purpose of the exercise is not to make you second-guess yourself but rather to call attention to the potential pitfalls as a defence against falling prey to them. To that end, the objective is to challenge the reader; to prompt you to hold up a mirror to your motivations, interrogate your intentions and consider your own conduct.

In that spirit, let's take a breath and go for it:

Why is engaging in sport important for your child? Are the benefits clear to them?

Why is your child's involvement in sport important to you? Is it more or less important to them?

Who are we doing this for? Whose needs are we serving?

Who is making the decisions in relation to your child's participation? Who should be?

What is driving your involvement?

What determines the extent of your involvement?

What would your child say about your reasons for being involved?

When your child encounters problems do you jump in or do you permit them to try to resolve it themselves?

Where do you go for advice and information?

How confident are you that you are doing the right thing?

How involved is your ego?

Appendix

Is it their dream or yours? Is making up for your own disappointments or unfulfilled ambitions part of the equation?

Is being the parent of a successful athlete part of your identity?

Is your kid enjoying participating in sport? Are you sure?

Is your child capable of organising themselves? Would they attend practice if you did not bring them?

Are you allowing your child to be challenged? Do you permit the coach to call them out when necessary and deliver critical feedback?

Are your decisions based on the best evidence available or are you just following what everybody else is doing?

Are you too invested? Are you more committed to your child's sporting career than they are?

Do you do things for your child that they are capable of doing for themselves?

Do you brag about your child's sporting achievements? Are you taking credit and sharing in the glory?

Do you act differently when your kids wins?

Do you take it personally when they lose? Does this affect how you behave?

If you watched video of yourself on the side-lines would it be uncomfortable viewing?

Well done to those who made it to the end! Rest assured, you are already ahead. Your dedication to the mission and desire to ensure you are doing the right thing are to your credit. Kudos to you. All the best to your child on their youth sports journey - they are in good hands...

Bibliography

1. Guthold R, Stevens GA, Riley LM, Bull FC. Global trends in insufficient physical activity among adolescents: a pooled analysis of 298 population-based surveys with 1·6 million participants. The Lancet Child & Adolescent Health. 2020;4(1):23-35.
2. Reilly JJ. When does it all go wrong? Longitudinal studies of changes in moderate-to-vigorous-intensity physical activity across childhood and adolescence. J Exerc Sci Fit. 2016;14(1):1-6.
3. Von Hofsten C. Action, the foundation for cognitive development. Scand J Psychol. 2009;50(6):617-23.
4. van der Fels IM, Te Wierike SC, Hartman E, Elferink-Gemser MT, Smith J, Visscher C. The relationship between motor skills and cognitive skills in 4-16 year old typically developing children: A systematic review. Journal of science and medicine in sport / Sports Medicine Australia. 2015;18(6):697-703.
5. Musculus L, Ruggeri A, Raab M. Movement Matters! Understanding the Developmental Trajectory of Embodied Planning. Front Psychol. 2021;12:633100.
6. Adolph KE, Hoch JE. Motor Development: Embodied, Embedded, Enculturated, and Enabling. Annual review of psychology. 2019;70:141-64.
7. Lozada M, Carro N. Embodied Action Improves Cognition in Children: Evidence from a Study Based on Piagetian Conservation Tasks. Front Psychol. 2016;7:393.
8. Stevens-Smith DA. Active bodies/active brains: The relationship between physical engagement and children's brain development. Physical Educator. 2016;73(4):719.
9. Erickson KI, Hillman CH, Kramer AF. Physical activity, brain, and cognition. Current Opinion in Behavioral Sciences. 2015;4:27-32.
10. Perez EC, Bravo DR, Rodgers SP, Khan AR, Leasure JL. Shaping the adult brain with exercise during development: Emerging evidence and knowledge gaps. Int J Dev Neurosci. 2019;78(1):147-55.
11. Takehara K, Togoobaatar G, Kikuchi A, Lkhagvasuren G, Lkhagvasuren A, Aoki A, et al. Exercise Intervention for Academic Achievement Among Children: A Randomized Controlled Trial. Pediatrics. 2021;148(5).
12. Ruiz-Ariza A, Grao-Cruces A, de Loureiro NEM, Martínez-López EJ. Influence of physical fitness on cognitive and academic performance in adolescents: A systematic review from 2005–2015. International Review of Sport and Exercise Psychology. 2016;10(1):108-33.
13. Haverkamp BF, Wiersma R, Vertessen K, van Ewijk H, Oosterlaan J, Hartman E. Effects of physical activity interventions on cognitive outcomes and academic performance in adolescents and young adults: A meta-analysis. Journal of sports sciences. 2020;38(23):2637-60.
14. de Bruijn AGM, Kostons DDNM, van der Fels IMJ, Visscher C, Oosterlaan J, Hartman E, et al. Importance of aerobic fitness and fundamental motor skills for academic achievement. Psychology of Sport and Exercise. 2019;43:200-9.
15. Garcia-Hermoso A, Ramirez-Velez R, Lubans DR, Izquierdo M. Effects of physical education interventions on cognition and academic performance outcomes in children and adolescents: a systematic review and meta-analysis. British journal of sports medicine. 2021;55(21):1224-32.
16. Shi P, Feng X. Motor skills and cognitive benefits in children and adolescents: Relationship, mechanism and perspectives. Front Psychol. 2022;13:1017825.
17. Klupp S, Mohring W, Lemola S, Grob A. Relations between fine motor skills and intelligence in typically developing children and children with attention deficit hyperactivity disorder. Res Dev Disabil. 2021;110:103855.

Bibliography

18. Pontifex MB, Saliba BJ, Raine LB, Picchietti DL, Hillman CH. Exercise improves behavioral, neurocognitive, and scholastic performance in children with attention-deficit/hyperactivity disorder. The Journal of pediatrics. 2013;162(3):543-51.

19. Chueh T-Y, Hsieh S-S, Tsai Y-J, Yu C-L, Hung C-L, Benzing V, et al. Effects of a single bout of moderate-to-vigorous physical activity on executive functions in children with attention-deficit/hyperactivity disorder: A systematic review and meta-analysis. Psychology of Sport and Exercise. 2022;58:102097.

20. Lambez B, Harwood-Gross A, Golumbic EZ, Rassovsky Y. Non-pharmacological interventions for cognitive difficulties in ADHD: A systematic review and meta-analysis. J Psychiatr Res. 2020;120:40-55.

21. Panksepp J. Can PLAY diminish ADHD and facilitate the construction of the social brain? J Can Acad Child Adolesc Psychiatry. 2007;16(2):57-66.

22. Nijhof SL, Vinkers CH, van Geelen SM, Duijff SN, Achterberg EJM, van der Net J, et al. Healthy play, better coping: The importance of play for the development of children in health and disease. Neurosci Biobehav Rev. 2018;95:421-9.

23. Siviy SM. A Brain Motivated to Play: Insights into the Neurobiology of Playfulness. Behaviour. 2016;153(6-7):819-44.

24. van Kerkhof LW, Damsteegt R, Trezza V, Voorn P, Vanderschuren LJ. Social play behavior in adolescent rats is mediated by functional activity in medial prefrontal cortex and striatum. Neuropsychopharmacology. 2013;38(10):1899-909.

25. Marquardt AE, VanRyzin JW, Fuquen RW, McCarthy MM. Social play experience in juvenile rats is indispensable for appropriate socio-sexual behavior in adulthood in males but not females. Front Behav Neurosci. 2022;16:1076765.

26. Danielson ML, Claussen AH, Bitsko RH, Katz SM, Newsome K, Blumberg SJ, et al. ADHD Prevalence Among U.S. Children and Adolescents in 2022: Diagnosis, Severity, Co-Occurring Disorders, and Treatment. J Clin Child Adolesc Psychol. 2024;53(3):343-60.

27. Kazda L, Bell K, Thomas R, McGeechan K, Sims R, Barratt A. Overdiagnosis of Attention-Deficit/Hyperactivity Disorder in Children and Adolescents: A Systematic Scoping Review. JAMA Netw Open. 2021;4(4):e215335.

28. Panksepp J, Burgdorf J, Turner C, Gordon N. Modeling ADHD-type arousal with unilateral frontal cortex damage in rats and beneficial effects of play therapy. Brain Cogn. 2003;52(1):97-105.

29. Hansen Sandseter EB, Kleppe R, Ottesen Kennair LE. Risky play in children's emotion regulation, social functioning, and physical health: an evolutionary approach. International Journal of Play. 2022;12(1):127-39.

30. Brussoni M, Gibbons R, Gray C, Ishikawa T, Sandseter EBH, Bienenstock A, et al. What is the Relationship between Risky Outdoor Play and Health in Children? A Systematic Review. International Journal of Environmental Research and Public Health. 2015;12(6):6423-54.

31. de Moraes YL, Varella MAC, Santos Alves da Silva C, Valentova JV. Adult playful individuals have more long- and short-term relationships. Evolutionary Human Sciences. 2021;3:e24.

32. Lisinskienė A, Lochbaum M. Links between Adolescent Athletes' Prosocial Behavior and Relationship with Parents: A Mixed Methods Study. Sports. 2018;6(1):4.

33. McCabe LP, Tsiros MD, Crozier AJ. Monkey see, monkey do? Exploring parent-athlete behaviours from youth athletes' perspective. Front Sports Act Living. 2023;5:1292812.

34. Nigg C, Niessner C, Nigg CR, Oriwol D, Schmidt SCE, Woll A. Relating outdoor play to sedentary behavior and physical activity in youth - results from a cohort study. BMC Public Health. 2021;21(1):1716.

Bibliography

35. Bolger LE, Bolger LA, O'Neill C, Coughlan E, O'Brien W, Lacey S, et al. Global levels of fundamental motor skills in children: A systematic review. Journal of sports sciences. 2021;39(7):717-53.

36. Cadenas-Sanchez C, Mena-Molina A, Torres-Lopez LV, Migueles JH, Rodriguez-Ayllon M, Lubans DR, et al. Healthier Minds in Fitter Bodies: A Systematic Review and Meta-Analysis of the Association between Physical Fitness and Mental Health in Youth. Sports medicine. 2021;51(12):2571-605.

37. Gu X, Zhang T, Chu TLA, Keller MJ, Zhang X. The direct and indirect effects of motor competence on adolescents' mental health through health-related physical fitness. Journal of sports sciences. 2019;37(17):1927-33.

38. Twenge JM, Spitzberg BH, Campbell WK. Less in-person social interaction with peers among U.S. adolescents in the 21st century and links to loneliness. Journal of Social and Personal Relationships. 2019;36(6):1892-913.

39. Twenge JM, Hisler GC, Krizan Z. Associations between screen time and sleep duration are primarily driven by portable electronic devices: evidence from a population-based study of U.S. children ages 0-17. Sleep Med. 2019;56:211-8.

40. Khan A, Burton NW. Electronic Games, Television, and Psychological Wellbeing of Adolescents: Mediating Role of Sleep and Physical Activity. Int J Environ Res Public Health. 2021;18(16):8877.

41. Fontanellaz-Castiglione CEG, Markovic A, Tarokh L. Sleep and the adolescent brain. Current Opinion in Physiology. 2020;15:167-71.

42. Pascoe M, Bailey AP, Craike M, Carter T, Patten R, Stepto N, et al. Physical activity and exercise in youth mental health promotion: a scoping review. BMJ Open Sport Exerc Med. 2020;6(1):e000677.

43. Paterson DC, Ramage K, Moore SA, Riazi N, Tremblay MS, Faulkner G. Exploring the impact of COVID-19 on the movement behaviors of children and youth: A scoping review of evidence after the first year. J Sport Health Sci. 2021;10(6):675-89.

44. Jenssen BP, Kelly MK, Powell M, Bouchelle Z, Mayne SL, Fiks AG. COVID-19 and Changes in Child Obesity. Pediatrics. 2021;147(5).

45. McGuine TA, Biese KM, Petrovska L, Hetzel SJ, Reardon C, Kliethermes S, et al. Mental Health, Physical Activity, and Quality of Life of US Adolescent Athletes During COVID-19-Related School Closures and Sport Cancellations: A Study of 13 000 Athletes. Journal of athletic training. 2021;56(1):11-9.

46. Twenge JM, Campbell WK. Associations between screen time and lower psychological well-being among children and adolescents: Evidence from a population-based study. Prev Med Rep. 2018;12:271-83.

47. Koepp AE, Gershoff ET. Amount and type of physical activity as predictors of growth in executive functions, attentional control, and social self-control across 4 years of elementary school. Dev Sci. 2022;25(1):e13147.

48. Neville RD, Guo Y, Boreham CA, Lakes KD. Longitudinal Association Between Participation in Organized Sport and Psychosocial Development in Early Childhood. The Journal of pediatrics. 2021;230:152-60 e1.

49. Zuckerman SL, Tang AR, Richard KE, Grisham CJ, Kuhn AW, Bonfield CM, et al. The behavioral, psychological, and social impacts of team sports: a systematic review and meta-analysis. The Physician and sportsmedicine. 2021;49(3):246-61.

50. Chang M, Bang H, Kim S, Nam-Speers J. Do sports help students stay away from misbehavior, suspension, or dropout? Studies in Educational Evaluation. 2021;70:101066.

Bibliography

51. Burns RD, Bai Y, Brusseau TA. Physical Activity and Sports Participation Associates With Cognitive Functioning and Academic Progression: An Analysis Using the Combined 2017-2018 National Survey of Children's Health. J Phys Act Health. 2020;17(12):1197-204.
52. Harbec M-J, Goldfield G, Pagani LS. Healthy body, healthy mind: Long-term mutual benefits between classroom and sport engagement in children from ages 6 to 12 years. Preventive Medicine Reports. 2021;24:101581.
53. Erickson KI, Hillman C, Stillman CM, Ballard RM, Bloodgood B, Conroy DE, et al. Physical Activity, Cognition, and Brain Outcomes: A Review of the 2018 Physical Activity Guidelines. Medicine and science in sports and exercise. 2019;51(6):1242-51.
54. Meijer A, Konigs M, Vermeulen GT, Visscher C, Bosker RJ, Hartman E, et al. The effects of physical activity on brain structure and neurophysiological functioning in children: A systematic review and meta-analysis. Dev Cogn Neurosci. 2020;45:100828.
55. Schmidt M, Egger F, Benzing V, Jager K, Conzelmann A, Roebers CM, et al. Disentangling the relationship between children's motor ability, executive function and academic achievement. PloS one. 2017;12(8):e0182845.
56. Marcori AJ, Okazaki VHA. Motor repertoire and gray matter plasticity: Is there a link? Med Hypotheses. 2019;130:109261.
57. Wade NE, Kaiver CM, Wallace AL, Hatcher KF, Swartz AM, Lisdahl KM. Objective aerobic fitness level and neuropsychological functioning in healthy adolescents and emerging adults: Unique sex effects. Psychology of Sport and Exercise. 2020;51:101794.
58. Ludyga S, Puhse U, Gerber M, Kamijo K. How children with neurodevelopmental disorders can benefit from the neurocognitive effects of exercise. Neurosci Biobehav Rev. 2021;127:514-9.
59. Pagani LS, Harbec MJ, Fortin G, Barnett TA. Childhood exercise as medicine: Extracurricular sport diminishes subsequent ADHD symptoms. Prev Med. 2020;141:106256.
60. Romer D, Reyna VF, Satterthwaite TD. Beyond stereotypes of adolescent risk taking: Placing the adolescent brain in developmental context. Dev Cogn Neurosci. 2017;27:19-34.
61. Eime RM, Young JA, Harvey JT, Charity MJ, Payne WR. A systematic review of the psychological and social benefits of participation in sport for children and adolescents: informing development of a conceptual model of health through sport. Int J Behav Nutr Phys Act. 2013;10(1):98.
62. Vella SA, Magee CA, Cliff DP. Trajectories and Predictors of Health-Related Quality of Life during Childhood. The Journal of pediatrics. 2015;167(2):422-7.
63. Matta PN, Baul TD, Loubeau K, Sikov J, Plasencia N, Sun Y, et al. Low sports participation is associated with withdrawn and depressed symptoms in urban, school-age children. J Affect Disord. 2021;280(Pt B):24-9.
64. Graupensperger S, Sutcliffe J, Vella SA. Prospective Associations between Sport Participation and Indices of Mental Health across Adolescence. J Youth Adolesc. 2021;50(7):1450-63.
65. Murphy J, Patte KA, Sullivan P, Leatherdale ST. Exploring the Association Between Sport Participation and Symptoms of Anxiety and Depression in a Sample of Canadian High School Students. Journal of Clinical Sport Psychology. 2021;15(3):268-87.
66. Vella SA, Swann C, Allen MS, Schweickle MJ, Magee CA. Bidirectional Associations between Sport Involvement and Mental Health in Adolescence. Medicine and science in sports and exercise. 2017;49(4):687-94.
67. Isaksson J, Selinus EN, Aslund C, Nilsson KW. Physical activity in early adolescence predicts depressive symptoms 3 years later: A community-based study. J Affect Disord. 2020;277:825-30.

Bibliography

68. Casali N, Cerea S, Moro T, Paoli A, Ghisi M. Just Do It: High Intensity Physical Activity Preserves Mental and Physical Health in Elite and Non-elite Athletes During COVID-19. Front Psychol. 2021;12(5242):757150.
69. Engels ES, Mutz M, Demetriou Y, Reimers AK. Levels of physical activity in four domains and affective wellbeing before and during the Covid-19 pandemic. Arch Public Health. 2021;79(1):122.
70. Latina D, Jaf D, Alberti R, Tilton-Weaver L. Can participation in organized sports help adolescents refrain from self-harm? An analysis of underlying mechanisms. Psychology of Sport and Exercise. 2022;59:102133.
71. Logan K, Lloyd RS, Schafer-Kalkhoff T, Khoury JC, Ehrlich S, Dolan LM, et al. Youth sports participation and health status in early adulthood: A 12-year follow-up. Prev Med Rep. 2020;19:101107.
72. Kwon S, Letuchy EM, Levy SM, Janz KF. Youth Sports Participation Is More Important among Females than Males for Predicting Physical Activity in Early Adulthood: Iowa Bone Development Study. International Journal of Environmental Research and Public Health. 2021;18(3):1328.
73. Eime R, Harvey J, Charity M, Westerbeek H. Longitudinal Trends in Sport Participation and Retention of Women and Girls. Front Sports Act Living. 2020;2(39):39.
74. Kemp BJ, Parrish AM, Cliff DP. 'Social screens' and 'the mainstream': longitudinal competitors of non-organized physical activity in the transition from childhood to adolescence. Int J Behav Nutr Phys Act. 2020;17(1):5.
75. Duckworth AL, Quirk A, Gallop R, Hoyle RH, Kelly DR, Matthews MD. Cognitive and noncognitive predictors of success. Proceedings of the National Academy of Sciences of the United States of America. 2019;116(47):23499-504.
76. Bernstein EE, McNally RJ. Exercise as a buffer against difficulties with emotion regulation: A pathway to emotional wellbeing. Behav Res Ther. 2018;109:29-36.
77. Piche G, Fitzpatrick C, Pagani LS. Associations Between Extracurricular Activity and Self-Regulation: A Longitudinal Study From 5 to 10 Years of Age. Am J Health Promot. 2015;30(1):e32-40.
78. Briere FN, Imbeault A, Goldfield GS, Pagani LS. Consistent participation in organized physical activity predicts emotional adjustment in children. Pediatr Res. 2020;88(1):125-30.
79. De Waelle S, Laureys F, Lenoir M, Bennett SJ, Deconinck FJA. Children Involved in Team Sports Show Superior Executive Function Compared to Their Peers Involved in Self-Paced Sports. Children. 2021;8(4):264.
80. Basterfield L, Gardner L, Reilly JK, Pearce MS, Parkinson KN, Adamson AJ, et al. Can't play, won't play: longitudinal changes in perceived barriers to participation in sports clubs across the child-adolescent transition. BMJ Open Sport Exerc Med. 2016;2(1):e000079.
81. Fraser-Thomas J, Côté J. Understanding Adolescents' Positive and Negative Developmental Experiences in Sport. The Sport Psychologist. 2009;23(1):3-23.
82. Newell KM. What are Fundamental Motor Skills and What is Fundamental About Them? Journal of Motor Learning and Development. 2020;8(2):280-314.
83. Lorenzo-Martinez M, Abelairas-Gomez C, Carballo-Fazanes A, Rey E. Prevalence of fundamental movement skill mastery in school-aged children and adolescents: a systematic review. BMJ Open Sport Exerc Med. 2025;11(4):e002439.
84. Duncan MJ, Roscoe CMP, Noon M, Clark CCT, O'Brien W, Eyre ELJ. Run, jump, throw and catch: How proficient are children attending English schools at the fundamental motor skills identified as key within the school curriculum? European Physical Education Review. 2019;26(4):814-26.
85. Chen Z, Zhu W, Ulrich DA, Qin M. Have the Fundamental Movement Skills of U.S. Children Changed? Research quarterly for exercise and sport. 2024;95(2):431-40.

Bibliography

86. O' Brien W, Belton S, Issartel J. Fundamental movement skill proficiency amongst adolescent youth. Physical Education and Sport Pedagogy. 2015;21(6):557-71.

87. Burton AM, Cowburn I, Eisenmann JC, Sawczuk T, Watson T, McDermott J, et al. Motor Competence, Physical Fitness, Psychosocial, and Physical Activity Characteristics in 9- to 14-Year-Olds: Sex Differences and Age and Maturity Considerations. Research quarterly for exercise and sport. 2025;96(1):171-82.

88. Weedon BD, Liu F, Mahmoud W, Burden SJ, Whaymand L, Esser P, et al. Declining fitness and physical education lessons in UK adolescents. BMJ Open Sport Exerc Med. 2022;8(1):e001165.

89. MacNamara A, Collins D, Giblin S. Just let them play? Deliberate preparation as the most appropriate foundation for lifelong physical activity. Front Psychol. 2015;6(1548):1548.

90. Pesce C, Masci I, Marchetti R, Vazou S, Saakslahti A, Tomporowski PD. Deliberate Play and Preparation Jointly Benefit Motor and Cognitive Development: Mediated and Moderated Effects. Front Psychol. 2016;7(349):349.

91. Rogers SA, Hassmén P, Alcock A, Gilleard WL, Warmenhoven JS. Intervention strategies for enhancing movement competencies in youth athletes: A narrative systematic review. International Journal of Sports Science & Coaching. 2020;15(2):256-72.

92. Popović B, Gušić M, Radanović D, Andrašić S, Madić DM, Mačak D, et al. Evaluation of Gross Motor Coordination and Physical Fitness in Children: Comparison between Soccer and Multisport Activities. International Journal of Environmental Research and Public Health. 2020;17(16):5902.

93. Stanković D, Horvatin M, Vlašić J, Pekas D, Trajković N. Motor Coordination in Children: A Comparison between Children Engaged in Multisport Activities and Swimming. Sports. 2023;11(8):139.

94. Biino V, Giustino V, Gallotta MC, Bellafiore M, Battaglia G, Lanza M, et al. Effects of sports experience on children's gross motor coordination level. Front Sports Act Living. 2023;5:1310074.

95. Pacheco MM, Dos Santos FG, Marques M, Maia JAR, Tani G. Transitional Movement Skill Dependence on Fundamental Movement Skills: Testing Seefeldt's Proficiency Barrier. Research quarterly for exercise and sport. 2021:1-10.

96. Lyle MA, Valero-Cuevas FJ, Gregor RJ, Powers CM. Lower extremity dexterity is associated with agility in adolescent soccer athletes. Scandinavian journal of medicine & science in sports. 2015;25(1):81-8.

97. Lyle MA, Valero-Cuevas FJ, Gregor RJ, Powers CM. Control of dynamic foot-ground interactions in male and female soccer athletes: females exhibit reduced dexterity and higher limb stiffness during landing. Journal of biomechanics. 2014;47(2):512-7.

98. Lawrence EL, Peppoloni L, Valero-Cuevas FJ. Sex differences in leg dexterity are not present in elite athletes. Journal of biomechanics. 2017;63:1-7.

99. Diekfuss JA, Hogg JA, Grooms DR, Slutsky-Ganesh AB, Singh H, Bonnette S, et al. Can We Capitalize on Central Nervous System Plasticity in Young Athletes to Inoculate Against Injury? Journal of Science in Sport and Exercise. 2020;2(4):305-18.

100. Jukic I, Prnjak K, Zoellner A, Tufano JJ, Sekulic D, Salaj S. The Importance of Fundamental Motor Skills in Identifying Differences in Performance Levels of U10 Soccer Players. Sports (Basel, Switzerland). 2019;7(7):178.

101. Ericsson KA. Towards a science of the acquisition of expert performance in sports: Clarifying the differences between deliberate practice and other types of practice. Journal of sports sciences. 2020;38(2):159-76.

102. Veldman SL, Jones RA, Okely AD. Efficacy of gross motor skill interventions in young children: an updated systematic review. BMJ Open Sport Exerc Med. 2016;2(1):e000067.

Bibliography

103. Rogers SA, Hassmén P, Roberts AH, Alcock A, Gilleard WL, Warmenhoven JS. Movement Competency Training Delivery: At School or Online? A Pilot Study of High-School Athletes. Sports. 2020;8(4):39.
104. Nepple JJ, Vigdorchik JM, Clohisy JC. What Is the Association Between Sports Participation and the Development of Proximal Femoral Cam Deformity? A Systematic Review and Meta-analysis. The American journal of sports medicine. 2015;43(11):2833-40.
105. Nguyen M, Bixby S, Yen YM, Miller P, Stracciolini A. Moderate and High Sport Specialization Level in Ice Hockey Athletes Is Associated With Symptomatic Cam Deformity. Sports health. 2023;15(5):753-9.
106. Al-Baldawi M, Pettit M, Khanduja V. The effect of exercise time and frequency on the development of cam morphology. BMC musculoskeletal disorders. 2025;26(1):903.
107. Doran C, Pettit M, Singh Y, Sunil Kumar KH, Khanduja V. Does the Type of Sport Influence Morphology of the Hip? A Systematic Review. The American journal of sports medicine. 2022;50(6):1727-41.
108. Palmer A, Fernquest S, Gimpel M, Birchall R, Judge A, Broomfield J, et al. Physical activity during adolescence and the development of cam morphology: a cross-sectional cohort study of 210 individuals. British journal of sports medicine. 2018;52(9):601-10.
109. Fernquest S, Palmer A, Gimpel M, Birchall R, Broomfield J, Wedatilake T, et al. A longitudinal cohort study of adolescent elite footballers and controls investigating the development of cam morphology. Scientific Reports. 2021;11(1):18567.
110. Pentidis N, Mersmann F, Bohm S, Schroll A, Giannakou E, Aggelousis N, et al. Development of Muscle-Tendon Adaptation in Preadolescent Gymnasts and Untrained Peers: A 12-Month Longitudinal Study. Medicine and science in sports and exercise. 2021;53(12):2565-76.
111. Bell DR, Post EG, Biese K, Bay C, Valovich McLeod T. Sport Specialization and Risk of Overuse Injuries: A Systematic Review With Meta-analysis. Pediatrics. 2018;142(3).
112. Arnold A, Thigpen CA, Beattie PF, Kissenberth MJ, Shanley E. Overuse Physeal Injuries in Youth Athletes. Sports health. 2017;9(2):139-47.
113. Takei S, Torii S, Taketomi S, Iizuka S, Tojima M, Iwanuma S, et al. Developmental stage and lower quadriceps flexibilities and decreased gastrocnemius flexibilities are predictive risk factors for developing Osgood-Schlatter disease in adolescent male soccer players. Knee surgery, sports traumatology, arthroscopy : official journal of the ESSKA. 2023;31(8):3330-8.
114. Rathleff MS, Winiarski L, Krommes K, Graven-Nielsen T, Holmich P, Olesen JL, et al. Activity Modification and Knee Strengthening for Osgood-Schlatter Disease: A Prospective Cohort Study. Orthop J Sports Med. 2020;8(4):2325967120911106.
115. Faigenbaum AD, Ratamess NA, Kang J, Bush JA, Rial Rebullido T. May the Force Be with Youth: Foundational Strength for Lifelong Development. Current sports medicine reports. 2023;22(12):414-22.
116. Edouard P, Mosser C, Chapon J, Depiesse F, Palmer D. Understanding the first injury in athletics and its effect on dropout from sport: an online survey on 544 high-level youth and junior athletics (track and field) athletes. BMJ Open Sport Exerc Med. 2024;10(1):e001767.
117. Reyes AC, Chaves R, Baxter-Jones ADG, Vasconcelos O, Barnett LM, Tani G, et al. Modelling the dynamics of children's gross motor coordination. Journal of sports sciences. 2019;37(19):2243-52.
118. Radnor JM, Oliver JL, Waugh CM, Myer GD, Lloyd RS. Muscle Architecture and Maturation Influence Sprint and Jump Ability in Young Boys: A Multistudy Approach. Journal of strength and conditioning research / National Strength & Conditioning Association. 2021.
119. Sokołowski B, Chrzanowska M. Development of Selected Motor Skills in Boys and Girls in Relation to Their Rate of Maturation - A Longitudinal Study. Human Movement. 2012;13(2).

Bibliography

120. Peek K, Ford KR, Myer GD, Hewett TE, Pappas E. Effect of Sex and Maturation on Knee Extensor and Flexor Strength in Adolescent Athletes. The American journal of sports medicine. 2022;50(12):3280-5.

121. Nuzzo JL, Pinto MD. Sex Differences in Upper- and Lower-Limb Muscle Strength in Children and Adolescents: A Meta-Analysis. European journal of sport science. 2025;25(5):e12282.

122. Round JM, Jones DA, Honour JW, Nevill AM. Hormonal factors in the development of differences in strength between boys and girls during adolescence: a longitudinal study. Annals of human biology. 1999;26(1):49-62.

123. Dadfar M, Soltani M, Novinzad MB, Raahemifar K. Lower extremity energy absorption strategies at different phases during single and double-leg landings with knee valgus in pubertal female athletes. Scientific Reports. 2021;11(1):17516.

124. Wild CY, Munro BJ, Steele JR. How Young Girls Change Their Landing Technique Throughout the Adolescent Growth Spurt. The American journal of sports medicine. 2016;44(5):1116-23.

125. Brant JA, Johnson B, Brou L, Comstock RD, Vu T. Rates and Patterns of Lower Extremity Sports Injuries in All Gender-Comparable US High School Sports. Orthop J Sports Med. 2019;7(10):2325967119873059.

126. Bunstine JL, Yang J, Kistamgari S, Collins CL, Smith GA. Differences in Overuse Injuries in Gender-Comparable Sports: A Nationally Representative Sample of High School Athletes. Journal of athletic training. 2024;59(9):962-8.

127. Sport Wi. Reframing sport for teenage girls: Tackling teenage disengagement. Women in Sport; 2022.

128. Ardern CL, Taylor NF, Feller JA, Webster KE. Fifty-five per cent return to competitive sport following anterior cruciate ligament reconstruction surgery: an updated systematic review and meta-analysis including aspects of physical functioning and contextual factors. British journal of sports medicine. 2014;48(21):1543-52.

129. Ryman Augustsson S, Ageberg E. Weaker lower extremity muscle strength predicts traumatic knee injury in youth female but not male athletes. BMJ Open Sport Exerc Med. 2017;3(1):e000222.

130. Herman DC, Onate JA, Weinhold PS, Guskiewicz KM, Garrett WE, Yu B, et al. The effects of feedback with and without strength training on lower extremity biomechanics. The American journal of sports medicine. 2009;37(7):1301-8.

131. Stearns KM, Powers CM. Improvements in hip muscle performance result in increased use of the hip extensors and abductors during a landing task. The American journal of sports medicine. 2014;42(3):602-9.

132. Tsukahara Y, Torii S, Yamasawa F, Iwamoto J, Otsuka T, Goto H, et al. Bone Metabolism, Bone Mineral Content, and Density in Elite Late Teen Female Sprinters. International journal of sports medicine. 2021;42(13):1228-33.

133. Bellver M, Del Rio L, Jovell E, Drobnic F, Trilla A. Bone mineral density and bone mineral content among female elite athletes. Bone. 2019;127:393-400.

134. Myer GD, Sugimoto D, Thomas S, Hewett TE. The influence of age on the effectiveness of neuromuscular training to reduce anterior cruciate ligament injury in female athletes: a meta-analysis. The American journal of sports medicine. 2013;41(1):203-15.

135. Myer GD, Ford KR, Palumbo JP, Hewett TE. Neuromuscular training improves performance and lower-extremity biomechanics in female athletes. Journal of strength and conditioning research / National Strength & Conditioning Association. 2005;19(1):51-60.

136. Greene DA, Naughton GA. Adaptive skeletal responses to mechanical loading during adolescence. Sports medicine. 2006;36(9):723-32.

Bibliography

137. Myer GD, Faigenbaum AD, Ford KR, Best TM, Bergeron MF, Hewett TE. When to initiate integrative neuromuscular training to reduce sports-related injuries and enhance health in youth? Current sports medicine reports. 2011;10(3):155-66.
138. Boccia G, Cardinale M, Brustio PR. Performance progression of elite jumpers: Early performances do not predict later success. Scandinavian journal of medicine & science in sports. 2021;31(1):132-9.
139. Brustio PR, Cardinale M, Lupo C, Varalda M, De Pasquale P, Boccia G. Being a top swimmer during the early career is not a prerequisite for success: A study on sprinter strokes. Journal of science and medicine in sport / Sports Medicine Australia. 2021;24(12):1272-7.
140. Barth M, Gullich A, Macnamara BN, Hambrick DZ. Quantifying the Extent to Which Junior Performance Predicts Senior Performance in Olympic Sports: A Systematic Review and Meta-analysis. Sports medicine. 2024;54(1):95-104.
141. Boccia G, Brustio PR, Moise P, Franceschi A, La Torre A, Schena F, et al. Elite national athletes reach their peak performance later than non-elite in sprints and throwing events. Journal of science and medicine in sport / Sports Medicine Australia. 2019;22(3):342-7.
142. Hill M, Scott S, Malina RM, McGee D, Cumming SP. Relative age and maturation selection biases in academy football. Journal of sports sciences. 2020;38(11-12):1359-67.
143. Sweeney L, Cumming SP, MacNamara Á, Horan D. A tale of two selection biases: The independent effects of relative age and biological maturity on player selection in the Football Association of Ireland's national talent pathway. International Journal of Sports Science & Coaching. 2022;18(6):1992-2003.
144. Niklasson E, Lindholm O, Rietz M, Lind J, Johnson D, Lundberg TR. Who Reaches the NHL? A 20-Year Retrospective Analysis of Junior and Adult Ice Hockey Success in Relation to Biological Maturation in Male Swedish Players. Sports medicine. 2024;54(5):1317-26.
145. Gullich A, Barth M. Effects of Early Talent Promotion on Junior and Senior Performance: A Systematic Review and Meta-Analysis. Sports medicine. 2024;54(3):697-710.
146. Barth M, Gullich A, Macnamara BN, Hambrick DZ. Predictors of Junior Versus Senior Elite Performance are Opposite: A Systematic Review and Meta-Analysis of Participation Patterns. Sports medicine. 2022;52(6):1399-416.
147. Murr D, Feichtinger P, Larkin P, O'Connor D, Honer O. Psychological talent predictors in youth soccer: A systematic review of the prognostic relevance of psychomotor, perceptual-cognitive and personality-related factors. PloS one. 2018;13(10):e0205337.
148. Ford PR, Ward P, Hodges NJ, Williams AM. The role of deliberate practice and play in career progression in sport: the early engagement hypothesis. High Ability Studies. 2009;20(1):65-75.
149. Gullich A, Macnamara BN, Hambrick DZ. What Makes a Champion? Early Multidisciplinary Practice, Not Early Specialization, Predicts World-Class Performance. Perspect Psychol Sci. 2022;17(1):6-29.
150. Boccia G, Moise P, Franceschi A, Trova F, Panero D, La Torre A, et al. Career Performance Trajectories in Track and Field Jumping Events from Youth to Senior Success: The Importance of Learning and Development. PloS one. 2017;12(1):e0170744.
151. Rommers N, Mostaert M, Goossens L, Vaeyens R, Witvrouw E, Lenoir M, et al. Age and maturity related differences in motor coordination among male elite youth soccer players. Journal of sports sciences. 2019;37(2):196-203.
152. Post EG, Rosenthal MD, Root HJ, Rauh MJ. Knowledge, Attitudes, and Beliefs of Parents of Youth Basketball Players Regarding Sport Specialization and College Scholarship Availability. Orthop J Sports Med. 2021;9(8):23259671211024594.

Bibliography

153. Hernandez MI, Biese KM, Schaefer DA, Post EG, Bell DR, Brooks MA. Different Perceptions of Parents and Children on Factors Influencing Sport Specialization. Journal of sport rehabilitation. 2020;30(2):190-7.

154. Staub I, Zinner C, Bieder A, Vogt T. Within-sport specialisation and entry age as predictors of success among age group swimmers. European journal of sport science. 2020;20(9):1160-7.

155. De Bosscher V, Descheemaeker K, Shibli S. Starting and Specialisation Ages of Elite Athletes across Olympic Sports: An International Cross-sectional Study. European Journal of Sport Sciences. 2023;2(5):9-19.

156. Oppici L, Panchuk D. Specific and general transfer of perceptual-motor skills and learning between sports: A systematic review. Psychology of Sport and Exercise. 2022;59:102118.

157. Güllich A, Cronauer R, Diehl J, Gard L, Miller C. Coach-assessed skill learning progress of youth soccer players correlates with earlier childhood practice in other sports. International Journal of Sports Science & Coaching. 2020;15(3):285-96.

158. Güllich A, Emrich E. Individualistic and Collectivistic Approach in Athlete Support Programmes in the German High-Performance Sport System. European Journal for Sport and Society. 2016;9(4):243-68.

159. Kliethermes SA, Nagle K, Cote J, Malina RM, Faigenbaum A, Watson A, et al. Impact of youth sports specialisation on career and task-specific athletic performance: a systematic review following the American Medical Society for Sports Medicine (AMSSM) Collaborative Research Network's 2019 Youth Early Sport Specialisation Summit. British journal of sports medicine. 2020;54(4):221-30.

160. Sweeney L, Horan D, MacNamara A. Premature Professionalisation or Early Engagement? Examining Practise in Football Player Pathways. Front Sports Act Living. 2021;3:660167.

161. Jayanthi NA, LaBella CR, Fischer D, Pasulka J, Dugas LR. Sports-specialized intensive training and the risk of injury in young athletes: a clinical case-control study. The American journal of sports medicine. 2015;43(4):794-801.

162. Jayanthi N, Kliethermes S, Dugas L, Pasulka J, Iqbal S, LaBella C. Risk of Injuries Associated With Sport Specialization and Intense Training Patterns in Young Athletes: A Longitudinal Clinical Case-Control Study. Orthop J Sports Med. 2020;8(6):2325967120922764.

163. Moesch K, Elbe A-M, Hauge M-LT, Wikman JM. Late specialization: the key to success in centimeters, grams, or seconds (cgs) sports. Scand J Med Sci Spor. 2011;21(6):e282-e90.

164. Gamble P. Informed: The Art of the Science of Preparing Athletes. Informed in Sport publishing; 2018.

165. Leyhr D, Murr D, Basten L, Eichler K, Hauser T, Ludin D, et al. Biological Maturity Status in Elite Youth Soccer Players: A Comparison of Pragmatic Diagnostics With Magnetic Resonance Imaging. Front Sports Act Living. 2020;2:587861.

166. Monasterio X, Gil SM, Bidaurrazaga-Letona I, Lekue JA, Santisteban J, Diaz-Beitia G, et al. Injuries according to the percentage of adult height in an elite soccer academy. Journal of science and medicine in sport / Sports Medicine Australia. 2021;24(3):218-23.

167. Terrell SL, Schuemann TL, Lynch J. Strategies to Deter Primary Cam Morphology in Youth Athletes: A Clinical Commentary and Call for Investigation. JOSPT Open. 2025;3(4):386-94.

168. Monasterio X, Cumming SP, Larruskain J, Johnson DM, Gil SM, Bidaurrazaga-Letona I, et al. The combined effects of growth and maturity status on injury risk in an elite football academy. Biology of sport. 2024;41(1):235-44.

169. Wik EH, Martinez-Silvan D, Farooq A, Cardinale M, Johnson A, Bahr R. Skeletal maturation and growth rates are related to bone and growth plate injuries in adolescent athletics. Scandinavian journal of medicine & science in sports. 2020;30(5):894-903.

Bibliography

170. van der Sluis A, Elferink-Gemser MT, Brink MS, Visscher C. Importance of peak height velocity timing in terms of injuries in talented soccer players. International journal of sports medicine. 2015;36(4):327-32.

171. Coughlan EK, Williams AM, McRobert AP, Ford PR. How experts practice: a novel test of deliberate practice theory. Journal of experimental psychology Learning, memory, and cognition. 2014;40(2):449-58.

172. Skenazy L. Free-range kids, giving our children the freedom we had without going nuts with worry. John Wiley & Sons; 2009.

173. Farrow D, Reid M, Buszard T, Kovalchik S. Charting the development of sport expertise: challenges and opportunities. International Review of Sport and Exercise Psychology. 2017;11(1):238-57.

174. Baker J, Young BW, Mann D. Advances in athlete development: understanding conditions of and constraints on optimal practice. Curr Opin Psychol. 2017;16:24-7.

175. Andrew M, Baptiste GZ, Reeves MJ, Roberts SJ, McRobert AP, Ford PR. The developmental activities of skilled youth CONCACAF soccer players and the contribution of their development system. International Journal of Sports Science & Coaching. 2021;17(6):1363-77.

176. Sieghartsleitner R, Zuber C, Zibung M, Conzelmann A. "The Early Specialised Bird Catches the Worm!" - A Specialised Sampling Model in the Development of Football Talents. Front Psychol. 2018;9:188.

177. Stegmann P, Sieghartsleitner R, Zuber C, Zibung M, Lenze L, Conzelmann A. Successful talent development in popular game sports in Switzerland: The case of ice hockey. International Journal of Sports Science & Coaching. 2021;16(3):710-21.

178. Vink K, Raudsepp L, Kais K. Intrinsic motivation and individual deliberate practice are reciprocally related: Evidence from a longitudinal study of adolescent team sport athletes. Psychology of Sport and Exercise. 2015;16:1-6.

179. Morton AT. 'One of the worst statistics in British sport': a sociological perspective on the over-representation of independently (privately) educated athletes in Team GB. Sport, Education and Society. 2021:1-14.

180. Emrich E, Fröhlich M, Klein M, Pitsch W. Evaluation of the Elite Schools of Sport. International Review for the Sociology of Sport. 2009;44(2-3):151-71.

181. De Bosscher V, De Knop P, Vertonghen J. A multidimensional approach to evaluate the policy effectiveness of elite sport schools in Flanders. Sport in Society. 2016;19(10):1596-621.

182. van Rens FECA, Elling A, Reijgersberg N. Topsport Talent Schools in the Netherlands: A retrospective analysis of the effect on performance in sport and education. International Review for the Sociology of Sport. 2012;50(1):64-82.

183. Hopwood MJ, Farrow D, MacMahon C, Baker J. Sibling dynamics and sport expertise. Scandinavian journal of medicine & science in sports. 2015;25(5):724-33.

184. Haider AH, Saleem T, Bilaniuk JW, Barraco RD, Eastern Association for the Surgery of Trauma Injury ControlViolence Prevention C. An evidence-based review: efficacy of safety helmets in the reduction of head injuries in recreational skiers and snowboarders. J Trauma Acute Care Surg. 2012;73(5):1340-7.

185. Lieberman DE, Venkadesan M, Werbel WA, Daoud AI, D'Andrea S, Davis IS, et al. Foot strike patterns and collision forces in habitually barefoot versus shod runners. Nature. 2010;463(7280):531-5.

186. Ryan MB, Valiant GA, McDonald K, Taunton JE. The effect of three different levels of footwear stability on pain outcomes in women runners: a randomised control trial. British journal of sports medicine. 2011;45(9):715-21.

187. Richards CE, Magin PJ, Callister R. Is your prescription of distance running shoes evidence-based? British journal of sports medicine. 2009;43(3):159-62.

Bibliography

188. Zech A, Venter R, de Villiers JE, Sehner S, Wegscheider K, Hollander K. Motor Skills of Children and Adolescents Are Influenced by Growing up Barefoot or Shod. Front Pediatr. 2018;6(115):115.

189. Hollander K, de Villiers JE, Sehner S, Wegscheider K, Braumann KM, Venter R, et al. Growing-up (habitually) barefoot influences the development of foot and arch morphology in children and adolescents. Scientific Reports. 2017;7(1):8079.

190. Mizushima J, Keogh JWL, Maeda K, Shibata A, Kaneko J, Ohyama-Byun K, et al. Long-term effects of school barefoot running program on sprinting biomechanics in children: A case-control study. Gait & posture. 2021;83:9-14.

191. Fuller JT, Bellenger CR, Thewlis D, Tsiros MD, Buckley JD. The effect of footwear on running performance and running economy in distance runners. Sports medicine. 2015;45(3):411-22.

192. Buszard T, Farrow D, Reid M. Designing Junior Sport to Maximize Potential: The Knowns, Unknowns, and Paradoxes of Scaling Sport. Front Psychol. 2019;10:2878.

193. Farber MJ, Kim MJ, Knodt AR, Hariri AR. Maternal overprotection in childhood is associated with amygdala reactivity and structural connectivity in adulthood. Dev Cogn Neurosci. 2019;40:100711.

194. Coutinho P, Ribeiro J, da Silva SM, Fonseca AM, Mesquita I. The Influence of Parents, Coaches, and Peers in the Long-Term Development of Highly Skilled and Less Skilled Volleyball Players. Front Psychol. 2021;12:667542.

195. Ryan Dunn C, Dorsch TE, King MQ, Rothlisberger KJ. The Impact of Family Financial Investment on Perceived Parent Pressure and Child Enjoyment and Commitment in Organized Youth Sport. Family Relations. 2016;65(2):287-99.

196. Stefansen K, Smette I, Strandbu Å. Understanding the increase in parents' involvement in organized youth sports. Sport, Education and Society. 2016;23(2):162-72.

197. Dorsch TE, Smith AL, Wilson SR, McDonough MH. Parent goals and verbal sideline behavior in organized youth sport. Sport, Exercise, and Performance Psychology. 2015;4(1):19-35.

198. Tamminen KA, McEwen CE, Kerr G, Donnelly P. Examining the impact of the Respect in Sport Parent Program on the psychosocial experiences of minor hockey athletes. Journal of sports sciences. 2020;38(17):2035-45.

199. Rosenthal RW, Jacobson L. Pygmalion in the Classroom. 1968.

200. Burns L, Weissensteiner JR, Cohen M. Lifestyles and mindsets of Olympic, Paralympic and world champions: is an integrated approach the key to elite performance? British journal of sports medicine. 2019;53(13):818-24.

201. Murray RM, Dugdale JH, Habeeb CM, Arthur CA. Transformational parenting and coaching on mental toughness and physical performance in adolescent soccer players: The moderating effect of athlete age. European journal of sport science. 2021;21(4):580-9.

202. Collins D, MacNamara A, McCarthy N. Super Champions, Champions, and Almosts: Important Differences and Commonalities on the Rocky Road. Front Psychol. 2015;6:2009.

203. Verner-Filion J, Vallerand RJ, Amiot CE, Mocanu I. The two roads from passion to sport performance and psychological well-being: The mediating role of need satisfaction, deliberate practice, and achievement goals. Psychology of Sport and Exercise. 2017;30:19-29.

204. Elliott S, Drummond MJN, Knight C. The Experiences of Being a Talented Youth Athlete: Lessons for Parents. Journal of Applied Sport Psychology. 2017;30(4):437-55.

205. Swann C, Crust L, Vella SA. New directions in the psychology of optimal performance in sport: flow and clutch states. Curr Opin Psychol. 2017;16:48-53.

Bibliography

206. Jackman PC, Dargue EJ, Johnston JP, Hawkins RM. Flow in youth sport, physical activity, and physical education: A systematic review. Psychology of Sport and Exercise. 2021;53:101852.
207. Visek AJ, Achrati SM, Mannix H, McDonnell K, Harris BS, DiPietro L. The fun integration theory: toward sustaining children and adolescents sport participation. J Phys Act Health. 2015;12(3):424-33.
208. Visek AJ, Mannix H, Chandran A, Cleary SD, McDonnell K, DiPietro L. Perceived importance of the fun integration theory's factors and determinants: A comparison among players, parents, and coaches. Int J Sports Sci Coach. 2018;13(6):849-62.
209. Madigan DJ, Stoeber J, Culley T, Passfield L, Hill AP. Perfectionism and training performance: The mediating role of other-approach goals. European journal of sport science. 2018;18(9):1271-9.
210. Vink K, Raudsepp L. Longitudinal Associations Between Perfectionistic Strivings, Perfectionistic Concerns, and Sport-Specific Practice in Adolescent Volleyball Players. Perceptual and motor skills. 2020;127(3):609-25.
211. Sapieja KM, Dunn JG, Holt NL. Perfectionism and perceptions of parenting styles in male youth soccer. Journal of sport & exercise psychology. 2011;33(1):20-39.
212. Vink K, Raudsepp L. Perfectionistic Strivings, Motivation and Engagement in Sport-Specific Activities Among Adolescent Team Athletes. Perceptual and motor skills. 2018;125(3):596-611.
213. Stoeber J, Madigan DJ, Gonidis L. Perfectionism is adaptive and maladaptive, but what's the combined effect? Personality and Individual Differences. 2020;161:109846.
214. Al-Yaaribi A, Kavussanu M. Teammate Prosocial and Antisocial Behaviors Predict Task Cohesion and Burnout: The Mediating Role of Affect. Journal of sport & exercise psychology. 2017;39(3):199-208.
215. Edison BR, Christino MA, Rizzone KH. Athletic Identity in Youth Athletes: A Systematic Review of the Literature. Int J Environ Res Public Health. 2021;18(14):7331.
216. Breske MP, Fry MD, Fry AC, Hogue CM. The effects of goal priming on cortisol responses in an ego-involving climate. Psychology of Sport and Exercise. 2017;32:74-82.
217. Gomes AR, Goncalves AM, Dias O, Morais C. Parental Behavior, Cognitive Appraisal, and Motivation in Young Athletes. Research quarterly for exercise and sport. 2019;90(1):80-94.
218. Kramers S, Thrower SN, Steptoe K, Harwood CG. Parental strategies for supporting children's psychosocial development within and beyond elite sport. Journal of Applied Sport Psychology. 2022:1-23.
219. Dahl RE, Allen NB, Wilbrecht L, Suleiman AB. Importance of investing in adolescence from a developmental science perspective. Nature. 2018;554(7693):441-50.
220. Suleiman AB, Dahl R. Parent–Child Relationships in the Puberty Years: Insights From Developmental Neuroscience. Family Relations. 2019;68(3):279-87.
221. Andrews JL, Ahmed SP, Blakemore SJ. Navigating the Social Environment in Adolescence: The Role of Social Brain Development. Biol Psychiatry. 2021;89(2):109-18.
222. Kavussanu M, Stanger N. Moral behavior in sport. Curr Opin Psychol. 2017;16:185-92.
223. Eime RM, Harvey JT, Charity MJ. Sport drop-out during adolescence: is it real, or an artefact of sampling behaviour? International Journal of Sport Policy and Politics. 2019;11(4):715-26.
224. Murray RM, Sabiston CM. Understanding Relationships Between Social Identity, Sport Enjoyment, and Dropout in Adolescent Girl Athletes. Journal of sport & exercise psychology. 2022;44(1):62-6.
225. Tomova L, Andrews JL, Blakemore S-J. The importance of belonging and the avoidance of social risk taking in adolescence. Developmental Review. 2021;61:100981.

Bibliography

226. Persson M, Espedalen LE, Stefansen K, Strandbu Å. Opting out of youth sports: how can we understand the social processes involved? Sport, Education and Society. 2019;25(7):842-54.
227. Lawler M, Heary C, Shorter G, Nixon E. Peer and parental processes predict distinct patterns of physical activity participation among adolescent girls and boys. International Journal of Sport and Exercise Psychology. 2021;20(2):497-514.
228. van Harmelen AL, Blakemore SJ, Goodyer IM, Kievit RA. The Interplay Between Adolescent Friendship Quality and Resilient Functioning Following Childhood and Adolescent Adversity. Adversity and Resilience Science. 2020;2(1):37-50.
229. Strandbu Å, Bakken A, Stefansen K. The continued importance of family sport culture for sport participation during the teenage years. Sport, Education and Society. 2019;25(8):931-45.
230. Wagnsson S, Lindwall M, Gustafsson H. Participation in organized sport and self-esteem across adolescence: the mediating role of perceived sport competence. Journal of sport & exercise psychology. 2014;36(6):584-94.
231. Knight CJ, Boden CM, Holt NL. Junior Tennis Players' Preferences for Parental Behaviors. Journal of Applied Sport Psychology. 2010;22(4):377-91.
232. Strandbu Å, Stefansen K, Smette I, Sandvik MR. Young people's experiences of parental involvement in youth sport. Sport, Education and Society. 2017;24(1):66-77.
233. Steinberg L, Lamborn SD, Darling N, Mounts NS, Dornbusch SM. Over-Time Changes in Adjustment and Competence among Adolescents from Authoritative, Authoritarian, Indulgent, and Neglectful Families. Child Development. 1994;65(3):754-70.
234. Morris AS, Ratliff EL, Cosgrove KT, Steinberg L. We Know Even More Things: A Decade Review of Parenting Research. J Res Adolesc. 2021;31(4):870-88.
235. Steinberg L, Elmen JD, Mounts NS. Authoritative Parenting, Psychosocial Maturity, and Academic Success among Adolescents. Child Development. 1989;60(6):1424-36.
236. Harwood CG, Barker JB, Anderson R. Psychosocial Development in Youth Soccer Players: Assessing the Effectiveness of the 5Cs Intervention Program. The Sport Psychologist. 2015;29(4):319-34.
237. Mesagno C, Beckmann J, Wergin VV, Gröpel P. Primed to perform: Comparing different pre-performance routine interventions to improve accuracy in closed, self-paced motor tasks. Psychology of Sport and Exercise. 2019;43:73-81.
238. Dohme L-C, Piggott D, Backhouse S, Morgan G. Psychological Skills and Characteristics Facilitative of Youth Athletes' Development: A Systematic Review. The Sport Psychologist. 2019;33(4):261-75.
239. MacNamara Á, Button A, Collins D. The Role of Psychological Characteristics in Facilitating the Pathway to Elite Performance Part 1: Identifying Mental Skills and Behaviors. The Sport Psychologist. 2010;24(1):52-73.
240. MacNamara Á, Button A, Collins D. The Role of Psychological Characteristics in Facilitating the Pathway to Elite Performance Part 2: Examining Environmental and Stage-Related Differences in Skills and Behaviors. The Sport Psychologist. 2010;24(1):74-96.
241. Winter S, O'Brien F, Collins D. Things Ain't What They Used to Be? Coaches Perceptions of Commitment in Developing Athletes. Journal of Applied Sport Psychology. 2019;33(3):357-76.
242. Zimmerman BJ. Becoming a Self-Regulated Learner: An Overview. Theory Into Practice. 2002;41(2):64-70.
243. Kitsantas A, Zimmerman BJ. Comparing Self-Regulatory Processes Among Novice, Non-Expert, and Expert Volleyball Players: A Microanalytic Study. Journal of Applied Sport Psychology. 2010;14(2):91-105.
244. Cowden RG. Mental Toughness, Emotional Intelligence, and Coping Effectiveness: An Analysis of Construct Interrelatedness Among High-Performing Adolescent Male Athletes. Perceptual and motor skills. 2016;123(3):737-53.

Bibliography

245. Neumann DL, McInnes M. A Brief Writing Intervention Assists Athletes to Cope With Performance Failures. Psych J. 2025;14(5):787-98.
246. Scott K. Radical Candor: Fully Revised & Updated Edition: Be a Kick-Ass Boss Without Losing Your Humanity. St. Martin's Press; 2019.
247. Knight CJ. Revealing Findings in Youth Sport Parenting Research. Kinesiology Review. 2019;8(3):252-9.
248. Knight CJ, Neely KC, Holt NL. Parental Behaviors in Team Sports: How do Female Athletes Want Parents to Behave? Journal of Applied Sport Psychology. 2011;23(1):76-92.
249. Thrower SN, Hamann M, Stokoe E, Harwood CG. Examining parent-child interactions in British junior tennis: A conversation analysis of the pre-competition car journey. Psychology of Sport and Exercise. 2022;60:102166.
250. Tamminen KA, Bissett JE, Azimi S, Kim J. Parent and child car-ride interactions before and after sport competitions and practices: Video analysis of verbal and non-verbal communication. Psychology of Sport and Exercise. 2022;58:102095.
251. Harwood C. Developmental Consulting in a Professional Football Academy: The 5Cs Coaching Efficacy Program. The Sport Psychologist. 2008;22(1):109-33.
252. Guo T, Ni Y, Li Q, Hong H. The Power of Faith: The Influence of Athletes' Coping Self-Efficacy on the Cognitive Processing of Psychological Stress. Front Psychol. 2019;10(1565):1565.
253. Sivaramakrishnan H, Spray C, Fletcher D, Ntoumanis N. John Henryism and fear of failure in competitive sport: predicting competitive standard and mental well-being. International Journal of Sport and Exercise Psychology. 2022;22(1):273-89.
254. Kaufman SB, Duckworth AL. World-class expertise: a developmental model. Wiley Interdiscip Rev Cogn Sci. 2017;8(1-2):e1365.
255. Toering T, Elferink-Gemser M, Jordet G, Jorna C, Pepping GJ, Visscher C. Self-Regulation of Practice Behavior Among Elite Youth Soccer Players: An Exploratory Observation Study. Journal of Applied Sport Psychology. 2011;23(1):110-28.
256. Dweck CS, Yeager DS. Mindsets: A View From Two Eras. Perspect Psychol Sci. 2019;14(3):481-96.
257. Ward AF, Duke K, Gneezy A, Bos MW. Brain Drain: The Mere Presence of One's Own Smartphone Reduces Available Cognitive Capacity. Journal of the Association for Consumer Research. 2017;2(2):140-54.
258. Mendoza JS, Pody BC, Lee S, Kim M, McDonough IM. The effect of cellphones on attention and learning: The influences of time, distraction, and nomophobia. Computers in Human Behavior. 2018;86:52-60.
259. Jones JJ, Kirschen GW, Kancharla S, Hale L. Association between late-night tweeting and next-day game performance among professional basketball players. Sleep health. 2019;5(1):68-71.
260. Crone EA, Konijn EA. Media use and brain development during adolescence. Nat Commun. 2018;9(1):588.
261. Canale N, Vieno A, Doro M, Rosa Mineo E, Marino C, Billieux J. Emotion-related impulsivity moderates the cognitive interference effect of smartphone availability on working memory. Scientific Reports. 2019;9(1):18519.
262. Wood AM, Froh JJ, Geraghty AW. Gratitude and well-being: a review and theoretical integration. Clin Psychol Rev. 2010;30(7):890-905.
263. Unanue W, Gomez Mella ME, Cortez DA, Bravo D, Araya-Veliz C, Unanue J, et al. The Reciprocal Relationship Between Gratitude and Life Satisfaction: Evidence From Two Longitudinal Field Studies. Front Psychol. 2019;10:2480.
264. Hussong AM, Langley HA, Rothenberg WA, Coffman JL, Halberstadt AG, Costanzo PR, et al. Raising Grateful Children One Day at a Time. Appl Dev Sci. 2019;23(4):371-84.

Bibliography

265. Morganti G, Kelly AL, Lascu A, Brustio PR, Padua E, Filetti C, et al. Relative age effects in European soccer: their association with contextual factors, impact on youth national teams' performance, and presence at the senior level. Front Sports Act Living. 2025;7:1546978.

266. Brazo-Sayavera J, Martinez-Valencia MA, Muller L, Andronikos G, Martindale RJJ. Identifying talented track and field athletes: The impact of relative age effect on selection to the Spanish National Athletics Federation training camps. Journal of sports sciences. 2017;35(22):2172-8.

267. Toum M, Tribolet R, Watsford ML, Fransen J. The confounding effect of biological maturity on talent identification and selection within youth Australian football. Sci Med Footb. 2021;5(4):263-71.

268. Till K, Baker J. Challenges and [Possible] Solutions to Optimizing Talent Identification and Development in Sport. Front Psychol. 2020;11:664.

269. Ford PR, Bordonau JLD, Bonanno D, Tavares J, Groenendijk C, Fink C, et al. A survey of talent identification and development processes in the youth academies of professional soccer clubs from around the world. Journal of sports sciences. 2020;38(11-12):1269-78.

270. Gullich A. Selection, de-selection and progression in German football talent promotion. European journal of sport science. 2014;14(6):530-7.

271. Collins DJ, Macnamara A, McCarthy N. Putting the Bumps in the Rocky Road: Optimizing the Pathway to Excellence. Front Psychol. 2016;7(1482):1482.

272. John JM, Gropper H, Thiel A. The role of critical life events in the talent development pathways of athletes and musicians: A systematic review. Psychology of Sport and Exercise. 2019;45:101565.

273. Twenge JM, Gentile B, DeWall CN, Ma D, Lacefield K, Schurtz DR. Birth cohort increases in psychopathology among young Americans, 1938-2007: A cross-temporal meta-analysis of the MMPI. Clin Psychol Rev. 2010;30(2):145-54.

274. Galatzer-Levy IR, Huang SH, Bonanno GA. Trajectories of resilience and dysfunction following potential trauma: A review and statistical evaluation. Clin Psychol Rev. 2018;63:41-55.

www.ingramcontent.com/pod-product-compliance
Lightning Source LLC
Chambersburg PA
CBHW080411170426
43194CB00015B/2774